SCHOOL VIOLENCE

And Children In Crisis

Community and School Interventions for Social Workers and Counselors

Edited by

Joshua Miller, Irene Rodriguez Martin, and Gerald Schamess
Smith College School for Social Work

LOVE PUBLISHING COMPANY®
Denver • London • Sydney

Chapter 2 is from *Children Who See Too Much* by Betsy McAlister Groves. Reprinted by permission of Beacon Press, Boston.

Chapters 4, is from *Focus on Exceptional Children, 33,* (1), 1–20. Reprinted by permission of Love Publishing, Denver.

Chapter 6 is from *Counseling and Human Development, 32,* (6) 1–18. Reprinted by permission of Love Publishing, Denver.

Chapter 7 is from *Counseling and Human Development 32,* (2) 1–14. Reprinted by permission of Love Publishing, Denver.

Some of the other chapters in this book are adapted from *Smith College Studies in Social Work, 71,* (169–377). Reprinted by permission of Smith College School for Social Work.

Published by Love Publishing Company
P.O. Box 22353
Denver, Colorado 80222
www.lovepublishing.com

Library of Congress Control Number: 2003101412

CONTENTS

iii

PREFACE

This volume encompasses a range of theoretical positions and practice initiatives directed toward understanding and ameliorating school violence and other crises children experience and enact behaviorally in school settings. The idea for the book originated during a conference entitled "Safe Schools: Building Fortresses or Opening the Doors to Community?" held in June 2000 at the Smith College School for Social Work. The conference was unusual in that both the presenters and the audience represented a diversity of disciplines, including social work, psychology, education, law enforcement, and public health. Some chapters in this volume were derived from presentations to that conference; other chapters were submitted, reviewed, and selected subsequently.

Because one of the book's central themes is the importance of interdisciplinary collaboration, and because contributors represent professional disciplines that sometimes disagree about fundamental values, priorities, and practice approaches, it seems important to emphasize the degree to which contributors and editors worked cooperatively in composing and editing this volume. Authors were enthusiastic about lending their voices to an edited volume that would be suitable for teaching practitioners and researchers in graduate and undergraduate programs and would also promote research, expand existing theoretical paradigms, encourage programmatic innovation, and provide guidelines for practice. From our viewpoint as editors, the volume will achieve its fundamental goal if it encourages the development of community partnerships where educators, professional helpers, and concerned citizens can join together to discuss the multiple causes of school violence and the range of interventions that seem most likely to alleviate crises on school campuses. School safety is a crucial issue for all Americans. It is central not only to promoting the health and well-being of today's children and families but also to ensuring our capacity to raise future generations of emotionally healthy, well-educated citizens.

Premises

In planning this volume, we were guided by certain premises. The first is that schools and communities are inextricably interconnected. Schools express community values and are deeply embedded in the fabric of community life. Communities depend on schools to prepare students for productive, prosocial lives as responsible citizens, however educational communities define such lives. Schools depend on communities for guidance in developing policy, providing financial support, and fulfilling a range of other essential functions. Because schools are inseparable from the communities they serve, it is counterproductive to think of them as freestanding educational institutions, independent of the local, state, and federal influences that determine their policies. This principle is not nearly as self-evident as it may seem. Programs designed to promote educational reform and/or to address particular school problems are regularly developed with little regard for community input, especially at the local level.

A second premise is that achieving an accurate and balanced understanding of school (or community) violence depends on the ability to utilize and integrate divergent theoretical perspectives. No single theory provides an adequate understanding of school violence, and no single intervention affords a viable "solution." Consequently, this volume presents a range of theoretical perspectives. For example Prothrow-Stith utilizes a public health paradigm; Garbarino discusses research findings on risk and resilience. Leone, Mayer, Malmgren, and Meisel use "nested ecological theory" to interpret and comment on a wide array of statistical data. Miller focuses on how some aspects of national social policy intentionally or unintentionally marginalize, neglect, and abuse particular subgroups of American children and their families. Weinhold emphasizes America's "culture of violence" as it affects the emotional climate of schools. Corbin discusses how group process theory can be utilized to reform the culture and administrative structures of school systems. Eismann explains how he adapts and applies principles drawn from the community mental health movement to treat children on the neighborhood streets where they play. Both Gelinas and McAlister Groves draw on trauma theory. Perez refers to socialization and role induction. Miller and Fanolis utilize crisis theory. Moriarty, Kalill, and Benander describe a psychosocially informed systemic approach that identifies children who are at risk of being harmed or of harming others. And Lightburn describes a community-wide systems of care model. Fortunately, these widely ranging theoretical perspectives complement one another remarkably well.

The third premise follows directly from the second. Understanding and responding helpfully to school violence requires a public health approach that emphasizes the importance of building partnerships between schools, families, and community agencies. Synergism develops when professionals from different disciplines collaborate with family members and community helpers. Collaboration makes it possible for partnership members to develop programs that are culturally sensitive, systemically oriented, psychologically attuned, developmentally informed, and syntonic with the values of particular communities. Moreover, there is reason to believe that the processes involved in creating partnerships, as well as the ongoing negotiations and discussions necessary to maintain collaborative relationships, play an essential role in facilitating constructive systemic, personal, and interpersonal change.

Format

This volume is divided into three parts. The first offers theoretical perspectives on understanding the etiology and consequences of school, family, and community violence. Included are chapters by Garbarino; McAlister Groves; Gelinas; Leone, Mayer, Malmgren, and Meisel; and Miller. Taken together, these contributions provide a theoretical overview of psychosocial factors that can either exacerbate or protect against the dire consequences of violent behavior. They also emphasize the degree to which trauma and violence interact to reinforce each other. Observing and/or personally experiencing interpersonal violence traumatizes children, whenever or wherever it occurs. It is most damaging, however, when it erupts in families and schools, environments where children ordinarily expect to be safe. In addition, a subset of traumatized children identify with the people who injure and/or frighten them. Among such children, traumatic exposure markedly increases the likelihood that they will act violently toward others. The idea that violence begets trauma and that trauma begets further violence is hardly new. As the authors in this section highlight, however, we cannot separate school violence from the violence that so frequently saturates American society. It seems evident, then, that if we really want to ameliorate school violence rather than simply broadcast pious sentiments, we must examine and modify some cherished policies that systematically work to undermine the well-being of vulnerable children and families.

The second section describes a number of school-based interventions. Weinhold observes and describes the existence of a schoolwide "culture of violence" that legitimizes widespread bullying. Horton-Parker also makes observations about a school-based culture of violence and presents thoughtful practical guidelines to help parents effectively teach their children prosocial behavior. Schamess discusses and evaluates some carefully researched group and schoolwide curricula directed toward reducing school violence. Corbin presents a comprehensive model for school reform that facilitates team building among and between the various constituencies that determine how schools actually function. Brassard and Butterfass explore the dynamics of escalation of violent situations in schools and offer suggestions to school personnel about how to de-escalate incipient conflict. Miller describes debriefing, an intervention that responds to the disorganizing effects of catastrophic events. Fanolis discusses the benefits of developing crisis intervention teams within schools. Moriarty, Kalill, and Benander present a "protocol approach" that assesses risk and provides guidelines for intervening with children who seem likely to victimize others or to be victimized. And finally, Sessions, Fanolis, Corwin, and Miller describe a collaborative project between a school for social work and an urban public school system in which closely supervised Master of Social Work interns provide clinical services to children and family members as well as offer developmentally and systemically informed consultation to teachers, administrators, and community helpers.

The third section presents community-based interventions. Prothrow-Stith advocates for a public health oriented, collaborative, community-wide response to violence. Rodriguez Martin discusses how in Springfield, Massachusetts, a graduate master of social work program, two public school systems, law enforcement agencies, and representatives from several community agencies are linked together to create a functional community partnership. Perez describes unexpected similarities between socialization processes in extended families and in organized street gangs and urges parents to take the time to teach prosocial traditions to their children. Lightburn discusses and evaluates the benefits inherent in utilizing the federally supported systems of care intervention model, which encourages collaboration between community institutions in addressing educational, health, and mental health issues. The section concludes with a description of how Eismann uses group-as-a-whole and psychodramatic techniques to create a street-level community of children in which older children nurture and care for nonrelated younger peers, thereby creating a supportive network of protective, symbolic brother/sister relationships.

Conclusion

Despite their theoretical and programmatic diversity, all of the contributions to this volume advance the theme of partnership building. By bringing together chapters written by practitioners who represent different theoretical orientations and practice experiences, we hope to encourage interdisciplinary discussion, expand the understanding of school violence, and find ways of responding more effectively to violent behavior when it occurs. Not surprisingly, the organization and contents of the volume reflect our collaboration as coeditors. In true parallel process, each of us brings a different theoretical orientation to the project. Rodriguez Martin is an expert in organizational theory and management practices, Miller adds a public policy/family systems/crisis intervention orientation, and Schamess is guided by psychodynamic, group process, and developmental theories. In spite of these differences, the collaboration has been both enjoyable and mutually instructive. Through our work on this book we have become increasingly convinced that interdisciplinary partnerships are essential for understanding and addressing the issues of reducing school violence, teaching prosocial behavior, and enhancing educational achievement as well as other issues in which social, educational, community, legal, family, cultural, interpersonal, and intrapsychic factors intersect dynamically.

By describing our positive experience as editors, we do not mean to imply that collaboration is either easy or conflict free. Under the best of circumstances, it entails hard work and determination, especially when fundamental conflicts emerge. In today's corporately oriented political climate, conflict breaks out between disciplines, not necessarily because of theoretical or methodological differences, but rather because of fierce interdisciplinary and interagency competition that discourages both collaboration and integration. At present, the U.S. government seems inclined to deal with many of its deeply contentious social conflicts by enacting public policies that have mutually exclusive objectives without acknowledging that it is impossible to achieve those objectives regardless of how much financial and political pressure funding agencies exert. To put it more simply, policy makers engage in a great deal of "doing" and "undoing" as they cobble together "solutions" to conflictual issues. In attempting to address school violence, for example, experts in both the public and private sectors explicitly promote programmatic cooperation while simultaneously implementing rationing systems that encourage ferocious competition for limited government and foundation financing. And, because most conflicts in this society stem from money issues, the dilemma is further exacerbated by policies that provide funding only for "innovative," time limited, research/demonstration projects that end when the original grant runs out. Theoretically, it makes good sense to ask local communities to pick up the funding for successful school-based programs, but such policy blithely ignores the fact that, typically, our cash strapped communities do not have the financial resources necessary to support new initiatives, even when those initiatives prove to be very effective. Accordingly, many efficacious programs end up on an Everest-sized scrap heap of discarded initiatives. Policies that (a) underfund school systems because of budgetary constraints, (b) increase performance expectations without a concomitant increase in state aid to local school districts, and (c) abandon programs that effectively address particular problems play a major role in creating an unrecognized and unacknowledged form of institutional violence directed against children and families. The consequences of such policies are frequently dire.

Some decades ago, family therapists and communications theorists introduced double-bind theory, a concept that addresses situations in which a family member is expected to pursue contradictory goals (e.g., staying home to care for a parent and leaving home to pursue a successful business career) without any acknowledgment that those goals are mutually exclusive. The theory asserts that double-bind messages tend to generate confused and irrational mental states that sometimes express themselves in psychotic or psychotic-like symptoms. In other words, double-bind expectations are frequently "crazy making." Although micro-theories do not necessarily provide useful explanations for macro-phenomena, this particular concept offers a thought-provoking framework for understanding the corrosive effects that presumably well-intended policies can create. What is "double binding" about contemporary educational policy is the tendency, for example, to couple the idea that competition is the best way of ensuring program efficacy with the idea that developing collaborative public-private partnerships is the most promising approach for reducing school violence. Because collaboration and competition are mutually exclusive goals, we cannot, reasonably, expect to achieve both simultaneously. In view of our apparent inability to agree about common objectives, the consequences of our disagreements would be far less problematic if we could at least acknowledge, publicly, that we are trying to advance in opposite directions at the same time.

Having raised this concern, we feel it important to also emphasize that the available statistics show that risk taking (e.g., carrying a weapon) and violent behavior have either leveled off or declined among schoolchildren over the past 6 years (Leone, Mayer, Malmgren, & Meisel, Chapter 4 in this volume). These changes are a tribute to the school-based violence reduction and crisis intervention programs reported here and elsewhere in the professional literature. Only time will tell whether or to what degree these statistics will be affected by the current economic downturn and the national emphasis on fighting terrorism. But at least for the moment, the news is encouraging.

Given what we currently understand about the interplay between individual behavior and social structure, it seems clear that we cannot eradicate school violence completely. Nonetheless, school violence can be reduced and its dynamics altered. Moreover, as our understanding of the multiple determinants of violent behavior increases, we should be better able to utilize a public health approach in developing programs that help students, educators, counselors, mental health providers, and other community helpers ameliorate the traumatogenic effects of such violence.

Both social work and education emphasize the importance of understanding and working with individuals within their social contexts. Although, oftentimes, the ideal outstrips the realities of our theoretical knowledge and practice capabilities, the level of collaboration represented in this volume and the growing support for public-private partnerships (when not undermined by conflicting policy mandates) take us a step closer to realizing the ideal. School violence affects everyone in America. It not only reflects the society we have created, but it also forces us to think about discrepancies between what we say we believe, the policies we enact, and the social institutions we create. Most Americans would agree that children have a fundamental right to feel safe and to be safe at school. As adults living in the richest, most powerful nation in the world, we owe at least that much to our children and to ourselves.

Joshua Miller
Irene Rodriguez Martin
Gerald Schamess

CONTRIBUTORS

Mark Benander, Ph.D., is a licensed psychologist in Massachusetts. Dr. Benander has extensive experience in the treatment of mental illness with a specialty in crisis intervention with adults, adolescents, and children. He has expertise in several forensic areas including both workplace and school violence, disability assessment, and psycho-diagnostic assessment for psychiatric commitment.

Marla Brassard, Ph.D., is Associate Professor of Psychology and Education at Teachers College, Columbia University. Her research focuses on the mental injuries and behavioral problems that result from parental psychological maltreatment and the contextual factors that moderate the effect of maltreatment, particularly the role of schools, teachers and peer relationships.

Michelle Butterfass, M.A., is an advanced doctoral student in School Psychology at Teachers College, Columbia University. Her research focuses on peer sexual harassment in early adolescence, particularly the factors that make some adolescents more vulnerable to experiencing sexual harassment by their peers. She has worked in schools, clinics, and hospitals with emotionally and behaviorally disturbed children and adolescents.

Joanne Corbin, Ph.D., is an assistant professor at the Smith College School for Social Work where she teaches child development, research methodology, and social work in school systems. Dr. Corbin has worked extensively in the field of mental health since 1979, focusing on the psychosocial issues of children, adults, and families, and on systemic work within public school systems.

Maria Corwin, Ph.D., is an associate professor at Bryn Mawr College Graduate School of Social Work and Social Research where she teaches clinical practice and HBSE courses. She is the author of a forthcoming book on time-limited clinical social work practice and has published articles and chapters on brief treatment, borderline personality disorder, and diversity issues in practice.

Edward P. Eismann, M.S.W., Ph.D., is founder and clinical director of Unitas Therapeutic Community in the South Bronx, New York City. He is also a member of the adjunct faculty at the Smith College School for Social Work, Northampton, Massachusetts.

Verba Fanolis, M.S.W., is the project coordinator of "Partners for Success," a community collaboration between the Smith College School for Social Work and the Springfield, Massachusetts School Department. She also worked at the Springfield Child Guidance Clinic, where she provided outpatient services to bereaved and traumatized clients.

James Garbarino, Ph.D., is a psychologist and co-director of the Family Life Development Center at Cornell University. He has focused his more than thirty-year career on the effects of violence on children. Dr. Garbarino has served as a consultant or advisor to a wide range of organizations including the National Committee to Prevent Child Abuse, the National Institute for Mental Health, and the American Medical Association. He is the author of numerous books including *Lost Boys: Why Our Sons Turn Violent and How We Can Save Them* (2000), *Children in Danger: Coping with the Consequences of Community Violence* (1998), and *Raising Children in a Socially Toxic Environment* (1995).

Denise J. Gelinas, Ph.D., is a member of the associate professional staff, Department of Psychiatry, Baystate Medical Center, Springfield, Massachusetts, where she founded and co-directed the Incest Treatment Program. She has presented nationally and internationally and has written extensively, most recently co-authoring *Addressing Child Sexual Abuse Allegations in Probate and Family Court: A Protocol.* She is an approved consultant in EMDR and conducts private practice and consultation in Northampton, MA.

Betsy McAlister Groves, Lic. S.W., is the founding director of the Child Witness to Violence Project at Boston Medical Center and assistant professor of pediatrics at Boston University School of Medicine.

Radha J. Horton-Parker, is an associate professor in the Department of Educational Leadership and Counseling at Old Dominion University in Norfolk, Virginia.

Paul M. Kalill, J.D., Ph.D., has a law degree and a degree in Forensic Psychology. He practices law in Springfield, MA, teaches at Springfield College, and is the co-author of the Protocol Approach Program. He is a consultant to corporations and governmental bodies and is a partner in Kalill, Moriarty, and Associates, Consultants and Workshops.

Peter E. Leone, Ph.D., is Professor at the University of Maryland and directs the National Center on Education, Disability, and Juvenile Justice, a project funded by the Office of Special Education Programs and the Office of Juvenile Justice and Delinquency Prevention.

Anita Lightburn, M.S.S., Ed.D., is a professor and Dean emeriti, Smith College School for Social Work. She is a consultant in the development of school based mental health services and is currently involved in research on community-based systems of care for children and adolescents with severe emotional disturbances and program evaluation of early childhood programs.

Kimber Malmgren, Ph.D., is an Assistant Professor in the Department of Special Education at the University of Maryland.

Irene Rodriguez Martin, B.S.W., MBA, is director of Graduate Enrollment and Continuing Education at the Smith College School for Social Work (SSW). She has extensive community outreach and organizational experience. From 1995–1999, she served as an organizational consultant to the SSW Partners for Success program, and in 2000 coordinated the conference *School Violence: Building Fortresses or Opening the Doors to Community?*

Matthew Mayer, Ph.D., is in the Department of Special Education at Michigan State University and specializes in school violence research.

Sheri Meisel, Ph.D., is Associate Director of the National Center on Education, Disability, and Juvenile Justice, a project funded by the Office of Special Education Programs and the Office of Juvenile Justice and Delinquency Prevention.

Joshua Miller, Ph.D., M.S.W., is an associate professor and co-chair of the Social Policy Sequence at Smith College School for Social Work. Before joining the faculty at Smith, he worked as a social worker, family therapist, community organizer, and agency director for more than twenty years. He is currently doing practice and research in the area of responses to community trauma and violence.

Ann Moriarty, Ph.D., is the director of the Clinical Health Graduate Counseling Program at Springfield College, Springfield, MA. She has extensive experience in psychological crisis intervention and is the co-author of *A Protocol Approach to School Violence*. Dr. Moriarty is a partner in Kalill, Moriarty, and Associates, Consultants and Workshops.

Monica H. Perez, J.D., is Associate Professor of Criminal Justice at Mount Holyoke Community College. She has worked with the Massachusetts Department of Youth Services providing Gang Awareness Training throughout New England and has instructed at the State Police Training Academy in Braintree.

Deborah Prothrow-Stith, M.D., is the associate dean at the Harvard School of Public Health, and is considered to be one of society's foremost authorities on the subject of violence. A graduate of Spellman College, she received her MD from Harvard Medical School in 1979. Her anti-violence efforts have led her from developing programs at neighborhood clinics and inner-city hospitals to serving as Massachusetts State Commissioner of Public Health. She is the author of the first violence prevention curriculum for school and communities *(Violence Prevention Curriculum for Adolescents)* and co-author of *Deadly Consequences,* which considers violence from a public health perspective.

Gerald Schamess, M.S.S., is Acting Associate Dean and Professor at the Smith College School for Social Work where he teaches advanced treatment courses in the school's master and doctoral programs. He has published on the therapeutic process, group psychotherapy with children and adolescents, trauma recovery, and managed mental health care. He also serves as the editor of the *Smith College Studies in Social Work.*

Phebe Sessions, Ph.D., is at the Smith College School for Social Work where she serves as Chair of the Social Work Practice Sequence. She currently has been exploring the relevance of narrative therapies, based on poststructural theories for collaborative models of practice in inner-city schools. She has directed the Partners for Success Program in Springfield since its inception.

Barry K. Weinhold, Ph.D., is at the University of Colorado–Colorado Springs in the Counseling and Human Services Program. He does research and training in conflict resolution, school violence, and leadership. He is the co-author of *Counseling Families* published by Love Publishing Company.

PART ONE

Children and Violence: Theoretical Perspectives

1

Why Our Children Turn Violent and How We Can Save Them

James Garbarino

There was a time not that long ago when the issue of lethal youth violence was marginalized. The worst example of this that I have encountered occurred about 10 years ago, when I worked in Chicago. I received a call from the office of a senator who was considering conducting hearings on youth violence. An aide was sent to spend time in Chicago and other major cities to collect background information. A month later, the aide called to say that he had completed his report for the senator. In his report, he concluded that the problem of lethal youth violence was primarily confined to poor minority kids. The senator's response had been, "Well, that's good news. Then we don't have to have hearings." His exact words were, reportedly, "Let them kill each other off."

Well, we are now a long way from that response, as evidenced by, for example, the 1999 White House summit on youth violence held in May in the wake of the Littleton shootings in Colorado. What has changed is that now all of America—including middle-class white America—can look in the newspaper and see their kids involved with or victim to violence. That makes youth violence a national issue worthy of presidential attention, hearings, and programs. We need to understand the legacy of racism and classism that informs this issue and defines it in many ways, but at the same time we need to make use of this mobilization of energy. Simply because energy is mobilized does not mean that people will do the right thing. Constructive change does not simply involve mobilizing energy and getting people's attention. It requires us to do something that we, as Americans, do not do very well—that is, think deeply about the issue.

With regard to action, Americans are number one. It is known around the world that if you want something done, you should get an American. The slogan "Just do it!" should probably be our national motto. This is really our strong suit. If a child is stuck in a well some place, we are the ones to handle it. We will mobilize, dig, raise funds for the child, and everyone will think it is terrific. But if what is needed is to think more deeply about the issue, it is necessary to lean on a much more European tradition, where theory and deep analysis have a longer history and a greater social credence.

There was a German psychologist named Kurt Lewin who worked in the United States and tried to bring this European approach to America. Lewin (1935) once wrote, "There is nothing so practical as a good theory," which to an American often sounds like a contradiction in terms. We tend to think theoretical is over *here* and practical over *there*. Lewin understood that to do good practice you have to understand things deeply. This is evident in many sound programs.

For example, in almost every state in the country, home visiting is being offered as a strategy for preventing child abuse, and with good reason. Research and program development done 20 years ago by psychologist David Olds and colleagues (1997) resulted in a home visiting program that was very effective in reducing child abuse. Olds spent a lot of time thinking through the interrelationship behind child development, family development, and intervention. When he got it all right theoretically, he came up with the nurse home visitor program, where nurses begin visiting during the prenatal period and continue for 2 years after birth. Now, 17 years later, Olds's research shows that the nurse home visitor is very powerful in protecting children from being abused. But the minute the program was turned over to the local health department, people who had not made the same investment in understanding the theory behind the program started making changes. Somebody said, "Well, you know, you've got caseloads of 10 families per nurse; we'll get a lot more bang for the buck if we have 30 families per nurse. Let's make it 30." Somebody else said, "Well, you have nurses doing this visiting. It would be a lot cheaper if we had volunteer lay-people do it—let's have volunteer laypeople." Somebody else said, "Well, you know, it's not convenient to begin visiting before the babies are born. Why don't we just wait until after they are born because then we'll have birth certificates?" When you start cavalierly changing the key elements that are grounded in the theory of a program, the program does not work the same way anymore. This is dangerous, but it is also very characteristic of America. "Just do it!"

To approach the issue of violence and safe schools, we need to think *more deeply*. Another way to make that point is with a parable. A parable, of course, is a teaching story, and this parable has something to teach us as Americans. It is called the parable of the lamppost. In the parable of the lamppost, Joe is on his way home from a meeting one night. He comes upon his friend George, who is on his hands and knees on the street, groping around under a lamppost. Joe stops and asks, "George, what's the matter?" George says, "Well, Joe, I have lost my car keys. I live 35 miles away, and I can't go home until I find them." "Well," says Joe, "Let me help you." So, like a good American, he rolls up his sleeves and he gets down on the street and starts groping around under the lamppost looking for the keys. Some time passes with no result, so Joe says, "Wait a moment, George. Maybe we need a more systematic approach. Maybe we need a *public health approach*." From his pocket he pulls a piece of chalk and draws a grid on the street under the lamppost and labels the boxes A through Z and 1 through 26. "Now," he says, "we can search systematically." So they search: Box A1, Box A2, Box A3, Box A4, on and on until they get to Box Z26. But they have not found the car keys. After thinking for a moment, Joe says, "Maybe we need a more *behaviorist approach*." So from his other pocket, he pulls a bag of candy. He says, "George, I am going to feed you this candy to get your behavior under control." He gets George moving left and right, and back and forth. It was very impressive, but they still had not found the car keys. So Joe says, "Maybe we need a more *psychoanalytic, psychodynamic approach*." He asks George about early experiences of loss in his life. Soon George remembers that when he was 4 years old he lost his teddy bear, and his feelings of loss come flooding back to him now with the loss of the car keys. Soon George is getting great insight, but he still cannot go home. "Well," says Joe, "maybe we need a *support group*." So he gets out his cell phone and calls other people who have lost their car keys. They talk to George, and soon George is feeling okay about losing his car keys. "Well," says Joe, "that didn't work. Maybe we need a more *educational approach*." So he pulls from his bag a book titled *History of the Key in Western Civilization*. They read how Ingmar Bergman used the key as a metaphor in his films and how Woody Allen picked up on that metaphor in his films; it was quite enlightening. But they still cannot find the keys. Finally Joe is really depressed and says, "All right, George, let's take a really radical approach. Where exactly were you when you dropped the keys?" George says, "I was about 150 yards up the road when I dropped the keys." So, of course, Joe asks, "Why are we looking here?" George replies, "The light is much better here!"

The reason this parable is applicable to us today is that there are so many forces at work around and inside us influencing us to look where the light is good: where we can get funding, where there are grants, where we can get corporate sponsors, where it does not rock the boat, and where we are personally comfortable. The point of the parable is that if the real issues lie up the road somewhere, in the dark places where people do not want to go, working where the light is good will yield few results beyond the appearance of action. If we do not look in those dark places, we will not solve the problem.

To dig deeper into the issue of youth violence, and not just offer some meager, popular response, we need to improve what I like to call our *conceptual toolbox*. Every professional carries around a toolbox, and there are five or six concepts I would put in our box to address the issue of violence. The first is an *ecological perspective on human development*. When you look at research on human development with your eyes wide open, you find rarely, if ever, a simple cause/effect relationship. Cause/effect relationships are always shaped and conditioned by culture, society, community, gender, race, ethnicity, and historical period. If the question is "Does X cause Y?" the best answer is "It depends on the context in which X and Y are occurring."

The issue of violence raises numerous striking examples of the importance of context. Twenty-five years ago a study by Mednick (1988) asked the question, "Are kids who are born with minor neurological damage more likely to end up as violent teenagers than biologically normal children?" (Well, now you know the answer: It depends.) It turned out if the children with minor neurological damage were growing up in well-functioning families, they were no more likely than biologically normal children to end up as violent teenagers. But if the children with neurological damage were growing up in abusive families and dysfunctional communities, they were 4 times as likely to end up as violent teenagers than biologically normal children were. The impact of biological risk, or disability, or vulnerability, depends on the context in which a child grows up.

This finding has tremendous implications for the practice of child welfare. If we are dealing with high-risk kids who have a tradition, a heritage, of risk, we had better be very careful about where we place them. That is one reason why kinship foster care is a risky proposition in many cases. Take, for example, the case of the 6-year-old boy in Michigan who shot and killed his first-grade classmate. He had been living with his mother, who was part of an illicit drug ring and his father was in prison. After the shooting he and his brother were sent to live with their uncle, their mother's brother, who was also part of the illicit drug ring. The kingpin of the drug ring was the boys' maternal grandmother. Would you want to place that child in foster care with his maternal grandmother? Eventually he was placed with his aunt, his mother's sister. You would surely want to know if she was a part of the same drug abusing family system, because if she was, you would be almost dooming that boy to replicate his father's criminal record and imprisonment.

Other studies on violence speak in the same way about the role of family context and community context. The point is that massive social risk, when it is present, tends to be overwhelming. The relevance of subtle difficulties in thinking and feeling may be diminished because of the overwhelming character of the context. Conversely, if zero risk exists in terms of social environmental factors, then it stands to reason that the only kids who are going to be in big trouble are those who have some neurological predisposition.

A study conducted in Germany tells a similar story. For a long time people have suspected or said they had known that kids who are prone to bullying are temperamentally not like other kids. By the same token, kids who are prone to victimization are not like other kids. The thinking goes that kids prone to victimization are kids who are hypersensitive, because bullies try their bullying out on everybody and eventually realize that some kids get really upset by it. The kids who are prone to bullying are that way because they have a belligerent temperament. The German study looked at the base heart rate of bullies, victims, and kids who were neither bullies nor victims; but the study also looked at context. To that end, the researchers measured the heart rates of kids in high-risk and low-risk families. They found that kids in low-risk families had different base heart rates if they were bullies, victims, or neither. The bullies had an average heart rate of 65 beats per minute, the victims had an average heart rate of 75 beats per minute, and the kids who were neither bullies nor victims had an average heart rate of 70 beats per minute. But in the high-risk families, all three groups had heart rates of 70 beats per minute. In a high-risk environment, it did not take a temperamental predisposition to produce a bully or a victim; the environment was so overwhelming that it crashed down on the kids.

The second key concept for our toolbox is the *accumulation of risk and opportunity* in children's lives. Research shows that rarely, if ever, does a single risk factor or a single opportunity factor account for much in the outcome of children. If we are trying to account for violence, we cannot look at one single factor. My book *Lost Boys* happened to come out the morning of the Littleton shootings, so it got a lot of extra attention. Journalists kept asking, "What is the cause for this tragedy?" And I kept trying to say that there is no *cause,* there is only the accumulation of risk. It is as if a boy is building a tower of blocks, block after block after block, and finally he puts one more block on the tower and it falls over. You cannot say that the last block is the cause of the fall because if that block were there by itself, it would not fall over. If some other block was put on last, it would appear to be the cause. Indeed, the research shows that it is the accumulation of risk factors that does the damage.

A classic study demonstrating this notion of accumulation of risk was done by University of Michigan psychologist Arnold Sameroff and his colleagues (Sameroff, Seifer, Barocas, Zax, & Greenspan, 1987). The Sameroff study looked at the accumulation of risk and its impact on intellectual development. Intellectual development is relevant to the issue of violence because it is known that average intellectual functioning is one of the pillars of resilience; it increases the ability to deal with adversity. The Sameroff study deals with how risk accumulation affects intellectual development, which ultimately plays a role in violence and aggression. Sameroff and colleagues looked at the following risk factors: poverty, absence of a parent, drug abuse in a parent, mental illness in a parent, low educational attainment in a parent, child abuse in the family, exposure to racism, and large family size. When none of these risk factors were present, the average IQ score was 119.

As risk accumulated, the story became very interesting. With one risk factor, the average IQ score was 116; with two risk factors, 113. Now that is really good news for the human enterprise—life does not have to be totally risk free for kids to thrive. Most kids can thrive with two risk factors, but for kids in the study with four risk factors, any four, the IQ scores went down to 93. Most kids can cope with two risk factors, but few can cope with four. For kids with eight risk factors, scores dropped to 85. That is the effect of the accumulation of risk. It has tremendous implications for our thinking about programs. Life does not have to be risk free, and no single risk factor is a problem in and of itself. The problem is not poverty, child abuse, or absent parents. Most kids can deal with any of those. The problem is too many of them. When we put too many burdens on a kid's shoulders, he or she cannot stand up under the weight.

But we also need to look at the accumulation of opportunity. More and more people are using the term "asset" to refer to these developmental opportunities. You may be familiar with the Search Institute in Minneapolis, Minnesota, and its research on developmental assets (Search Institute, Website). The 40 assets studied ranged from things inside the child and inside the family to attributes inside the school and inside the community. The list is incredibly diverse, including such assets as family life provides high level of support; child goes to church or religious institutions at least an hour a week; and young person is optimistic about his or her future. It is an incredible range of items. The researchers found that the more assets a child has in his or her life, the less likely he or she is to have problems.

Let us look at violence from this perspective. In the Search Institute study, a child fell into the violent category if he or she had engaged in three or more acts of hitting, fighting, injuring a person, carrying a weapon, or threatening physical harm in the past 12 months. Of the children who had 31 to 40 assets, only 6% were found to be in the violent category. Of the children who had 21 to 30 assets, 16% were in the violent category. Of the children who had 11 to 20 assets, 35% were in the violent category. And of the children with 0 to 10 of these assets, 61% were in the violent category. The issue is not which asset you have but, rather, how many assets you have. It is a mirror image of risk accumulation.

An issue worth considering, however, is the 6% of the children with between 31 and 40 assets who *were* in the violent category. How could they be violent? With kids who have between 0 and 10 assets we can say, "Well, sure, what do you expect?" But notice that even with 0 to 10 assets, 39% *are not* in the violent category. A third of these kids were hanging in there being prosocial. Kids are resilient even when they have nothing going for them. The 6% of the kids who were violent even though they had many assets might be called asset-resistant. Think about a boy like Dylan Klebold, one of the shooters at the school in Littleton, Colorado. Dylan had numerous assets: loving, competent, caring parents; good school; no poverty; affluence—you name it, he had it. What right did he have to be so screwed up? Well, maybe he was an asset-resistant kid with a troubled inner life. When you look at kids who kill, 90% are not surprising at all. Their lives are full of abuse, trauma, deprivation, impoverishment, and oppression. But 10% of the kids who kill are of this more mysterious kind that comes out of nowhere socially.

This assets approach also provides insight into opportunities for intervention. For example, of the assets studied by the Search Institute, about 10 are very much a function of the school a child attends. Some school climates provide a caring, encouraging environment; parents are actively involved in helping young people succeed in school; youngsters feel safe at home, at school, and in the neighborhood; school provides clear rules and consequences, and so forth. What kinds of schools are most likely to provide these assets to students, making the schools safer for the students, from the students, and for the community? One issue to consider is size.

Research from the 1950s (Barker & Gump, 1964) showed us that small high schools create a different social climate than big high schools do. The assets associated with schools in this study included such things as participation in music, theater, or art at least 3 hours a week; participation in sports or youth organizations; and parents actively involved with school programs. Another asset is that everyone is needed, not because the teachers and the principal go to inclusiveness workshops or have had their consciousnesses raised, but because the context demands participation. The research found that in small high schools, kids were much more likely to be provided with all of these assets than in a big high school. This was particularly important for marginal students, those at risk of dropping out, those who were disaffected, those whose parents did not support their education, those with lower IQ scores; for those kids, the research found that small schools were better.

In a big school, students try out for activities, and those who do not make the cut cannot participate. These students do not feel they are in a caring environment. They do not participate in activities; they do not feel safe. The research found that when student population got larger than about 500 for grades 9 to 12, the schools very quickly crossed over into the dynamic of bigness. In 1955, the average student population of America's high schools was 500; by 1975 it was about 1,500.

The third concept we need to bring to our toolbox is *humility about resilience.* I have used that term earlier: resilience, the ability to deal with adversity, the idea that we can cope but we also have limits. In American society, however, the term resilience has a kind of dark side. In this judgmental society, it's a short step between celebrating coping and being judgmental of those who are not coping. The worst example I encountered occurred when I was testifying in the murder trial of a 16-year-old boy. My job was to explain to the jury how the accumulation of risk in the absence of assets should be understood to help make sense of what the boy did—not just to excuse what he did, but to make sense of it. In the cross-examination the prosecutor asked, "What's wrong with this boy that he isn't resilient?" And I realized that instead of celebrating coping, we were making a deficiency judgment.

Two studies give an intellectual foundation for the humility we need to have in thinking about resilience. Brigadier General S. L. A. Marshall, the official U.S. military historian of World War II in Europe, commissioned the first study. He asked the following question: If regular soldiers go into combat and stay in combat for 60 days, what percentage end up as psychiatric casualties? The data showed that after 60 days of combat, 98% of the soldiers became psychiatric casualties. One has to question the intellectual justification for judging those soldiers as being deficient, when 98% became psychiatric casualties, particularly because the 2% who did not break down were found to not be robust healthy, well-adjusted men—they were all psychopaths. That gives us a perspective on resilience—the only people who did not go crazy already were crazy (Grossman, 1996).

Psychologist Pat Tolan from the University of Illinois did the domestic equivalent to that study when he asked what percentage of kids would break down under the burden of various levels of additional risk factors (Tolan, 1996). The researchers measured "breaking down" in both academic terms (needing remedial special education) and mental health terms (needing professional mental health intervention). The risk factors considered included living in violent, impoverished neighborhoods; abuse and neglect; being between the ages of 13 and 15; being male; and being a person of color. Tolan wondered what percentage of children with all five of these risk factors would show one or both forms of breakdown. Not surprisingly, the answer was 100%. Having so many risk factors does not mean such kids' lives are over. Many of them find a way back, but anyone with that burden takes a major hit.

To make the concept even more concrete to you personally, think about whether you consider yourself in good physical shape because you work out or do aerobics or in less good shape—that is, a couch potato. If I were to ask which group has better lung capacity, better resilient breathing, surely it would be the aerobic group. But then if I asked which group would last longer on the surface of the moon, the answer would be neither group. All the aerobic breathing in the world is not going to protect you on the surface of the moon. That is the starting point for humility about resilience, resilience in context. And there but for the grace of God go any of us.

The fourth concept for our toolbox is the issue of *temperament*—the recognition that children come to us with different packages of attributes: active, passive, soothable, unsoothable, and so forth. Temperament, however, is not destiny. It is probability. Temperament is what the child offers up to the world as a possibility and a challenge, or a direction. Without knowledge, without resources, without intelligence, without insight, temperament shapes patterns of behavior that lead kids down different pathways. In *The Challenging Child* (1996), Stanley Greenspan looks at five different kinds of difficult temperaments and shows how to succeed with each one. If temperament is a challenge, how do parents succeed in meeting that challenge? It is important to understand how the child sees and experiences the world. As I said before, temperament takes place in context too; temperament predicts violence in some situations but not in others. We can override temperament to a large degree.

The next key concept for the toolbox is *rejection.* Anthropologist Ronald Rohner (1975) studied rejection in 118 cultures around the world and found that in every one of the cultures, kids who are rejected turn out badly, and they turn out badly in ways that are culturally appropriate. They develop whatever is bad in that culture, so much so that Rohner called rejection a psychological malignancy or psychological cancer. This is important for understanding youth violence because one of the themes for kids who are violent is the problem of rejection. It may be interpersonal rejection in the family or in school, or it may be linked to homophobia or to racism. In any case, it is internalized as rejection of who you are as a person, of your identity. Rejection produces shame, shame produces anxiety about psychic annihilation (you feel you will cease to exist), and violence is one sure way to demonstrate to yourself and to others that you do indeed exist. A man in prison once said to a colleague of mine, "I'd rather be wanted for murder than not be wanted at all." If positive acceptance is not provided, there is always the negative route. The experience of being wanted and needed is one of the psychological anchors that keeps kids steady.

The last concept for the toolbox is *spirituality*—the recognition that human beings are not simply animals with complicated brains but are spiritual beings as well. Not meeting your spiritual needs can produce damage in much the same way as not meeting your physical, nutritional, emotional, and intellectual needs does. Of all the characteristics I have found in common in the kids I have interviewed who have killed, spiritual emptiness is perhaps the most common thread. I think there are at least three reasons why a spiritually empty child is in jeopardy. First, a spiritually empty child has a kind of hole in his or her heart, and that hole must be filled with some sense of meaningfulness. If it is not filled by the positive meaningfulness of a universe of love and a reverence for life, then it will be filled with a kind of demonically meaningful interpretation of life. Second, a child who is spiritually empty has no sense of limits. Spiritually grounded children have a sense that they exist in a meaningful spiritual universe, that they are not acting alone, and that there are limits on them and on what they can do. Reverence for life comes naturally. A spiritually empty child says, "I'm on my own in here, it's me and you. You make me angry, you deserve to die. You make me afraid, you deserve to die. You make me feel bad, you deserve to die." Third, a spiritually empty child has no emotional floor to fall back on when he or she gets sad. A grounded child could say, "I may feel lousy, but at least I know I live in a meaningful universe and there's a comfort to that." The spiritually empty child is on his or her own. He or she can go into emotional free fall and can fall as low as a human being can possibly go.

If you start to put all these concepts together—spirituality, rejection, temperament, accumulation of risk, ecological perspective, humility about resilience—you have the tools for beginning to look at the different pathways that kids take. When these tools are used, it becomes clear that 90% of the kids who are put on the pathway that includes abuse, deprivation, and oppression develop a chronic pattern of aggression, bad behavior, acting out, and violation of others' rights by the time they are 10. These are behaviors that might meet the diagnostic standard for conduct disorder. We know that 30% of kids diagnosed with conduct disorder by age 10 end up as delinquents in adolescence (Dodge, Pettit, & Bates, 1997). But even here, context has its effects: In some neighborhoods, the figure is 65%; in other neighborhoods, it is 15%—same patterns of behavior, different ramifications. The outcome depends on the context in which the children grow up, the context of peer support, the context of gun availability, the context of media imagery and so forth.

I was in Canada a few weeks ago on the day of a school massacre. In Ottawa, a 15-year-old boy attacked his school. The TV images looked just like U.S. TV images: ambulances, police cars, girls crying into one another's shoulders, boys trying to hold back their tears, distraught parents. Five kids were sent to the hospital, all of whom were released with minor injuries because the only weapon the attacker could come up with was a knife. Put that same boy on our side of the border and there would have been a gun, and it would not have caused minor injuries. That is part of the toxicity in which these troubled kids are drowning.

A few years ago a survey of the youth prison system (Edens & Otto, 1997) found that 85% of the boys in prison have conduct disorders. How surprising! How else do you end up in a prison except by showing a chronic pattern of aggression, bad behavior, acting out, and violating the rights of others?

Now remember that 90% of the kids who develop a chronic pattern of aggression, bad behavior, acting out, and violating others' rights come from backgrounds including abuse, deprivation, and oppression. They go down the route of conduct disorder. Whether they end up as killers depends a lot on how toxic or benign the culture is around them. But as I said before, there are also the other 10% who are not abused, who do not develop early conduct disorder, but who become so troubled in their thinking and feeling that they really lose their way in the world. Ironically, they often try to keep that a secret. They develop a secret life because they do not want to disappoint their parents; their parents love them. They do not want to disappoint their teachers; their teachers care for them. Boys in particular keep this secret world.

We are doing a study at Cornell called "The Secret Life of Teenagers" in which we are asking college students to talk about the most dangerous/illegal things they did when they were teenagers, things their parents still do not know about. Some of the stories we are hearing are hair-raising. And this is among Ivy League students who are in human development.

Kip Kinkel, the school shooter in Springfield, Oregon, was hearing voices and never told anybody because he did not want to disappoint his parents. Michael Carneal, the boy from West Paducah, Kentucky, who shot up a prayer meeting, had a photographic memory—total recall for every insult he had ever experienced in his life going back to age 3. Nobody knew this; it did not leak out until his secret life burst forth in a barrage of bullets.

The real challenge for us in thinking about school safety and safe schools is to find a way to use these concepts to understand the development of every kid who walks in the doors of our schools, whether they are prone to be in the 90% or the 10%. We need to develop the infrastructure of mental health services, of caring, of participation, of character education, to support, accept, and nurture kids in a way that will meet their spiritual and their emotional needs. And if we do all of this and we keep our eyes open, we can probably have safer schools.

**References**

Barker, R., & Gump, P. (1964). *Big school, small school.* Stanford, CA: Stanford University Press.

Dodge, K. A., Pettit, G. S., & Bates, J. E. (1997). How the experience of early physical abuse leads children to become chronically aggressive. In C. Cicchetti & S. L. Toth (Eds.), *Developmental psychopathology: Vol. 9. Theory, research, and intervention* (pp. 263–288). Rochester, NY: University of Rochester Press.

Edens, J. F. F., & Otto, R. K. (1997, Spring). Prevalence of mental disorders among youth in the juvenile system. *Focal Point: A National Bulletin on Family Support and Children's Mental Health, 1,* 6–7.

Garbarino, J. (1999). Lost boys: why our sons turn violent and how we can save them. NY: the Free Press.

Greenspan, S. (1995). The challenging child. NY: Perseus.

Grossman, D. (1996). On killing. NY: Little, Brown.

Lewin, K. (1935). *A dynamic theory of personality.* New York: McGraw-Hill.

Mednick, S. (1988). *Biological bases of antisocial behavior.* Norwell, MA: Keuwer.

Olds, D., Eckenrode, J., Henderson, C. R., Jr., Kotzman, H. K., Powers, J., Cole, R., et al. (1997). Long-term effects of home visitation on maternal life course and child abuse and neglect: 15-year follow-up of a randomized trial. *Journal of the American Medical Association, 278,* 637–643.

Rohner, R. (1975). *They love me, they love me not.* New Haven, CT: Human Relations Area Files Press.

Sameroff, A., Seifer, R., Barocas, R., Zax, M., & Greenspan, S. (1987). Intelligence quotient scores of 4-year-old children: Social environmental risk factors. *Pediatrics, 79,* 343–350.

Search Institute. (2000). *Developmental assets: An overview.* Retrieved from http://www.search-institute.org/assets/

Tolan, P. (1996, October). How resilient is the concept of resilience? *Community Psychologist, 4,* 12–15.

2

When Home Isn't Safe: Children and Domestic Violence

Betsy McAlister Groves

When we speak to groups of parents or professionals about our work with children who witness violence, they frequently ask about our findings: What kinds of violence are children being exposed to? What is the worst form of violence for children? As we have accumulated experience with many children and families, we have reached conclusions about the answers to those questions. Despite the fact that the Child Witness to Violence Project began as a response to children's exposure to community violence, we have learned that children are most affected by exposure to the more private and insidious violence that occurs inside their homes. Domestic violence, violence that occurs between adult caregivers in the home, seems to be the most toxic form of exposure to violence for children. Furthermore, we now believe that young children are far more likely to be exposed to violence in the home than violence on the street. For many children, the first lessons they learn about violence are not from television or from the streets, but are learned at the feet of their parents. These lessons are generally the wrong lessons: that it is acceptable to use threats or force to get one's way; that violence has a place in an intimate relationship; that adults can hurt one another and not apologize or take responsibility for their actions.

This is not to say that exposure to murder or mayhem on the streets does not affect children. Children talk extensively about their fear of going outside or going to school, their worries about their parents and families, and their sense of vulnerability.

From *Children Who See Too Much* by Betsey McAlister Groves; Copyright 2002 by Betsey McAlister Groves; Reprinted by permission of Beacon Press, Boston.

Parents speak with frustration and hopelessness about not being able to let their children go to the park or having to impose limits on their children, not because they do not trust them, but because they do not believe the environment is safe. Sometimes these limits become the source of conflict, as young children want to spend time with peers and parents simultaneously are frightened to allow their children to pursue this age-appropriate desire.

The violence that occurs within the home, however, is worse for children. They are more intensely affected and the consequences are more long-lasting. This form of violence has been shielded from the public eye. There has been little media attention about domestic violence unless it was a fatal or particularly horrific episode of abuse. In retrospect, as we looked back upon our initial expectations of who we would serve in the Child Witness to Violence Project, we realized that we, too, underestimated the prevalence of domestic violence. It was easier to look at the violence on the street than to face the horrors of what people who ostensibly loved one another could do to each other within the seclusion of their homes.

The conspiracy of avoidance was particularly obvious in the case of Charles and Carole Stuart in 1989. This case, which drew national attention, involved the murder of a young pregnant woman. Her husband reported that they had been assaulted and robbed by armed black men as they drove home from childbirth classes at a local hospital. The murder occurred in a predominantly black neighborhood of Boston. The coverage of the case played on stereotypes: black men are dangerous, especially to white women. Black neighborhoods are notoriously unsafe for white people. Police began a massive hunt for the assailant and arbitrarily rounded up many young black men to interview. They made a quick arrest and were prepared to close the case when the husband committed suicide by jumping off a bridge. It was then revealed that Charles Stuart had murdered his wife as part of a scheme to collect insurance money. The aftermath of that highly publicized event was a soul-searching debate about the assumptions we make about people and behavior.

In a similar manner, we discovered that it was easier for the Child Witness to Violence Project to focus on the effects of community violence on children than to look at the violence within children's homes. We wanted to disbelieve or minimize the stories that children told. These cases of domestic violence raised complex and difficult issues. They almost always involved other systems: police, child protection services, and the courts. Sometimes it was hard to tell the "good guys" from the "bad guys." We found ourselves angry with mothers for staying in the relationships, for not protecting their children. We felt helpless because there were no easy solutions for most of these cases. We were forced to look at our own attitudes and beliefs about relationships, conflict, and what is best for children.

Domestic violence (also termed spousal abuse, partner violence, family violence, intimate partner violence, wife-beating) technically refers to any act of interpersonal violence between or among family members, including child abuse. For purposes of this book, domestic violence refers to threats of intimidation or violence or actual acts of violence between adult partners. In our project, the large majority of cases involve acts of violence or threats made by men against women. This trend is borne out in the national statistics of reported domestic violence incidents. According to the Bureau of Justice Statistics at the U.S. Department of Justice, 85% of the victims of domestic assault are women. Domestic violence is sometimes described as a "women's issue" or a "feminist concern." From our experience, we believe it is everyone's problem and a critical issue for children. For anyone who is concerned about youth violence or violence prevention, the issue of domestic violence must be among the first to receive attention.

Wife abuse is not a new phenomenon. The current attention paid to this issue, however, is a result of the resurgence of the feminist movement in the 1960s and 1970s. In her book, *Heroes of Their Own Lives: Politics and History of Family Violence,* Linda Gordon provides a fascinating historical perspective on the evolution of domestic violence as a social problem.[1] Her analysis of child abuse/neglect records between 1880 and 1960 cites repeated references to wife abuse. This abuse, however, was neither identified as a problem nor directly addressed by social services. The focus was, instead, on children. At varying times, caseworkers responded with moral condemnation of mothers and fathers, with efforts to reform behavior, or with psychological condemnation, particularly of women, who were generally seen as either deserving or wanting the abuse. Women themselves appeared to ignore the abuse. They came forward for help with their children, rarely dwelling on their own abuse.

Throughout much of the 20th century, the courts routinely upheld sexually discriminatory laws reflecting the proper relationship between men and women, relationships that were based on English common law. This body of law held that women (and children) were the husband's property. These laws had far-reaching implications for women in terms of divorce law, domestic relations, and definitions of marital rape. The abuse of women was not acknowledged, much less labeled as criminal behavior. With the post–World War II prosperity, however, women became less dependent on men, both financially and psychologically, and the seeds of the women's movement were sown.

In the early 1960s with the beginning of the feminist movement, there was a new consciousness about violence within marital relationships. For the first time, this problem was framed as a social problem as opposed to a psychological or interpersonal problem. This important shift in definition laid the groundwork for the beginning of the battered women's movement in the 1970s. By this time, marital violence was defined as an abuse of power, to be viewed in the context of our tradition of patriarchal law.

This shift in definition of marital violence from personal to social problem redrew the lines between private behavior and public interest. Victims of domestic violence were heard in many forums. Laws were created to protect their rights and to criminalize wife abuse. An array of services, shelters, and counseling programs were created to serve victims and perpetrators of domestic violence. In short, the notion

---

[1]Gordon L. *Heroes of Their Own Lives: Politics and History of Family Violence,* New York: Viking, 1988.

of a man's house being his castle was dramatically changed as his private behavior landed in the public domain.

The history of public awareness of children as the hidden victims of domestic violence is even shorter than the history of awareness of domestic violence. There is scant mention in the child mental health literature of child witnesses to domestic violence before 1990. Even within the battered women's movement, there was little mention of children and few programmatic resources for them. The early advocates for victims of domestic violence believed that the focus should be on women's safety. Diverting resources to children reinforced the patriarchal attitudes of women's needs being placed last. In addition, there was the pressure of limited resources. Shelters operated on a limited budget and there was understandable reluctance to divert money to children's programming.

Services for the children of battered women began to grow in the early 1990s. This growth was probably due to two influences. First, there was a growing awareness in the child mental health community of the devastating impact of environmental trauma for children.[2-5] Research yielded valuable findings about the impact of early experiences on brain development and child functioning. The second factor that supported the growth of children's services was the influx of federal and state money for services to battered women. Perhaps the largest amount of money was made available by the federal government through the passage of the Violence Against Women Act in 1994, which provided more than one billion dollars for increased funding to battered women's shelters, training for police and prosecutors, and legal resources to prosecute domestic violence cases. This increase in resources has spilled over into children's services. Children of battered women are no longer the hidden victims.

 **Children and Conflict in the Home**

Conflict is an inherent part of family relationships. Most, if not all, parents have raised their voices toward their spouse or children. Couples argue, children fight, parents yell. How does this conflict affect children? At what point does parental arguing become abusive or harmful to children? This question has been carefully studied and the findings are interesting. According to Mark Cummings and his colleagues, who have published extensively in this area, children, even in their infancy,

[2]Pynoos RS, & Eth S. (1985). Children traumatized by witnessing acts of personal violence, homicide, rape or suicide behavior. In Eth S, & Pynoos RS, eds. *Post-Traumatic Stress Disorder in Children*. Washington, DC: American Psychiatric Association Press, 19–43.

[3]Garbarino J, Dubrow N, Kostelny K, & Pardo C. (1992). *Children in Denver: Coping With the Consequences of Community Violence*. San Francisco, CA: Jossey-Bass.

[4]Terr LC. (1990). *Too Scared to Cry: Psychic Trauma in Childhood*. New York: Harper and Row.

[5]Jaffe PG, Wolfe DA, & Wilson SK. (1990). *Children of Battered Women*. Newbury Park, CA: Sage Press.

show reactions of distress when they are exposed to "background anger," defined as adults verbally arguing and yelling.[6] In one series of experiments, 20-month-old toddlers showed increased amounts of aggression with their playmates after they had been exposed to anger or loud arguing between adults.[7] This research underscores the fact that even very young children are aware of conflict in the home, and that the conflict affects their behavior.

Another interesting dimension of this research is children's response to conflict. Children are likely to become involved in the marital conflict, either by attempting to distract, comfort, or problem solve for the arguing parents. These responses may be seen in children as young as age 2. By age 5 or 6, children actively attempt to mediate parent arguments.

One might assume that children who grow up in homes where there is constant arguing or yelling would adapt. They would get used to it, and therefore be less affected. Contrary to expectations, however, Cummings discovered that repeated exposure to parent arguing does not diminish children's reactions. Children react more strongly by becoming more anxious and aggressive. The notion of becoming desensitized to parental fighting was not supported by this research.

Finally, Cummings and colleagues have found that if parents resolved the arguments, children were much less likely to be affected.[8,9] Even partial resolution, such as changing the subject, or agreeing to drop the argument, seemed to dramatically reduce the impact on children. In their simulated experiments with children, they instructed some of the adults to resolve arguments in front of children and others to leave the room and return with indications that the fight was over. Although children who had heard the resolution to the argument benefited the most, the stress of all children was markedly reduced.

The take-home message for all parents from this series of studies is that marital conflict is not inherently bad for children. Children may even learn positive and pro-social lessons from seeing their parents argue and then resolve the conflict. If the argument is resolved, children can cope. If the arguments are chronic and unresolved, however, children react negatively. In the Cummings' research, fighting which included physical aggression was much more psychologically harmful for children than verbal arguing. This is not surprising, but the consistency of their findings builds a powerful case for the ways in which physical fights or even threats of personal injury overwhelm children's abilities to cope. Children who lived with physical

---

[6]Cummings EM, & Davies P. (1994). *Children and Marital Conflict: the Impact of Family Dispute and Resolution.* New York: Guilford Press.

[7]Cummings EM, Iannotti RJ, & Zahn-Wexler C. (1985). The influence of conflict between adults on the emotions and aggression of young children. *Developmental Psychology, 21,* 495–507.

[8]Cummings EM, Vogel D, Cummings JS, & El-Sheikh M. (1989). Children's responses to different forms of expressions of anger between adults. *Child Development, 60,* 1392–1404.

[9]Cummings EM, Ballard M, El-Sheikh M, & Lake M. (1991). Resolution and children's responses to interadult anger. *Developmental Psychology, 27,* 472–470.

aggression were more likely to blame themselves and to see themselves negatively. This distorted self-appraisal affected children in all areas of social functioning.

When the War Zone Is in the Home

Since 1990, nearly 100 studies of the effects of exposure to domestic violence on children have been published, most focusing on children between the ages of 6 and 17.[10] These studies have thoroughly analyzed the risks of domestic violence for children. It is quite clear that exposure to domestic violence affects children in a range of deleterious ways. It affects their emotional development, their social functioning, their ability to learn and focus in school, their moral development, and their ability to negotiate intimate relationships as adolescents and adults. It is associated with greater rates of juvenile delinquency, anti-social behavior, substance abuse, and mental illness. It also increases the risk of direct physical injury. Children who are bystanders to conflict often become the direct victims of abuse. Young children lack the ability to remove themselves from the fighting: a toddler clings desperately to his mother; an infant is held by her mother who is being beaten. Older children may try to intervene and are injured as a result of their attempts to mediate or protect.

Why is domestic violence so toxic for children? Researchers who have studied this question have enumerated several characteristics. Exposure to a violent event will be more psychologically threatening for children, especially young children, if the child perceives himself to be in danger, if he perceives that his caretaker is in danger, and if he is physically close to the violent event.[11,12] All of these attributes apply to situations involving domestic violence. In another study, researchers looked at a number of records of children who had been diagnosed with Post Traumatic Stress Disorder.[13] Because these children were in the court system, the researchers had access to detailed and extensive records on the children, some of which extended over a number of years. They were curious to learn more about what stresses might be most strongly correlated with the child's diagnosis of Post Traumatic Stress Disorder. They found two factors to be the strongest predictors: a history of sexual abuse and witnessing chronic domestic violence. In fact, exposure to domestic violence seemed to be more harmful overall than being a direct victim of child abuse. Thus we are reminded that if the violence is close at hand, if it involves caretakers,

---

[10]Edleson JL. (1999), Children's witnessing of adult domestic violence. *Journal of Interpersonal Violence, 14*(8), 839–870.

[11]Zeanah CH. (1994). Assessment and treatment of infants exposed to violence. In Osofsky J. & Fenechel E., eds. *Hurt, Healing and Hope.* Arlington, VA: Zero to Three, 29–37.

[12]Drell M, Siegal C, & Gainsbauer T. (1993). Post-traumatic stress disorder. In Zeanah CH, ed. *Handbook of Infant Mental Health.* New York: Guilford Press, 291–304.

[13]Famularo R, Fenton R, & Kinscherff R. (1993). Child maltreatment and the development of post-traumatic stress disorder. *American Journal of Diseases of Children, 147,* 755–759.

if it puts the child at harm, this child is much more likely to suffer serious and long-lasting emotional consequences.

Another powerful by-product of the domestic violence between parents is the lessons children learn about the use of force and intimidation. Young children learn social roles by imitating what they see and hear. They dress up like Dad, do housework with Mom, practice the moves of cartoon figures on television. If children observe that physical force is a part of their parents' relationships, they will also imitate this behavior. In violent homes, children learn that aggression is a part of intimate relationships, or that it is acceptable to relieve stress by yelling or threatening another family member. It is normal to use force to get one's way, and no apologies are necessary. When these children enter day care or pre-school and hear rules such as "use your words, not your hands" or "no hitting allowed," they have no context to rely on. These rules make no sense. Instead, these children have constructed their own understandings of the social order: might makes right. An accidental bump from another child is interpreted as purposeful aggression. One must always be on guard for violence. Thus, a child who grows up with violence behaves in a distrustful, aggressive fashion. This stance works at home, but fails miserably in pre-school settings.

Perhaps the greatest distinguishing feature of domestic violence for young children is that it psychologically robs them of both parents. One parent is the terrifying aggressor; the other parent is the terrified victim. For young children who depend exclusively on their parents to protect them, there is no refuge. These situations are different from those of families who face community violence. In most of those cases, parents are not fearful for their own lives and can be both heroic and resourceful in their efforts to protect their children. (This is not to imply that women who are victims of domestic violence are not heroic and resourceful; however, if they are fighting for their own survival, there are limits as to what they can do to protect their children.) Parents' emotional availability makes a big difference in how children respond to the trauma of a violent event. In the Child Witness to Violence Project we learned about the buffering effects of parents in memorable ways.

One of the first cases referred to us was that of Lisa, a 9-year-old girl who lived with her family in a tough neighborhood in Boston where street crime was common. Lisa woke one night to see a man at her window, attempting to open her screen. She was terrified by this vision and began to scream for her mother. By the time her mother entered the room, there was no sign of the intruder. The mother reassured Lisa that it must have been a bad dream. Lisa was not convinced, and spent the remainder of the night in a terrified state. The next morning, her mother checked the window and found signs of an attempted forced entry. Lisa's nightmare had been real.

Within a week of that incident, Lisa became afraid to go out of the house. She begged her mother to change bedrooms; she could not sleep at night. When she began to miss school, her mother took Lisa to her pediatrician. The mother was exasperated, saying that she needed help in convincing Lisa to forget about this incident. The mother had bought strong latches for all the windows and she believed the house to be safe from intruders. She believed that the best thing to do was to stop thinking and talking about the incident. It was apparent, however, that no amount of security could help Lisa feel safe. The pediatrician asked for a consultation from our program and I agreed to sit in as the doctor talked with Lisa about her fears.

Before the meeting, the doctor and I agreed that he should be the person to interview Lisa since he had known her for many years. With her mother and me in the room, he gently asked her to talk about what had happened. Lisa talked about waking up to see this scary face at the window. She became animated as she remembered his face and the sounds of him cutting the screen. She reviewed her confusion and disbelief when he disappeared. Maybe it had been a dream, she speculated. However, with the corroborating evidence, she now felt terrified that he would return. She tried to imagine what he would have done if he had entered the room. She talked about seeing scary movies where girls are kidnapped and killed. Within a few days, she began to worry that he was following her and she was afraid to go to school. She also talked about how hard it was to close her eyes at night. We understood that she was not sleeping, which further contributed to her reluctance to go to school. The doctor asked many questions about how often she thought about the man at the window, when she was most afraid, and what her greatest fears were. In short, he allowed her to talk openly about the incident from her perspective, and he validated her feelings. He neither minimized her feelings nor attempted to give reassurance. He just listened.

As the mother heard her daughter explain what this incident had done to her, she became visibly upset. Speaking through her guilt, she explained that she had thought it would be best if they didn't dwell on what happened, and therefore, she had not allowed her daughter to express how scared she was. As Lisa spoke directly about the aftermath of this incident, her mother also became angry. She revealed for the first time that she had a good idea of who the intruder was. By her report, their house bordered an area that was known for drug selling, and the suspected intruder was a drug dealer who was known in the neighborhood. In an animated and determined voice, she told her daughter that she would make sure this did not happen again. Lisa's mother was a large woman who by her own description could be forceful if necessary. I began to worry that she might take matters into her own hands in ways that were potentially dangerous for her. She was resolute, however, that she would take care of matters. As she provided reassurances, I observed that Lisa, who had been tense and withdrawn, was now animated and relaxed.

The doctor then asked Lisa what she thought might be helpful in a plan to get her back to school. He discussed a plan with Lisa and her mother to change her bedroom around so that her bed was facing away from the window. (This was Lisa's request.) He asked them to return in 2 weeks for a follow-up session. The family did not return, but phoned instead to say that Lisa was much better and had returned to school.

How was Lisa helped in this encounter? I observed Lisa's non-verbal behavior carefully during the interview and was struck by her connection to her mother. Although the doctor was asking the questions, Lisa talked to her mother about her feelings. She wanted her mother to know what this experience was like for her. I was also impressed by the power of this mother's reassurances. It was evident that Lisa savored her mother's fury. Her mother's absolute confidence that she could take care of this situation was the optimal intervention for Lisa. Children want (and need) to believe that their parents can protect them. This mom was eloquent in that regard. I believe this strength was contagious and helped Lisa conquer the fears she had developed.

This case shows how parents can psychologically assist their children in coping with the aftermath of trauma. If the parents are themselves traumatized, however, their capacity to emotionally protect their children is often compromised. The double jeopardy of exposure to domestic violence is that children are both directly traumatized by their exposure to trauma and robbed of the refuge of their parents. Consider this story.

Michelle, a 28-year-old mother of three children, Mark, age 7, Sally, age 6, and Eric, age 4, brought her children to the Child Witness to Violence Project for counseling services at the suggestion of the local battered women's shelter where she had been staying. The shelter staff was concerned about the children's behavior, particularly that of Mark, who was very aggressive and moody in the shelter. At the first evaluation session, we began by seeing the mother and children together. This standard practice gives children a chance to feel more comfortable in the setting and to discuss among all family members the reason for seeking services from us. We decided to assign two therapists to this family because of the number of children. My colleague asked the mother to tell us something about why she brought the children in. The mother began by telling us that they had lived in a small town about 40 miles from Boston until two weeks ago when she fled from her husband and came to Boston. Michelle, who sat hunched in the chair, began to tell a horrific story about the abuse that led to her decision to leave home. She described that her husband had hit her for years, culminating in an incident where he attempted to strangle her with an extension cord. This incident happened one morning after the older children were in school. Eric was at home and witnessed the event. Michelle recounted every detail of what led up to this assault and told us about how she had been able to break loose by kicking her husband. She grabbed Eric and fled from the house, hailing a taxi that took her to the older children's school. From the school she called the police. The police transported her and her children to the domestic violence shelter. She later learned that her husband had been arrested and charged with attempted murder.

As she told the story, I observed the children. They began the session by sitting quietly in three chairs. However, as Michelle began to talk, the children fidgeted and began to bicker among each other. Mark reached over and hit Sally. Eric moved to the play area and looked at the toys. Soon all three children were in the play area. The older children began to pull toys off the shelf. A dispute broke out over one toy. In a flash, they began to throw them at each other. Eric sat in the corner, looking stunned. This escalation in action and aggression took place within a five-minute span. The children became so disruptive that I could not hear Michelle talk. She made no attempt to intervene or calm her children. She finally stopped talking when Mark threatened to pull a bookcase over onto the floor.

As difficult as it was for me to sit passively, I knew that the children's behavior was communicating a powerful message and that I should refrain from intervening unless the situation was dangerous. This unfolding of events gave us rich information about the family. We later realized that the increasing chaos that the children produced was their way of telling their mother that they could not bear to hear the story she was telling. It was too overwhelming. They got her to stop by using the time-honored strategy of escalating their misbehavior to the point of danger. Obviously they had used this strategy before and it was a familiar sequence of interactions for them. It worked. Michelle stopped talking and began to yell at the children to clean up the mess they made.

Equally striking to me was Michelle's single-minded focus on re-telling her story to the extent that she seemed completely unaware of her children. As she told the story, she was re-living the horror and she was unable to tune in to her children's distress. She was so traumatized that she could not see how scared and upset her children were to hear the story told again. We have learned from many of the women we work with that this numbness and decreased ability to recognize when children are frightened or distressed is a hallmark of their trauma. Despite her good intentions, Michelle's ability to emotionally protect her children is compromised by her own experiences with violence.

This case illustrates the particular risks of exposure to domestic violence for children and how parental response makes a difference. When parents are overwhelmed, they are unable to read their children's cues of distress and the situation often deteriorates rapidly.

The following stories show how individuals in families struggle with the existence of violence within the home. They also show the relentless toll that this behavior takes on children. Finally, these stories provide a reminder that domestic violence cuts across all social classes.

The Stories of Jenna and Ben

We received a request from a family court judge to help determine what kind of visitation schedule should be established for two children who had witnessed physical violence between their parents. They were in the custody of their mother; their father was seeking access to his children by asking the court to set up a schedule for visits. The judge wanted to impose a schedule that was fair to the parents but also took into account the children's emotional reactions to the violence. In order for us to make informed recommendations, we arranged to spend time with each child and each parent to get to know them, to hear from each member of the family about their perspectives of the parents' conflict and their ideas for how the visits should be scheduled.

The family lived in a wealthy suburb of Boston. Both parents worked full-time. The father was an attorney; the mother, a college professor. The children, Jenna, age 9, and Ben, age 7, attended private day school. The third child, 6-month-old Jacob, was not part of the request for visitation. Both parents agreed that he was too young to be a part of the visitation plan for the immediate future. Before we met the family, we learned from the court that there had been at least one incident of physical violence between the parents that resulted in police intervention. In fact, Ben had called 911 during the fight. A police report was sent to us, along with a copy of the judge's temporary custody orders. The report documented injuries to the mother and the resulting arrest of the father. He was held for a few hours. His wife asked that he be released, on the condition that he not stay at home. Other than this meager information, we knew little about the family.

We interviewed the father and the mother separately, asking them each the same questions: Could they tell us about the marital conflict? What was it about? How long had it been going on? What did the children understand about the conflict? Who talked with the children about it? How did the children seem to be affected? We also asked each parent about his/her relationship with their children. We asked them to describe the children, to talk about what they liked to do with the children, about each child's strengths and talents, what concerns they had about the children, and about what their ideas were about a good plan for visitation.

As is often the case with parents who are locked in struggle, their perspectives and recommendations were dramatically different. The father, whom I interviewed first, was bitter and angry about being denied access to his children. He saw this refusal as an attempt of the mother to gain power and turn his children against him. He admitted that the parental relationship had been stormy with angry fights and poor communication. When asked about the physical violence, he was dismissive. He told me that things got out of hand once in a while, but that she was an equal participant. He explained that the incident involving the police had been overblown. They had a fight, she picked up a knife, and he tried to protect himself, resulting in injuries to both of them. When asked specifically about other incidents of physical fighting, he said that there had been one or two times when they had pushed or grabbed each other. There had been no injuries and, to the best of his knowledge, the children had not been aware of these fights because they usually happened in the evening after the children were in bed.

I then asked him about his children and how he saw their strengths. He described them both as smart, doing well in school, and enjoying sports. However, as I asked more specific questions, he said that he actually did not spend much time with them because of the demands of his job. His description of his children was vague and without animation. He wanted to change the subject to address his anger at being denied access to the children. I also asked in some detail about his work and his background. By his report, he was a hard-working and successful lawyer. When he was a child, his family had little money; he was the first member of his family to graduate from college. He worked hard to get through law school. He was particularly proud that he had been able to afford to buy a new home within the past year in an expensive neighborhood. He mentioned also his satisfaction in being able to send his children to private school, an advantage he had not had.

I then interviewed the mother. As I expected, her story was quite different. She said that their relationship began to deteriorate when he was in law school. She taught part-time and provided most of the care for their young daughter, Jenna. Her husband had little to do with Jenna and provided no support at home. She resented his lack of involvement. They argued about this from time to time. Occasionally the arguments were heated. She recalled the first time he pushed her. She was shocked and left home for a couple of days to stay with her mother. By the time Ben was born, she described her marriage as "miserable." She barely saw her husband; their only communication seemed to be through their fights. There were occasional episodes of fighting that escalated to physical abuse. She reported that he would berate her, and sometimes she would be so angry that she slapped him. On one occasion, he pushed her against the kitchen cabinets and bruised her arm badly. She remembered being worried that her colleagues would ask about the bruises, but she knew she could easily make up a story. She also remembered being relieved that the bruises weren't on her face. It would have been more obvious and harder to lie if the injury had been on her face.

The mother described the incident involving the police. By her report, her husband had listened to a telephone message of hers from a male colleague. He became suspicious, accusing her of having an affair. The fight, which began in the kitchen, quickly escalated. He grabbed her by the hair and took out a kitchen knife. She was terrified and called to the children to summon the police. The baby was asleep upstairs; she did not know where the older children were at the time, but she remembered that she was afraid for her life. She managed to kick the knife out of his hand and run out the door. The police arrived as she was running from the porch. They saw evidence of the fight in the kitchen and made an arrest on the spot. The father was removed and put in jail.

Afterwards, she collected the children, who were terrified. She made the decision at that point to leave her husband. She told me that the intensity of his anger was unlike anything she had experienced before, and she knew at that point that she could stay with him no longer. Despite her fear and anger at her husband, she also felt guilty about having him arrested. She knew this arrest would affect his career, and she did not want to bring shame or dishonor to him. Because of her worry about his status at work, she decided to drop charges if he would agree to leave the household. He was released the following day. The police accompanied him back home to pick up his belongings, and he moved into an apartment in the neighboring town.

The mother reported that her husband contacted a lawyer to begin separation proceedings and requested visitation with the children. Meanwhile, she had talked to the children about what had happened. She was surprised to learn from the children that they had heard their parents fighting for the past year or so, and that they were terrified of their father. They had no interest in seeing him. At that point, she hired an attorney and the case went to court.

The next step in this evaluation involved direct interviews with the children. I decided to interview them separately. I knew this approach would be more stressful for the children, but I wanted to give each of them the chance to tell the story from his/her perspective and to do so in private. I interviewed Jenna first. She was a mature and verbal 9-year-old. She came calmly into the office, sat across from me and looked directly at me. I asked her some initial questions about school, her favorite subjects, and television shows. This preamble was both to put her at ease and to assess her mood and communication skills. She did not want to color or draw, but wished to get to the point of the interview. I asked her what she had been told about why she was here. She replied that she knew that I was the person who would tell the judge whether she should see her father and she wanted to let me know that she did not want to see her father "ever again." As I asked Jenna to tell me more about this decision, she explained to me that her father and mother had been fighting for as long as she could remember. She fell asleep every night to the sounds of their fighting. When I asked her what the worst part of the fighting was, her voice dropped and she said that she was afraid her mother would get killed. This was the first sign of emotion from this calm and mature little girl. I then asked her to tell me about the fight in which the police had responded. Again, her facial expression changed. She sat forward in her chair and began to fiddle with the papers in front of her. For the first time, she looked away as she began to talk. Soon, she had forgotten I was there and was re-living the fight.

She was waiting to go to school when the fight began, sitting in the living room that was next to the kitchen. From where she sat, she saw everything. She saw her parents yelling and saw her father grab her mother. He then turned and picked up a "big knife." "I thought he was going to cut her throat," she said. Her mother began to scream at the children to call the police. Her father yelled, "If you call the police, I'll beat you." Jenna described being frozen with fear and indecision. In a panic she had run out of the house. As Jenna concluded the story, she burst into tears and sobbed uncontrollably. I gave her a tissue, and when she had regained her composure, I asked her what the worst part of this experience had been for her. She cried quietly and said, "I left my mom. I was too scared he would hurt me and I couldn't call the police."

The response was heartbreaking. This brave and frightened girl was wrenched with guilt over her perceived failure to protect her mother. As we discussed this episode further, the depth of her shame and self-blame was striking. She re-played the event over and over in her head, she said, to try to figure out why she had "run away." The fact that her father had made a direct threat to her safety wasn't enough to assuage her guilt. In her eyes, she had failed her mother.

When I asked about her ideas for current visits, she again said that she had no interest in seeing her father. She said that the house was peaceful now, and she didn't care if he ever came back. While I doubted that her emotional reactions to her father were quite that simple, I was struck with how adamantly she reacted to the idea of visits.

My final interview was with 7-year-old Ben. As I would have predicted with someone his age, he was less verbal and had a shorter attention span. Instead of one longer interview, I decided to interview him twice for shorter periods of time. In the first interview, he seemed very nervous, fidgeting in his seat and avoiding eye contact. He declined the offer to draw a picture. I asked what his understanding was of our visits, and he said that it was to decide about seeing his father. I asked why his parents were separated. He said that they fought a lot. I asked if he could tell me about the scariest fight, and he began to talk about the time the police had come.

His description was somewhat different from his sister's, both because of his age and because he actually saw little. As he told the story, he was upstairs playing in his room when he heard shouting and arguing downstairs. He stayed in his room because he did not like the sounds of what he was hearing. Then he heard his mom screaming to call the police. He got "very scared" and thought about what he had learned at the school about calling 911. He placed the call. He could hear his father yelling. He said that he was so scared that he went back into his room, barricaded the door, and hid in the closet. I asked what he was most afraid of. He replied that he thought his father would hurt him. The police found him in his closet a short while later. As Ben told this story, he looked more and more anxious. He stopped talking and asked if he could leave the room. I commented that it must have been very scary for him and that he didn't have to talk about it anymore if he didn't want to. He appeared to be visibly relieved and sank back in his chair. He then asked if he could draw a picture. His picture was of a cat "with blood all over his face." He declined to tell me more about the picture.

In the second interview, he was more relaxed and talked about school. He didn't have many positive things to say about school: He didn't like his teacher; he got into trouble for fighting, but it wasn't really his fault. I asked about what he missed with his dad not being home. He said his dad used to play baseball with him and he missed that. When I asked Ben what he thought was important to think about if he was to have visits with his dad, he was quiet for a long time and then replied, "Well, I think maybe we could have visits, but not for a long time." I asked about how long would be good. "When I am old enough to get away if I have to," Ben responded.

This case went to court with my recommendation that visits be postponed for the next 6 months until these children had been able to see a therapist and resolve some of their initial reactions to the violence they had witnessed.

As I thought about this case, one of the truths that emerged was the hidden nature of this family's life in an affluent suburb. I began to think about the ways in which class and privilege become their own forms of prison. It turned out that this mother had previously gone to the police about her husband's abusiveness. The police had offered her legal remedies and counseling. She declined, however, explaining to me that she did not want to ruin her husband's reputation. All she wanted, she said, was an end to the abuse. She had no desire to embarrass him or jeopardize his job. The public nature of seeking a restraining order or having him arrested was humiliating, and she wanted to avoid this loss of privacy. It wasn't until she feared for her life that she decided to act. Even then, she declined a full restraining order, opting instead for a milder order that he stay away from the home. She wanted to help her husband save face.

Similarly, the children's needs went unrecognized. I talked with both teachers to get information about their functioning in school. Jenna, as I could have predicted, was an excellent student and a leader in the classroom. The teacher, who spoke with great affection about Jenna, was surprised to hear from the mother that the parents had separated. Ben's teacher gave a more mixed report. Ben was quite aggressive at times and had trouble focusing on his work. He seemed preoccupied with fighting, bringing action figures of wrestlers to school and engaging in pretend battles with them in the classroom. In fact, the teachers had recommended a learning evaluation for him. Not unexpectedly, the mother did not tell either teacher about the abuse. She didn't want anyone at school to know. Although one can readily understand the mother's reticence to confide in the teachers, it ultimately made their job more difficult, and limited their abilities to help the children. I could imagine that Jenna's teacher could have been an important refuge for Jenna if she had known. Jenna desperately needed to talk with someone about what was going on in her parents' home. The secrecy resulted in Jenna's feeling more singularly responsible for the situation. If Ben's teacher had received more complete information, his aggressive behavior and his short attention span would have been understood in a different light.

Another lesson from this family's story is about how differently children react to an event. This abuse had very different meanings for Jenna and Ben, and they showed their reactions in different ways. Jenna assumed responsibility for protecting her mother, and her mother's injuries were visible symbols of failure. I speculate that this assumption of responsibility was Jenna's because she was the oldest child. She was bright, verbal, and mature. These attributes made her both vulnerable and strong: vulnerable because she was burdened with expectations she could not fulfill; strong because, in fact, these attributes helped her cope with the stress at home. Jenna is doing well in school. Her intellect and engaging personality will hopefully continue to benefit her.

Ben, on the other hand, appears to be more vulnerable. Perhaps this is because of age (boys at this age usually lag behind girls in cognitive and social development), and because of gender (the role model of a father who is abusive presents complications for Ben in his own development). Ben has already been identified in school as a troublemaker. He is both intrigued with aggression and frightened by its consequences. Perhaps his fascination is an attempt to neutralize his fear.

Both children have been affected in ways that their parents do not fully understand. Unfortunately, in this comfortable community, there is little support for anyone talking more openly about these occurrences.

Maria, Anna, and Billy

Maria, a 25-year-old mother of two children, Anna, age 5, and Billy, age 3, was referred to the Child Witness to Violence Project by the children's pediatrician because he was concerned about their behavior. In a health visit, Maria had told him that Billy was impossible to manage and that she was worried that he might get hurt. As an example of his behavior, Maria reported the occasion when Billy got out of his bed at night and left their apartment. Fortunately, Maria heard him open the door and stopped him immediately. She was quite worried, however, that he might try to leave again. They live in an urban neighborhood that Maria described as unsafe. His day-care provider was also frustrated with him because he hit other children, and he would not heed limits in day care. When the doctor asked about stresses at home that might be contributing to Billy's behavior, Maria confided that she had obtained a restraining order from the court for protection against her abusive husband. The pediatrician was surprised; despite the fact that he had cared for the children since their birth, he did not know about these family problems. As he asked about the abuse, Maria told him that it had been severe at times. She then pulled up her skirt to show scars on her legs from cigarette burns, inflicted by her husband. The doctor told her about the Child Witness to Violence Project and made a referral.

At the Project, as we discussed the referral in our team meeting, we decided this case was urgent. The mother had been seriously abused. The 3-year-old child was behaving in ways that were dangerous to himself, and we worried that this mother might not be able to keep him safe. One of the counselors called Maria to set up an initial evaluation. Despite her apparent interest in coming to see the counselor, she failed to keep the appointment. The counselor called her back, this time spending more time with her on the telephone to assess the level of crisis. She found out that Maria had been a victim of abuse for the past 3 years and that the children witnessed numerous episodes of violence, including one instance of forced rape. It was this horrifying event that propelled Maria to go to court to seek protection. However, even after a restraining order was issued, her husband continued to come to the neighborhood. He was frequently seen outside their house. One morning, Maria discovered that someone had broken into her basement; she suspected her husband. She called the police each time she or the children saw him; however, he would flee before the police arrived, thus avoiding arrest. Maria also stated that she had little money and could not afford to move. In fact, she barely had enough money to feed and clothe her children. She had depended on her husband's income. Without it, she was desperate. Again, the counselor scheduled an appointment for Maria to bring the children to our program. Maria did not keep this appointment.

This pattern of making appointments and failing to keep them lasted for several weeks. We were very worried about the situation and struggled as a team to decide whether we should notify the state's Child Protection Services about our safety concerns for the children. However, more information about the family emerged as the counselor continued to talk with Maria on the telephone, convincing us to hold off on notifying Child Protection Services. First, Maria told the counselor that she had gone to stay with her mother in another part of the city. She believed she was safe. There were other adults in the home, and she would not be at this home alone. Second, Maria confided that she had been in foster care as a child because her father was abusive to her. She hated the system and felt it created many more problems for her than it solved. Because of her time in this system, she refused to consider a battered women's shelter as an option for safety. She told the counselor that she had lived in group homes before and felt that they were terrible places for children. Her worst fear was that her children would eventually be removed from her care and put into the foster care system. Ironically, Maria believed that keeping herself and her children out of a shelter was the best way to ensure their safety. This fear also kept Maria from bringing her children to see us.

The counselor explained her dilemma to Maria: If she could not meet the children and get some sense of their well-being, she would be legally mandated to notify Child Protection Services. The counselor assured Maria that she understood her fears and that, as a program, we were dedicated to helping mothers establish safe environments for their children. The counselor's patience and respect for Maria, along with her genuine empathy for Maria's dilemma, paid off: Maria brought her children in for an evaluation approximately 3 weeks after the first call to the program.

In the first interview Maria was exhausted and overwhelmed. She had enrolled in a vocational training program, and it was important to her that she be able to finish so she could get a job. However, she was forced to commute long hours from her mother's home, and the children were not faring well. Billy was in day care. The center director had communicated her concern about his behavior, along with the warning that if things did not improve, Billy would be asked to leave. The day-care staff worried that they could not protect the other children from Billy's aggression. Maria thought about going to a shelter, but decided against it. In addition to her memories of her own shelter experiences, a move to a shelter would result in the loss of the day-care slot for Billy.

The counselor interviewed both children. Billy was very active and unfocused in the session, running from one toy to another, but not able to engage with any specific activity. He said to the counselor that his dad hit his mom, but that she would be okay because he would protect her. When the counselor asked how he would do so, he replied that he had a knife. Anna, the 5-year-old girl, was subdued and shy. She sat quietly in the room as the counselor talked with the mother. When she was interviewed alone, she was at first reluctant to talk. Her mother had said that Anna had trouble sleeping at night. The counselor began with that topic, asking Anna about nighttime. Anna replied that she was scared. When pressed to say more about her fears, Anna replied that she worried that her mother would die. She thought about this fear in school, and it made her sick to her stomach. She looked very sad as she talked about this fear. It was clear that she was suffering as much as Billy, only in a less obvious way.

Within 3 days of that interview, Maria called to say that her husband had appeared at the school bus stop as she picked Anna up. She also said that Billy had climbed out the window of her second story apartment early that morning. With this news, the counselor was convinced that the situation had deteriorated to a dangerous level and urged Maria to take Billy to the local hospital's emergency room for a psychological evaluation. The counselor also told Maria that she was so concerned about the children that she must notify Children's Protection Services about the crisis. The counselor worried that Maria would be angry and frightened and would cut off contact with everyone. Although Maria told the counselor that she was angry and felt betrayed, she took Billy to the hospital, and he was admitted for an in-patient stay. The counselor made a report to the local Child Protection Services office, and an investigation was begun.

The counselor heard nothing from Maria for the next 3 weeks. Finally, Maria called to tell the counselor that although she had been very angry, she knew that the counselor was doing her best to help the family be safe. She agreed to come in again to talk. This exchange seemed to be crucial in helping Maria accept help and commit to a relationship with the counselor. She and our counselor worked together for the next year. Progress was slow and erratic. Billy was released from the hospital and enrolled in a therapeutic day-care program. His behavior improved dramatically. Maria left her vocational training program, but later took pleasure in becoming a room parent at Billy's school. The Children's Protection Service agency helped Maria secure an apartment in another part of the city. This move was a great relief to everyone: They could now feel safer at home. As the initial crisis subsided, however, Maria grew more depressed and immobilized. She began to confide in the counselor her own history of abuse, something she had never before discussed with anyone. Together, Maria and her counselor decided that Maria should be hospitalized to help manage her sense of hopelessness and desolation. This hospitalization was somewhat helpful for Maria, but devastating for the children. Their fears and worries about their mother were vividly revived.

Anna continued to have significant difficulty in school. She was afraid of other children and began to fall behind in her work. She begged her mother to be allowed to stay at home. Maria once commented that Anna seemed to prefer punishment to going to school. She developed chronic head and stomach aches. During one session with the counselor, Anna explained that she was particularly afraid to ride the bus to school. The counselor was curious about this fear. Anna told her that she had been struck by a ball that someone tossed around the bus. In addition, a girl sitting near her had recently been hit with a rock that was thrown into the window by a person on the street. She also said that the bus was often late picking her up and that there were too many children on the bus. In short, Anna began each day by feeling scared and vulnerable. With her previous exposures to dangerous violence, Anna was highly sensitive and fearful about random or unexpected danger in her environment. It was no wonder she had trouble focusing on her work in school. The counselor assisted the mother in contacting school officials about the bus situation. Although it was finally improved, Anna lost most of that academic year in terms of achievement in school. Because she was quiet and caused little trouble, neither her teachers nor the school officials were aware of her distress.

At the end of 15 months of counseling, Maria and Billy were greatly improved. Anna was no longer afraid at school, although she continued to have academic difficulties. Stable, safe housing was perhaps the most important component of the family's improvement. High-quality day care made a dramatic difference for Billy. Maria re-enrolled in the vocational program, leading to job placement. Throughout this time, the counselor continued to provide a steady, warm, and accepting relationship with Maria and the children. She provided great stability throughout much of the initial crisis. Maria articulated the value of this relationship in a letter she wrote to the counselor, thanking the counselor for caring about her family and believing that they could make it through the crises they endured.

This case is a grim reminder about the intermingling effects of exposure to domestic violence and poverty. Unlike the first family, Maria and her children lacked the basic necessities of safe housing. Maria had no safety net of savings. She could barely feed her children. She had few friends and did not access community resources. For reasons that are quite different from those of the first family, Maria also refused shelter. Her own history of abandonment and abuse made her distrustful of most people and institutions. Perhaps because she was poor and lived in a high-crime neighborhood, the police were also less responsive. They failed to apprehend her husband, thus making it possible for him to continue a reign of terror over the family. In short, neither the legal nor the community support systems worked for Maria. What began as a problem between Maria and her husband magnified to include each family member. The child Anna, who was perhaps the most seriously affected by the violence, displayed the least obvious symptoms and therefore initially did not get the help she needed. The schools were particularly unresponsive to Anna's needs.

These cases illustrate both the immediate and long-lasting effects of exposure to domestic violence on children. We see that children are affected in unique ways that are partially dependent on their personalities, their strengths, their ages, and their pre-existing relationships with their parents. We can also understand how the effects of chronic trauma on adults affect their capacities to parent their children. Maria's extensive history of abuse affected her ability to make good judgments about keeping her children safe. It wasn't until she began to recognize the severity of her own trauma that she could improve her parenting relationships with her children.

These cases also raise complex intervention and policy questions. In the first case, the question of what contact Ben and Jenna should have with their father is unresolved. How does the court balance the children's rights to feel safe with the right of a parent to have access to his children? How does the court weigh the importance of children maintaining an on-going connection with both parents with the needs of the mother to be free from her abusive husband? In the second case, the counselor struggles with the definition of child abuse or neglect. Is it abusive or neglectful on the part of parents to physically hurt one another in front of the children? Who should be charged with the neglect in this case? The father for his terrifying and dangerous behavior? The mother for her failure to protect the children? There are no easy answers to these questions.

Obstacles to Seeking Help: Why Domestic Violence Is Still a Shameful Secret

Despite the differences in the worlds of the two families described above, the mothers' responses were similar. They shared a sense of shame and secrecy about what happened to them. Both mothers worried about being judged as bad mothers. This legacy of secrecy and shame associated with domestic violence is powerfully described in Linda Gordon's analysis, mentioned at the beginning of this chapter, of 1,500 child abuse/neglect cases in the city of Boston between 1880 and 1960. There was no systematic protocol for inquiring about or documenting the presence of domestic violence in the home. References to domestic violence therefore appeared in records erratically, as part of caseworkers' descriptions of family functioning. Even without systematic assessment, however, as many as ⅓ of the records surveyed mentioned adult abuse. If caseworkers had systematically inquired, the number may have been twice as high. The unwritten code of behavior for women of that era minimized the significance of wife abuse, even while the reporting began to legitimize child abuse as a social issue.

Today, domestic violence is widely recognized and accepted as a pressing family problem. There have been extensive media campaigns, television dramas, novels, and magazine articles that have made domestic violence an issue for our society. However, women continue to tell us they are ashamed to admit that they are in abusive relationships, particularly if there are children involved. Obstacles to seeking help include the fear of being judged as a failure, the sense of deserving the abuse, and the fear of being blamed for not leaving the relationship. In our interviews with women, they express deep shame; they listen carefully to our questions to find evidence of our judgment or condemnation. As they recount instances of abuse, they look to see if we are repulsed or disbelieving. Despite the increasing societal recognition of domestic violence, many women continue to find it unacceptable to disclose their personal struggles.

In a pattern that is consistent with this sense of self-blame and self-hate, some women make their way to our services precisely because there are children. When we ask why a woman is seeking services now, she tells us she is concerned about the children. In other words, some women cannot seek help for themselves, but they will go public about the violence on behalf of children. This is the same pattern Linda Gordon found in her research of the late 1800s.

Another reason that women find it difficult to come forward about domestic violence is the fear that they will be judged as negligent and bad parents and that the state will intervene to take their children. In Maria's case, described above, Maria articulates this fear as an obstacle for seeking help. Recent legislative initiatives in several states give this fear legitimacy. As the public has recognized the plight of children who live with domestic violence, some states have enacted legislation aimed at penalizing abused women for their failure to protect children. A recent article in the *New York Times* focused on a 1998 state court decision that declared incidents of domestic violence committed in the presence of children to be sufficient grounds for a woman to be charged with neglect.[14] These policies, while enacted with

---

[14]Sengupta S. (2000, July 8). Tough justice: Taking a child when one parent is battered. *New York Times,* A1, A11.

the well-intended hope of protecting children, have the unintended consequences of discouraging women from disclosing domestic violence, which, in the long run is probably much more devastating for the children involved.

Another important dimension of a woman's decision to seek help is the way in which her culture views marital relationships and efforts to seek help outside the family. There are both cultural and religious beliefs that define behavior and relationships between the sexes and within marriage. Several women seen in the Child Witness to Violence Project have told us that their religion prohibits their leaving their husbands or that their marriage vows dictate that they stay in the relationship at any cost. In some cultures, spousal separation is shameful and divorce is rare. The notion of counseling is unheard of. To talk about family problems outside the home brings disgrace on the family.

In conclusion, the problems faced by children and women affected by domestic violence are complex. The particular horror of domestic violence for children is that it robs them of the basic sense of home as a safe haven. They learn at an early age that it may not be safe to depend on adult caregivers for respite. These lessons are learned behind closed doors, away from the eyes or ears of the community. The adult victim and the perpetrator of the violence each have their own reasons for keeping the silence. In the history of a patriarchic society, fear of judgment and shame keep the victim quiet. Fear of sanction and the need for control silence the perpetrator. In order to create interventions that help in these situations, we must create a social climate that breaks the code of silence and brings the devastating phenomenon of domestic violence into the public light.

3

Witnessing Violence: The Effects on Children and Adolescents

Denise J. Gelinas

Witnessing violence puts children and adolescents at significant risk for experiencing anxiety and depression and for developing phobias, conduct disorders, and especially post-traumatic stress disorder (PTSD) (Pynoos & Eth, 1985). It is interesting that this fact is little realized or appreciated, but as Benedek noted, there has been a "long tradition of denying psychological and psychiatric sequelae" in children exposed to traumatic events (1985, p. 4). This denial extends to the mental health professions as well as to society at large.

A few early clinicians drew our attention to these matters. Anna Freud and Dorothy Burlingham (1943) wrote about the responses of children and parents separated during World War II, and Solomon (1942) reported on children's reactions to air raids and blackouts during that same period. Friedman and Lynn (1957) wrote about reactions of children aboard the *Andrea Doria* after it sank. Spitz (1943) and Bowlby (1973, 1980) wrote about the trauma of loss of attachment, and Summit and Kryso (1978) wrote about child sexual abuse. But their work, though well received, did not spark general professional interest. Similarly, although the inclusion of post-traumatic stress disorder in the third edition of the *Diagnostic and Statistical Manual* (American Psychiatric Association, 1980) stimulated robust research about adult combat participants and victims of disasters and civilian violence, little attention and no diagnostic categories were devoted to the possible post-traumatic effects of events on children. This began to change in the late 1970s and mid-1980s when noted clinicians in child and adolescent work began to turn their attention in this direction, culminating in such edited volumes as *Post-Traumatic Stress Disorder in Children*

(Eth & Pynoos, 1985) and *Sexual Abuse: Incest Victims and Their Families* (Goodwin, 1989) and in Terr's work with the children kidnapped in Chowchilla, California, in 1976 (1979, 1981, 1983). In these volumes, clinicians wrote that the best way to think about the symptoms showed by their young patients was to conceptualize them as signifying post-traumatic stress disorder.

In 1987, the first major study of PTSD in children appeared that was comparable to the adult studies in its empirical structure and ability to investigate systematically a large number of individuals exposed to the same isolated, traumatic violent event (Pynoos et al., 1987). This event was a lethal sniper attack on an elementary school playground. Clearly, the empirical study of children witnessing trauma has a very recent beginning. What did this study reveal to us?

Witnessing Violence in the School

The children witnessed the following event. On February 24, 1984, just after the dismissal bell, a sniper began firing from a second-story apartment window across the street from an elementary school in Los Angeles. As described by Pynoos et al. (1987),

> he shot repeated rounds of high-powered ammunition at children on the playground. One child and a passerby were killed, 13 other children were injured, and scores were pinned on the playground under gunfire. Some ran screaming across the yard trying to get out of the line of fire; others hid behind playground trees or trash cans; some dropped to the ground and remained motionless. The bullets pierced metal school doors, shattered school windows located on the other side of the schoolyard, and left holes in the nearby monkey bars. Groups of children trapped in several classrooms were told by their teachers to hide in closets or under tables. Some teachers taped paper over the door window so potential intruders would be unable to see into the classroom. The majority of children had already reached home or scurried home at the sound of the shooting. Many were separated from their brothers and sisters, and parents were denied access to the school grounds by a police barricade. (p. 1058)

This particular elementary school was one of 12 in the Los Angeles school district that was on a year-round schedule, so one quarter of its 1,100 students were on vacation at that time and were not exposed to the event, except by media reports (Pynoos et al., 1987). Approximately 1 month after the shootings, members of the psychiatric crisis team who had joined the school psychological counselors conducted consultations in nearly all classrooms. Five teachers refused to allow their classes to participate; 33 other classes were visited. During the classroom consultation phase, all of the children were engaged in a structured drawing and storytelling exercise. Team members conducted structured interviews and tested 5 to 8 children from each classroom of about 25 children (using the PTSD Reaction Index for all children and the Coddington Life Events Scale for parents of some of the children). Children were randomly selected for the study; investigators had no knowledge about their exposure levels or their responses to the shooting. Degrees of exposure included the following categories: out of vicinity, absent, at home, in neighborhood, on the way home, in the school, and on the playground itself. These categories were later collapsed to four levels: in the playground, in the school, and two levels signifying being away from the school. The authors interviewed, tested, and obtained complete study information on 159 children (14.5% of the student body) who ranged in age from 5 to 13 years old. The gender (50.3% male, 49.7% female) and ethnic (50% African-American, 50% Hispanic) distributions of the sample were comparable to those of the total student body. Children who had been wounded were not part of the study.

Pynoos et al. (1987) found that, not surprisingly, the shooting had disrupted the entire school community. The absentee rate peaked at 268 children per day within the first week after the shootings and did not return to the normal average of 64 children per day until a month later (p. 1058). In addition, there was a 100% rise in visits to the school nurse, from 1,250 to 2,500 during the 6 months after the shootings. Of the 159 children studied, Pynoos et al. found that 38.4% had either moderate or severe PTSD symptoms after the event, 22% reported mild symptoms, and nearly 39.6% had no symptoms. The children showed significant differences in the severity proportions across the four exposure levels. That is, severe or moderate PTSD was described by 77% of the children who had been on the playground at the time of the shooting and by 67% of those in the school building, whereas mild or no PTSD was described by 74% of those children no longer at school and 83% of the children on vacation. As exposure increased, so did the number of stress symptoms reported by the children, with a marked drop-off in symptoms among children who were away from the school that day. Age, gender, and ethnicity did not influence either the type or the severity of symptom picture; degree of exposure to the trauma, as with adults, was the most powerful factor.

Besides degree of exposure to the trauma, one other factor powerfully influenced how traumatic the shooting was, and that factor was attachment. Within each level of trauma exposure, the children who knew the girl who had been killed had significantly more severe symptoms. Pynoos et al. (1987) felt that the positive correlation of PTSD symptoms with level of acquaintance with the child who was killed explained the presence of a severe or moderate post-traumatic stress reaction in some children who had been in the low exposure groups. Also, the 43% of children who had siblings attending the school identified worry about the sibling's safety during the shooting as a source of extreme stress and reported continuing to worry even after the event.

The children with severe to moderate PTSD complained of a cluster of symptoms that included intrusive thoughts about the shooting, reexperiencing the event, avoidance of reminders, reduced involvement with the external world, and estrangement from people. These symptoms are similar to the biphasic numbing/constriction and intrusive reexperiencing found in adults with PTSD. The children did not describe numbing per se. Pynoos et al. noted Terr's (1979) observation that the kidnapped children she had worked with did not usually describe feeling numb. The highly exposed children in the Los Angeles shooting did, however, describe more specific symptoms that suggest numbing, including a lessened interest in play or other usually enjoyable activities, feeling more distant from their parents or friends, feeling more alone with their emotions, and not wishing to be aware of their feelings. In addition, symptoms of increased fear and anxiety were found across severity levels. Disturbed sleep, bad dreams, thoughts of the event interfering with learning, and difficulty paying attention at school were most prevalent among the children with severe PTSD.

A follow-up study done approximately 1 year later (Nader, Pynoos, & Frederick, 1990) found that while there was some decrease in PTSD symptoms in all groups of children—those on the playground, in the school, and at home—"74% of the children who were most exposed to the violence and who witnessed a death (on the playground) continued to have significantly more severe persistent PTSD symptoms than the other groups of children (quoted from Brown, Scheflin, & Hammond, 1998).

Clearly, exposure to violence in the school puts children at significant risk to develop a number of symptoms and problems, and for PTSD specifically. Such school shootings are what we tend to think of when we consider children or adolescents witnessing violence, but there are other contexts we need to consider as well. In fact, children and adolescents are exposed to a great deal of violence, with well-documented destructive effects.

Exposure to Community Violence

Early studies on the prevalence and effects of community violence were conducted with high-risk populations, usually defined as male, inner-city, minority, and economically disadvantaged adolescents and children. In these studies, as many as 97% of adolescents and children disclosed being a witness to community violence, and as many as 70% reported being victimized by some sort of community violence (Fitzpatrick & Boldizar, 1993; Martinez & Richters, 1993; Osofsky, Wewers, Hann, & Fick, 1993). Martinez and Richters (1993) found greater depression, anxiety, intrusive thoughts, and sleep problems among children who had either witnessed or been victims of community violence. Among 6- to 10-year-old children, witnessing violence has been significantly correlated with concurrent antisocial behavior (Miller, Wasserman, Neugebauer, Gorman-Smith, & Kamboukos, 1999).

Recent work (Scarpa, 2001) has examined witnessing violence and direct victimization by violence in a sample of students who were just beyond the adolescent years and were selected from what would be considered a relatively low-risk population— that is, university students in a rural western state university. Scarpa's sample included 476 students, mean age of 20 years, with further testing conducted with a subset of 54 students. Respondents were 66% white, 4.2% African-American, 4.4% Hispanic, 1.1% Native American, and 6.3% Asian. For 5.3%, ethnicity was not reported.

Overall, 95.6% of these young adults reported witnessing some form of violence, and 90.2% reported witnessing violence at least 3 times in their lifetime. Exposures were not always to the same form of violence; 81.6% of the students reported witnessing at least three different forms of violence. Zero to five percent of the students reported witnessing someone being killed, sexually assaulted, shot, or committing suicide. Ten to thirty percent reported witnessing the stabbing of a person, the break-in of another's home, a dead body (other than at a funeral or a wake), or a break-in at their own home. Thirty-five to seventy-four percent reported seeing someone wounded by violence or gunfire, hitting by a family member, chases by gangs or individuals, someone being beaten, mugged, or threatened with harm, hitting by a non-family member, or a gun or knife being used as a weapon. Generally, prevalence rates were 1.3 to 4 times higher for witnessing than for being directly victimized; the exceptions reported were for being hit by a family member, with approximately equal risk of witnessing and direct victimization, and for sexual assault, for which the prevalence rate was 3.5 times higher for victimization than for witnessing. Women were at higher risk than men for experiencing sexual assault, but men were at higher risk than women for witnessing violence in general. Scarpa (2001) noted that the rates of both witnessing and direct victimization of violence in her low-risk population were very similar to those reported for high-risk populations (Fitzpatrick & Boldizar, 1993), but the severity of the witnessed acts varied significantly. The difference in violence exposure between high- and low-risk populations, according to Scarpa, appears "to be one of quality, not quantity . . . high-risk samples are more likely to be exposed to severe life-threatening forms of violence. Low-risk samples, on the other hand, are exposed to high rates of less severe forms of violence" (p. 49).

The respondents in Scarpa's study who had witnessed violence reported higher levels of depression and aggressive behavior than did those who had not witnessed violence. Unlike Fitzpatrick and Boldizar (1993) and Martinez and Richters (1993), Scarpa did not report increased distress and PTSD. However, her study did not assess clinical diagnoses, so it reveals no findings in either direction on this question. Additionally, Scarpa noted that the small subsample of 54 tested respondents reduced the statistical power to detect significant differences in anxiety, even though the mean scores showed increased anxiety in the high-exposure groups. Further, her self-report measures might not have been sensitive enough to discern PTSD. Scarpa's study is particularly tantalizing, because depressive features are often the leading clinical picture for underlying PTSD (Gelinas, 1983). Although it does not address PTSD, Scarpa's work does fill in the picture of how frequently children, adolescents, and young adults are witnesses to interpersonal violence and how, in all studies, the effects are neither benign nor negligible.

Violence in the Home

Finally, we should look within the home. We have known for some time that children are far more likely to witness violence within the confines of their own homes than in their schools. This knowledge, however, is much more difficult for us to tolerate and to keep in our memories. It is important for us to remember this fact, because the violence children and adolescents witness in their homes carries the potential for greater destructive impact.

Large-scale surveys have drawn attention to the extent of violence in the home (Strauss, Gelles, & Steinmetz, 1980). Children witness battering and/or the rape, suicide, or homicide of a parent in surprisingly large numbers. Battering of spouses and child abuse not only account for the largest number of victims but also result in even larger numbers of child and adolescent witnesses (Pfouts, Schopler, & Henley, 1982). Russell (1982) concluded from a large survey of households that 14% of married women in the United States reported experiencing marital rape at least once in their lifetimes. In 11% of those cases, one or more of the respondents' children knew about or witnessed the rape. This finding is unexpected but is easily understood given the demographics of rape. As noted in Pynoos and Eth (1985):

> At a minimum, there is a 10:1 ratio of unreported to reported rapes, with an estimated actual annual incidence of approximately 800,000 rapes. . . . 40% of all rape victims are in the 20–39-year-old, child-bearing age group, and over 40% of all rapes occur in the home. If, estimating *conservatively* [original emphasis], a child is in the home when a rape occurs in one out of five instances, then as many as 25,000 children are exposed to this form of violence each year. (p. 22)

The demographic pattern for children witnessing homicide is similar. For the year 1980, the reported number of homicides in the United States was 23,967 (Centers for Disease Control, 1984), and approximately 40% of the reported homicides were the result of domestic violence. The vast majority of the victims were ages 20 to 39; that is, they were of the common child-rearing age. Suicide and suicidal behavior are also violent acts and constitute a major source of childhood exposure to violence (Pynoos & Eth, 1985). Here, too, the epidemiological characteristics of suicidal behavior put children at substantial risk for witnessing it.

Pynoos and Eth (1985) studied 100 uninjured children who had witnessed the major violence of the rape, murder, or attempted or completed suicide of a parent. The children showed a wide range of problems, with symptoms including confusion, anxiety, fear, guilt, intrusive visual and cognitive reexperiencing, trauma reenactment in play, frightening dreams and other sleep disturbances, nausea, constricted affect, and declining school performance.

Overall, nearly 80% of these children met the full diagnostic criteria for PTSD. The structure of the PTSD shown by the children was the same as the classic picture found in adults exposed to trauma, a biphasic symptom picture of numbing and constricting alternating with repetitive intrusions and persistent physiological hyperarousal. The children, however, expressed these sequelae in ways that were influenced by their developmental level. Terr (1979) first reported some of the differences in the childhood expression of traumatic sequelae. In the DSM-IV (American

Psychiatric Association, 1994), these differences in expression are reflected by modifications of the adult criteria to reflect developmental level in children. Thus, instead of describing feelings of fear, helplessness, or horror, such as found in adults, children may express their overwhelming affects through agitated or disorganized behavior. In adults, reexperiencing often is expressed as recurrent and intrusive distressing recollections, in dreams of the traumatic event, or in acting or feeling as if the event were recurring. In children, however, reexperiencing may take the form of reenactments of the trauma or of repetitive play in which themes or aspects of the trauma are enacted. The numbness and constriction found in adults may, in children, be expressed as feelings of estrangement from the outside world or descriptions of not wanting to have the feelings they are experiencing. The persistent symptoms of increased arousal may be expressed as irritability and disorganized or agitated behavior. (These expressions of PTSD in children can sometimes be difficult to differentiate from attention deficit/hyperactivity disorder [ADHD] [Putnam, 1997]. The disorganized or agitated behavior seen in childhood PTSD can easily be misunderstood as the motoric overflow, disorganized, or very active behavior seen in ADHD.) Finally, the violent injury or death of a parent can serve as "a psychic organizer" (Pynoos & Eth, 1985) that profoundly alters a child's view of the world and of him- or herself. This effect probably contributes to some of the pervasive changes we see in the self-systems, relationships, and functioning of adults who have had extensive childhood histories of trauma and who we would diagnose as having complex PTSD (Herman, 1992).

Witnessing violence in the home may carry an intergenerational effect as well. A large survey of marital aggression in the general population conducted by Kalmuss (1984) found that childhood witnessing of battering was the most significant predictor of intergenerational marital aggression. Kalmuss also indicated that the intergenerational transmission of marital violence is role-specific rather than gender-specific. That is, a child or adolescent witnessing his or her father hitting his or her mother increases the likelihood not only that sons could be victims as well as offenders but also that daughters could be offenders as well as victims.

Among homicidally aggressive young children, Lewis et al. (1983) found that the most significant factor contributing to their violence was having had a father who behaved violently or, sometimes, even homicidally. The researchers also noted that some of these children were at increased risk for suicidal behavior.

Why Children Who Witness Violence Are Vulnerable to PTSD

There are a number of reasons why children and adolescents are vulnerable specifically to PTSD as a result of witnessing violence. First, as is the case with adult PTSD, the traumatic sequelae for children and adolescents are more severe and longer lasting if the stressor is of human origin (American Psychiatric Association, 1980), and clearly violence is of human origin. Witnessing violence can be sufficiently traumatic that a case of PTSD is induced. Issues of facticity and agency are important here. If we fall on the ice and break a leg, that is facticity. The event is not pleasant, but such an accident generally carries limited psychological consequences. If, however, someone intentionally breaks our leg, that is agency, and it is much worse. If the injury occurs because someone *meant* it to happen, the meaning of the event changes and the consequences change as well. As the old saying goes, even a dog can tell the difference between a stumble and a kick. Children are as vulnerable as adults to the factors in interpersonal violence that reflect the intentionality of the injuries they are witnessing.

Second, children are more vulnerable than adults to the traumatic impact of events because of their developmental level. There are many ways to think about vulnerability related to developmental level, one of which is Pierre Janet's (1889) original formulation about the development of traumatic disorders. Janet proposed that during trauma, information is processed differently and adaptive behavior can be disrupted (Van der Kolk & Van der Hart, 1989). Most *normal* experiences are automatically integrated into an individual's existing "cognitive schema" and appropriate action can be taken. Cognitive schemas are the conceptual frameworks within which the individual understands the world and organizes new experiences. Thus, if a person is sitting in a conference and becomes chilly, he or she might put on a sweater without really breaking off attention from the material being presented. The individual can do this because becoming chilled is a familiar experience and he or she knows how to respond. But what makes an experience traumatic is the arousal of vehement emotion in the face of some event that the individual is unable to fit within any existing cognitive schema. Janet contended that intense emotions can interfere with normal information processing. There is some contemporary support for this view. For example, it appears that the intensity of emotion during trauma affects the mode of memory storage (Squire, 1987). In Janet's view, the severity of vehement emotion depends on the "emotional state of the victim at the time of the event and on the cognitive appraisal of the situation" (Van der Kolk & Van der Hart, 1989, p. 1533). In the face of such vehement emotions, the usual cognitive schemas may be "inadequate to create a mental construct which places the experience in the perspective of prior knowledge schemes, causing it to be left unintegrated" (Van der Kolk & Van der Hart, p. 1534). The unintegrated material, usually somatosensory, motoric, or cognitive, enters dissociative storage to reappear at intervals as unsought traumatic reexperiencing.

This formulation for the development of post-traumatic stress disorder is particularly relevant for children and adolescents for two reasons. First, their cognitive schemas—their conceptual frameworks for understanding the world and organizing new experience—are inevitably smaller and less well developed than those of adults. They have a smaller experience base and fewer years of various learning, so their cognitive schemas are far more easily overwhelmed.

Second, children and adolescents are just as likely as adults to experience vehement emotion if an object of attachment is threatened, but they are more likely to be developmentally dependent on these objects of attachment. Also, we know that the dynamics of attachment clearly influence the impact of traumatic events, the development of post-traumatic disorders, and recovery along a variety of dimensions (Gelinas, 1996). For instance, the impact of sexual abuse is much greater if the child is abused by a loved one than by a stranger (Gelinas, 1983; Herman, 1981, 1992; Russell, 1986). When the abuser is a family member, the child's relational structure is disturbed and distorted in addition to the child developing the biphasic PTSD sequelae (Gelinas, 1983, 1997). The child loses the safety in the relationship, which can be devastating. As Van der Kolk has described:

> The earliest and possibly most damaging psychological trauma is the loss of a secure base. When caregivers who are supposed to be sources of protection and nurturance become simultaneously the main sources of danger, a child must maneuver psychologically to reestablish some sense of safety, often becoming fearfully and hungrily attached, unwillingly or anxiously obedient, and apprehensive lest the caregiver be unavailable when needed. (1987, p. 32)

Along another dimension, the presence of individuals to whom we are attached ordinarily confers some protection against the impact of traumatic events. For example, the most powerful element protecting men from acute traumatic disorder in combat during World War II was the social cohesion—the network of attachments—within the immediate combat unit (Grinker & Spiegel, 1945). Recovery from trauma is robustly helped by the availability of people to whom we are attached and with whom we can talk about the traumatic events. In children, the responsiveness of loved ones is crucial to recovery. As noted by Van der Kolk (1987), "the most powerful influence in overcoming . . . psychological trauma seems to be the availability of a caregiver who can be blindly trusted when one's own resources are inadequate" (p. 32). Finally, attachment affects witnessing as well. When a loved one is seen injured, the impact is deeper than when one witnesses the injury of a stranger. If there is strong loyalty or protectiveness toward the other, the impact is greatly exacerbated. Shay (1994) has written about how protective men in combat units are to one another, noting that "men become mothers to one another in battle" (p. 49). The "berserker" rages Shay investigated among American combatants in Vietnam were, without exception, precipitated by witnessing the death of another soldier toward whom the "berserker" felt particularly protective.

Similarly, for children witnessing violence, the impact is greater if they are attached to the target of the violence. For instance, Pynoos et al. (1987) found that within every level of exposure among children who directly or indirectly witnessed the sniper shooting in the playground, children who knew the victim well had significantly ($p<.001$) more severe symptoms.

Finally, if a child witnesses violence in the home, it may be impossible for the child to talk about what has happened or even to have his or her experience validated. The family may have no resources with which to work through what has happened, they may adamantly deny the trauma, or they may be among the injured (or dead) victims. The children may be trapped with what has happened, or what may still be happening, and have no way to work through the trauma. This is particularly unfortunate because we know that recovery depends on the individual's ability to find people to attach to, with whom he or she can talk about and can feel what has happened.

When we talk about violence in the home, we are talking about what is essentially ground zero of the child's attachment network. Witnessing the injury or death of a parent within the home is profoundly destructive and disruptive. It represents the convergence of dynamics regarding witnessing violence, immature development, and attachment effects. If the perpetrator is an attachment figure as well, the situation is clearly most pernicious. Witnessing such events can cause profound changes in a child's sense of the safety of, and his or her notions about the advisability of, future close relationships (Pynoos & Eth, 1985). It can also create a foreshortened sense of the future, which may be one of the most significant markers of childhood trauma (Terr, 1983).

The response of the community and especially of important others is crucial here, as is the reestablishment of supportive community structures as quickly as possible. Psychotherapy should be available, and it should be appropriate, focusing on the traumatic events' sequelae and their impact on development. Sometimes "people along the way" who take an appropriate interest in a child and treat him or her in a civilized and respectful manner can make a significant difference in a child's ability to cope, persevere, and retain some positive self-esteem (Rhodes, 1990).

However, it has become clear that these situations cannot be solved only by changes in clinical treatments or by informal personal interventions. Respected clinician-theoreticians continue to call for societal and policy efforts to change society's denial about violence (Chu, 1998; Goodwin, 1989; Herman, 1992; Putnam, 1997). The degree to which children and adolescents are exposed to violence, whether as victims, witnesses, or participants, can be changed only if clinical efforts are joined by a social, cultural, and political agenda that genuinely addresses and seeks to reduce this exposure and heal its effects.

Total Exposure to Violence

Children and adolescents in our society are exposed, one way and another, to an astonishing amount of violence. Besides the effects of witnessing violence, some of which have been discussed here, children and adolescents are often the targets of violence. For example, three sequential studies monitored the prevalence of child abuse and neglect from 1979 to 1993 (U.S. Department of Health and Human Services, 1981, 1988, 1996). The most recent of these national incidence studies on child abuse and neglect estimated that, in 1993, 1,553,800 children were moderately or severely harmed as a direct result of abuse or neglect, representing a 2.3% prevalence rate among all children. An estimated 1,500 children died as a result of their abuse in 1993. It is particularly disturbing to note that the numbers of abused and neglected children were two-thirds higher in 1993 than in 1986. Even adjusting for an increased population, a child had more than 1.5 times the risk of experiencing abuse or neglect in 1993 than in 1986.

In a different vein, Garbarino (Garbarino, Kostelny, & Dubrow, 1991) has for years been writing about the saturation levels of violence that children and adolescents are exposed to in inner cities. He has argued that inner-city exposure can be equated to the violence in combat zones. Further, he has drawn our attention to what he has termed the "accumulated assets and deficits" that accrue and influence the developmental trajectory (Garbarino, 2000).

We must also recognize the saturation level of violence in our fabulously productive and wealthy entertainment industry's products: in films, television programs, MTV loops, music cassettes and CDs, film trailers, magazines and so-called comics, animated films and shorts, and arcade, video, and computer games. These offerings may be mind-numbingly violent on one level, but there also exists a large body of academic work documenting the deleterious effects of exposure to the violence in these products.

As a society, we have a problem with violence. We are attracted, fascinated, disgusted, stimulated, injured, and made wealthy by violence. The question arises of whether we, in our unexamined fascination and absorption with violence, are destructively influencing what the historian Fernand Braudel called the "deep structures" of our society. Braudel (1987) wrote that civilizations have superficial manifestations (plays, artwork, fashion) and periods (the romantic period, the Renaissance) as well as turning points signaled by important events or "heroes." He wrote that civilizations also have "deep structures"—foundations that are simultaneously conscious and subconscious (e.g., "religious beliefs . . . or a timeless peasantry or attitudes towards death, work, pleasure and family life" [p. 28]. These foundational structures are enduring, distinctive, and original. They give civilizations their characteristic qualities. For example, Braudel wrote that "the role of women is always a structural element in any civilization . . . it is a long-lived reality, resistant to external pressure, and hard to change overnight" (p. 29). These deep structures change, but very slowly and usually only subconsciously at first.

It would appear that converging lines of information are telling us that we must, as a society, become more conscious of our uses of violence and what its effects are. Violence affects everyone: targets, perpetrators, witnesses, consumers, and the ostensibly uninvolved who live in the fabric of our civilization. Every society's relationship with violence constitutes a Braudelian deep structure, and ours, at this point, should be examined much more closely.

 **References**

American Psychiatric Association. (1980). *Diagnostic and statistical manual of mental disorders* (3rd ed.). Washington, DC: Author.

American Psychiatric Association. (1994). *Diagnostic and statistical manual of mental disorders* (4th ed.). Washington, DC: Author.

Benedek, E. (1985). Children and psychic trauma: A brief review of contemporary thinking. In S. Eth & R. Pynoos (Eds.), *Post-traumatic stress disorder in children* (pp. 3–16). Washington, DC: American Psychiatric Press.

Bowlby, J. (1969). *Attachment and loss: Vol. 1. Attachment.* New York: Basic Books.

Bowlby, J. (1973). *Attachment and loss: Vol. 2. Separation.* New York: Basic Books.

Bowlby, J. (1980). *Attachment and loss: Vol. 3. Loss.* New York: Basic Books.

Braudel, F. (1987). *A history of civilizations* (American ed.). New York: Allen Lane–The Penguin Press.

Brown, D., Scheflin, A., & Hammond, C. (1998). *Memory, trauma treatment and the law.* New York: Norton.

Centers for Disease Control, Violence Epidemiology Branch. (1984). *Violent crime: Summary of morbidity.* Atlanta, GA: Author.

Chu, J. (1998). *Rebuilding shattered lives: The responsible treatment of complex post-traumatic and dissociative disorders.* New York: Wiley.

Eth, S., & Pynoos, R. (Eds.). (1985). *Post-traumatic stress disorder in children.* Washington, DC: American Psychiatric Press.

Fitzpatrick, K., & Boldizar, J. (1993). The prevalence and consequences of exposure to violence among African American youth. *Journal of the American Academy of Child and Adolescent Psychiatry, 32,* 424–430.

Freud, A., & Burlingham, D. (1943). *War and children.* London: Medical War Books.

Friedman, P., & Lynn, L. (1957). Some psychiatric notes on the *Andrea Doria* disaster. *American Journal of Psychiatry, 14,* 426–432.

Garbarino, J. (2000, June). *The human face of violent youth.* Conference address, "Safe Schools: Building Fortresses or Opening the Doors to Community?" Smith College School for Social Work.

Garbarino, J., Kostelny, K., & Dubrow, N. (1991). What children can tell us about living in danger. *American Psychologist, 46,* 376–383.

Gelinas, D. (1983). The persisting negative effects of incest. *Psychiatry, 46,* 312–332.

Gelinas, D. (1996, December). Attachment and trauma: Phased treatment of relational disturbances. Conference address, "Psychological Trauma: Relationships and Recollections," Harvard Medical School and Massachusetts Mental Health.

Goodwin, J. (1989). *Sexual abuse: Incest victims and their families* (2nd ed.). Chicago: Year Book Medical Publishers.

Grinker, R., & Spiegel, J. (1945). *Men under stress.* Philadelphia: Blakiston.

Herman, J. (1981). *Father-daughter incest.* Cambridge, MA: Harvard University Press.

Herman, J. (1992). *Trauma and recovery.* New York: Basic Books.

Janet, P. (1889/1973). L'automatisme psychologique: essai de psychologie experimentale sur les formes inferieures de l'activite humaine. Paris: Felix Alcan; Paris: Societe Pierre Janet/Payot. Cited in Van der Kolk, B., & Van der Hart, O. (1989). Pierre Janet and the breakdown of adaptation in psychological trauma. *American Journal of Psychiatry, 146,* 1530–1540.

Kalmuss, D. (1984). The intergenerational transmission of marital aggression. *Journal of Marriage and the Family, 46,* 11–19.

Lewis, D., Shanok, S., Grant, M., & Ritvd, E. (1983). Homicidally aggressive young children: Neuropsychiatric and experiential correlates. *American Journal of Psychiatry, 140,* 148–153.

Martinez, P., & Richters, J. (1993). The NIMH Community Violence Project: II. Children's distress symptoms associated with violence exposure. *Psychiatry, 56,* 22–35.

Miller, L., Wasserman, G., Neugebauer, R., Gorman-Smith, D., & Kamboukos, D. (1999). Witnessed community violence and antisocial behavior in high-risk urban boys. *Journal of Community Psychology, 28,* 417–425.

Nader, K., Pynoos, R., & Frederick, C. (1990). Children's PTSD reactions one year after a sniper attack at their school. *American Journal of Psychiatry, 147,* 1526–1530.

Osofsky, J., Wewers, S., Hann, D., & Fick, A. (1993). Chronic community violence: What is happening to our children? *Psychiatry, 56,* 36–45.

Pfouts, J., Schopler, J., & Henley, H. (1982). Forgotten victims of family violence. *Social Work, 27,* 367–368.

Putnam, F. (1997). *Dissociation in children and adolescents: A developmental perspective.* New York: Guilford Press.

Pynoos, R., & Eth, S. (1985). Children traumatized by witnessing acts of personal violence: Homicide, rape or suicide behavior. In S. Eth & R. Pynoos (Eds.), *Post-traumatic stress disorder in children.* Washington, DC: American Psychiatric Press.

Pynoos, R., Frederick, C., Nader, K., Arroyo, W., Steinberg, A., Eth, S., et al. (1987). Life threat and post-traumatic stress in school-age children. *Archives of General Psychiatry, 44,* 1057–1063.

Rhodes, R. (1990). *A hole in the world: An American boyhood.* New York: Simon & Schuster.

Russell, D. (1982). *Rape in marriage.* New York: Macmillan.

Russell, D. (1986). *The secret trauma: Incest in the lives of girls and women.* New York: Basic Books.

Scarpa, A. (2001). Community violence exposure in a young adult sample. *Journal of Interpersonal Violence, 16,* 36–53.

Shay, J. (1994). *Achilles in Vietnam: Combat trauma and the undoing of character.* New York: Atheneum.

Solomon, J. (1942). Reactions of children to blackouts. *American Journal of Neuropsychiatry, 12,* 361–362.

Spitz, R. (1946). Hospitalism: A follow-up report. *Psychoanalytic Study of the Child, 2,* 113–117.

Squire, L. (1987). *Memory and the brain.* New York: Oxford University Press.

Strauss, M., Gelles, R., & Steinmetz, S. (1980). *Behind closed doors: Violence in the American family.* New York: Anchor Books.

Summit, R., & Kryso, J. (1978). Sexual abuse of children: A clinical spectrum. *American Journal of Orthopsychiatry, 48,* 237–251.

Terr, L. (1979). Children of Chowchilla: Study of psychic trauma. *Psychoanalytic Study of the Child, 34,* 547–623.

Terr, L. (1981). Psychic trauma in children: Observations following the Chowchilla school-bus kidnapping. *American Journal of Psychiatry, 138,* 14–19.

Terr, L. (1983). Chowchilla revisited: The effects of psychic trauma four years after a school bus kidnapping. *American Journal of Psychiatry, 140,* 1543–1550.

U. S. Department of Health and Human Services, Administration for Children and Families, National Center on Child Abuse and Neglect. (1981). *The first national incidence study of child abuse and neglect (1979).* Washington, DC: U.S. Government Printing Office.

U. S. Department of Health and Human Services, Administration for Children and Families, National Center on Child Abuse and Neglect. (1988). *The second national incidence study of child abuse and neglect (1986).* Washington, DC: U.S. Government Printing Office.

U.S. Department of Health and Human Services, Administration for Children and Families, National Center on Child Abuse and Neglect. (1996). *The third national incidence study of child abuse and neglect (1993).* Washington, DC: U.S. Government Printing Office.

Van der Kolk, B. (1987). The separation cry and the trauma response: Developmental issues in the psychobiology of attachment and separation. In B. Van der Kolk (Ed.), *Psychological trauma.* Washington, DC: American Psychiatric Press.

Van der Kolk, B., & Van der Hart, O. (1989). Pierre Janet and the breakdown of adaptation in psychological trauma. *American Journal of Psychiatry, 146,* 1530–1540.

4

School Violence and Disruption: Rhetoric, Reality, and Reasonable Balance

**Peter E. Leone, Matthew J. Mayer,
Kimber Malmgren, and Sheri M. Meisel**

During the past few years the specter of school violence has caused many parents, teachers, and administrators to rethink their basic assumptions about the safety of schools. Tragic and senseless shootings of students by students in public schools in the United States have left us stunned and distraught. Images of school shootings and the demand that schools become safe for all children have shaped responses by politicians, parents, and school administrators (Sheley, 2000).

Recent and widely publicized school shootings raise a number of questions: Are public schools less safe than they were 10 years ago? Twenty years ago? Can teachers teach and children learn in an atmosphere where concerns about safety interfere with instruction and management? In addition to these questions, parents and others want to know who has been involved in these school shootings and whether schools have taken steps to ensure that these incidents don't happen in their schools.

Most parents and members of communities believe that schools should be places where children develop intellectually and socially. The idea that school violence, in whatever form, interferes with the orderly operation and safety of schools is anathema to the public. Beyond concerns about physical injury to children, disruption of the school environment interferes with others' learning and can create a climate of fear in which children avoid school or engage in behaviors to protect themselves (Chandler et al., 1998). There is also the concern that minor problems, if ignored, will escalate into major events.

51

The most current data on school violence and youth victimization in the United States indicate that violence has been declining since 1993. Data reported by the Federal Bureau of Investigation as part of the Uniform Crime Reports (Rand, 1998), as well as students' self-report of victimization that are part of the National Crime Victimization Surveys (Brener et al., 1999), indicate that violence perpetrated by and against youth continues to fall. In spite of this, many segments of the public believe that school violence is increasing (Brooks, Schiraldi, & Ziedenberg, 2000). Some of this misperception may be associated with the widely publicized school shootings at Columbine High School in Colorado and similar incidents in Kentucky, Oregon, and Michigan in the past few years.

Nevertheless, Uniform Crime Reports and data from other sources indicate that schools are the safest places for children to be. Fewer homicides and violent crimes are committed against children at school than in their homes or on the streets (Kaufman et al., 1998; Kaufman et al., 1999; Snyder & Sickmund, 1999). Students are greater than 100 times more likely to be the victim of a homicide away from school than at school (Kaufman et al., 1998).

Another issue that occasionally surfaces when the discussion turns to school violence is the role played by students with mental health problems or other disabling conditions. Some critics believe that special education rules and regulations have tied school principals' hands with regard to discipline and students with disabilities (Hymowitz, 2000). The most recent reauthorization of IDEA (Individuals With Disabilities Education Act) in 1997, however, gave schools a great deal of latitude in responding to disciplinary problems exhibited by students with disabilities. Principals can unilaterally remove special education students involved in weapons or drug offenses and those at risk of harming themselves or others and place them in interim alternative programs (Bear, 1999).

In this chapter we examine issues related to school violence and disruption. We begin by examining the sociocultural context within which school violence occurs, using a nested ecological schema. The first section presents a review of major changes in the status of children and their families, a discussion of availability and consequences of easy access to firearms, and the increase in prevalence of violence in popular media. We also examine media coverage of recent, widely publicized school shootings and the effect that media coverage has on parents' and students' perceptions of school safety. In the second section of the chapter, we examine prevalence and trends in school violence, with particular attention to the use of firearms on school property. This discussion explores some of the difficulty associated with defining and measuring school violence.

We then discuss the challenge of balancing the right to education with the importance of maintaining safe and orderly schools. In particular, we look at available data on the role of students with disabilities in school suspensions and discuss possible interpretations of these data. Finally, we examine how local schools and school districts have addressed violence and disruption in their buildings and communities. We describe violence-prevention initiatives and present guidelines for parents, teachers, and administrators to assist in ensuring that their schools are safe places that promote academic achievement and healthy behavior among all children and adolescents.

The Contexts of School Violence

School violence is a multifaceted phenomenon. Preventing school violence and responding to violent acts that occur within schools require an understanding of the larger community and society. Human behavior is shaped by social-ecological contexts that include individuals with whom we interact daily as well as broad societal contexts that deliver messages about appropriate behavior and relationships among people (Bronfenbrenner, 1979). A widely accepted model (Tolan & Guerra, 1994) of youth and family violence depicts a nested ecological system (see Figure 4.1) of

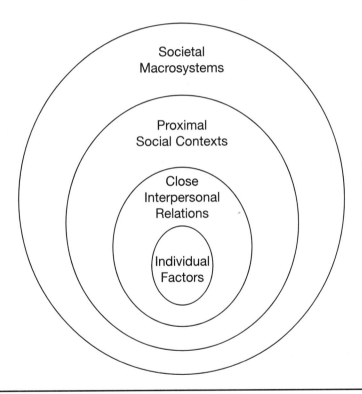

Figure 4.1

A Nested Ecological System of Influences on Youth Behavior

Source: Adapted from "Prevention of Delinquency: Current Status and Issues," (1994), by P. H. Tolan & N. G. Guerra, *Applied & Preventive Psychology, 3,* 254.

individual factors, close interpersonal relations (e.g., peers and family), proximal social contexts (e.g., school and neighborhood), and societal macrosystems (e.g., media and laws governing gun use). Schools have created prevention activities and developed school-wide management plans that have reduced disciplinary referrals and suspensions, addressing risk factors and needs at multiple levels (Taylor-Green et al., 1997; Sugai, Sprague, Horner, & Walker, 2000). These efforts and similar community-based initiatives have the potential to make schools more safe and orderly places for children. In this chapter, we will address aspects of the outer three levels of this nested system that surround the individual, looking at several school, family, and larger societal level factors.

The problem of school violence is linked to changes within our culture and society. Significant changes in family structure and changes in the status of children contribute to the problems that educators see in schools. Violence in the entertainment and news media has increased dramatically in recent years (Lichter, Lichter, & Amundson, 1999) and contributes to a sense that youth are being negatively influenced by the movies they see, the television they watch, the popular music they hear, and the video games they play.

Many youths have easy access to guns (Ward, 1999). At the same time, print and broadcast news media regularly report on a wide range of violent crime committed not just in our own communities but in any hamlet served by an affiliate or a subsidiary of a large media conglomerate (Goldstein, 1994). It is difficult to establish causal relationships between school violence and changes in family structure, violent themes in popular entertainment, the availability of guns, and the reporting of violence by the news media. In each of these areas, however, there have been significant changes in recent years.

Family Structure and Poverty

Changes in family structure and changes in the relative distribution of income within society in recent decades have affected children. In 1950, fewer than 20% of all children in the United States lived in households that were dual-earner nonfarm families and one-parent families. At present, nearly two thirds of all children live in dual-earner nonfarm and one-parent families (Hernandez, 1995). The effect of this drastic change in living arrangements is that fewer adults are at home and available to support students during the non-school hours. Although some of this change may have been offset by an increase in number of parents who work at home, evidence suggests that less time is available for parents to assist and monitor their children. Survey-based estimates suggest that from 4% to 23% of children regularly care for themselves, and several major surveys found that about 12% of children ages 5–12 were in self-care at least once a week (Kerrebrock & Lewit, 1999; U.S. Department of Education, 1999b).

Another major change since 1980 that affects children has been a shift in the distribution of family income. While the mean income of families in the United States has risen, there has been an increasing gap between children in families living at the lowest income levels and those at the highest levels. From 1968 to 1994, income inequality in the United States increased 22.4% (Weinberg, 1996). While the percentage of children living in luxury approaches 20%, an even larger percentage of children live in relative poverty or near-poor frugality (Hernandez, 1995; U. S. Bureau of the Census, 1998; Weinberg, 1996).

More recent data from the U.S. Bureau of the Census, based on the *Gini Index* and quintile shares of aggregate household income (widely used measures of income inequality), show for the most part, from 1993 to 1998, no significant change in income distribution (A. Jones, personal communication, July 17, 2000). Poverty and the availability of parents to supervise their children do not directly create or cause school violence or disruption. Nevertheless, poverty is one of a number of factors that place youth at-risk for school failure, dropout, and delinquent behavior (Walker & Sprague, 1999), and inadequate monitoring and supervision of children is associated with the development of antisocial behavior and delinquency (Patterson, 1982; Farrington, 1995; Hawkins et al., 2000).

Violence in the Entertainment Industry

A study by the Center for Media and Public Affairs documented the frequency with which violent images are featured in popular entertainment (Lichter et al., 1999). It examined made-for-television movies, television series, music videos, and movies to determine the prevalence with which violent content was featured. The study found that, across all forms of entertainment, serious violent images or scenes were featured on the average of 14 times per hour of viewing. When just high violence shows were examined, there was an average of 54 violent acts per hour. Although causal effects between viewing violent images and engaging in violent or disruptive behavior in school are difficult to establish, evidence suggests that exposure to television violence does have an effect on violent behavior (American Psychological Association, 1993; Felson, 1996; Reiss & Roth, 1993).

Media Coverage of School Violence

During the past few years, news media have ratcheted up their coverage of violence in communities and across the country. The evening news and the daily paper chronicle violent acts, both local and across the country, involving juveniles and adults. In the wake of the tragic events and the massive media blitz at Columbine High School in April, 1999, a *USA Today* poll found that 68% of Americans surveyed thought that it was likely or very likely that a school shooting could occur in their town. Other polls of parents' perceptions of school safety revealed similar results (Brooks, Schiraldi, & Ziedenberg, 2000).

Consolidation within the media industry has placed control of radio, television, and newspapers in the hands of fewer and fewer companies (Howard, 1995). As corporate giants compete for audience share or circulation, reporting of violence has become a marketing tool to increase market share (Felson, 1996). Local events in one part of the country become national events as affiliate television and radio stations and newspapers carry reports throughout the country. Although juvenile crime rates fell in the 1990s, the public, informed by media coverage of violence, largely believed that juvenile crime was up and that schools were unsafe (Brooks et al., 2000).

Access to Guns

Handguns and other firearms are more widely available in the United States than in any other industrialized nation in the world, reflecting a permissive policy approach. A 1997 National Institute of Justice report estimated that approximately one third of all households in the United States have guns, with two thirds of gun owners possessing more than one gun (Cook & Ludwig, 1997). At the time of a recent survey 20% of gun owners reported having unlocked, loaded guns in their houses (Cook & Ludwig, 1997). In 1997, more than 4,200 children ages 0–19 were killed by firearms in the United States. More than 2,500 of these killings were homicides and another 1,200 were suicides (Ward, 1999).

Proportionately, young black males are more likely than white youths to be the victims of gun violence. Though federal law restricts sales of guns to minors by licensed gun dealers, in some states children as young as 12 can legally possess semi-automatic weapons and other firearms (Ward, 1999). Yet, unmistakably, the horrific killing of students by students in schools in recent years could not have happened without easy access to firearms by children.

Accountability, Achievement, and Zero Tolerance at the School Level

Our public schools also have changed dramatically. Among other things, there has been an increased focus on accountability, information technology, and achievement. At the same time, there has been a decrease in tolerance of deviant behavior. Accountability and an emphasis on literacy for the Information Age have created a greater sense of urgency among educators. Teachers, principals, and superintendents are being asked to measure and demonstrate tangible academic gains in their students' performance. In this climate, disruptive students, particularly those who score poorly on tests that measure the performance of the classroom, school, or school district, are at-risk for being excluded from the education community.

Under the mantle of zero tolerance, schools and school boards have instituted policies that suspend students from school for a wide variety of rule infractions that range from threats of violence to possession of weapons to use or possession of drugs on school property. Zero tolerance has created situations in which principals have no latitude or discretion in administering disciplinary sanctions. Thus, students have been suspended for sharing Midol tablets, for bringing a plastic knife to spread peanut butter at lunch, for sharing cough drops, for displaying a manicure kit with a

1-inch knife, and for sharing a prescription inhaler with a student experiencing ana-phylactic shock (Tebo, 2000; Skiba & Peterson, 1999).

In sum, changes in the family and the status of children, increases in violent images in popular entertainment, changes in media coverage of violent events, increased availability of guns, and increased accountability at school all set the stage for understanding the current state of school violence and disruption. In the next section, we examine authoritative reports concerning school violence and discuss the difficulty of measuring school violence.

Understanding School Violence

Interest in school violence is a relatively recent phenomenon. How we conceptualize and define school violence shapes how schools think about and respond to the problem (Furlong & Morrison, 2000). Depending upon one's definition of the term, acts of school violence can range from threats of physical violence, to bullying, physical assaults, and homicide.

Data on School Violence

Schools are safer than individual homes and neighborhoods. Children are more likely to encounter serious violent crime away from school than at school. Multiple sources suggest that students are approximately three times safer in school than away from school (Elliott, Hamburg, & Williams, 1998; Kaufman et al., 1999; Snyder & Sickmund, 1999). There is less than a one in a million chance of a student experiencing a school-related violent death. Furthermore, the vast majority of school-related injuries are not violence-related and the majority of school crime is non-violent theft (U.S. Department of Education, 1999a).

The picture of school violence that has emerged over the past decade provides reason for concern, yet optimism for the future. The findings are mixed. In 1997, there were 202,000 serious violent crimes (rape, sexual assault, robbery, and aggravated assault) against students ages 12–18 in school and 2.7 million total school crimes (Kaufman et al., 1999). Centers for Disease Control (CDC) data collected in 1999 from the Youth Risk Behavior Surveillance (YRBS) (Kann et al., 2000) found:

- 6.9% carried weapons at school nationally during 30 days prior to the survey, with males (11.0%) reporting much higher rates of weapon-carrying than females (2.8%)
- 7.7% of students nationally reported having been threatened or injured with a weapon on school property during the past 12 months
- 14.2% of students had been in a physical fight at school during the prior 12 months.

Some longer-term data show that certain measures of violence in schools have remained fairly constant over the past 20 years while other measures of violence have shown a clear pattern of decrease during the 1990s. For example, YRBS data (Centers for Disease Control and Prevention, 2000) show a steady, dramatic decline in students reporting having carried a weapon on school property during the 30 days prior to the survey, from 11.8% in 1993 to 6.9% in 1999 (see Figure 4.2).

The same YRBS data show a similarly impressive decline in students reporting having carried a gun during the 30 days prior to the survey, from 7.9% in 1993 to 4.9% in 1999. Also, from 1993 to 1999, the percentage of students who reported having been in a physical fight at school during the 30 days prior to the survey dropped from 16.2% to 14.2%. The *Annual Report on School Safety* (U.S. Department of Education, 1999a) also reports a decline in several measures of school violence during the 1990s.

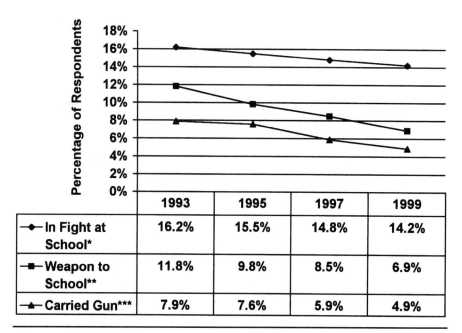

	1993	1995	1997	1999
◆ In Fight at School*	16.2%	15.5%	14.8%	14.2%
■ Weapon to School**	11.8%	9.8%	8.5%	6.9%
▲ Carried Gun***	7.9%	7.6%	5.9%	4.9%

Figure 4.2

Self-Report of Risk Related Behaviors: 1993–1999 Trends

Source: Centers for Disease Control and Prevention. (2000). *Fact Sheet: Youth Risk Behavior Trends*

* Involved in a fight *on school property* at least one time during the 12 months preceding the survey
** Carried a weapon *on school property* at least one time during the 30 days preceding the survey
*** Carried a gun at least one time during the 30 days preceding the survey

Several indicators of school violence have remained fairly constant over the past 20 years. For example, from 1976 to 1997, approximately 5% of high school seniors report having been injured with a weapon at school during the previous 12 months, according to data from the ongoing *Monitoring the Future* study (University of Michigan). During the same period, approximately 12% of seniors report having been injured without a weapon and about 12% report having been threatened with a weapon at school during the previous 12 months (U.S. Department of Education, 1999b; Institute for Social Research, 1997). Other data sources, such as the so-called Principals' and Disciplinarians' Report (U.S. Department of Education, 1998a), show relatively less crime in the schools. That report was based on incidents in which the school called the police. Understandably, administrators may be reluctant to call police or to submit reports suggesting that their school environment is out of control.

This discussion demonstrates that reported measures of school violence differ somewhat depending on the source. A reasonable question to ask is: Why do we see clear signs of decline in some measures, yet relative stability in other measures? Also, how do we decide whether, and to what extent, school violence and disruption is a serious problem? To begin to answer these questions, we need to consider a number of issues surrounding school violence, as well as community-based violence data collection and reporting.

Making Sense of the Numbers

National data on school violence come from several sources. Some sources focus on criminal acts per se; others focus on injury from a health agency perspective; and some privately commissioned surveys (e.g., Metropolitan Life Survey of the American Teacher) focus on various aspects of school violence. The FBI Uniform Crime Reporting (UCR) Program gathers reports from local law enforcement agencies directly or through respective state agencies (Cook & Laub, 1998). As illustrated by Cook and Laub, the UCR data can seriously underestimate true levels of violent crime and provide no information on age of victim or assailant.

Furthermore, some data on juvenile crime are presented in terms of arrests, whereas other data represent convictions. These two categories are quite different, as arrest figures can include innocent individuals (Loeber, Farrington, & Waschbusch, 1998, p. 21). Arrests records do not offer a viable sample of actual crime perpetrators (Cook & Laub, 1998). In addition, law enforcement agencies vary considerably in their reporting of data to the UCR system, thus making year-to-year and other comparisons risky.

A separate source of national level data on violence comes from the National Crime Victimization Survey (NCVS), using household interviews conducted every 6 months (since 1973), and from the School Crime Supplement (SCS) to the NCVS, which is conducted every 4 or 5 years. The NCVS provides information on victimization of youths age 12 and older. Like other forms of self-report, however, this one is subject to errors from a variety of sources, including sampling frame problems, instrument problems, and respondent errors such as inaccurate recall, comprehension problems, omissions, and telescoping effects (Biemer et al., 1991).

Data gathering methods to assess school violence vary considerably, and perceived violence is consistently reported at higher levels than self-reports of violent incidents (Furlong & Morrison, 1994). Methodologically, studies on school violence usually take a [confirmatory] hypothesis verification approach. That is, school violence is assumed to exist, and survey questions elicit responses that confirm its existence. A Congressional Research Service report (U.S. Library of Congress, 1994) found problems in data collection efforts regarding school violence in terms of inconsistent definitions and wording of indicators, varying time frames among studies, and underreporting of criminal acts.

Reiss and Roth (1993) offer a detailed analysis of data collection issues pertaining to violence. They cite differences among UCR, NCVS, and National Center for Health Statistics (NCHS) data in terms of: "(a) domain of events, (b) unit of count, (c) timing of counting, and (d) sources of discretion and error in recording and counting events."

Furthermore, events that are measured are social constructs that depend on society's view of crime—something that changes over time. Reiss and Roth also note that crime incidents can be described differently as a function of the location and circumstance, whether they are defined in terms of the perpetrator (arrest) or victim (injury), and whether multiple offenders or offenses are involved. All of these issues can contribute to varying depictions of violent activity in the community as well as in schools.

Agencies responsible for data collection, analysis, and reporting have attempted to ameliorate the situation throughout the 1980s and 1990s. The CDC has supported many efforts to standardize definitions and reporting of injury-related data (CDC, 1997; Mercy, Ikeda, & Powell, 1998). The National Education Statistics Agenda Committee (U.S. Department of Education, 1996) assessed the current status of data collection and reporting among the states regarding criminal and violent behaviors in schools. The committee issued a report describing the existing state of affairs, providing model definitions for data collection and a description of a model data system that states could choose to implement.

Reconciling the differences between CDC data showing a clear decline in school violence and *Monitoring the Future* data showing stability over two decades is a challenge. The participants, time frames, and wording of questions differ between these surveys. For example, several of the CDC-YRBS survey questions pertain to frequency of weapon-carrying and involvement in a fight. Several of the questions from the *Monitoring the Future* survey pertain to being threatened or injured with a weapon, and having property damaged or stolen.

Although we may choose to think of these questions as proxy variables for school violence and disruption, just because they fall under a common umbrella concept does not necessarily mean that they measure the same behaviors. They each need to be evaluated within the context of the specific survey effort. Unfortunately, no existing procedure allows clear reconciliation of these data differences. The best one can do is to conclude that some serious problems remain with school violence, but that there are several clear signals of an improving situation and that, generally speaking, schools are safe.

Balancing Educational Rights with an Orderly School Environment

Public schools are charged with providing all children with educational opportunities. School administrators and teachers have a vested interest in creating environments in which their students can best learn. Given the diversity and the numbers of children who walk through the public school doors, this is no small feat. School systems and personnel must constantly balance the need for orderliness and efficiency in schools with the rights and entitlements of individual students. Although the needs and desires of school systems often are aligned with the needs and desires of the students they serve, at times the two are at odds.

In the following sections we will discuss some of the entitlements due students in general and how these entitlements have affected schools' abilities to provide appropriate educational environments. We also will discuss the impact of those additional entitlements afforded students with disabilities, including some of the pitfalls and misperceptions associated with these entitlements.

Educational Entitlements

Compulsory school-attendance laws give children the right, as well as the responsibility, to attend school. Schools must serve all the children in their communities—even children who prefer not to attend. The public schools cannot pick and choose whom they serve, even if picking and choosing would result in more efficiency, higher achievement scores for the school as a whole, or less disruption.

Over time, compulsory school-attendance laws have created problems for schools in jurisdictions where schools and school districts have not adapted to their changing school clientele. Problems have included truancy, disruptive or disrespectful behavior, drug use, threats of violence, and acts of violence. As problems have cropped up, individual schools, school districts, and governmental agencies have crafted ways for schools to deal with those problems. Responses have included (and continue to include) the use of behavioral modification strategies, timeouts, and corporal punishment. For serious violations of the school code, schools have expelled students and placed them into alternative education settings (Yell, 1990; Yell, Cline, & Bradley, 1995; Yell, 1998, ch. 15). Sometimes these responses have been effective in restoring order to the school environment. Other times these responses have gone too far and threatened the rights of the students to whom they are applied.

The U.S. Supreme Court has examined the issue of school discipline on several occasions. In 1977, the Court examined the constitutionality of corporal punishment

(*Ingraham v. Wright,* 1977). Although the Court eventually decided that corporal punishment did not constitute "cruel and unusual punishment" and that students were not entitled to a hearing prior to the administration of corporal punishment (under the due process clause of the 14th Amendment), the justices did reiterate that individual teachers or administrators could be held liable or subject to criminal penalties if the corporal punishment administered was later found to be excessive. Even though the *Ingraham v. Wright* decision did not change the legal status of corporal punishment, the very fact that the Supreme Court heard this case influenced state legislatures to pass additional laws governing the use of corporal punishment (Yell, 1990; Yell, 1998, ch. 15). Corporal punishment remains an option for schools in some states, but its use is limited by requirements such as approval by the principal, presence of an adult witness, and prior parental approval. These limitations protect individual students from capricious and overzealous use of corporal punishment by frustrated school personnel.

Another disciplinary action that has been called into question is suspension from school. In 1975, the U.S. Supreme Court heard *Goss v. Lopez,* in which nine high school students alleged that their constitutional right to due process (under the 14th Amendment) had been violated when they were each suspended for up to 10 days without a formal hearing. In this case, the Court sided with the students, declaring that schools must provide evidence of a student's misconduct at a hearing prior to (or immediately following) the suspension. The Court ruled that students' rights to attend school supersede schools' rights to unilaterally exclude students for misconduct. Although school suspensions for disciplinary purposes are allowable, the process must include oral or written notice of the offense and the right to be heard (Yell, 1998, ch. 15).

In *Honig v. Doe* (1988), the Supreme Court set the stage for revised procedures in dealing with aggressive and violent students. This contributed to a change in attitudes among educators, politicians, and the public with regard to the behavior of students with disabilities. Bill Honig, Superintendent of Instruction for California schools, argued that a dangerousness exclusion to the "stay-put provision" of disability law existed, whereby schools could exclude students who threatened the safety of others. The Court denied his argument and made it clear that the stay-put provision held, and that schools could not unilaterally remove students considered dangerous while their change of placement was being appealed.

The Court's ruling also supported the position that a suspension of more than 10 days is a change of placement. The court affirmed that normal procedures, including temporary suspensions of up to 10 days, timeout, study carrels, and detention could be used with dangerous students (Sorenson, 1993; Tucker, Goldstein, & Sorenson, 1993; Yell, 1998).

In the 1990s, particularly in the aftermath of the *Honig* decision, a number of state and local education agencies revised school disciplinary codes to reflect the tenor of recent Safe and Drug-Free Schools legislation (Skiba & Peterson, 1999, 2000). This legislation was aimed at eliminating weapons and controlled substances on school grounds. This type of disciplinary approach—popularly referred to as zero tolerance—has serious flaws in its implementation. Some administrators have overlooked small infractions by otherwise well-behaved students (e.g., an honor student who forgets to remove a miniature Swiss army knife from his keychain), and others have enforced the letter of the law to such an unyielding extent that they attract national media attention (e.g., the second-grader who brought his grandfather's watch to show and tell; a 1-inch mini-pocketknife was attached; the student was suspended and sent to an alternative school for 1 month).

The real problem with a zero-tolerance posture is that serious punishments, such as suspensions from school, have been handed out in an arbitrary and inconsistent manner (Harvard University Civil Rights Project, 2000; Skiba & Peterson, 1999; Tebo, 2000). Students with disabilities who have behavioral problems and who typically have few advocates in the schools, as well as African-American students, are particularly vulnerable to harsh disciplinary tactics (Harvard University Civil Rights Project, 2000; Townsend, 2000).

Entitlements of Students With Disabilities

Although basic educational entitlements apply to all students, those with disabilities are afforded separate, additional protections under the IDEA, amended and reauthorized in 1997. Provisions of IDEA pertaining to discipline are frequently a source of contention. For example, if a student engages in aggressive or disruptive behavior as a consequence of his or her disability, a school is not at liberty to unilaterally suspend that child from school for that very behavior. This is not to say, however, that schools have no recourse whatsoever when a student with a disability misbehaves.

A wide-range of commonly used discipline tactics are still available to use with students with disabilities. These include behavior management strategies, restrictions on privileges, and in-school suspension. Even suspension from school is still an option as long as that suspension does not last 10 days or become part of a pattern of suspensions that accumulate up to 10 days in length.

The stay-put provision of IDEA (IDEA Regulations, 34 C.F.R. § 300.514) is a common concern for teachers and administrators. When a student with a disability engages in serious acts of misconduct that could result in that student's removal from his or her current placement, school administrators and the student's parents often concur on a plan of action. When parents and school administrators disagree and parents request a due-process hearing, the stay-put provision comes into play. Under the stay-put clause, schools are not allowed to remove a student from his or her current placement while the disciplinary action is under review.

The stay-put provision often is misinterpreted to mean that children with disabilities can engage in dangerous conduct without fear of ever being removed to a more restrictive setting. To the contrary, if a student with a disability brings a weapon or controlled substance to school, that student is subject to the same disciplinary actions that apply to a student without a disability. The student then can be referred to an Interim Alternative Education Placement (IAEP).

Regardless of the disciplinary outcome, the school system must provide special education services to any student with a disability who ends up being suspended from school for more than 10 cumulative days in a school year. In addition, if a child with a disability engages in behavior that school administrators believe is likely to result in injury to self or others in the school community, the child with a disability can be removed to an IAEP for up to 45 days (Bear, 1999). The critical element is that the child with a disability not lose access to his or her educational services. The educational services provided to children with disabilities—including services designed to address their behavioral and social-skill deficits—are critical to their eventual success.

Occasionally schools use homebound instruction as an IAEP. These cases seem to violate both the spirit and intent of IDEA discipline provisions. Homebound instruction typically is limited to about 6 hours per week. In such circumstances, it is virtually impossible to provide appropriate academic instruction, and this level of service precludes meaningful implementation of a student's IEP.

Behaviors of Students With Disabilities

How often are students with disabilities involved in school violence and disruption? Apart from anecdotal accounts, it is difficult to find authoritative analyses, as data sources are limited. Several sources from recent years, however, present a partial picture and enable us to draw some tentative conclusions. We will examine two reports on implementation of the Gun-Free Schools Act, an analysis of suspensions and expulsions in Kansas, an analysis from Kentucky schools, a look at recent data from Maryland, and data regarding suspensions in Delaware and Minnesota. We also examine a national-level study of suspensions and expulsions by the Research Triangle Institute, a survey of state and local practices from state directors of special education services, and findings in the 21st Annual Report to Congress on IDEA.

Gun-Free Schools Reports

Subsequent to passage of the Gun-Free Schools Act of 1994, Congress mandated that annual reports be issued concerning implementation of the Act, including data on involvement of students with disabilities. The Act required each state receiving federal funds under the Elementary and Secondary Education Act (ESEA) to have a state law in effect mandating a minimum 1-year expulsion of students who brought a firearm to school, allowing chief administering officers the right to modify expulsion terms on a case-by-case basis.

During the 1996–97 school year, 6,093 students were expelled from school under the Act. Of the 43 states reporting on shortened expulsions, 39 states reported on the disability status of these students. Of the 699 students reported, 37% had disabilities under IDEA (U.S. Department of Education, 1998b). During the 1997–98 school year, 3,930 students were expelled from school under the Act. Of the 49 states reporting on shortened expulsions, 48 states reported on the disability status of these students. Of the 1,459 students reported, 38% had disabilities under IDEA (U.S. Department of Education, 1999c).

Suspensions and Expulsions in Kansas

Cooley (1995) examined suspension/expulsion data in Kansas, using survey data from 441 secondary school principals. This study found that students with disabilities had more than double the likelihood of suspension/expulsion than students without disabilities. Students with learning disabilities and behavior disorders were disproportionately represented among the students with disabilities who were suspended/expelled, compared to their proportions among students with disabilities in Kansas.

According to the researchers, however, students receiving special education services were no more likely than nondisabled students to engage in injury-causing behaviors. Furthermore, the acts committed by the suspended students with disabilities were found to be no different than those committed by nondisabled students. The report concluded that the students with disabilities were not receiving IEP-related services appropriate to their needs.

Analysis of Records in Kentucky

An analysis of records of 465 students in an Eastern Kentucky school district (Fasko, Grubb, & Osborne, 1995) found that about 20% of the suspended students were disabled, although students with disabilities composed about 14% of students included in the study. Approximately 83% of the suspensions were given to male students, and 17% to females. Males and females made up 53% and 47% of the student population, respectively.

Maryland Data

Data from Maryland (Maryland State Department of Education, 2000) showed that statewide, 64,103 students were suspended during the 1998–99 school year. Of those students, 15,669 (24.4%) were students with disabilities. Students with disabilities made up 13.1% of the statewide enrollment that year. Prior Maryland data for the 1997–98 school year (Maryland State Department of Education, 1999) provided an inconclusive picture of suspensions of students with disabilities because duplicated and unduplicated counts were mixed, using both incident- and person-specific data. This made comparisons to statewide percent of students with disabilities impossible, because, depending on relative rates of multiple offenses among disabled and nondisabled populations, different conclusions could be drawn.

Suspensions in Delaware

Along a similar vein, data from a study of suspensions in Delaware (cited in Sinclair and others, 1996) found that 23% of the incidents resulting in out-of-school suspensions during the 1994–95 school year involved special education students. These data were based on *incident* counts, not *person* counts. Therefore, we cannot conclude that 23% of the suspended students were special education students. Interestingly, the 1997–98 Maryland data (also not conclusive for similar reasons) found that 23.5% of short-term suspension incidents were associated with students with disabilities.

Suspensions in Minnesota

A University of Minnesota policy research brief (Sinclair et al., 1996) reported that in Minnesota, the overwhelming percentage of suspensions of students with disabilities involved students with learning disabilities and behavior disorders. The study found that, based on data from several other state studies, about 25% of suspension incidents were associated with students with disabilities.

Research Triangle Institute Report

Fiore and Reynolds (1996) conducted an exhaustive study gathering data on discipline issues in special education. The researchers found that for aggregated data from responding states and districts, approximately 20% of suspended students were students with disabilities, a percentage much larger than their proportion of the student population. Approximately 80% of the misconduct by students with disabilities was considered less serious, with about 20% of the misconduct falling into more serious categories. Also, the vast majority of students with disabilities who were suspended were males. Students with emotional disabilities were overrepresented among students with disabilities who were suspended.

The authors noted the paucity of available data on suspension/expulsion of students with disabilities. Only six states and 16 districts provided data on suspensions that included information on students with disabilities. The report demonstrated a tremendous variability among the states with regard to data systems on suspensions and on students with disabilities. The authors urged caution in interpreting the results, as many jurisdictions either had no such data-recording system or failed to provide the requested data. In turn, the available data cannot be construed as a nationally representative sample for students with disabilities.

21st Annual Report to Congress

The 21st Annual Report to Congress on IDEA (U.S. Department of Education, 2000) addressed school discipline and students with disabilities and reviewed some of the research cited above. Citing a 1994 Office of Civil Rights (OCR) report that found no overrepresentation of students with disabilities among suspended students, the Department of Education report discussed discrepant findings concerning discipline and students with disabilities.

Survey of State Departments of Education

A survey of state departments of special education (Morgan, Loosli, & Striefel, 1997) found improvements in maintaining and disseminating behavior standards compared to a similar survey done 5 years earlier. Of the 41 state respondents, 14 states reported that they had no such standards on behavioral procedures. The researchers found considerable variability among the states with regard to maintaining an information dissemination, monitoring, and training system for behavioral procedures for students with disabilities.

Conclusions Drawn From Studies

Although the data discussed above do not constitute a nationally representative sample of students with disabilities, we can still draw several tentative conclusions from these studies.

1. Mounting evidence suggests that a disproportionately high percentage (possibly close to 20%) of suspended students are students with disabilities, compared to a national proportion of about 11% of students ages 6–21 receiving services under IDEA. One OCR study (cited in the 21st Annual Report to Congress) contradicts this conclusion. Several studies demonstrate that students with learning disabilities and emotional disturbance are overrepresented among suspended students with disabilities.
2. Several studies have found that the majority of suspension-related behaviors seem to be nonviolent and generally do not result in injuries to others.
3. The nature of the suspension-related behaviors of students with disabilities may not be substantively different than the behaviors of the students' nondisabled peers.
4. Some evidence suggests that procedures to guarantee a system of consistent behavioral procedures for students with disabilities vary tremendously among the states and that students in some states may not be receiving appropriate services. Rather, suspension may be the procedure of choice in lieu of more proactive, supportive approaches.

Research by Mayer and Leone (1999), as well as publications by the Justice Policy Institute and the American Policy Forum (Brooks, Schiraldi, & Zeidenberg, 2000; Mendel, 2000) suggest that punitive, controlling approaches do little to solve continuing problems of school violence and disruption or juvenile crime in the community.

More data regarding specific school experiences with violence, individual school practices, and the role of students with disabilities will be gathered with the new School Survey on Crime and Safety (SSOCS), sponsored by the U.S. Department of Education, National Center for Education Statistics (NCES). NCES plans to conduct the SSOCS every 2 years, and the first SSOCS report is due in December 2000.

Gun-Free Schools Act suspension data revealed 37%– 38% representation by students with disabilities among cases shortened to less than one year for states reporting disability-related data. While it is logical that a relatively high percentage of cases meriting chief administering officer review would involve examination of disability-related factors, these data raise several concerns. *First,* the data (U.S. Department of Education, 1998b, 1999c), is a small and possibly unrepresentative subset of the complete dataset, precluding thorough analysis of the situation. The data must be interpreted with caution.

Second, there is reason to believe that often, students with disabilities get caught more often than nondisabled peers, because of problems with social communication, poor judgment, poor planning skills, and attributional biases that can lead to more confrontation with authority figures. These students may be more easily identified by the system for their infractions. That is not to lessen the egregiousness or unacceptability of such behaviors. Rather, it may simply point to a state of affairs in which students with disabilities are represented disproportionately in such cases, in part, because their nondisabled peers are more adept at eluding detection.

Third, the 37%–38% data could be fairly accurate, in which case schools need to develop new understandings and find more effective interventions to reduce weapon-carrying, particularly by students with disabilities. Additional research may shed more light on the exact nature of this phenomenon.

Schools clearly face many challenges in maintaining a safe and orderly environment. The next section presents several approaches to school- and community-based programming.

How Schools Have Responded to Problems of School Violence

Understanding and Shaping School Environments

School-based violence prevention initiatives are considered a best-practice approach to foster positive youth development (Dwyer & Osher, 2000; Mendel, 2000; Walker & Horner, 1996). Federal and state policy makers increasingly are viewing schools as excellent sites for prevention activities, although federal expenditures for these efforts are relatively modest (Gottfredson, 1997). Schools provide consistent access to youth in the early developmental years, and they employ staff members who are focused on ensuring successful academic and behavioral outcomes for students. Another critical advantage is that many risk factors (see Figure 4.3) associated with youth violence are school-related and therefore may be modified within school settings.

Schools should consider three fundamental principles when planning violence prevention initiatives. *First,* evidence strongly supports the effectiveness of *school-wide violence prevention* initiatives based conceptually on a public health model. This model organizes prevention efforts so that schools can systematically address the needs of all students, including those with severe academic, emotional, or behavioral problems.

Second, approaches that emphasize punishment, control, and containment have been demonstrated to be ineffective in preventing or intervening in disruption and violence; punitive orientations may actually exacerbate school disorder (Mayer & Leone, 1999).

Third, effective school-wide prevention initiatives are comprehensive, have several components, and involve a broad range of services and supports provided over a sufficient period. Because the antecedents of youth violence are highly correlated (Dryfoos, 1990; Hawkins et al., 2000), prevention programs that address a range of interrelated risk and protective factors have greater potential than single-focus programs.

INDIVIDUAL RISK FACTORS	PEER RISK FACTORS
• Poor academic skills • Impulsivity • Substance use • Poor social problem-solving skills • Inability to understand the perspective of others • Poor conflict-resolution skills • Difficulties in understanding the moral consequences of actions	• Low social status • Rejection by peers • Gang involvement • Shared deviant peer norms • Association with delinquent peer groups
FAMILY RISK FACTORS	**SCHOOL/COMMUNITY RISK FACTORS**
• Inconsistent discipline • Reliance on coercion • Harsh or abusive discipline • Poor monitoring of activities • Insecure attachments • Defensive communication • Deviant shared values • A high percentage of negative interactions • Low levels of emotional closeness • Inefficient use of family resources	• Lack of student/parent involvement • Low academic achievement • Lack of social organization and social support • Few opportunities for recreation • Unemployment and economic disparities • High levels of community crime • Availability of firearms

Figure 4.3

Risk Factors for Youth Violence

Source: *A Program Planning Guide for Youth Violence Prevention* (1996, p. 15), by N. G. Guerra and K. R. Williams (Boulder, CO: Center for the Study and prevention of Violence). Copyright © 1996 by the Institute of Behavioral Science, Regents of the University of Colorado. Reprinted by permission.

The public health approach underlying school-wide violence prevention initiatives was defined by the Institute of Medicine (1994) as a three-tiered ecological perspective incorporating a continuum of strategies at graduated levels of intensity. This model promotes the use of a comprehensive framework of *universal, selective*, and *indicated* prevention strategies (Tolan, Guerra, & Kendall, 1995).

■ Universal strategies are the foundation of school-wide prevention efforts because they apply a primary prevention approach to the entire school population.

FOCUS ON SCHOOLS: CALVERTON MIDDLE SCHOOL

Calverton Middle School in Baltimore serves nearly 1,200 students in grades 6 through 8. The school has had a history of low achievement test scores, high rates of student and teacher absenteeism, and discipline problems. Seventy percent of the students at Calverton are eligible for free or reduced-price lunches. During the 1999– 2000 school year, 56 of the 85 teachers at the school held provisional or probationary certification. Seven teachers were on long-term leave.

Performance at Calverton was among the lowest for middle schools in the state of Maryland. Daily attendance by students for the 1998–1999 school year averaged 69%, and during the Fall of 1999, more than 300 students were tardy to school each day. The school was chaotic and experienced frequent interruptions resulting from pulled fire alarms, fights, and classroom disruptions.

Scores on the statewide Maryland School Performance Assessment Program (MSPAP) from 1993–99 indicated that fewer than 6% of eighth grade students scored excellent or satisfactory in reading and fewer than 5% of eighth graders scored excellent or satisfactory in mathematics. On the Maryland State Department of Education's Middle School Performance Index (SPI), Calverton scored from 22.57 to 28.24 each year from 1993 to 1999. The SPI is the weighted average of a school's relative distance from the satisfactory standards, where a score of 100 is considered satisfactory. Several years ago, Calverton was placed on a list of schools eligible for reconstitution or takeover by the Maryland State Department of Education.

In February, 2000, a new principal, Karl Perry, assumed administrative responsibility for Calverton. To begin the process of turning Calverton into an effective and caring school, Perry, with the support of staff, instituted a series of measures designed to refocus the attention of staff and students on academic excellence. Following consultation with other administrative staff, the Five Ps—be Present, Punctual, Prepared, Polite, and Positive—were introduced. Perry's primary objectives in assuming the principalship were to gain control of the school and improve the school climate. Principal Perry also introduced the *Drop Everything And Read* (DEAR) program, a regular part of the school day at Calverton. He met with parents, local business owners, and members of the community to develop shared strategies to combat truancy and tardiness.

As a result of using an appropriately tailored combination of universal and selective level interventions, Calverton Middle School has showed early signs of improvement. For example, student attendance has risen from about 69% to over 76%. Tardy arrivals have dropped from about 300 per day during the Fall to about 150 during the Spring semester. Office referrals dropped from more than 2,600 during the Fall semester of 1999 to under 2,200 during the following semester.

Consistent use of these strategies provides sufficient support for a majority (80%–90%) of students in each school, thereby avoiding most instances of new problem behavior. Examples of universal prevention strategies include unambiguous behavioral expectations, proactive classroom management strategies, teacher expectations that support positive student outcomes, opportunities for positive attachment to school, consistent use of incentives and consequences, and school-wide literacy programs.

■ Selective strategies provide increased support for a smaller number of students (10%–15%) in each school. Secondary prevention strategies such as small-group instruction, social-skills training, behavioral contracting, and mentoring are designed to avoid the escalation of emerging academic and behavioral problems.

■ Indicated strategies support a relatively small number of students in each school (1%–5%) who demonstrate significant academic or behavioral problems requiring the most intensive level of support. Prevention strategies for these youth are individualized and often involve long-term involvement of education, mental health, social service, and juvenile justice agencies. Wraparound planning (Burns & Goldman, 1999) and school-based mental health services (Weist & Warner, 1997; Woodruff et al., 1999) are widely regarded as important advances in violence prevention for high-risk youth.

The variety of strategies incorporated in school-based violence prevention plans can be organized as individual or as environmental approaches. Prevention plans may focus on individual risk factors including alienation from school, truancy, poor academic performance, low levels of social competency, and antisocial behavior in the early grades. More broadly, prevention plans may focus on risk factors in the school and community, such as availability of drugs and weapons, negative peer experiences, and inadequate academic or behavioral support. Although examples of prevention strategies at the individual and environmental level are presented separately below, the interdependence of risk factors calls for integrated approaches that incorporate more than a single type of support.

Strategies frequently included in school-wide prevention plans that target individual risk factors include:

1. Instructional programs (identified as the most common prevention strategy used in schools) (Womer, 1997; Larson, 1994). These curriculum-based approaches focus on a range of social competency and academic skills with the goals of preventing or remediating academic failure, heightening awareness and knowledge of social influences on violent behavior, and teaching appropriate responses to these influences.

2. Behavior-management techniques designed to change antisocial behaviors and promote positive behavioral skills. These strategies will be most effective when based on systematic screening to identify students at risk for antisocial behavior (Sprague & Walker, 2000).

3. Peer strategies including peer coaching, mediation, and counseling.
4. Counseling and mentoring strategies.

Examples of environmental strategies are a strong academic mission, defining norms for appropriate behavior, promoting student attachment to school, and modifying organizational and structural conditions in the school by decreasing class size and providing a consistent climate of emotional support (Leone, 1997). In this context, prevention strategies should become a normative part of the school routine. For example, programs that teach nonviolent problem-solving strategies have a greater chance for success when the school climate regularly supports and models that approach to conflict (Gottfredson, 1997). School-wide prevention plans should be a high priority for the school and school system, a commitment reflected by strong administrative leadership at the school and district level and the provision of sufficient fiscal resources.

Efficacy of These Approaches

Although prevention science strongly supports the efficacy of school-wide approaches that incorporate multiple interventions and link schools and their environmental contexts, research on the impacts of these approaches is lacking (University of Vermont, 1999). As a result, numerous prevention initiatives have been implemented but reliable data of their effectiveness are not widely available. Despite the limited availability of rigorous evaluation studies in the 1990s, efforts to document the effectiveness of youth violence prevention programs are increasing. Schools using prevention plans report positive outcomes including improved academic performance and staff morale (Dwyer & Osher, 2000), as well as reduced behavior problems, reflected by fewer disciplinary referrals and suspensions (Sugai, Sprague, et al., 2000).

In an exhaustive study of school-based crime prevention efforts, Gottfredson (1997) found positive effects for programs that clarify behavioral norms, offer comprehensive instruction in a range of social-competency skills over a long period, provide behavior modification, and restructure schools to create smaller and more supportive units of instruction. Evidence also points to approaches that are *not* effective, including insight-oriented individual counseling and peer counseling (Gottfredson, 1997; Tolan & Guerra, 1998).

Our discussion of the advantages and strategies associated with school-wide prevention approaches is extended in the next section. We also present examples of research-based, school-wide prevention programs that show promise in reducing school disorder and promoting successful academic and social outcomes.

Promising Approaches

Numerous programs across the United States have shown positive results. Although it is beyond the scope of this chapter to review specific programs, we highlight three promising approaches to provide a perspective of the wider prevention and early

FOCUS ON SCHOOLS:
RICHARD MONTGOMERY HIGH SCHOOL

Richard Montgomery High School (RMHS) in Rockville, Maryland, serves approximately 1,650 students in grades 9–12 in a suburban Washington, DC, school district. The school serves a diverse student body that is 12% African-American, 15% Asian, 16% Latino, and 55% non-Latino Caucasian students. Nearly 9% of students receive services because of limited English proficiency, 7% of the students receive special education services, and 10% of the students receive free and reduced-price meals. The mobility rate at RMHS is 6%. Students at RMHS perform well academically; approximately 500 students in the school are enrolled in the International Baccalaureate program—a rigorous college preparatory program—and 69% of students attend 2- or 4-year colleges after graduation.

In spite of average daily attendance above 90% and a strong academic program, the school has had an unacceptably high number of serious disciplinary incidents in recent years. In the 1997–98 school year, there were 35 serious disciplinary incidents at the school, including racial incidents, major vandalism, fights, and drug incidents. Mark Kelsch, a new principal appointed at the beginning of the 1998–99 school year, set out to reduce serious disciplinary incidents and improve academic performance of the school through greater participation and involvement of students and teachers in all aspects of the school.

Kelsch's approach—a form of universal or primary prevention—combines a strong emphasis on relationships between adults and students and among students with rules that count and are fairly enforced.

The changes Kelsch has brought to RMHS include a daily 10-minute televised program produced by students and broadcast throughout the school. The program includes information from the principal, student groups, teaching staff, and others. Other changes include a focus on student achievement and recognition, reorganization of the school schedule so that all teachers in an academic area have common planning time, and consistent enforcement of attendance and tardy policies. These changes appear promising. During the 1999–2000 school year, 12 serious disciplinary incidents occurred—a reduction of nearly two thirds from just 2 years ago. The number of students losing course credit because of unexcused absences and being tardy to class dropped by 50% from the previous year. This past year Richard Montgomery High School received the Blue Ribbon Award for excellence from the U.S. Department of Education. For more information about the school, visit the web site: http://www.mcps.k12.md.us/schools/rmhs/

intervention landscape. The listing of resources and websites (at the end of the chapter) leads to many other excellent program approaches and models.

Positive Behavioral Interventions and Supports: PBIS

Positive behavioral interventions and supports (PBIS) is a systems approach to creating and sustaining school environments that foster academic and behavioral competence for all students. As compared with traditional school-based approaches that target problem behavior demonstrated by individual students, PBIS focuses broadly on identifying policies and practices of the school itself that support or impede successful outcomes.

In this approach, classroom management and instructional practices are viewed as parallel processes; effective teaching of both academic and social skills involve strategies such as direct instruction, positive reinforcement, modeling, and precorrection (Sugai, Kameenui, et al., 2000). The PBIS framework emphasizes data-based assessment of the school climate and individual student progress through measures such as disciplinary referrals, attendance rates, and suspension rates. Functional behavior assessments are used in response to more intense problem behaviors.

Skill-Building: Violence Prevention Curricula

Violence prevention curricula based on social learning theory are used widely in school settings to improve students' problem-solving and anger-management skills, and to increase their knowledge of nonviolent responses to interpersonal conflict (Kenney & Watson, 1999). Conflict resolution and social skills are taught directly as a distinct curriculum or through integration in other coursework.

Numerous models for violence prevention through problem solving are available. For example, an interpersonal cognitive problem-solving approach with demonstrated effectiveness focuses on primary prevention in the elementary grades (Shure, 1999). In this approach, parents and teachers are trained to instruct children directly in using specific thinking and communication skills designed to prevent conflict in school and at home. *Second Step* is a violence prevention curriculum designed for use in preschool through ninth grade (Frey et al., 2000). The curriculum emphasizes building protective social and emotional competencies and reducing aggressive and antisocial behaviors.

The Violence Prevention Curriculum for Adolescents (Prothrow-Stith, 1987) is designed to teach alternatives to aggressive behavior and to create supportive classroom environments in urban schools. Evidence suggests that the program is effective in reducing aggressive conflicts among students.

Mental Health and Social Services in Schools: Linkages to Learning

Linkages to Learning is a primary prevention model for the delivery of mental health, health, and social services for at-risk children and their families at 11 elementary and middle schools in Montgomery County, Maryland. The program was established in 1992 as a joint effort among public and private nonprofit agencies to respond to the increased needs of low- income children and their families. Parents are viewed as partners in this effort, taking an active role in developing solutions to individual, family, and community challenges. The overall goal of the program is to address social, emotional, and somatic health problems that undermine children's ability to succeed in school.

Participating children and families receive mental health assessment and counseling; assistance in obtaining shelter, food, housing, and employment; medical/dental care; assistance with immigration, translation, and transportation; and educational support including academic tutoring, mentoring, and adult education classes. Researchers at the University of Maryland completed a comprehensive longitudinal impact evaluation of children in a participating school and a control school (Fox et al., 1999). The evaluation found positive outcomes for children and parents, including improved academic achievement and behavioral functioning at home and school, increased consistency in parenting practices and overall family cohesion.

Developing a Plan to Prevent School Violence

In this section we present an overview of the major steps involved in establishing an effective school-wide violence prevention plan.

1. Assessing school needs.

Even though fundamental principles for organizing effective prevention plans can be identified and consistently applied, schools cannot follow "one size fits all" formulas or blueprints. The first step in developing a violence prevention plan that incorporates promising practices and responds to the local school context is to conduct a needs assessment.

A systematic needs assessment enables the staff to understand the structural, economic, cultural, linguistic, and developmental variations that influence the functioning of specific schools. The unique features of schools that would be addressed in needs assessment include differences in size and physical structure; personal and cultural attributes of students, staff, and the community; prior experiences with prevention strategies; and current perceptions of the level of order and disorder. Using information gathered in needs assessment helps to shape a school-wide prevention plan that incorporates specific performance goals tailored to the strengths and priorities of each school and community (Walker & Horner, 1996).

2. Developing parent and community support.

Because schools operate within environmental contexts, prevention initiatives that incorporate strong parent and community partnerships can mediate positive outcomes for youth. Kellam (2000) underscores the promise or perils associated with school/community partnerships when he emphasizes that "how prevention program leaders relate to community concerns will dictate the fate of their efforts (p. 2)."

Effective school-wide prevention plans operate best when they involve individual parents and parent organizations in meaningful ways. Parent/school collaboration enhances opportunities for schools to work successfully with troubled youth, extending prevention initiatives beyond schools and into local communities.

Links between the school and the larger community may take many forms, including collaboration among child-serving agencies, local business, law enforcement, and advocacy organizations. An important consideration in developing community support is to ensure that violence prevention initiatives are culturally competent. This is especially critical given the differential application of school disciplinary practices that result in the disproportionate suspension of African American youth (Townsend, 2000).

3. Developing a leadership team.

School-wide prevention plans that are actively supported by school- and district-level personnel, students, and families will likely produce the most effective and durable results. Team-based decision making can enhance ownership and acceptance of school violence prevention plans. Such a leadership team would be composed of staff members representing the various disciplines and roles within the school (e.g., general and special education teachers, counselors and school psychologists, administrators, paraprofessionals), and may include students, parents, and community members. Given the many risk factors associated with youth violence, the leadership team also could function as the organizational mechanism for systematic collaboration with mental health, social service, law enforcement, and other community agencies.

The leadership team conducts and analyzes the needs assessment, formulates short- and longer-term goals, identifies potential prevention strategies, monitors progress, and evaluates results (Dwyer & Osher, 2000). Teams can be formed specifically to address school-wide prevention efforts, or they can be built from and coordinated with other school-based management teams that exist in many schools.

4. Providing staff development.

As is the case in all school reform efforts, staff training is essential to ensure understanding, support, and consistent use of the school-wide violence prevention plan. Carefully designed and implemented training, available for *all* school staff, operationalizes the concept of a school-wide violence prevention agenda. This training involves teachers, counselors, bus drivers, cafeteria workers, clerical staff, and others working in the school. An important focus of training is skill development that supports achievement of instructional and behavioral competence for all students.

The content of training is also tailored for staff with specialized responsibilities, such as members of the leadership team. Further, given the complex nature of youth violence, staff development should reflect sustained rather than isolated training activities. Inservice training that follows this approach supports the reliable and consistent application of prevention strategies throughout the school.

5. Evaluating the plan.

Evaluation is the systematic collection and analysis of relevant data to inform decision making (Muraskin, 1993). Despite growing evidence supporting the use of school-wide violence prevention plans, specific prevention programs and practices have not typically been evaluated through rigorous research. Without benefit of evaluation, school staff and policy makers may respond to troubling behavior based more on political expediency than empirically validated practice.

Evaluation begins with needs assessment and can extend to process, outcome, and cost-benefit research (Flannery, 1998). When examining school-wide prevention programs one or more of the major types of evaluation may be appropriate to use.

- *Process evaluations* address the qualities that make school-wide prevention programs work or not work.
- *Outcome evaluations* focus on determining the impact of school-wide prevention programs on the school climate and for individual students.
- *Cost-benefit evaluations* identify whether specific programs are cost-effective.

Evaluation design has been constrained by difficulties in identifying and measuring outcomes related to prevention of violence in schools (discussed in previous section). Further, the impact of violence prevention programs has not been measured reliably because most evaluations have focused on immediate results in a limited number of sites rather than on longer-term results and replication in different types of schools and communities.

Challenges Ahead: Next Steps

Many reports have shown that school and community-based adolescent violence has been declining in recent years and that schools are considerably safer than surrounding neighborhoods. At the same time, addressing school violence remains an appropriate concern for educators, parents, political leaders, and other members of the community. We've learned from program evaluations, as well as a vast body of research in the fields of education, mental health, social services, and juvenile justice, that school violence must be addressed on the individual, family, school, neighborhood, and larger societal levels. Multifaceted interventions must target specific risk factors, be developmentally appropriate, and be culturally sensitive. In addition, interventions should involve parents and members of the community, promote interagency collaboration, address multiple levels of the child's life (e.g., school, family, neighborhood), and involve an evaluation component.

Schools will continue to face challenges while working with students with disabilities. State and local school systems must develop, disseminate, and monitor the interventions used in addressing behaviors of students with disabilities, using research-based best practices. Schools need to explore alternatives to school suspension, keeping students engaged in their school responsibilities and promoting their academic success. Responsive and flexible approaches require, and real progress demands, long-term investment and commitment. There are no quick fixes. Schools should examine their climate and programming to ensure that they are addressing their students' needs. Successful school programs require a buy-in by *all* school staff—teachers, support staff, and school administration—not just by a particular program's leadership team.

Data collection and analysis of prevention efforts should be ongoing, using rigorous methodology, as exemplified by the PBIS approach (Sugai, Kameenui, et al., 2000). School- and community-based programs have to maintain ongoing data collection and record keeping and should evaluate student and family needs and progress. At present, the role of students with disabilities in school violence and disruption is not well understood. Meaningful prevention and intervention efforts require thorough understanding of the challenges facing school administrators in serving students with disabilities, particularly those with behavioral problems.

In the face of pressure to offer politically expedient responses to media accounts of school violence and disruption, all members of the community must cultivate a balanced approach to the problem. Parents, educators, administrators, local officials, and other community members should gather accurate information relevant to their community circumstances and needs. A wide range of resources and supports now available from federal agencies, public interest advocacy groups, and private foundations are listed below.

A Final Note

Professionals sometimes are affected by the pressures and circumstances of their daily working environment and may react to problems by seeking the most expedient solution. In addressing the complex needs of students with behavioral difficulties, we must force ourselves to take stock of the situation and proceed thoughtfully, in a reasonable and balanced manner. Teamwork and collaboration among all stakeholders, careful study and thorough planning, and a commitment to reflection and self-evaluation all hold the promise of ultimate success.

References

American Psychological Association. (1993). *Violence and youth: Psychology's response.* Washington, DC: Author.

Bear, G. G. (1999). *Interim alternative educational settings: Related research and program considerations.* Alexandria, VA: National Association of State Directors of Special Education, Project Forum.

Biemer, P. P., Groves, R. M., Lyberg, L. E., Mathiowetz, N. A., & Sudman, S. (1991). *Measurement Errors in Surveys.* New York: Wiley.

Brener, N. D., Simon, T. R., Krug, E. G., & Lowry, R. (1999). Recent trends in violence-related behaviors among high school students in the United States. *Journal of the American Medical Association, 282*(5), 440–446.

Bronfenbrenner, U. (1979). *The ecology of human development: Experiments by nature and design.* Cambridge, MA: Harvard University Press.

Brooks, K., Schiraldi, V., & Ziedenberg, J. (2000). *School house hype: Two years later.* Washington, DC: Justice Policy Institute.

Burns, B. J., & Goldman, S. K. (Eds.) (1999). Promising practices in wraparound for children with serious emotional disturbance and their families. *Systems of care: Promising practices in children's mental health, 1998 series, Vol. IV.* Washington, DC: Center for Effective Collaboration and Practice, American Institutes for Research.

Centers for Disease Control and Prevention. (1997). *Recommended framework for presenting injury mortality data.* Morbidity & Mortality Weekly Report, 1997; 46 (No. RR-14): 4–5.

Centers for Disease Control and Prevention. (2000). *Fact sheet: Youth risk behavior trends.* [online], http://www.cdc.gov/nccdphp/dash/yrbs/ trend.htm

Chandler, K. A., Chapman, C. D., Rand, M. R., & Taylor, B. M. (1998). *Students' reports of school crime: 1989 and 1995.* Washington, DC: U.S. Departments of Education and Justice. (NCES 98-241/NCJ-169607)

Cook, P. J., & Laub, J. H. (1998). The epidemic in youth violence. In M. Tonry, & M. H. Moore (Eds.), *Youth Violence* (pp. 27–64). Chicago: University of Chicago Press.

Cook, P. J. & Ludwig, J. (1997, May). Guns in America: National survey on private ownership and use of firearms. *Research Brief* (NIJ Rep. No. NCJ-165476). Washington, DC: U.S. Department of Justice, National Institute of Justice.

Cooley, S. (1995). *Suspension/expulsion of regular and special education students in Kansas: A report to the Kansas State Board of Education* (ERIC Document Reproduction Service No. ED 395 403). Topeka: Kansas State Board of Education.

Dryfoos, J. (1990). *Adolescents at risk.* New York: Oxford University Press.

Dwyer, K. & Osher, D. (2000). *Safeguarding our children: An action guide.* Washington, DC: U. S. Departments of Education and Justice, American Institutes for Research.

Elliott, D., Hamburg, B., & Williams, K. (Eds.). (1998). *Violence in American schools.* New York: Cambridge.

Farrington, D. P. (1995). The challenge of teenage antisocial behavior. In M. Rutter (Ed.), *Psychological disturbances in young people: Challenges for prevention* (pp. 83–130). New York: Oxford University Press.

Fasko, D., Grubb, D. J., & Osborne, J. S. (1995, November). *An analysis of disciplinary suspensions.* Paper presented at annual meeting of Mid-South Educational Research Association, Biloxi, MS. (ERIC Document Reproduction Service No. ED 393 169)

Felson, R. B. (1996). Mass media effects on violent behavior. *Annual Review of Sociology, 22,* 103–128.

Fiore, T. A., & Reynolds, K. S. (1996). *Analysis of discipline issues in special education.* Research Triangle Park, NC: Research Triangle Institute. (ERIC Document Reproduction Service No. ED 425 607)

Flannery, D. J. (1998). *Improving school violence prevention programs through meaningful evaluation.* New York: ERIC Clearinghouse on Urban Education. (ERIC Document Reproduction Service No. ED 417 244)

Fox, N., Leone, P., Rubin, K., Oppenheim, J., & Friedman, K. (1999). *Final report on the linkages to learning program and evaluation at broad acres elementary school.* Unpublished manuscript, University of Maryland at College Park.

Frey, K. S., Hirschstein, M. K., & Guzzo, B. A. (2000). Second step: Preventing aggression by promoting social competence. *Journal of Emotional & Behavioral Disorders, 8*(2), 102–112.

Furlong, M. & Morrison, G. (1994). Introduction to miniseries: School violence and safety in perspective. *School Psychology Review, 23*(2), 139–150.

Furlong, M., & Morrison, G. (2000). The *school* in school violence: Definitions and facts. *Journal of Emotional & Behavioral Disorders, 8*(2), 71–82.

Goldstein, S. Z. (1994). Corporate communication: A futurist vision. *Communication World, 11*(1), 26–28.

Goss v. Lopez, 419 U.S. 565 (1975).

Gottfredson, D. C. (1997). School-based crime prevention. In L. W. Sherman, D. C. Gottfredson, D. L. MacKenzie, J. Eck, P. Reuter, & S. D. Bushway. *Preventing crime: What works, what doesn't, what's promising: A report to the United States Congress.* [online] http://www.preventingcrime.com/report/index.htm

Gun-Free Schools Act, 20 U.S.C. § 1415 (e) (3).

Harvard University Civil Rights Project. (2000). *Opportunities suspended: The devastating consequences of zero tolerance and school discipline policies.* [online] http://www.law.harvard.edu/groups/civilrights/conferences/zero/zt_report2.html

Hawkins, J. D., Herrenkohl, T. I., Farrington, D. P., Brewer, D., Catalano, R. F., Harachi, T. W., & Cothern, L. (2000, April). Predictors of youth violence. *Juvenile Justice Bulletin.* Washington, DC: U.S. Department of Justice, Office of Juvenile Justice and Delinquency Prevention.

Hernandez, D. J. (1995). Changing demographics: Past and future demands for early childhood programs. *The Future of Children, 5*(3), 145–160.

Honig v. Doe, 479 U.S. 1084 (1988).

Howard, H. H. (1995). TV station group and cross-media ownership: A 1995 update. *Journalism & Mass Communication Quarterly, 72*(2), 390–401.

Hymowitz, K. S. (2000). Who killed school discipline? *City Journal, 10*(2), 34–43.

Ingraham v. Wright, 430 U.S. 651 (1977).

Institute of Medicine (1994). *Reducing risks for mental disorders.* Washington, DC: National Academy Press.

Institute for Social Research. (1997). *Monitoring the future study.* Ann Arbor: University of Michigan.

Kann, L., Kinchen, S. A., Williams, B. I., Ross, J. G., Lowry, R., Grunbaum, J. A., & Kolbe, L. J. (2000). Youth risk behavior surveillance—United States, 1999. *Morbidity & Mortality Weekly Report, 49* (SS–5).

Kaufman, P., Chen, X., Choy, S. P., Chandler, K. A., Chapman, C. D., Rand, M. R., & Ringel, C. (1998). *Indicators of school crime and safety, 1998.* Washington, DC: U.S. Departments of Education and Justice. (NCES 1998-251/NCJ-172215).

Kaufman, P., Chen, X., Choy, S. P., Ruddy, S. A., Miller, A. K., Chandler, K. A., Chapman, C. D., Rand, M. R., & Klaus, P. (1999). *Indicators of school crime and safety, 1999.* Washington, DC: U.S. Departments of Education and Justice. (NCES 1999-057/NCJ-178906)

Kellam, S. G. (2000). Community and institutional partnerships for school violence prevention. In S. G. Kellam, R. Prinz, & J. F. Sheley, *Preventing school violence: Plenary papers of the 1999 Conference on Criminal Justice Research and Evaluation—Enhancing Policy and Practice Through Research* (Vol. 2, pp. 1–21). Washington, DC: U.S. Department of Justice, National Institute of Justice.

Kenney, D. J., & Watson, S. (1999, July). Crime in the schools: Reducing conflict with student problem solving *Research brief* (NIJ Rep. No. NCJ-177618). Washington, DC: U.S. Department of Justice, National Institute of Justice.

Kerrebrock, N., & Lewit, E. M. (1999). Children in self-care. *The Future of Children, 9*(2), 151–160.

Larson, J. (1994). Violence prevention in the schools: A review of selected programs and procedures. *School Psychology Review, 23,* 151–164.

Leone, P. E. (1997). The school as a caring community: Proactive discipline and exceptional children. In J. Paul, M. Churton, W. Morse, A. Duchnowski, B. Epanchin, P. Osnes, & L. Smith (Eds.), *Special education practice: Applying the knowledge, affirming the values, and creating the future.* (pp. 91–103). Pacific Grove, CA: Brooks-Cole.

Lichter, S. R., Lichter, L. S., & Amundson, D. (1999). *Merchandizing mayhem: Violence in popular culture.* Washington, DC: Center for Media and Public Affairs.

Loeber, R., Farrington, D. P., & Waschbusch, D. A. (1998). Serious and violent juvenile offenders. In R. Loeber & D. P. Farrington (Eds.), *Serious and violent juvenile offenders* (pp. 13–29). Thousand Oaks, CA: Sage.

Maryland State Department of Education (1999, January). *Suspensions from Maryland public schools (1997–98)*. Baltimore: MSDE Results Branch.

Maryland State Department of Education (2000, January). *Suspensions from Maryland public schools (1998–99)*. Baltimore: MSDE/PRIM-Information Management Branch.

Mayer, M. J., & Leone, P. E. (1999). A structural analysis of school violence and disruption: Implications for creating safer schools. *Education & Treatment of Children, 22,* 333–358.

Mendel, R. (2000). *Less hype, more help.* Washington, DC: American Youth Policy Forum.

Mercy, J. A., Ikeda, R., & Powell, K. E. (1998). Firearm-related injury surveillance: An overview of progress and challenges ahead. *American Journal of Preventive Medicine, 15*(38), 6–16.

Metropolitan Life Insurance Company. (1999). *Metropolitan Life survey of the American teacher, 1999: Violence in America's Public Schools.* New York: Author.

Morgan, R. L., Loosli, T. S., & Striefel, S. (1997). Regulating the use of behavioral procedures in schools: A five year follow-up survey of state department standards. *Journal of Special Education, 30*(4), 456–470.

Muraskin, L. D. (1993). *Understanding evaluation: The way to better prevention programs* [online], http://ed.gov.offices/OUS/eval/primer1. html

Patterson, G. R. (1982). *Coercive family process.* Eugene, OR: Castalia.

Prothrow-Stith, D. (1987). *Violence prevention curricula for adolescents.* Newton, MA: Education Development Center.

Rand, M. (1998). *Criminal victimizations 1997: Changes 1996–97 with trends 1993–97.* Washington, DC: US Department of Justice, Bureau of Justice Statistics.

Reiss, A. J. & Roth, J. A. (Eds.). (1993). *Understanding and preventing violence.* Washington, DC: National Academy Press.

Sheley, J. F. (2000). Controlling violence: What schools are doing. In S. G. Kellam, R. Prinz, & J. F. Sheley, *Preventing school violence: Plenary papers of the 1999 Conference on Criminal Justice Research and Evaluation—Enhancing Policy and Practice Through Research* Vol. 2, pp. 37–57). Washington, DC: US Department of Justice, National Institute of Justice.

Shure, M. B. (1999, April). Preventing violence the problem-solving way. *Juvenile Justice Bulletin.* Washington, DC: U.S. Department of Justice, Office of Juvenile Justice & Delinquency Prevention.

Sinclair, M. F., et al. (1996, December). On a collision course? Standards, discipline, and students with disabilities, *Policy Research Brief, 8*(4). Minneapolis: Institute on Community Integration, University of Minnesota. (ERIC Document Reproduction Service No. ED 404 793)

Skiba, R. J., & Peterson, R. L. (1999). The dark side of zero tolerance: Can punishment lead to safe schools? *Phi Delta Kappan, 80*(5), 372–378.

Skiba, R. J., & Peterson, R. L. (2000). School discipline at a crossroads: From zero tolerance to early response. *Exceptional Children, 66*(3), 335–347.

Snyder, H. N., & Sickmund, M. (1999). *Juvenile offenders and victims: 1999 national report.* Washington, DC: Office of Juvenile Justice and Delinquency Prevention.

Sorenson, G. (1993). Update on legal issues in special education discipline. *Education Law Reporter, 81,* 399–411.

Sprague, J. & Walker, H. (2000). Early identification and intervention for youth with violent behavior. *Exceptional Children, 66*(3), 367–379.

Sugai, G. M., Kameenui, E. J., Horner, R. H., & Simmons, D. C. (2000). *Effective instructional and behavioral support systems: A school-wide approach to discipline and early literacy.* [online], http://ericec.org/ osep/eff-syst.htm

Sugai, G. M., Sprague, J. R., Horner, R., & Walker, H. M. (2000). Preventing school violence: The use of office discipline referrals to assess and monitor school-wide discipline interventions. *Journal of Emotional & Behavioral Disorders, 8*(2), 94–102.

Taylor-Greene, S., Brown, D., Nelson, L., Longton, J., Gassman, T., Cohen, J., Swartz, J., Horner, R. H., Sugai, G., & Hall, S. (1997). School-wide behavioral support: Starting the year off right. *Journal of Behavioral Education, 7,* 99–112.

Tebo, M. G. (2000). Zero tolerance, zero sense. *ABA Journal, 86,* 40–45.

Tolan, P. H. & Guerra, N. G. (1994). Prevention of delinquency: Current status and issues. *Applied & Preventive Psychology, 3,* 251–273.

Tolan, P. H., & Guerra, N. G. (1998). *What works in reducing adolescent violence: An empirical review of the field.* Boulder, CO: Center for the Study and Prevention of Violence, University of Colorado.

Tolan, P. H., Guerra, N. G, & Kendall, P. C. (1995). Introduction to special section: Prediction and prevention of antisocial behavior in children and adolescents. *Journal of Consulting & Clinical Psychology, 63*(4), 515–517.

Townsend, B. L. (2000). The disproportionate discipline of African American learners: Reducing school suspensions and expulsions. *Exceptional Children, 66*(3), 381–391.

Tucker, B. P., Goldstein, B. A., & Sorenson, G. (1993). *The educational rights of children with disabilities: Analysis, decisions and commentary.* Horsham, PA: LRP.

U.S. Bureau of the Census, Current Population Reports (1998). *Measuring 50 years of economic change using the March current population survey* (Rep. No. P60-203). Washington, DC: U.S. Government Printing Office.

U.S. Department of Education, National Center for Education Statistics. *Recommendations of the crime, violence, and discipline reporting task force* (Rep. No. NCES 97-581). 1996. Washington, DC: National Education Statistics Agenda Committee.

U.S. Department of Education, National Center for Education Statistics (1998a). *Violence and discipline problems in U.S. public schools: 1996–1997* (Rep. No. NCES 98-030). Washington, DC: Author, 1998.

U.S. Department of Education, Office of Elementary and Secondary Education and Planning and Evaluation Service. (1998b). *Report on state implementation of the gun-free schools act— School Year 1996–97.* (Contract N0. EA94052001). Prepared by Westat, Rockville, MD.

U.S. Department of Education (1999a). *Annual report on school safety.* Washington, DC: Author.

U.S. Department of Education, (1999b). *The Condition of Education 1999.* Washington, DC: National Center for Education Statistics. (ERIC Document Reproduction Service No. ED 430 324)

U.S. Department of Education, Office of Elementary and Secondary Education and Planning and Evaluation Service. (1999c). *Report on state implementation of the Gun-Free Schools Act— school year 1997–98.* (Contract No. EA94052001). Prepared by Westat, Rockville, MD.

U.S. Department of Education (2000). *Twenty-first annual report to Congress on the implementation of the Individuals with Disabilities Education Act.* Washington, DC: Government Printing Office. Author.

U.S. Library of Congress, Congressional Research Service. *Violence in schools: An overview* (CRS Report for Congress No. 94-141 EPW). Washington, DC: Author.

University of Vermont. (1999). Prevention strategies that work: What administrators can do to promote positive student behavior. Burlington, VT: Department of Education, School Research Office.

Walker, H. M., & Horner, R. H. (1996). Integrated approaches to preventing antisocial behavior patterns among school-age children and youth. *Journal of Emotional or Behavioral Disorders, 4*(4), 194–220.

Walker, H. M. & Sprague, J. R. (1999). The path to school failure, delinquency, and violence: Causal factors and some potential solutions. *Intervention in School and Clinic, 35*(2), 67–73.

Ward, J. M. (1999). *Children and guns.* Washington, DC: Children's Defense Fund.

Weinberg, D. H. (1996). *A brief look at postwar U.S. income inequality* (Rep. No. P60-191). Washington, DC: U.S. Bureau of the Census.

Weist, M. D., & Warner, B. S. (1997). Intervening against violence in the schools. *Annals of Adolescent Psychiatry, 21,* 235–251.

Womer, S. C. (1997). *What kinds of school-based prevention programs are publicized?* Ellicott City, MD: Gottfredson Associates.

Woodruff, D. W., Osher, D., Hoffman, C. C., Gruner, A., King, M. A., Snow, S. T., & McIntire, J. C. (1999). The role of education in a system of care: Effectively serving children with emotional or behavioral disorders. *Systems of care: Promising practices in children's mental health, 1998 Series* (Vol. 3). Washington, DC: Center for Effective Collaboration and Practice, American Institutes for Research.

Yell, M. L. (1990). The use of corporal punishment, suspension, expulsion, and timeout with behaviorally disordered students in public schools: Legal considerations. *Behavior Disorders, 15,* 100–109.

Yell, M. L., Cline, D., & Bradley, R. (1995). Disciplining students with emotional and behavioral disorders: A legal update. *Education & Treatment of Children, 18,* 299–308.

Yell, M. L. (1998). *The law and special education.* Upper Saddle River, NJ: Prentice-Hall.

Disclaimer: The opinions stated in this chapter are those of the authors and do not represent U.S. Department of Education, Office of Special Education Programs or U.S. Department of Justice, Office of Juvenile Justice and Delinquency Prevention (OJJDP) policy. No endorsement of the Office of Special Education Programs, the U.S. Department of Education, or the OJJDP should be inferred.

5

Societal Neglect and Abuse of Children

Joshua Miller

On May 26, 2000, the last day of school at Lake Worth Community Middle School in Lake Worth, Florida, 13-year-old Nathaniel Brazill shot and killed a popular language arts teacher, Barry Grunow. According to reporter Jeff Goodell (2000), Nathaniel had been raised by his mother and prior to the murder had been a good student with a perfect attendance record and no history of violent acts or affiliation with violent people. His mother worked full-time at a retirement home, earning $22,500 a year. Although she was attentive to her son, her work schedule sometimes meant she was not home when Nathaniel left to go to or return from school. His contact with his father had become more sporadic, and he had witnessed domestic violence toward his mother by her partners. The day of the incident he had been suspended and sent home for getting into a water balloon fight with a girl. He wanted an adult to return to school to advocate for him, but his mother was at work, his grandmother's car was not working, and his aunt was not home. He apparently did not return to school planning to kill Grunow, who had not been involved with his suspension and whom he liked; the tragedy occurred impulsively and without premeditation.

Nathaniel was indicted for murder and tried as an adult. He faced the possibility of a life sentence without parole. In late 2001, when Nathaniel was 14, he was sentenced to 28 years in prison. He had taken the stand in his own defense, which was broadcast by Court Television. After the verdict, a Palm Beach Post on-line opinion poll found that 90% of respondents felt that Brazill's sentence was not enough (Palm-Beach Post.com, 2002).

85

In 1996, the *New York Times* published an article about the increase in shootings occurring in schools (Appelbome, 1996). The article described a number of incidents: a 15-year-old pregnant girl killed by another teenager with a semiautomatic pistol; a teacher left in critical condition after being hit in the head by a stray bullet from a gang battle outside; a 14-year-old honors student who killed a teacher and two students with a high-powered rifle and handguns in a math class; a student who opened fire in a school corridor killing a student and a teacher; a student who killed a teacher, wounded another, then shot himself. The article cited a recent Harris poll that found that ⅛ of the students surveyed (⅖ of the inner-city students) had at some time carried a weapon for protection. That article was written prior to the tragedy at Columbine High School in Colorado in 1999 in which 2 students killed 12 students, a teacher, and themselves.

The story of Nathaniel Brazill and Barry Grunow, like too many other stories we have sadly heard over the past decade, is a more horrific manifestation of the lesser violence in schools that typically involves threats, bullying, assaults, and destruction of property. Whatever the nature of violent incidents in schools, the focus is usually on the perpetrators involved and their families. The question we ask is, How could this happen? At times, as in the case of Nathaniel Brazill, the students are portrayed as monsters without feelings, empathy, or remorse. This portrayal has spawned a movement to treat these children as adults, to no longer grant them special developmental status (Talbot, 2000). When 11-year-old Nathaniel Abraham killed an 18-year-old man, he was tried and convicted as an adult (Bradsher, 2001). The media will often focus on families of the perpetrators, searching for clues of parental abuse, neglect, mismanagement, and indifference.

It is understandable that when violent incidents involving child perpetrators occur in schools, there is an effort to try to understand who the children are, what their family contexts are, and what led to the acts of violence. But as Prothrow-Stith and Rodriguez Martin discuss elsewhere in this book, there is also a community context within which schools and families are embedded. For families to be able to provide their children with secure emotional, psychological, social, and economic foundations, they depend on safe, economically viable communities with adequate social capital and resources (Miller, 2001).

As Garbarino has illustrated in Chapter 1 of this volume, there are national social and cultural trends that go beyond local communities that exacerbate and even foster youth violence. And there are national and state social welfare policies that reflect our national commitment to care for our children. In this chapter, I argue that our society is neglecting children and that some of our policies can even be viewed as forms of child abuse. I will describe 10 ways in which I believe our society is harming our children and diminishing their parents' ability to care for them. The neglect and abuse occur through a mixture of intentional policies and a reliance on unfettered market forces, aided and abetted by a reductionistic public discourse that appropriates apparently reasonable ideas in the service of justifying policies that harm and damage our most vulnerable citizens. The list in this chapter is not inclusive. For example, I do not consider how society neglects children by not protecting them from unsafe drinking water, polluted air, and other environmental hazards. Rather, I have concentrated on 10 areas that directly affect children in schools and that social workers and educators are better able to address.

Ten Ways in Which Our Society Is Harming Our Children

1. By Allowing Children to Be Poor

The United States has seen worse economic times for children than now. At the turn of the 20th century, more than half of the people in the United States were poor (Levitan, 1990). In 1949, nearly half of all children were still poor (Danziger & Danziger, 1993). By 1964, the situation had improved, with 14% of children living below the poverty line. More recently, however, the trend has become variable. In 1994, for example, the figure was 28% (Children's Defense Fund [CDF], 1995). In 1997, the rate had dropped to 22% (National Center for Children in Poverty [NCFCP], 2000), but that was still 50% higher than the low point in 1964. The poverty rate for Latino, African American, and Native American children is about 3 times as high as the poverty rate for white children (NCFCP, 2000; Staveteig & Wigton, 2000).

I used the wording "*allowing* children to be poor" because their poverty is not inevitable. Rather, it is the result of intentional social policy. For example, the relative poverty rates for children in other industrialized countries are far lower than the rates in the United States. In Sweden, the poverty rate for children is 2.6%; in France, 7.9%; in Germany, 10.7%; in Australia, 12.6% (United Nations Children's Fund [UNCF], 2000). It is not that these countries started with lower child poverty rates than that in the United States, rather the discrepancy, is the result of tax and social welfare policies. France reduced its child poverty rate in the late 1990's from 28.7% to 7.9%; Australia reduced its rate from 28.1% to 12.6%. The United States started with a 26.7% poverty rate and reduced it to 22.4%. Among industrialized countries, only Mexico has a higher relative child poverty rate than the United States. A report from the United Nations Children's Fund (2000) p. 3 noted: "The persistence of child poverty in rich countries undermines both equality of opportunity and commonality of values. It therefore confronts the industrialized world with a test both of its ideals and its capacity to resolve many of its most intractable social problems."

Not only does the United States have the second highest relative poverty rate among industrialized nations, but it has the greatest rates of income inequality between children: Our richest children are very rich, and our poor children are very poor (Rainwater & Smeeding, 1995). This trend exists throughout the population. Since the early 1980s, income has been redistributed to the highest echelons of society (Phillips, 1991). The wealthiest 1% (or 2.5 million people) of the population has about as much income after taxes as does the poorest 40% (or 100 million people)

(CBPP, 1995). According to the Congressional Budget Office, in both the 1980s and 1990s income inequality grew in the United States. During those two decades the average after-tax income of the poorest 20% of the population was stagnant, for the middle fifth the income rose by 18%, and for the top 1% of the population it grew by 157% (Shapiro, Greenstein, & Primus, 2001). And these figures predate the recent tax cut signed by President Bush, which has further exacerbated these trends. The gap between rich and poor in the United States is significantly greater than the gap between rich and poor in any other industrial countries (Bradsher, 1995).

In 1996 President Bill Clinton signed the Personal Responsibility and Work Opportunity Act (the Welfare Reform Act). This removed the safety net for poor children that exists in most other industrialized countries and had the following provisions (Children's Defense Fund, 1996c):

- It rescinded the federal entitlement for public assistance to children in need and placed time limits (5 years) on the length of time that a family can receive cash assistance for the care of their poor children.
- It increased work requirements for the parents of poor children without adequately funding job training or day care.
- It reduced food stamp eligibility and benefit levels.
- It reduced the number of children eligible for Supplement Security Income.
- It denied many children whose parents are immigrants access to food stamps or SSI.

Five years after the passage of this act, many parents who had been receiving public assistance have left the welfare rolls and are working. However, most of their jobs pay low wages and have not lifted them and their families out of poverty (National Campaign for Jobs and Income Support [NCJIS], 2001; Polit, Widom, Edin, Bowie, London, Scott & Valenzuela, 2001; Sherman, Amey, Duffield, Ebb, & Weinstein, 1998). Many who have left the welfare rolls have had spells of unemployment, regularly experience hunger and housing problems, and lack access to health care (NCJIS, 2001; Polit et al., 2001).

Poverty undermines families. Not only are poor families economically more fragile, not only do they have fewer resources, not only do the parents in these families often have lower self-esteem and higher anxiety, but because the parents need to work harder to get by, they spend more time working and less time with their children. Thurow (1995) estimated that parents spend 40% less time with their children than parents did 30 years ago. For poor families, the figure is likely higher.

Poverty and inequality hurt children in many ways. Children living in poverty are twice as likely to have birth defects, 4 times as likely to die from a fire, and 6 times as likely to die from infectious diseases (Edelman, 1994). Poverty depletes children physically, emotionally, psychologically, and spiritually. It destroys their sense of hope, their sense of fairness and justice, their belief in their parents and themselves, and their belief in the society in which they live. Poverty is also significantly correlated with school violence (Goodell, 2000).

2. By Denying Children Health Care

In the United States in 1999, 10.8 million children (over 14% of the country's children) had no health care (CDF, 2001c). In Texas, 25.2% of children are uninsured (Sherman et al., 1998). And as with poverty, the uninsured rates for children of color are much higher than the rate for white children. For example, in 1997, 34.9% of Native American children and 22.8% of Hispanic children were uninsured, compared to 8.8% of white children. The United States is the only wealthy industrialized country that does not provide universal health coverage for all of its children (Kamerman & Kahn, 1988).

The U.S. gross domestic product per capita is the highest in the world (United Nations Development Programme [UNDP], 1993). So how do we explain our failure to provide medical care to our children? Universal health coverage is not an economic necessity but a political and moral issue, a reflection of our national values and priorities.

Health care includes therapy, counseling, and other mental health services. Nathaniel Abraham, the 11-year-old mentioned earlier in this chapter, did not receive counseling despite having manifested signs of psychological, emotional, and behavioral problems for 3 years prior to committing murder (Bradsher, 1999). Children who are emotionally, psychologically, and physically healthy are more likely to have good self-esteem, to concentrate on their classes, and to exercise socially acceptable impulse control.

3. By Not Protecting Children From Guns

As discussed earlier, there have been many incidents in the United States involving firearms with school-aged children. In 1992, 3,351 children were murdered with firearms (CDF, 1996a). To put this statistic another way, every day 15 of our children and youth are killed with firearms (CDF, 1996a). To break it down into minutes, every 98 minutes a child is killed with a firearm (CDF, 1996b).

A major reason for the shootings is that more people have guns in the United States than in other countries. In Japan 1% of the population has guns; in England, 4.4% of the population has guns and in the United States, the official estimate of percentage of households with guns is 48% (Kristof, 1996), a figure that is likely to increase after the tragic events of September 11, 2001.

The homicide rate in the United States is 8 per 100,000 people (UNDP, 1993). The next closest country is Denmark with a 5.7 rate; Japan's rate is 1.5, Canada's is 2.6, England's is 1.6 (UNDP). Is the higher U.S. rate because we have more killers in our midst? Are there more demented and murderous people in the United States than in other countries? Somehow, we have become a society where high levels of homicides are the norm and over 3,000 children a year die from guns. Goodell's (2000) description of the events leading up to the murder of Barry Grunow by Nathaniel Brazill strongly suggest that the shooting was an impulsive act and that if Brazill had not had access to the gun, which he found in a drawer at a friend's house, Grunow would be alive today.

4. By Not Funding Education Properly

Our basic system of funding education is to rely on property taxes. As the tax base in a city goes down and educational need rises, funding for schools diminishes. Some say that money is not the answer, but our wealthier citizens and communities pay more money for their children to be educated, whether by sending them to private schools or by spending more per child than in poor communities.

Obviously, education is a critical form of human capital investment. It is strongly correlated with social and economic success. The United States spends a comparable amount per capita on education as a percentage of its gross domestic product as do other industrialized countries (UNDP, 1993). The problem is the unequal way the money is spent in the United States. We have poor children attending poorly resourced schools. Consequently, they have higher dropout rates, lower achievement rates, and much lower rates of college attendance (CDF, 1994). Students who, as a consequence of poverty, live in communities lacking economic and social capital require the most attention, enriched curricula, remedial services, and on-site counseling and therapy. Yet they attend schools least able to provide these services. If any one societal trend challenges the myth of equality of opportunity in this country, it is the vastly unequal system of education.

5. By Allowing Children to Go Hungry and Be Homeless

The National Coalition for the Homeless has estimated that 1.1 million U.S. children are living in emergency shelters at any given moment (Edelman, 2001). This figure underestimates the number of homeless children, because many shelters cannot serve all of the requests for shelter that they receive from families and because many homeless families do not seek these services. As with poverty, health insurance, and access to quality education, children of color suffer disproportionately. The homeless rate for African American, Hispanic, and Native American families is twice as high as that for whites (Staveteig & Wigton, 2000).

A closely related problem to homelessness is childhood hunger. America's Second Harvest (2001) has estimated that 9 million children receive food from a food pantry or shelter and that 2.6 million households with children are "food insecure." Again, the rates for Hispanic, Native American and African American families are twice as high as for whites (Staveteig & Wigton, 2000).

Hungry and/or homeless children are more likely to be malnourished and to live in environments that lack the structure, safety, consistency, and resources necessary to support their physical and mental health. Their cognitive capabilities, ability to concentrate in school, and capacity to study at home are compromised at the same time that their exposure to violence and distracting stimuli is increased.

6. By Stranding Parents Without the Means to Care for Their Children

It is difficult for parents in our country to survive in today's market economy. The passage of the Personal Responsibility and Work Opportunity Act of 1996 cut a major hole in an already frayed safety net for poor families. Many parents relied on the system of public assistance to support them in times of need, a system including what had been known as Aid to Families With Dependent Children (AFDC), food stamps, Earned Income Tax Credits, Supplementary Security Income, and Medicaid. Most studies indicate that the majority of people who newly registered to use AFDC did so temporarily (Corbett, 1993)—it really did serve as a safety net. And all families in America receive welfare. The better-off families receive it in the form of tax deductions, but the net result for all families is the same: government funded transfers that go to families. However, the poorest families particularly rely on the programs mentioned earlier, and it is these programs—AFDC, food stamps, Earned Income Tax Credits, Supplementary Security Income, and Medicaid—that have been dismantled, reduced, or are facing cuts, at a time when poor families are economically vulnerable. As the Children's Defense Fund (1994) has stated, these are "child survival programs."

Parents are placed in a bind by being expected to work, even when there are fewer jobs that pay enough to survive on, and at the same time, being expected to care for their children, although there is inadequate affordable, quality child care. Structurally, it has always been a challenge for parents to manage the fact that their children's schooling ends at 3:00, when most jobs continue for another 2 hours or more. Yet the recent "welfare reform act" did not increase after-school day care. This creates a tension for working parents between their roles as caretakers and their roles as workers, a strain that recent laws and policies have exacerbated rather than reduced.

Parents need to work to provide for their families, at a time when the conditions of work are less secure and remunerative than in the past, except for the very wealthy. With large numbers of dual-earner and single-parent families, it has become increasingly difficult for parents to directly supervise their children before and after school. Parents making $22,500 for full-time jobs, as was Nathaniel Brazill's mother, cannot afford to cut back their work schedules or to pay for private baby-sitting services. Yet, there is a paucity of public programs that provide care when parents cannot be available and government support for such programs has been cut over the past decade. This lack of programs is also related to the tax-cutting fever that has swept the nation and states for the past 20 years, because typically the rationale for cutting social service programs is that there is not enough money to fund them. Taken together, these factors result in children not receiving adequate care and supervision because it is not possible for their parents to provide (for) such services while working to keep their families financially afloat. Relating the problem to the subject of this book, unsupervised and under-supervised children are at greater risk for being the victims of violence and exploitation and are more vulnerable to becoming violent perpetrators themselves.

7. By Stranding Children in the Child Welfare System

It is estimated that each year over a third of children reported to child welfare authorities are abused and neglected by their caretakers (General Accounting Office [GAO], 1995), and nearly 3 million children are reported each year (CDF, 2001b). Annually over 550,000 children are placed in foster care (CDF, 2001b). Child neglect and abuse are perhaps the clearest examples of situations for which society has an obligation to care directly for children. Yet, across the country, budgets for child welfare services are being cut, and child welfare worker's caseloads are far above the recommended limits. Children in foster care, who have complex needs, are placed in overcrowded foster homes that are supervised by overtaxed social workers. Children have been further abused and neglected in foster care, and some have even died. The adoption process is clogged, and significant numbers of children do not have workable permanent plans (Kamerman & Kahn, 1989). Although there has been a decrease in the number of children entering foster care, they remain in foster care for longer periods of time (CDF, 2001b). It is not an overreaction to describe child welfare as being in a state of crisis.

Some politicians have sought to revive institutional care for children, an idea abhorred even by those who work in institutions for children. Abuse, neglect, exploitation, and lack of stable, nurturing parent figures for children have marked the history of such institutional care.

It is ironic that children are removed from their parents because their parents do not feed or supervise them properly, or because they are exposed to violence and exploitation, yet that is often the role model provided by the way in which our society cares for children in out-of-home placements. And it is chilling to contemplate that 80% of the Illinois prison population were formerly foster children (Johnson, 1996).

As with the other types of societal abuse and neglect of children, the stranding of children in the child welfare system is not necessary or inevitable. Family preservation programs help keep families together and prevent children from entering foster care, but they are labor-intensive and require adequate funding. Child welfare workers and foster parents do better work with children when they have sufficient training and lower caseloads. Juvenile and family courts were established to respond to the unique needs of children, but judges presiding over these courts have overflowing dockets and fewer diversion and referral options. All of these barriers to the prevention of societal abuse and neglect of children are surmountable but require political and economic commitment.

8. By Cutting Successful Programs That Support Children and Families

One of the more insidious aspects of the current public discourse about children and families is that the social service system as a whole is often criticized, providing justification for dismantling it. This attack occurs despite reams of empirical evidence validating the success of many programs that support children and families, as well as chronic underfunding of the very programs that are under fire.

Prenatal care works. It lowers the infant mortality rate and stops babies from dying. Health care works. It raises life expectancy and the overall quality of life. Head Start works. It prepares children for success in school (Schorr, 1988). Family support programs help to keep families together and provide networks of support within communities (Kagan, Powell, Weissbourd, & Zigler, 1987). Therapy helps children and parents to understand themselves, change behaviors, and improve relationships. (And for a sexually abused child or for a child who has witnessed the shooting of a friend therapy is not a short-term proposition that can be completed in the 5 to 10 sessions authorized by a managed care corporation.) Quality child care works. It can be socially and educationally beneficial to children, and it allows parents to work. Comprehensive, school-based programs have been demonstrated to increase the likelihood of keeping at-risk students in school (GAO, 1993). This is but a small list of the many programs documented as having helped children and families. Most of these programs are under siege, being underfunded, defunded, or in some instances discontinued.

9. By Incarcerating People as Social Policy

People should be punished for their crimes, and apparently many Americans, if not the majority, believe that 14-year-old Nathaniel Brazill should be incarcerated for at least 28 years. But it is difficult to understand the scale of the unprecedented rise in the prison population in this country as solely a response to crime. In fact, the number of people incarcerated since the 1980s has risen by over 168% despite the fact that the crime rate has remained steady (Butterfield, 1992; Rothman, 1994). More than 2 million Americans are in prison (Justice Policy Institute [JPI], 2000; Lynch, 2000), and this figure excludes the more than 2.5 million people on parole and 475,000 on probation (Rothman, 1994). Although African Americans make up only 13% of the national population, they constitute 50% of the state and federal prison population (JPI, 2000). In addition to our locking more people up, there have been movements in many states to deny prisoners educational services, one of the few pathways that have helped to prepare them for life outside of prison.

Tougher sentencing laws and mandatory prison terms probably contribute to the growth of the prison population. There is also the trend of treating serious juvenile offenders as adults and placing them in prison or sending them to "boot camps." Perhaps some would argue that these are pro-child strategies because people who pose a potential danger to children are taken off the streets. However, many prisoners return to communities, embittered and without skills or jobs. Prisons are also a major recruiting site for gangs, which for the most part do not make neighborhoods particularly safe for children. But locking up so many adults, the vast majority for nonviolent crimes, also has other disastrous consequences for families and communities. Placing parents in prison destabilizes families, removes adult breadwinners from families, undermines families' economic viability, and leaves children without consistent parent figures.

There are alternatives to massive rates of incarceration. All industrialized countries with the exception of Russia have significantly lower incarceration rates than the United States (The Sentencing Project [TSP], 2001). The United States is home to 5% of the world's population but houses about 25% of the world's prison population. Sixty percent of the inmates in federal U.S. prisons are sentenced for drug-related infringements (Lynch, 2000). Massive incarceration is intentional social policy because it chooses punishment over rehabilitation. Tax dollars are spent on prison construction and maintenance rather than on education, counseling, and prevention. The Justice Policy Institute (2000) reported that the United States spends 50% more money imprisoning 1.2 million nonviolent offenders than it spends on welfare programs that serve 8.5 million people. It spends 6 times more on prisons than it spends on child care for 1.25 million children. While public university spending decreased in most states in the past decade, prison construction increased. In California, five African American men are in prison for every man in a state college or university (Taqi-Eddin, Macallair, & Shiraldi, 1998). The United States has chosen to incarcerate massive numbers of adults as a central social policy initiative, a by-product of which has been to maroon many children in families and communities that are bereft of adults.

10. By Promulgating a Discourse of Denigration

A final aspect of the societal abuse of children unfortunately, is the public discourse that surrounds children and their needs. Instead of conducting a rational, nuanced, balanced public dialogue that considers the needs of children, our society has conducted a discourse that objectifies others, truncates dialogue, and leads to punitive and simplistic solutions (Miller & Schamess, 2000). Perhaps it is not surprising that the needs of children are being ignored when political leaders repeat bromides about "shrinking government," when people who advocate for children's needs are automatically called "tax and spend liberals," and when the rationale for lifting restrictions on assault guns is "freedom of expression."

As wealth has been redistributed upward and children have become poorer, we have had a public discourse about denying benefits to "welfare queens," closing our borders and denying benefits to immigrants, returning responsibilities to states while defunding federal programs, and calling for welfare reform while gutting the safety net for children. This public narrative has followed a course that resembles what Whillock (1995) has described as a strategy of hate speech: Angry and disenfranchised people, such as the American middle class, are encouraged to direct their anger at scapegoats; the target group is dehumanized and denigrated; political opposition to harmful policies is associated with the defense of the denigrated group and is therefore discredited; and groups directing hate speech seek to subjugate and destroy the opposition while compromise and rational dialogue are sacrificed. Extreme rhetoric uses the expression of love and concern (for example, concern for poor children) to justify actions that harm poor children (reducing their income and making them poorer) (Muir, 1995). Hate speech becomes shrill and monological: Its speakers contend that there is only one way of viewing the situation; any opposing views are unacceptable (Whillock & Slayden, 1995). Mythical others, such as "the American people," are invoked to justify extreme views and actions (Slayden, 1995). Ultimately, such a public discourse legitimizes neglect and abuse toward vulnerable people in society (Whillock & Slayden, 1995), including children.

None of This Is Inevitable

What I have described is not inevitable, nor is it the result of ineluctable forces, such as the "market," that must remain unfettered. Societal abuse and neglect of children result from a discourse that legitimizes these acts and the policies that support them. Other industrial countries consistently take better care of their children, in part by providing more support for children's families. They recognize that taking care of children involves taking care of their parents. Other countries provide child benefits (they pay parents to fulfill their societal responsibility of caring for children), day care (for example, universal government-supported day care in France), and education benefits. They also provide transitional benefits for people temporarily unable to work who are caring for children, housing allowances, child support collection, and universal health insurance for all children (Kamerman & Kahn, 1988). Some use their policies to support mothers who stay at home to care for their children (as in Great Britain), others gear their policies toward keeping parents in the work force (Germany and France), while others use social policy as a means of reducing societal inequities, such as the wage differentials between men and women (Sweden) (Kamerman & Kahn, 1988). None use imprisonment as a central social policy initiative.

Although I have directed much of my criticism toward the government, employers also set policies that help or hurt children. A decade ago, many corporations were responding to the needs of parents by providing on-site day care—an initiative that is certainly stalled if not reversed. Yet such cutbacks are often not an economic necessity. Over the past decade many corporations have reaped significant profits for their investors and directors. CEOs are making record salaries, often tens of millions of dollars, regardless of whether they have overtly helped their companies. In the 1960s, the ratio between the typical worker salary and the chief executive salary was 30 to 1; in the 1990s, it was 100 to 1 (Uchitelle, 1996). The mean salary for chief executives at large companies in the United States is over $2 million, and we can add to that nearly $5 million in other forms of compensation, such as stock options (Uchitelle, 1996). And, as mentioned earlier, companies are now far less generous with their health insurance benefits, routinely hiring temporary workers who receive no benefits.

What Can We Do?

Although there are not simple answers to these vexing, disturbing issues, it is important to consider what can be done to support children and prevent society from neglecting and abusing them. A starting point is to *have a genuine dialogue* about this very topic. If hate speech is monological and suppressing, dialogue is cleansing (Whillock & Slayden, 1995). One thing we can all do is promote and contribute to a serious dialogue to discuss these complex and complicated issues. Whether that is through conferences, hearings, meetings with political leaders, writing letters to the editor, or calling in to radio talk shows, every little bit of nuanced, reasoned discussion helps. It is important to analyze and challenge anti-child diatribes, to deconstruct misleading metaphors and inappropriate analogies. And we must model respectful dialogue that does not scapegoat, polarize, reduce, and unite some at the expense of scapegoating others. Children need concerned adults to initiate and foster such public dialogues, but they should also be participants in them. Children describing their experiences in foster care or their fears of guns can have a powerful impact on adults who listen.

A more concrete suggestion is to *support programs that support families*. Children grow up best in families, and policies and programs that support families support children. Further, we should challenge policies that seek to undermine or dismantle programs that support families, such as Earned Income Tax Credits. It is true that criticisms directed at family support programs might identify some legitimate societal concerns, such as a belief in the value of self-sufficiency. But these concerns do not justify tearing the safety net without having in place viable alternatives that are at least as supportive as the existing programs. Such dismantling flirts with disaster for children and ultimately for all of society (Moynihan, 1996). When safety nets are removed to punish adults, children suffer; when incarceration becomes the policy of choice over education, prevention, and rehabilitation, we harm children. The central criterion for all social policy initiatives should be whether they support the ability of families to care for children.

Adults should also *support anti-gun legislation* as a way of protecting children. Too many children in this country die from being shot. The reasons for this situation are complex, but fewer guns on the street, particularly hand guns and assault rifles, might protect some children without interfering with the rights of legitimate hunters.

In addition, we must *stand behind and strengthen our child welfare system*. It is unacceptable to remove children from abusive and neglectful caretakers and then place them in inadequate or risky situations. Foster parents are our representatives for children in need, and they and the rest of the child welfare system need substantial public support. A society that continues to abuse and neglect children who have already been maltreated sets a poor example for its citizens and other nations.

In the area of societal neglect and abuse of children, there are large, challenging, political, social, and moral issues for the nation to consider. Do we want a society in which the gap between the wealthiest and poorest children is the largest in the industrial world? This did not occur by chance. It has been the result of conscious social policy, evidenced through changes in tax rates, the value of the minimum wage, and income support programs. Do we want to live in a society where more than 10 million children have no health insurance? All European countries and Canada have decided that such a situation is unacceptable. Are we living up to our ideals as a nation if children of color, when compared to white children, consistently have higher rates of poverty, have more health problems, have less access to health care, have higher rates of hunger and homelessness, attend underfunded schools, have more parents imprisoned, and are more highly represented in the nation's system of substitute care? This is not a nation of equal opportunity and equal rights. We need to "achieve" the nation that we say we believe in (Rorty, 1998), which means imagining it and working to obtain it.

All adults should think of themselves as advocates for all children. Children do not make social policy, they do not run corporations, they do not shape the public discourse, they do not vote, and they are unable to create the conditions to protect and care for themselves. They are children and should be treated as such. All adults have an obligation to *care* for our collective children. But we, as educators and social workers, have a unique obligation to *advocate* for them. Kamerman (1996, p. 464) has stated, "Social work practitioners need to remember that they are the eyes and ears of the profession." Children need adults who will listen to them, observe how they are being treated, and raise their voices on their behalf. We can achieve safer communities and schools for our children if we hold our society and ourselves accountable as their caretakers.

**References**

America's Second Harvest. (2001, December 6). *Who's hungry?* URL: www.secondharvest.org/childhunger/child_hunger_facts.html

Appelbome, P. (1996). Shootings at schools prompt new concerns about violence. *New York Times,* March 3, p. A12.

Bradsher, K. (1995, October 27). Widest gap in incomes? Research points to U.S. *New York Times,* pp. A1, A22.

Bradsher, K. (1999, November 23). Need for counseling unmet in boy who became a killer. *New York Times,* p. A14.

Bradsher, K. (2001, November 17). Michigan boy who killed at 11 is convicted of murder as an adult. *New York Times,* p. A1.

Butterfield, F. (1992, July 19). Are American jails becoming shelters from the storm? *New York Times,* pp. A1, A22.

Center on Budget and Policy Priorities. (1995). *Only high-income households have recovered fully from the recession.* Washington, DC: Author.

Children's Defense Fund. (1994). *Wasting America's future.* Boston: Beacon Press.

Children's Defense Fund. (1995, November). *CDF reports 16*(12), Washington, CD: Author.

Children's Defense Fund. (1996a, January). *CDF Reports, 17*(2).

Children's Defense Fund. (1996b, February). *CDF Reports, 17*(3).

Children's Defense Fund. (1996c, August 8). Summary of final welfare conference bill. *Handsnet* [online newsletter]. Availabe: e-mail hn3208@handsnet.org

Children's Defense Fund. (2001a, Nov. 30). *Booming economy leaves millions of children behind: 12.1 million children still living in poverty.* URL: www.childrensdefense.org/release000926.htm

Children's Defense Fund. (2001b, November 30). *The Children's Defense Fund reviews the state of America's children and says it's time to do whatever is necessary to leave no child behind.®* URL: www.childrensdefense.org/release010417.html

Children's Defense Fund (2001c, November 30). *Uninsured children under age 19 in the U.S., 2000.* URL: www.childrensdefense.org/hs_resadv_numunins.php.

Corbett, T. (1993). Child poverty and welfare reform: Progress or paralysis? *Focus, 15*(1), 1–17.

Danziger, S. K., & Danziger, S. (1993). America's childhood. *Daedalus, 122*(1), 57–83.

Edelman, M. W. (1994). Introduction. In A. Sherman, *Wasting America's future; The Children's Defense Fund report on the cost of child poverty* (pp.xv-xxix). Boston: Beacon Press.

Edelman, M. W. (2001, November 30). *CDF Reports: A voice for children.* URL: www.childrens-defense.org/voice1298.html

General Accounting Office. (1993, December). *School-linked human services: A comprehensive strategy for aiding students at risk of school failure* (GAO/HRD94-21). Washington, DC: Author.

General Accounting Office. (1995, September). *Child welfare: Complex needs strain capacity to provide services* (GAO/HEHS95-208). Washington, DC: Author.

Goodell, J. (2000, October 26). Nathaniel Brazill's last day of school. *Rolling Stone, 852.* URL: www.jeffgoodell.com/articles/natbraz.html

Johnson, D. (1996, April 1). Program creates community for foster care. *New York Times,* pp. A1, B9.

Justice Policy Institute. (2000). *The punishing decade: Prison and jail estimates at the millennium.* Washington, DC: Author.

Kagan, S. L., Powell, D. R., Weissbourd, B., & Zigler, E. F. (Eds.) (1987). *America's family support programs.* New Haven, CT: Yale University Press.

Kamerman, S. B. (1996). The new politics of child and family policies. *Social Work, 41*(5), 453–465.

Kamerman, S. B., & Kahn, A. J. (1988). *Mothers alone: Strategies for a time of change.* Dover, MA: Auburn House Publishing.

Kamerman, S. B., & Kahn, A. J. (1989). *Social services for children, youth, and families in the United States.* Greenwich, CT: Annie E. Casey Foundation.

Kristof, N. D. (1996, March 3). Guns: One nation bars, the other requires. *New York Times,* Sect. 4, p. 3.

Levitan, S. A. (1990). *Programs in aid of the poor* (6th ed.). Baltimore: Johns Hopkins University Press.

Lynch, T. (2000, February 20). All locked up. *The Washington Post,* [Editorial] p. B7.

Miller, J. (2001). Family and community integrity. *Journal of Sociology and Social Welfare, 28*(4), 23–44.

Miller, J., & Schamess, G. (2000). The discourse of denigration and the creation of other. *Journal of Sociology and Social Welfare, 27*(3), 39–62.

Moynihan, D. P. (1996, January 11). Congress builds a coffin. *New York Review of Books, 43*(1), pp. 33–36.

Muir, J. K. (1995). Hating for life: Rhetorical extremism and abortion clinic violence. In R. K. Whillock & D. Slayden (Eds.), *Hate speech* (pp. 163–195). Thousand Oaks, CA: Sage.

National Campaign for Jobs and Income Support. (2001, October 2). *Leaving welfare, left behind: Employment status, income and well-being of former TANF recipients.* Washington, DC: Author.

National Center for Children in Poverty. (1999, June 7). *Young Children in Poverty: A statistical update,* (June 1999) edition, http://www.nccp.org/99uptext.html

Phillips, K. (1990). *The politics of rich and poor: Wealth and the American electorate in the Reagan aftermath.* New York: Harper Perennial.

Polit, D. F., Widom, R., Edin, K., Bowie, S., London, A. S., Scott, E. K., et al. (2001, November 21). *Is work enough? The experiences of current and former welfare mothers who work.* URL: www.mdrc.org/Reports2001/UC-IsWorkEnough/IsWorkEnough.htm

Rainwater, L., & Smeeding, T. M. (1995). *Doing poorly: The real income of American children in a comparative perspective* (Luxembourg Income Study, Working paper no. 127). Syracuse, NY: Syracuse University, Maxwell School of Citizenship and Public Affairs.

Rorty, R. (1998). *Achieving our country.* Cambridge, MA: Harvard University Press.

Rothman, D. J. (1994, February 17). The crime of punishment. *New York Review of Books, 41*(4) pp. 34–48.

Schorr, L. B. (1988). *Within our reach: Breaking the cycle of disadvantage.* New York: Doubleday.

Shapiro, I., Greenstein, R., & Primus, W. (2001). *Pathbreaking CBO study shows dramatic increases in income disparities in 1980s and 1990s: An analysis of the CBO data.* Washington, DC: Center on Budget and Policy Priorities.

Sherman, A., Amey, C., Duffield, B., Ebb, N., & Weinstein, D. (1998). *Welfare to what? Key findings on family hardship and well being.* Washington, DC: Children's Defense Fund and National Coalition for the Homeless.

Slayden, D. (1995). Holy wars and vile bodies: The politics of an American iconography. In R. K. Whillock & D. Slayden (Eds.), *Hate speech* (pp. 196–225). Thousand Oaks, CA: Sage.

Staveteig, S., & Wigton, A. (2000, March 4). *Racial and ethnic disparities: Key findings from the National Survey of America's Families.* URL: http://newfederalism.urban.org/html/series_b/b5/b5/html

Palm Beach Post.com (2002, December 3) Teacher Barry Grunow shot by student Nathaniel Brazill. URL: www.gopi.com/post/pbpost/news/grunow.html

Talbot, M. (2000, September 10). The maximum security adolescent. *New York Times Magazine,* p. 41.

Tagi-Eddin, K., Macallir, D., & Shiraldi, V. (1998). *Class dismissed: Higher education vs. corrections during the Wilson years.* San Francisco: Justice Policy Institute.

The Sentencing Project (2001). *Americans behind bars: U.S. and International rates of incarceration, 1995.* Washington, DC: Author.

Thurow, L. (1995, September 3). Companies merge; families break up. *New York Times,* Sect. 4, p. 10.

Uchitelle, L. (1996, March 29). 1995 was good for companies, and better for a lot of CEOs. *New York Times,* pp. A1, D8.

United Nations Children's Fund. (2000). *A league table of child poverty in rich nations.* Florence, Italy: UNICEF Innocenti Research Centre.

United Nations Development Programme. (1993). *Human development report 1993.* New York: Oxford University Press.

Whillock, R. K. (1995). The use of hate as a stratagem for achieving political and social goals. In R. K. Whillock & D. Slayden (Eds.), *Hate speech* (pp. 28–54). Thousand Oaks, CA: Sage.

Whillock, R. K., & Slayden, D. (1995). Introduction. In R. K. Whillock & D. Slayden (Eds.), *Hate speech* (pp. ix–xvi). Thousand Oaks, CA: Sage.

PART TWO

Interventions in Schools

6

Uncovering the Hidden Causes of Bullying and School Violence

Barry K. Weinhold

Because the bulk of the iceberg that the Titanic hit on April 14, 1912, was invisible to the ship's captain, this great ship sank to the bottom of the ocean. On April 20, 1999, our great nation also hit a largely invisible iceberg at Columbine High School. Since then, the public eye has been focused on the tip of this metaphoric iceberg, known as the "culture of violence." In trying to find ways to avoid further school violence, the larger culture of violence remains hidden from our collective view. Unless this nation changes its course, it surely is headed for more collisions with this invisible iceberg that can cause the deaths of many more innocent people.

Ever since the Columbine tragedy, people have been asking, "How could this have happened?" and "What can we do to prevent it from happening again?" Much of the public commentary about the causes of the Columbine massacre has been directed at assigning blame and finding quick-fix solutions. What might be more useful is uncovering the hidden causes of this tragedy and developing long-range primary prevention strategies to deal with these hidden causes. The goals of this chapter are to (a) examine the hidden elements of the culture of violence that were present in the Columbine tragedy, (b) expose the pervasive nature of bullying and school violence, (c) show how school violence is only a small part of a larger pattern of violence that is fed by the culture of violence, and (d) describe effective long-range prevention methods that address the hidden elements of the culture of violence.

What is the Culture of Violence?

The most visible forms of the culture of violence that make up the tip of the iceberg of violence are

- youth violence
- domestic violence
- road rage
- gang violence
- hate crimes
- community crime and violence
- global conflict and war.

Ample evidence documents the increasingly negative effects of the culture of violence. For example, juvenile crime is up 47 percent nationally, and almost 3 million violent crimes occur annually at or near schools. The number of violent crimes committed by youth is expected to double by the year 2010 (Perry, 1996a). Similar increases have occurred in reported cases of child abuse and domestic violence (Portner, 1997). According to Sebastian (1996), half of all married women will experience some form of violence from their partners during their marriage and more than one-third are beaten repeatedly.

Feeding this rapidly growing culture of violence is the prevalence of violence on television and in movies and interactive videos. The World Wrestling Federation (WWF), which sponsors professional wrestling matches, particularly glorifies violence by portraying bullies as heroes. Teachers report the influence of WWF wrestling on their students, describing a marked increase in the number of children imitating aggressive WWF gestures and behaviors at school. Many of these teachers also report that parents are becoming more threatening and intimidating toward the teachers when they come to school to complain about something they think is unfair.

Public opinion surveys show that violence in the schools is the number-one education-related concern of Americans (Adler & Springen, 1999). Many schools have adopted get tough policies to deal with violence in the schools. These include initiating zero-tolerance policies, installing metal detectors, hiring more police to patrol the halls, and placing video cameras in school buildings for increased surveillance.

The Hidden Elements in the Culture of Violence

The culture of violence has at least six hidden elements that point toward the occurrence of more Columbine-type shootings:

1. A dominator value system that supports violence
2. An over-focus on negative behaviors

3. The pervasiveness of bullying behavior
4. Collective denial of the effects of bullying behavior
5. The role of post-tramatic stress disorder (PTSD) in the perpetration of violence
6. The effects of parental neglect and emotional abandonment on children.

This chapter addresses each one of these relatively hidden elements of the culture of violence and describe effective primary prevention methods for dealing with these underlying causes of violence.

A Dominator Value System That Supports Violence

What supports this pervasive culture of violence is a system of dominator values (Weinhold & Weinhold, 2000). These values are behind the increase in aggressive and bullying behaviors. Those who live by these dominator values:

■ Use power plays involving violence, threats of violence, intimidation, and exploitation to get their way and to bully others.
■ Have little regard for the rights, needs, or even the lives of others, particularly if they see these others as a threat.
■ Exploit the needs and rights of others when they perceive them as having less power, status or influence, including women, children, and minorities.
■ Are on the defensive and never admit mistakes.
■ Blame others for causing their problems.
■ Believe that "might makes right."

As evidence of the widespread influence of the dominator system, a study reported that one in three women worldwide has been beaten, raped, or somehow mistreated by men (Heise, Ellsberg, & Gottemoeller, 1999). Dominator values are so tightly woven into the fabric of our culture that they are virtually invisible. For example, most Americans agreed with the United States' bombing of Iraq and Kosovo, even though they knew that thousands of innocent civilians were being killed.

Dominator values are actively promoted by the sports and entertainment industries. For example, hardly anyone even questions the gratuitous violence in wrestling matches sponsored by the World Wrestling Federation or World Championship Wrestling. These matches have some of the highest ratings on cable television. Regular television channels are no better, with daytime shows exemplifying dominator values, such as the *Jerry Springer* and *Jenny Jones* programs, commanding huge ratings. Movies such as *The Terminator* glorify violence and pack the theaters. Violent video games such as *Doom* had considerable influence on Eric Harris and Dylan Klebold, the Columbine killers. Violence is a profitable business. Unless these values are changed or supplanted by kinder and more humane values, the culture of violence will continue to grow and flourish in the United States, further undermining all of our democratic institutions.

As a counter balance to the dominator value system is another value system that some call the "humanistic or democratic value system" (Eisler, 1987). Those who espouse these values are people who:

- Strive to resolve their conflicts with others in peaceful, nonviolent ways so everyone gets their needs met.
- Use the "rule of law" and seek common ground to settle racial, cultural, religious, and political disputes.
- Understand cultural relativity and are able to show tolerance and respect toward people of different cultures.
- Seek equalitarian relationships based on mutual respect, trust, and caring.
- Admit mistakes and strive to learn from them.
- Take responsibility for their actions.

These are the values of democracy that we strive to teach our children, but dominator values are undermining the very foundation of our democracy. The dominator value system lurks behind all domestic violence, child abuse, elder abuse, workplace violence, school violence, road rage, hate crimes, and wars.

Over-Focus on Negative Behaviors

Much of people's behavior is motivated by a desire to meet the basic needs for recognition, attention and approval. Over the past 6 years, I visited more than 100 schools, and asked students and faculty members the following question: "Is it easier for you to get noticed or get attention in this school by doing something positive or something negative?" Almost 100 percent of them have replied "negative" (Weinhold, 1999a). This consistent feedback from children and faculty members indicates that children and adults adapt and learn to use negative behaviors to meet their need for recognition because their positive behaviors usually go unnoticed. This is not just a school problem. If someone were to ask the same question of kids in families or workers in companies or in organizations such as the military, they likely would get the same answer.

This focus on negativity is hidden below the tip of our social iceberg and supports the visible culture of violence that we see in the media. For example, have you ever noticed how characters on television sitcoms get the most audience laughter when they make a mistake? This culture of negativity in schools, families, the workplace, and the highway creates an overall climate that breeds violence.

A basic law of psychology says: "What you pay attention to is what you are going to get more of." If we focus too much of our attention on negative behaviors and not enough on positive behaviors, negative behavior will increase. An overwhelmingly negative school climate is damaging to the self-esteem of kids. For example, when kids in kindergarten were asked if they like themselves, 95 percent or more said "yes." By fourth grade, the percentage of these kids who reported liking themselves was down to 60 percent. By eighth grade, the percentage was down to 40 percent, and by twelfth grade, it was down to 5 percent (Weinhold, 1999a).

Columbine High School was no exception. At this upper middle-class suburban high school, every student who was the least bit insecure about himself or herself was worried about being different in some way. A senior girl at Columbine summed it up: "It's a rat race inside the school to see who's going to be more popular. Everybody's thinking: 'Am I going to look cool for the popular kids? Are they going to accept me?'" Another student said, "With all the animosity between the various social groups at Columbine, something like this was bound to happen" (Dube, 1999).

Pervasiveness of Bullying

From firsthand accounts (Dube, 1999; Prendergast, 1999) and from the killers' own videos (Gibbs & Roche, 1999), we know that Harris and Klebold were repeatedly bullied and subjected to verbal put-downs, leading to their plan of violent revenge. Initially, the role of bullying in the Columbine killings was played down. The role of bullying in the Columbine shootings is discussed in more detail later in this chapter.

Bullying is the most common form of violence in our society, and it is what drives the culture of violence. Dominating males and females bully people whom they perceive as weaker and less powerful. Men bully their female partners, women bully their children, older children bully their younger siblings, and younger children bully their pets.

Bruce Perry (1996b) calls this phenomenon the "vortex of violence." He says that violence always travels from the strongest to the weakest or from the most powerful to the least powerful. Known as the *talionic response*, it is part of the adage in the *Bible,* "an eye for an eye and a tooth for a tooth" (Weinhold, 1991). Men and women who are adult bullies are violent toward less powerful men and women. Men who are adult bullies are violent toward less powerful women. Women who are bullies commit the most violence against children. Older children who bully are the most violent toward younger children. Younger children who have been bullied take it out on their pets. Young children, who are at the bottom of this vortex, often do not have anyone to pass it on to, so they absorb it, accumulate it, and wait until they are old enough, big enough, or strong enough to erupt in some dramatic way that hurts other people.

Bullying in Schools

Although more than 97 percent of U. S. schools report having some sort of violence-prevention program, very few of them are effective, according to the U. S. Department of Education. In a study of the top 84 violence-prevention programs, only 10 were seen as effective (Lederer & Varela, 1998). Less than 10% of the nation's 85,000 public schools have comprehensive school-based mental-health services for kids (Joseph, 1999). Most of the violence-prevention initiatives and studies of the causes of violence, not just those dealing with bullying or school violence, focus on violence of a specific type—family violence, school violence, gang violence, and so on. They do not understand the interrelatedness of the culture of violence, and they usually start too late.

Few programs feature early intervention and primary prevention even though primary prevention programs cost significantly less and are far more effective. Most people are inclined to wait until the problem is acute, and then they try to fix it. In addition, few programs look at the culture of violence for the underlying causes of bullying and school violence. Many homes actually instill in their children dominator values that support bullying and school violence. Instead, we need to instill partnership values in our schools to counter some of the dominator values that kids bring with them to school. Using reactive and shortsighted approaches to try to prevent violence is like trying to avoid hitting an iceberg by rearranging the deck chairs on the Titanic. It has no effect on the outcome.

What is bullying? There is some confusion about what constitutes bullying. Bullying is defined as something that someone repeatedly does or says to gain power over or to dominate another person. The following are some typical examples of bullying:

- name calling, put-downs, cruel teasing
- saying or writing nasty things about others
- deliberately excluding certain people from activities
- not talking to certain people
- threatening others with bodily harm
- taking or damaging others' things
- hitting or kicking
- making people do things they don't want to do.

Among several kinds of bullies are the following (Marano, 1995).

1. *Proactive bullies* need no provocation and are naturally more aggressive toward others. This group frequently has poor social and relational skills and compensates for this lack of skills by picking on others.
2. *Reactive bullies* often are victimized by other bullies and then retaliate by becoming bullies as well.
3. *Provocative victims* provoke fights or aggressive encounters with others. They are quick to become oppositional or defiant and cry or display exaggerated responses in conflict situations. This group is mostly rejected by their peers and has the fewest friends.

It is often difficult for even peers to identify who are the bullies and who are the victims because the vortex of violence is so prevalent and so many participate in it (Paulk et al., 1999).

Brown's Broken Toy Project

Tom Brown (1999), the founder of the Broken Toy Project and conductor of school workshops on bullying, asked kids to describe bullying. Here is what they told him, in their own words:

- new kids

- fat kids
- skinny kids
- boys that "suck" in sports
- boys that act like "fags"
- lesbians
- kids who are smart
- kids who are dumb
- geeks
- computer-freaks
- kids who wear geeky out-of-style clothes
- kids who stink and smell
- teacher's pets
- kids with unkempt hair
- retarded kids
- kids who talk funny
- kids who walk funny
- minority kids
- kids in wheelchairs
- kids who get good grades
- kids who get poor grades
- girls with blonde hair
- kids with curly hair
- kids with freckles
- kids with funny looking ears or noses
- kids with diseases

As you can see from this list, just about any kid in school could become a target of a bully. All they have to do is be different in some way that causes them to stand out.

The kids in Tom Brown's study were explicit about *where* kids get bullied. They said:

the bus
the bathroom
the halls
recess
P.E. class

When Tom Brown asked the students why they thought bullies picked on other kids, the students gave the following answers:

They have low self-esteem.
Other kids egg them on.
For attention.
They're mean and don't care about other kids' feelings.
It's cool. You get a lot of friends when you're a bully.

Tom Brown's kids were explicit about why they don't tell grown-ups about bullying incidents:

Fear of a parent or guardian going to school and yelling at the bullies or teachers or principal.
Fear of being told to fight back when they have no desire to fight back.
Shame.
Not wanting to scare or worry their parents.

Tom's kids indicated that they got mixed messages from grown-ups:

Fight back.
Walk away.
Tell your teacher.
Quit being a baby. Start taking up for yourself.

The kids gave their reasons why kids are afraid to confront bullies:

You get instant retaliation.
You get ganged up on by bullies and their friends.
You get in trouble with the school.
You get a reputation of being a bully yourself.
The bully's older brother or sister will get after you.
You might hurt the bully and get sued or in trouble with the police.

When Tom Brown asked kids what three things kids usually do when they see someone being bullied, he got an answer that is at the heart of why bullying persists. The students said:

Run over and watch.
Run over and watch.
Run over and watch.

What keeps bullying going isn't just the bullies and the victims. It is also the bystanders who watch the incidents of bullying and do nothing to stop them. Bystanders provide an audience for the bully and give bullies the peer attention they crave. Any intervention designed to stop bullying must address the role of the bystanders.

What do kids do when they are bullied? Again Tom Brown's kids told it like it is:

Walk or run away.
Get a teacher to help.
Use humor.
Tell the bully to leave you alone.
Yell to attract a lot of attention.

Brown (1999) summarized some of the most ineffective methods that educators use to deal with bullying:

Punish both the bully and the victim.

Look the other way; ignore bullying behavior, passing it off as horseplay or kids being kids.

Bring the bully and the victim together in one room and ask the bully if he or she has been bullying the victim.

Tell the victim to quit being a crybaby and start standing up for himself or herself.

Tell the victim to make better friends.

Tell the victim to quit tattling on other kids.

Punish the bully without any attempt to resolve the situation—for example, setting up a meeting between the bully and a counselor or someone else who can talk to this student without coming off as a threat.

Yell at either or both the victim and the bully in front of other children.

Show an educational film dealing with bullying without processing the contents of the film before or afterward.

Spend money to bring an anti-bullying program into a school without doing follow-up activities.

Brown (1999) summarized his research by saying, "This is what I hear from children everywhere I go to present my program. It doesn't matter what kind of school or if the child is a first or a sixth grader. Kids know exactly what is going on."

Olweus' Research on Bullying

Dan Olweus (Olweus, 1994), from the University of Bergen in Norway, did an extensive study of bullying. Here are his definition and conclusions:

Bullying occurs when one or more persons deliberately and repeatedly try to hurt another person through words or actions. Relevant conclusions are:

- Bullying is an act of violence, and it is against the law.
- The bully's ultimate goal is to achieve domination and control over another person.
- Bullies often are not good students and have academic problems in school, such as a learning disability.
- Bullies often lack power in their own lives and compensate for it by dominating others.
- Children who bully become adults who bully unless they receive help.
- Bullying is a cry for help.

Why is bullying important to us?

1. *All school violence begins with bullying.* All serious school violence starts with seemingly innocent bullying or put-downs which eventually can escalate into

violence involving guns or knives. The lack of respect for another person's human rights—the most common factor in all criminal behavior—begins with school bullying. Schools that do not deal with bullying when it first appears can become a breeding ground for criminal behavior and pose a serious threat to public safety.

2. *Serious school violence is on the increase.* One of the first cases of school violence to reach the national press occurred in 1994. Fifteen-year-old Brian, from Woodstock, Georgia, cried out in his school classroom, "I can't take this any more," and then, with a single gunshot, ended his life. After his death, his parents and the school officials learned that Brian had been the victim of repeated harassment, humiliation, and bullying at school. Actually, since 1992, there have been 250 violent deaths in schools that involved multiple victims, culminating with the Columbine massacre (Joseph, 1999).

The great majority of these deaths occurred in cities and towns with populations of under 80,000 people, showing us that there is no safe place for our kids. Almost all the killers were white males from relatively affluent families, not gang members or teens from the inner city. In virtually every school shooting, bullying has been a factor. As in the Columbine shootings, most of the students who committed these violent crimes were "reactive bullies" who finally decided to get revenge against the other bullies who had picked on them.

Some of the other school shootings that involved bullying are as follows.

Feb. 2, 1996: Two male students in Moses Lake, Washington, were shot to death by a 14-year-old male honor student who had been the target of repeated bullying by those students.

Mar. 24, 1998: An 11-year-old boy and a 13-year-old boy shot and killed four girls and a female teacher in a Jonesboro, Arkansas, Middle School. They had made repeated threats to others in the school about their intent to do violence, but they were ignored. The 13-year old was described as a bully.

Sept. 1998: Two school outcasts in Green River, Wyoming, 18-year-old Cody Bradley and 16-year-old David Taylor, who were ostracized and bullied by other students, stabbed and killed a 17-year-old boy who they said stole Bradley's girlfriend, and then they shot themselves a day later in a suicide pact.

Oct. 1998: A 12-year-old middle-school student from Woodstock, Georgia, was beaten up by a known 15-year-old bully as he got off the bus at school. The victim went into a coma and a few days later was taken off life support.

Nov. 1998: Five Burlington, Wisconsin, boys were arrested for plotting the deaths of their teachers, administrators, and the other students who they said were picking on them. They told school officials that the other students "treated them like trash."

3. *Bullying was at the root of the Columbine massacre.* We must learn the lessons of the Columbine massacre if we are to prevent it from happening again. The

group of Columbine students identified as the "trenchcoat mafia," which included Eric Harris and Dylan Klebold, was harassed, bullied and put down daily for years. This practice was initiated by a clique of student athletes and later joined many other Columbine students.

Every day when Harris and Klebold came to school, they were met at the door by a group of students who harassed them by pouring orange juice on their trenchcoats so they would have to wear the sticky stuff all day. Harris, Klebold, and others in this group who were bullied tried to sneak into school through a side door or back door to avoid this daily ritual. They also were harassed in the hallways and cafeteria and were called names. Frequently the football players would throw a body block on them, knocking them into the lockers or the wall, and call them "dirt bags" or "dirt balls." One 15-year-old Columbine student said, "It must have been hell for them" (Dube, 1999).

Time magazine (Gibbs & Roche, 1999) quoted a 255-pound defensive lineman at Columbine as saying,

> Columbine is a clean, good, place except for those rejects. Sure, we teased them. But what do you expect with kids who come to school with weird hairdos and horns on their hats? It's not just the jocks; the whole school's disgusted with them. They're a bunch of homos, grabbing each other's private parts. If you want to get rid of someone, usually you tease 'em. So the whole school would call them homos, and when they did something sick, we'd tell them, "You're sick and that's wrong."

Even though this happened in front of many students and teachers, no one tried to stop it. The killers wore weird clothing to call attention to themselves and even wore armbands that said, "I hate people." As they opened fire on their classmates, Harris and Klebold were heard to say, "This is for all the people who made fun of us all these years" (Dube, 1999).

Notwithstanding their obvious cries for help, no one gave these boys the kind of attention they really needed. They were very bright and very lonely, yet no one seemed to try to redirect their behavior in more positive ways. Further, cliques like those that bullied and harassed Harris and Klebold at Columbine High School exist in every school in this country. In most schools, the athletes are at the top of the heap. They act out the dominator behaviors that many school athletic programs highly value.

Killing is a learned behavior. Children don't naturally kill. They learn it from their experience of violence in their home and, most pervasively, from violence as entertainment on television, in the movies, and by playing interactive video games. Killing requires the availability of weapons and training because there is a built-in aversion to killing one's own kind. Law enforcement and military personnel know this because they have to go through rigorous training before they are able to shoot someone, if necessary. And then they are trained not to kill but, instead, to maim or disarm a dangerous person with a weapon (Grossman, 1998).

Research on the effects of television is clear. In nations or regions where television is introduced for the first time, the murder rate doubles within 15 years. The American Medical Association concluded that long-term childhood exposure to television is a causal factor behind approximately half of the violent crimes committed in the United States, or about 10,000 homicides, 70,000 rapes, and 700,000 injurious assaults (Grossman, 1996).

David Grossman (1998) said:

> The result is a phenomenon that functions much like AIDS, which I call AVIDS—Acquired Violence Immune Deficiency Syndrome. AIDS has never killed anybody. It destroys your immune system, and then other diseases that shouldn't kill you become fatal. Television violence by itself does not kill you. It destroys your violence immune system and conditions you to derive pleasure from violence. And once you are at close range with another human being and its time for you to pull that trigger, Acquired Violence Immune Deficiency Syndrome can destroy your midbrain resistance. (p. 36)

Further, violent video games are teaching our children how to shoot to kill with increasing accuracy. In the Jonesboro, Arkansas, killings, one boy had no experience shooting guns and the other had only some experience in shooting guns. Yet, they fired 27 shots from 100 yards and hit 15 people. That's pretty good shooting. Why were they so good? They both had played violent video games for hours at a time that taught them how to hit targets. Video games train kids to shoot a gun to kill someone (Grossman, 1998).

On a dare from a friend, a 15-year-old boy in South Carolina tried to rob a local convenience store. In the process, he reflexively shot and killed the clerk. From 6 feet away, he pointed a snub-nosed .38-caliber pistol at the back of the clerk's head, and when the clerk turned around to face the boy, the boy shot the clerk right between the eyes. This boy had spent hundreds of hours playing video games, learning to point and shoot, point and shoot. When asked why he did it, the boy replied, "I don't know. It was a mistake. It wasn't supposed to happen" (Grossman, 1998).

Those who have been in the military or law enforcement know that the correct option is often not to shoot. But when kids put their quarter in a video machine, their intention is to shoot to kill. In a video game, there is always a stimulus that sets them off and instructs them to start shooting.

In the case of the 15-year-old boy in South Carolina—he said he got excited and scared when the convenience clerk turned around; his heart rate went up; the flow of adrenaline closed down his forebrain, he panicked and reflexively he did what he was conditioned to do: He pulled the trigger, shooting just as accurately as he had done hundreds of times before when he was playing video games. Our children are learning to kill and to enjoy it (Grossman, 1998).

Here are some additional statistics:

■ 60 percent of men on TV dramas are depicted in violent scenes; 11% are killers (Grossman, 1998).

■ In the media in general, the majority of victims are women and children. (Grossman, 1998).

■ 20 percent of suburban high-school students endorsed the idea of shooting someone "who has stolen something from you." (Grossman, 1996).

Bullying is pervasive in most schools. Some statistics that bear this out are:

■ Half of all violence against teenagers occurs in school buildings, on school property, or on the street in the vicinity of the school. Most begins as bullying or put-downs (NIDR, 1999).

■ The National School Safety Center estimates that more than 525,000 attacks, shakedowns, and robberies occur per month in public secondary schools in the United States (Weinhold & Weinhold, 1998).

■ The National Education Association estimates that 160,000 students miss school every day (totaling 28 million missed days per year), because of fear of attack or intimidation by a bully (Fried & Fried, 1996).

■ Students receive an average of 213 verbal put-downs per week, or 30 per day (Fried, personal communication, 1996).

■ In a survey of 558 students in a Midwestern middle school, the researchers found that 80 percent of the students had engaged in bullying behaviors in the previous 30 days (Espelage et al., 1999).

■ 80 to 90 percent of adolescents report some form of victimization from a bully at school (Espelage et al., 1999).

■ 90 percent of all students thought that bullying caused social, emotional, or academic problems for the students who were bullied (Weinhold & Weinhold, 2000).

■ 69 percent of all students believe that schools respond poorly to bullying and victimization (Weinhold & Weinhold, 2000).

How does bullying differ from grade to grade? (Olweus, 1994).

■ Bullying occurs in every grade, but it happens most frequently in grades 4 through 8.

■ Bullying usually starts as teasing and put-downs with younger bullies and then becomes more physical and more violent as bullies get older.

■ Bullies can be easily identified in each grade by the sixth week of the school year.

■ Potential bullies can be easily identified as early as preschool if we recognize the early warning signs.

How does bullying differ between boys and girls? (Saunders, 1997).

■ Boys tend to use direct physical and verbal attacks to bully others.

■ Girls tend to use more indirect, subtle, and social methods such as exclusion, manipulation, and spreading rumors.

■ Boys tend to bully other boys (80 percent) and girls (60 percent).

■ Boys are more likely than girls to be both perpetrators and victims of aggressive physical and verbal bullying by peers.

■ In middle-school, girls who mature early are often bullied and sexually harassed by boys.

■ Girls tend to bully only other girls.

■ Boys usually bully alone, and girls bully in groups.

Bullying Outside of School

How pervasive is bullying outside of schools? Considering that bullying is a hidden part of the overall culture of violence that is supported by dominator values, you can see that it occurs almost everywhere—at home, at work, and on the road.

At home, some key points in bullying are as follows.

■ Older siblings often bully their younger brothers and sisters.

■ Bullies and victims of bullying often grow up to become batterers. Adult perpetrators of domestic violence often have been identified as bullies or victims of bullying while they were in school (Straus & Gelles, 1988).

Bullying occurs in the workplace as well. Bully OnLine (1999) reported the results of a study, as follows.

■ Bullies at school who get away with it often become serial bullies at work.

■ Children who get bullied at school tend to become targets for bullying at work.

■ More than one million U. S. workers are assaulted annually.

■ The most common reasons people are bullied on the job are that they are good at their job and they are popular with other employees (the workplace bully is driven by jealousy and envy).

■ In the United Kingdom, one in three people leave their job because of bullying.

■ The same study showed that 53 percent of UK employees have been bullied during their working life.

Road rage has become recognized in recent years. Nerenberg (1999) reported the following:

■ Road rage is another form of bullying.

■ In 1996, 28,000 Americans died because of aggressive driving.

■ There are 2 billion episodes of road rage per year in the United States.

■ Violent incidents of road rage have increased 51 percent over the last five years.

Collective Denial About Effects of Bullying

The most common way that schools deal with bullying is to ignore it. Many teachers don't see anything wrong with bullying. One Columbine student reported,

"Teachers would see them push someone into a locker, and they'd just ignore it" (Prendergast, 1999). A junior at Columbine said, "I can't believe the faculty couldn't figure it out. It was so obvious that something was wrong" (Dube, 1999). In another study, teachers were able to identify only 10 percent of the students who reported being a victim of a bully (Paulk et al., 1999). A prevailing attitude among some teachers is that those who get bullied probably had it coming to them. In families, fewer than one in 10 incidents of bullying involving suspected child abuse or domestic violence ever get reported, and of the incidents that are reported, few are ever investigated and almost none result in any criminal charges (Weinhold, 1991).

How does bullying differ from normal peer conflicts? The collective denial is supported by misconceptions about how bullying situations differ from normal peer conflicts. There is a big difference between these situations (Weinhold, 1999a). A bullying situation has six defining factors:

- *Intent to harm.* The perpetrator finds pleasure in taunting or trying to dominate the victim and continues even when the victim's distress is obvious.
- *Intensity and duration.* The bullying continues over a long period and the extent of bullying is damaging to the self-esteem of the victim.
- *Power of the bully.* The bully has power over the victim because of age, strength, size, or gender.
- *Vulnerability of the victim.* The victim is more sensitive to teasing, cannot adequately defend himself or herself, and has physical or psychological qualities that make him or her more prone to victimization.
- *Lack of support.* The victim feels isolated and exposed. Often, the victim is afraid to report the bullying for fear of retaliation.
- *Consequences.* Damage to the victim's self-esteem is longlasting and leads the victim to markedly withdraw from school or, conversely, to become aggressive.

In a normal peer conflict situation, in contrast, none of these elements is present. Those who are involved in a normal peer conflict

- do not insist on getting their own way.
- give reasons why they disagree.
- apologize or offer win-win suggestions.
- are free to bargain and negotiate to get their needs met.
- can change the topic and walk away.

Effects of Bullying

What are the short-term effects of bullying in our schools? Here are some examples of the immediate or short-term effects of bullying in schools:

- 10 percent of students who drop out of school do so because of repeated bullying (Weinhold & Weinhold, 1998).
- 20 percent of all high school students surveyed report avoiding the restrooms out of a fear of being bullied (NIDR, 1999).

- In the United States, about 2 million teenagers carry guns, knives, clubs, and razors (NIDR, 1999).
- As many as 135,000 take these weapons to school (NIDR, 1999).
- Nearly one-third of the students have heard a classmate threaten to kill someone (Langer, 1999).
- 78 percent who knew of the threats to kill someone said they didn't report them to an adult (Langer, 1999).
- 40 percent of high school students say there are potentially violent cliques at their school (Langer, 1999).
- One in five of the students say they personally know a classmate who has brought a gun to school (Langer, 1999).
- Of those who knew a classmate who brought a gun to school, 83 percent say they did not report it to an adult (Langer, 1999).
- 54 percent of the students say it would be easy for them to get a gun. (One student said it was as easy as buying candy at the corner store.) (Langer, 1999).
- 67 percent say it would be easy for them to make a bomb (Langer, 1999).

What are the known long-term effects of bullying? Some of the conclusions of the Olweus (1993, 1994) studies are:

Studies on those who are bullied (Olweus, 1993)

- Being bullied during middle school is predictive of low self-esteem 10 years later.
- By age 23, children who were bullied in middle school were more depressed and had lower self-esteem than their peers who had not been bullied.
- Bullied children feel more isolated than their peers, who often reject them out of fear that they, too, will become a target of bullies if they are seen with targeted students.
- Being bullied can lead to suicide.
- Some victims of bullies resort to eventual violent retaliation against the bully.

Studies on the bullies themselves (Olweus, 1994)

- By age 23, about 60 percent of the boys identified as bullies in middle school had at least one conviction of a crime, and 35 percent to 40 percent had three or more convictions.
- 50 percent of all identified school bullies became criminals as adults.
- Bullies at age 8 are three times more likely to be convicted of a crime by age 30.
- Bullies are less likely than nonbullies to finish college or locate a good job.

Why do children bully and put others down? There is a clash between the old and the new thinking on the causes of bullying and school violence. The new thinking is based on the recent research findings cited in this chapter. Table 6.1 presents a comparison.

Table 6.1	CONVENTIONAL VERSUS NEW THINKING
Conventional Thinking	**New Thinking**
Bullying is genetic. Bullies are born that way.	Bullying is shaped by early childhood experiences.
Bullies should just be expelled.	Bullying is a cry for help.
Bullying is normal kids' behavior.	Bullying is a symptom of untreated trauma.
Bullying is harmless.	Bullying is traumatic for those being bullied.
Bullies will grow out of it.	Without intervention, bullying leads to further violence.
Bullies are influenced by peer modeling.	Bullies are influenced more by media and family modeling.
Watching violence on TV or movies is harmless.	TV and movie violence traumatizes kids.
Violent video games are harmless fantasy.	Traumatized kids can't separate reality and fantasy.

Causes of Bullying

If we are going to eliminate the causes of bullying, a multitude of risk factors have to be addressed. Consider the following risk factors.

Family factors

- ■ The home is the most violent place in the United States (Straus, 1994).
- ■ Children from violent homes are three to four times more likely to become bullies. Contrary to popular belief, most of the violence directed at young children in the home comes from the mother and older siblings (Straus & Gelles, 1988).
- ■ Three primary predictive family factors are (Weinhold & Weinhold, 2000):
  - — a lack of solid bonding/attachment with the young child.
  - — poor supervision and neglect of the child's needs.
  - — acceptance and modeling of aggressive or bullying behaviors by parents or older siblings.
- ■ Few early identification and intervention programs are available to help young children who show aggressive tendencies.

Personality factors

- ■ Children with an impulsive temperament are more inclined to develop into bullies (Olweus, 1994).
- ■ Bullies often have attachment disorders (Weinhold, 1999).

■ Boys who are physically bigger or stronger than peers of the same age are more likely to become bullies (Olweus, 1993).

■ Bullies like to be in charge, dominate, and assert their power. They like to win at any cost (Olweus, 1993).

■ Bullies crave attention, so they show off and act tough to get it from peers (Olweus, 1994).

■ Bullies lack empathy for their victims and have difficulty feeling compassion (Olweus, 1993).

■ Bullies believe that the victim provoked the attack and deserves the consequences (Olweus, 1994).

■ Bullying is a cry for help (Olweus, 1994).

School Factors

■ The amount of adult supervision is directly tied to the frequency and severity of bullying in schools (Saunders, 1997).

■ A negative school climate where negative behavior gets most of the attention encourages the formation of cliques and bullying (Espelage et al., 1999).

■ Some teachers threaten, tease, shame, or intimidate students to maintain control of their classroom (Olweus, 1994).

■ 25 percent of teachers see nothing wrong with bullying and put-downs. Schools often condone this behavior and do nothing to prevent bullying and put-downs (Olweus, 1994).

■ The learning environment can be poisoned by bullying and put-downs, raising the fear and anxiety of all students (Johnson & Johnson, 1995).

■ Early identification and intervention programs are lacking. Bullies can be identified as early as preschool (Olweus, 1994).

Community Factors (Hawkins, Catalano et al., 1992).

■ Schools in poor urban neighborhoods experience more violence in and around schools.

■ People feel less safe in neighborhoods that show evidence of crack houses, drug dealing, and related violence. This spills over into the neighborhood schools, where there is more drug-dealing and related violence.

■ Schools located in neighborhoods with high turnover mobility and transiency also have more bullying.

■ State and local policies about early prevention, identification, and intervention are lacking.

Role of PTSD and Trauma as a Hidden Cause of Violence

A book on conflict resolution, *Conflict Resolution: The Partnership Way* (Weinhold & Weinhold, 2000), presents research indicating that most conflict situations involve stimulus conditions that remind those involved of previously unresolved conflicts and traumas. In a conflict situation, people frequently show symptoms resembling a post-traumatic stress reaction, or when they witness violent conflicts involving others, they may actually regress to an earlier trauma or conflict. They are actually existing in two realities at once, and usually they are unaware of why they are reacting the way they are.

Symptoms of PTSD

Clinical symptoms of post-traumatic stress disorder (PTSD) (APA, 1996) are as follows:

- *Reexperiencing old traumas*—Recurrent and intrusive recollections, distressing dreams, flashbacks, intense reactions to ordinary events.
- *Persistent avoidance of triggering situations and a "numbing" effect on general responsiveness*—Compulsive efforts to avoid people, thoughts, or feelings that arouse memories, depression, or detachment from others; a restricted range of affect.
- *Increased hypervigilence.* Difficulty sleeping, irritability and outbursts of anger, difficulty concentrating, an exaggerated startle response.

Activation of the Adrenal Stress Response

Another effect of repeated exposure to conflict and violence is that people become desensitized to violence. When I give talks on violence, I typically ask members of the audience to raise their hand if they have personally witnessed violence or if they were the victim of violence. Typically, about one-third of the audience members raise a hand. To not have witnessed any violence, they would not have seen a violent television show or a violent movie and would not have seen anyone in the family, workplace, highway, school, or neighborhood being violent. Highly unlikely! Why did they not raise their hand then?

They likely had to dissociate so they could cope with the amount of violence they were exposed to. At the same time, they remain in a constant hypervigilent state to avoid being triggered by memories of past violence. If people are in a persistent hyperaroused state, adrenal horomones are flowing through their bloodstream, and they are likely to fight, flee, or freeze if the current conflict situation contains even the slightest hint of an earlier conflict situation that they did not resolve. These classic adrenal stress reactions are wired into us to help us deal with situations in which we perceive danger. We don't even have to think about it (Weinhold & Weinhold, 2000).

When bullies pick on others, they likely have been triggered into the fight mode of the adrenal stress reaction. They hope they can discharge the accumulated fear, anger, and hurt from an earlier traumatic incident by picking on those they perceive as weaker. Untreated symptoms of PTSD may be a major factor in why people own more than 250 million guns in the United States. They just don't feel safe.

Accompanying the fear of violent encounters is a companion factor that causes people to be attracted to and fascinated by violence. The natural learning style of humans is to repeat a behavior until it is learned or understood or the trauma is healed. Freud called this *repetition compulsion*. Thus, we are drawn to what we fear. That is why so many people like to watch violent events, such as wrestling and seem to enjoy being scared out of their wits by violence on TV and in the movies.

People actually seem to be addicted to violence at the same time they are still trying to understand and heal what happened to them when they were traumatized by it during early childhood. Children see violence on TV and it traumatizes them. They then either compulsively try to stay away from anything that might remind them of this kind of violence and at the same time are drawn to it (Weinhold & Weinhold, 2000).

Parental Neglect and Emotional Abandonment of Our Children

In Ken Magid's and Carol McKelvey's book *High Risk: Children Without a Conscience* (1989), they state that severely abused and neglected children will grow up to become violence-seeking adults unless there is an intervention in their lives before age 16. These authors estimate that up to 20 million adults fall in this category and the numbers are growing more rapidly than the population. They advise that we must do a better job of protecting these children and intervening in the lives of young children who exhibit symptoms of attachment disorder. If we don't, Magid predicts that "soon there will be more of them than us and then we will be in real trouble" (Magid, 1992).

Research by Dr. Bruce Perry of Baylor College of Medicine (1996a, 1996b) has pointed to a particular family environment that will turn a normal child into a killer. He uncovered the effects on the brain of repeated stress caused by abuse, neglect, or terror, which cause physical and maybe permanent changes in young children. He found that the constant flood of adrenaline causes the brain to reset the brain's alarm system on an almost constant hair-trigger alert. Children who are constantly exposed to abuse or who witness the abuse of others, such as a sibling or a parent, can also cause their brains' system of adrenal stress horomones to become unresponsive.

These are the high-risk kids that Magid is talking about. They have antisocial personalities and typically have a low heart rate and impaired emotional sensitivity including a lack of empathy. They often kill or torture animals (Begley, 1999).

A Profile of the Character-Disturbed Child

Cline (1979) was one of the first to profile the characteristics of a high-risk child who has an attachment disorder. He listed the following characteristics:

- Lack of ability to give and receive affection.
- Self-destructive behavior.

- Cruelty to others.
- Phoniness.
- Severe problems with stealing, hoarding, and gorging on food.
- Marked control problems.
- Lack of long-term friends.
- Abnormalities in eye contact.

The three types of maternal attachments are: secure, avoidant, and anxious/ambivalent. Campos, Barrett, et al. (1983), found that 62 percent of infants are securely attached, 23 percent are avoidant, and 15 percent are insecure/ambivalent. The type of early attachment a child has causes him or her to develop what is called an internal "working model" of the world (Ainsworth, 1989; Bowlby, 1988). There are also three identifiable sub-types of avoidantly attached children: (a) the lying bully who blames others; (b) the shy, dissociated loner who seems emotionally flat, and (c) the obviously disturbed child with repetitive twitches and tics who daydreams and shows little interest in his or her environment. The two ambivalent sub-types are: (a) the fidgety, impulsive child with poor concentration who is tense and easily upset by his or her failures, and (b) the fearful, hypersensitive, clingy child who lacks initiative and gives up easily (Karen, 1998).

The *DSM-IV* (APA, 1996) has updated these characteristics in its diagnosis of a "Conduct Disorder." This diagnosis applies to anyone under 18 years of age, and for those over 18, it usually is called an Antisocial Personality Disorder. The symptoms are as follows:

Aggression toward people and animals:

- Often bullies, threatens, or intimidates others.
- Often initiates physical fights.
- Has used a weapon that can cause serious physical harm to others.
- Has been physically cruel to people.
- Has been physically cruel to animals.
- Has stolen while confronting a victim.
- Has forced someone into sexual activity.

Destruction of property:

- Has deliberately engaged in fire-setting with the intention of causing serious damage.
- Has deliberately destroyed others' property (other than by fire-setting).

Deceitfulness or theft:

- Has broken into someone else's house, building, or car.
- Often lies to obtain goods or favors or to avoid obligations.
- Has stolen items of nontrivial value without confronting a victim.

Serious violations of rules:

◼ Often stays out at night despite parental prohibitions, beginning before 13 years of age.

◼ Has run away from home overnight at least twice while living in parental or parental surrogate home.

◼ Is often truant from school, beginning before 13 years of age.

To be diagnosed with this disorder, a persistent pattern of three or more of these behaviors must be present over the past 12 months, with the presence of at least one of the behaviors for the past 3 months. Most of these behaviors are similar to the ones that Cline found in his study on the effects of poor bonding and attachment. Clearly, parental neglect, abuse, and emotional abandonment play an important role in creating the internal "working model" of these kinds of young people. If we are going to stop bullying and school violence as well as the rest of the antisocial behaviors of children and adults, we have to help parents achieve a secure bond or attachment with their children.

In addition, Perry's research has indicated that parents who are withdrawn and remote, neglectful and passive or depressed, are at risk of causing their child's brain to stop developing. Perry found that neglect impairs the development of the brain's cortex, where feelings of belonging and attachment occur. According to Perry, these neglected kids desperately need positive adult attention to compensate for the lack of attention or negative attention they received early in life from their parents or family members (Perry, 1996b).

Violato and Russell (1994) conducted a Canadian meta-analysis of 88 published research studies on the effects of nonmaternal care on the development of infants and young children. They found that if the mother is gone for more than 20 hours a week, it can seriously effect the social-emotional, behavioral development and maternal attachment of infants and young children. Lero, Goelman, et al. (1992) found that 70 percent of Canadian mothers with children under 6 years old are working fulltime. In the United States, the figure is estimated to be 75 percent. This form of neglect has serious implications for our national policy of federal and state support for daycare so mothers can work.

Other research has confirmed that once the internal working model of the world is formed in early childhood, it persists into adulthood virtually unchanged (Pearson, Cowen, et al. 1993). Krause and Haverkamp (1996) summarize the research this way:

> Existing research does suggest that the bond between parent and child is likely to remain in effect across the life span and plays an important role in later life parent-child relations. (pp. 85–86)

From their meta-analysis cited above, Violato and Russell (1994) concluded that the absence of the mother for more than 20 hours per week during infancy and early childhood increases the prevalence of insecure/ambivalent attachments by approximately 50 percent.

Developmental Trauma

As a part of the author's research on conflict resolution, he has identified the presence of developmental traumas during early childhood as the main cause of a later fear of or fascination with violence. These traumas often are caused more by neglect than abuse and, therefore, are harder to identify because "nothing happened," except that the child's needs were neglected and the significant adults disconnected from them (Weinhold & Weinhold, 2000).

From the author's research (Weinhold & Weinhold, 2000), the following are the usual causes of developmental traumas:

- Child abuse, neglect, or emotional abandonment during the first 2 years of life.
- Disruptions in the normal sequence of development.
- Prolonged or repeated separations between mother and child during early bonding because of illness.
- Daily small disconnects between mother and child.
- Repeated encroachment of the child's physical, psychological, and emotional boundaries.
- A lack of understanding of the child's needs.
- Lack of support for safe exploratory behavior.
- Using the child to satisfy the parent's needs.

This research (Weinhold & Weinhold, 2000) has shown that developmental traumas may be the cause of the following problems:

- Developmental delays—"late-bloomers."
- Attachment disorders (ambivalent or anxious/avoidant).
- Attention deficit/hyperactive disorder.
- Cognitive impairment because of cognitive neglect.
- Primitive problem-solving strategies that involve use of violence.
- Dissociation in females.
- Aggressive, impulsive, reactive, and hyperactive behaviors in males.

The author of *Real Boys* (Pollack, 1998) says that when parents or other adults disconnect from young boys, the boys learn to suffer in silence and, rather than crying tears, they eventually "cry bullets." This fits with the description of events in the lives of Eric Harris and Dylan Klebold. Their pent-up abandonment rage, exacerbated by the marginalization at school, discharged through violence. By studying brain scans, Perry found that neglected children had more damage to the cognitive functions of their brain than did abused children. The brain actually atrophies when it isn't stimulated enough. Another of Perry's findings is that children who were traumatized early in life develop more primitive, less mature styles of conflict resolution. They tend to be more impulsive, more easily triggered by stimulus events, and less likely to consider the consequences of their actions. Looked at through this lens, bullying can be seen as adapting to the effects of early traumas and using bullying as a protective mechanism to try to feel safe again (Perry, 1996b).

Conclusions from this research can be summarized as follows (Weinhold & Weinhold, 2000):

- Many bullies and victims of bullying show classic signs of PTSD and possibly suffer from the effects of the neglect of their basic attachment needs early in life.
- Bullying incidents usually begin with a triggering event that leads to a traumatic reenactment of previous unresolved developmental traumas or conflicts experienced by the bully, the victim, or both.
- Bullies and victims need counseling that teaches them trauma-reduction techniques and conflict-resolution skills, and provides them with the positive attention they missed in their early childhood experiences.

The Kindness Campaign: A Primary Prevention Program To Curb Bullying and School Violence

The Kindness Campaign was started in July 1994 under the National Program for the Study and Prevention of Youth and Family Violence at the University of Colorado at Colorado Springs. It was designed as a primary prevention program to address the rising tide of violence among youth, in families, and in schools. Though the National Program receives in-kind support from the university, it depends upon grants and contributions from individuals and corporations. The Kindness Campaign is based on the idea that the best way to eliminate a negative behavior (bullying, put-downs, aggressive behaviors) is by focusing everyone's attention on the opposite of these behaviors: kindness. The program addresses each of the hidden elements of the culture of violence. Below is a summary of how the Kindness Campaign addresses these hidden elements and the results achieved thus far:

Promoting Humanistic Values

The predominant message of the Kindness Campaign is that domination and violence can be stopped if schools and communities use their resources to promote humanistic values such as kindness, respect for the law, peaceful resolution of conflicts, and understanding and tolerance of differences. The campaign's co-sponsor, the local CBS television affiliate, conducted a random sample interview of its viewers in late 1994 and found that 75% of its viewers believed the Campaign was having a positive impact on the community (Weinhold, 1996). Since then, the Kindness Campaign has co-sponsored many community events designed to build common ground and increase understanding and tolerance. These events include an Annual Interfaith Celebration of Kindness and neighborhood ceremonies to recognize the positive activities of residents.

Kindness Campaign programs have been started in more than 105 schools, reaching over 70,000 students in Colorado Springs. Ten other U.S. cities have adopted the Kindness Campaign in their community and schools. As a result of the efforts of the Kindness Campaign's programs, in 1997 the city of Colorado Springs was one of three U.S. cities to be named a "Community of Kindness."

Creating a Positive School and Community Climate

More than 105 area schools have used the Kindness Campaign to improve their school climate. Their results indicate that children who get more recognition for positive behaviors don't have to bully others or wear trench coats to get attention. The Kindness Campaign has produced a curriculum guide, *Spreading Kindness: A Program Guide for Preventing Peer Violence in Schools,* which contains 154 activities for schools to use in designing their own program.

One suggested activity shows how to develop a school Kindness Code that would include the following:

1. "We will say and do kind things to others in this school."
2. "We will recognize the kind things that other people say and do."
3. "We will help those who are having trouble being kind."

In most schools that started the Kindness Campaign, student to student put-downs dropped significantly. One elementary school reduced put-downs by 94 percent after the Kindness Campaign was introduced (Weinhold, 1999a).

Reducing Bullying and Aggressive Behaviors

When bullies see other kids getting recognized for positive behaviors, they begin exhibiting more positive behaviors. In three different middle schools where the Kindness Campaign was introduced, discipline referrals to the office dropped by more than 30 percent. The Kindness Campaign's Creating Kind and Safe Schools program helps schools develop an anti-bullying policy. Faculty and students learn about the negative effects of bullying and then collaborate to create a schoolwide anti-bullying policy. Such a policy might include the following:

1. "Teachers and staff agree to confront all incidents of bullying and put-downs that they see."
2. "Students agree to help those being bullied or put down by speaking out and/or getting adult help."
3. "All students, faculty, and staff agree to include everyone in their activities. No one is marginalized."

Dealing With Student Traumas

One of the best ways to deal with untreated trauma is the use of peer mediation programs and schoolwide conflict-resolution classes. Peer mediation involves identifying a group of students, who are selected for their leadership and interpersonal qualities, to become identified as peer mediators. These peer mediators are trained to intervene in peer-conflict situations, where they attempt to get the parties to resolve their conflict peacefully or get adult help, if necessary. This helps prevent peer conflicts from escalating into more aggressive actions. They are trained to approach students engaged in a peer conflict and to offer to help them mediate the conflict.

Usually the agreement is that if the parties can resolve the conflict to everyone's satisfaction, the matter is ended. If not, the peer mediator takes the parties to see a teacher, a counselor, or an administrator, who then will intervene. In combination with a conflict-resolution curriculum, peer mediation helps prevent peer conflicts from escalating and helps prevent bullying. Again, excellent peer-mediation training materials are available on the market. More than 8,500 of the some 85,000 schools in the United States teach conflict resolution to all students (NIDR, 1999).

Research (Johnson & Johnson, 1995) shows that a conflict-resolution curriculum in the schools:

■ decreases physical violence in the school,
■ leads to less disruptive behavior,
■ improves academic performance,
■ empowers kids to solve their own problems, and
■ increases student leadership.

Developing Cooperative Learning Methods to Resolve Conflicts

Many schools have found that, by adding cooperative learning to their curriculum, they are able to reduce bullying and related school violence. In the 1960s, David and Roger Johnson (1995) from the University of Minnesota created a cooperative learning program called Teaching Students to be Peacemakers. This K–12 program has been operating for more than 30 years and teaches all students:

■ to recognize what is a conflict and what is not a conflict,
■ to negotiate win-win solutions to conflicts, and
■ to help mediate schoolmates conflicts.

After conducting numerous research studies to determine the effectiveness of this program, they found that it resulted in a schoolwide discipline program focused on empowering students to regulate and control their own and their classmates' actions. As a result of this program, when a conflict occurred, the students involved would first try to negotiate a resolution. If that failed, they would ask a classmate to help mediate the conflict. If that failed, they would ask a teacher to help mediate the conflict. If that failed, the teacher would be asked to arbitrate the conflict. If that failed, they would ask the principal to help mediate the conflict, and if that failed, they would have the principal arbitrate the conflict (Johnson & Johnson, 1995).

In addition, teachers and counselors need to be trained to identify the symptoms of PTSD and how to intervene effectively in these cases. I have developed training materials and, through the Kindness Campaign, offer inservices and train teachers and counselors in these skills. The whole field of traumatology has had a number of breakthroughs that have led to the development of new trauma reduction techniques that school counselors and teachers can learn to use when they encounter students who are experiencing symptoms of PTSD (Weinhold & Weinhold, 2000).

Addressing Parental Abuse and Neglect

The Kindness Campaign has produced an activity guide for parents, *Raising Kind Kids: An Activity Guide for Fostering Kindness in Families* (Weinhold, 1999b). This guide contains 25 family-kindness activities that parents can use to instill more kindness into their families. Working through the PTAs in schools, the Kindness Campaign offers inservices to parents who want to increase their ability to relate to their children in positive ways. In addition, the Kindness Campaign has produced a guide for preschools, *Kind Beginnings: An Activity Guide for Fostering Kindness in Pre-schools* (Weinhold, 2000). This activity guide contains 36 field-tested activities that preschool teachers can utilize to teach young children how to be kind and respectful toward each other.

Businesses Adopting a Kind and Safe School

One of the main intervention programs of the Kindness Campaign in schools is the Adopt a Kind and Safe School project. Area businesses that are interested in helping make area schools kinder and safer for the children of their employees have "adopted" schools. The business donates funds for the Kindness Campaign to work intensively with their adopted school to create a positive learning climate and put in place an anti-bullying policy. The business also arranges for its employees to volunteer at the school as aides or tutors in the classroom. The Kindness Campaign conducts inservices with the faculty and students, plans school assemblies, and installs follow-up evaluation procedures. An outline of the process that the Kindness Campaign uses to deliver this program follows.

  I. Conduct a needs assessment.
     A. Determine what is needed to make this a kind and safe school.
     B. Meet with faculty and students.
     C. Develop a contract with the school to provide the program it needs.

 II. Establish the Kindness Campaign to change the overall school climate.
     A. Conduct inservices with faculty and staff.
     B. Select a Kindness Committee and School Coordinator(s).
     C. Help committee design program to meet school needs (Utilize the Program Guide: *Spreading Kindness*).
     D. Organize kick-off assembly for the students.

E. Do follow-up consultation with faculty and students.

F. Start Kind Kids Council(s).

G. Conduct ongoing evaluation of outcomes.

III. Create an all-school policy on bullying and put-downs.

A. Conduct student and teacher survey/needs assessment.

B. Do inservice for faculty and staff.

C. Design classroom activities for students.

D. Develop classroom and school rules.

E. Do follow-up in-service/consultation.

F. Design and conduct ongoing evaluation (formative and summative).

IV. Help the school establish primary prevention/school safety methods (optional).

A. Help establish a peer mediation program.

B. Help establish a conflict-resolution curriculum for all students.

C. Help create an emergency disaster plan.

D. Help create an overall school safety plan.

V. Conduct in-service trainings (optional).

A. Trauma Reduction Techniques for Counselors and Teachers.

B. Understanding Gender Differences: Real Boys and Real Girls.

C. High-Risk Kids: Early Identification and Intervention.

D. Kids' Rights: The Legal Rights of Children to Protection Against Violence.

E. Conflict Resolution/Peer Mediation Training.

VI. Provide other services, if needed. Sometimes schools need help with special projects such as designing a better system to deal with students who are disruptive. The Kindness Campaign has designed community and school service programs as an alternative to school suspension.

VII. Help develop long-term cooperative relationships between the school and the business sponsor. The Kindness Campaign staff attempts to encourage the development of a cooperative, long-term relationship between the school and the business. This varies with each school and business. Most businesses arrange to have their employees volunteer at the school they have adopted. Some tutor or read to students who don't get much help at home, and others assist the teacher in the classroom in various ways. Some businesses encourage their adopted schools to provide them with a wish list of equipment or supplies that the school needs and then, if possible, the business provides it.

VIII. Develop programs for the business employees and their families. This is a vital link in the Adopt a Kind and Safe School project. Here, the staff of the Kindness Campaign offers inservice training to the employees of the businesses that have adopted a school. These programs include parenting classes for employees who have families, teaching them how to discipline using kindness and nonthreatening methods. An ambulance company was noticing that its employees were suffering from vicarious trauma and burn-out because of their daily exposure to traumatic and crisis situations. The staff of the Kindness Campaign offered to teach the employees how to recognize their own trauma symptoms and then teach them practical trauma reduction techniques that they could use with each other and with themselves.

Will we wake-up in time? George Kennan, former Secretary of State, likened the American public to a sleeping dinosaur. He said every now and then something would disturb the dinosaur and it would wake up and flail about, trying to find who or what was to blame for waking it up. In the process, it would destroy or damage much of its surroundings. Finding no one to blame, it would go back to sleep.

It seems to me that we are in danger of having a repeat of the Columbine shootings. We may say, "It isn't going to happen here, so we don't have to worry" or, "We can't seem to find who is to blame." So we may go back to sleep until something wakes us up again. I assure you that the next time will be an even more dramatic wake-up call.

The Cost of Failure to Act

Unless we take action to deal with the hidden elements of the culture of violence, the problem will get worse. We will see some of the following:

- The dropout rate as a result of bullying will continue to rise. (It is currently 10 percent).
- The number of high school students who are afraid to go to restrooms at school will increase. (It is now 20 percent of high school students).
- The number of kids who report being bullied will increase. (Currently it is 80 to 90 percent among middle school students).
- The number of kids who stay home to avoid bullying will increase. (Currently, 162,000 students stay home each day because they are afraid to go to school.)
- More short-sighted, reactive solutions, such as installing metal detectors, hiring more police to patrol the halls, and putting in more surveillance cameras, will be tried with no tangible results.
- More school shootings will occur. (64 percent of adults believe it will happen in their own community).
- The government will be forced to intervene and pass restrictive legislation holding schools and parents legally accountable. (A description of a first attempt at this is presented below.)

Bullying and Human Rights

Bill and Rita Head, Georgia parents of a 15-year-old who shot himself in front of his classmates after suffering repeated bullying, have proposed new legislation to better protect our children. As a result, a bill was introduced into the Georgia State Legislature that amends the Georgia Criminal Code to give children the same protection under the law that persons 21 years old and older have.

Currently, the Criminal Code in Georgia, as well as some other states, excludes children from protection under the law concerning five types of violent behavior: simple assaults, simple battery, battery, stalking, and using so called "fighting words" or engaging in disorderly conduct. The Heads also want mandatory posting of the rights of children under the law in all schools and mandatory reporting of violations of these laws by the teachers (Brown, 1999).

This is an attempt to classify bullying and put-downs as violations of the rights of children "to be secure and protected from fear, intimidation and physical harm caused by the activities of violent groups and individuals." This represents an intriguing proposal because, using the standard definitions of assaults and battery, stalking, fighting words, bullying, and put-downs are violations of human rights under the laws that cover adults. The same human rights clearly should be extended to children and youth under 21 years of age. This would get the attention of school officials who until now have essentially turned their backs on bullying and put-downs. If such a law had existed in Colorado, the Columbine shootings may not have occurred. The Juvenile Code in Colorado covers these five categories of violent behavior, but it does not call for posting these laws in schools and it does not call for mandatory reporting by teachers. You might check on the Criminal Code in your state.

Summary

Hidden aspects of the culture of violence that keep it going include the dominator value system, an over-focus on negativity, the pervasiveness of bullying, collective denial of the effects of bullying, the presence of PTSD, and an increase of parental abuse and neglect. These hidden factors must be addressed if we are going to change the culture of violence. The Kindness Campaign is an effective primary prevention program that addresses these hidden elements of the culture of violence in schools and communities.

References

Adler, J. & Springen, K. (1999). How to fight back. *Newsweek,* May 3, 1999, p. 37.

Ainsworth, M. (1989). Attachments beyond infancy. *American Psychologist, 44,* 709–716.

American Psychiatric Association (APA). (1996). *The diagnostic and statistical manual (DSM-IV), (4th ed.).* Washington, DC: American Psychiatric Association Press.

Begley, S. (1999). Why the young kill. *Newsweek,* May 3, 1999 p. 32–37.

Bowlby, J. (1988). *A secure base: Parent-child attachment and healthy human development.* London: Routledge.

Brown, T. (1999, January 18). *The bullying reference*, 1(4), Zanesville, OH: The Broken Toy Project. Retrieved February 6, 1999 from World Wide Web: http:/members.tripod.com/-Ghoul2x/Bully1.html

Brown T. (1999). *The broken toy project*. 846 1/2 McIntire Ave. Zanesville, OH, 43701.

Bully OnLine. (1999). *Web Site of the UK National Workplace Bullying Advice Line*. URL: <www.successunlimited.co.uk/costs.htm>

Campos, J., Barrett, K., et al. (1983). Socioemotional development. In M. M. Haith & J. J. Campos (Eds.), *Handbook of child psychology: Vol. 2. Infancy and psychobiology*. New York: Wiley, pp. 783–915.

Cline, F. (1979). *Understanding and treating the severely disturbed child*. Evergreen, CO: Evergreen Consultants in Human Behavior.

Dube, J. (1999). High school hell. *ABC NEWS.com,* April 24, 1999, p. 1.

Eisler, R. (1987). *The chalice and the blade*. San Francisco: Harper & Row.

Espelage, D., et al., (1999, Aug.). Interviews with middle school students: Bullying, victimization, and contextual factors. Presentation at American Psychological Association Annual Conference, Boston, Aug. 21.

Fried, S., & Fried, P. (1996). *Bullies and victims: Helping your child survive the schoolyard battlefield*. New York: M. Evans & Co.

Gibbs, N., & Roche, T. (1999). The Columbine tapes. *Time,* 154 (25), 40–51.

Grossman, D. (1996). *On killing: The psychological cost of learning to kill in war and society*. New York: Little, Brown & Co.

Grossman, D. (1998). Trained to kill. *Christianity Today*, Aug. 10, 1998, pp. 31–39.

Hawkins, D., Catalano, R., et al. (1992). *Communities that care: Action for drug abuse prevention*. San Francisco: Jossey-Bass.

Heise, L., Ellsberg, M., & Gottemoeller, M. (1999, Dec.). *Ending violence against women.* (Population Reports, Series L, No. 11). Baltimore: Johns Hopkins University, School of Public Health, Population Information Program.

Johnson, D. W., & Johnson, R. (1995). *Teaching students to be peacemakers*. Edina: MN: Interaction Book Co.

Joseph, J. (1999). Sugar, spice and ready to kill. *ABCNEWS.com*, April 28, 1999, pp. 1–2.

Karen, R. (1998). *Becoming attached*. New York: Oxford University Press.

Krause, A. & Haverkamp, B. (1996). Attachment in adult child-older parent relationships: Research, theory, and practice. *Journal of Counseling & Development, 75,* 83–92.

Langer, G. (1999). Students report violent peers. *ABCNEWS.com*, April 26, 1999, pp. 1–2.

Lederer, L., & Varela, S. (1998). *Safe schools, safe students: A guide to violence prevention strategies*. Washington DC: Substance Abuse & Mental Health Services Administration.

Lero, D., Golman, H., et al. (1992). *Parental work patterns and childcare needs* (Catalogue 89-529E) Ottawa: Canadian National Child Care Study.

Magid, K., & McKelvey, C. (1989). *High risk: Children without a conscience*. New York: Bantam Books.

Marano, H., (1995). Big. bad. bully. *Psychology Today*, 28, 50–68.

National Institute for Dispute Resolution. (1999). *Conflict resolution education facts*. URL: <www.CRFnet.org>

Nerenberg, A. (1999). *Road rage*. Web Site URL: <www.roadragenerenberg.com>

Olweus, D. (1993). Victimization by peers: Antecedents and long-term consequences. In K. H. Rubin & J. B. Asendorf (Eds.), *Social withdrawal, inhibition, and shyness in childhood*. Hillside, NJ: Erlbaum.

Olweus, D. (1994). *Bullying at school: What we know and what we can do*. Oxford, UK: Blackwell Publishers.

Paulk, D. et al. (1999). Teacher, peer and self-nominations of bullies and victims of bullying. Presentation at American Psychological Association Annual Conference, Boston, August 21, 1999.

Pearson, J., Cowen, P., et al. (1993). Adult attachment and adult child-older parent relationships. *American Journal of Orthopsychiatry*, 63, 606–613.

Perry, B. (1996a). Aggression and violence: The neurobiology of experience. *AACAP Developmentor*. Spring.

Perry, B. (1996b). Neurodevelopmental adaptations to violence: How children survive the inter-generational vortex of violence. In *Violence and childhood trauma: Understanding and responding to the effects of violence on young children*. Cleveland, OH: Gund Foundation Publishers, 66–80.

Pollack, W. (1998). *Real boys*. New York: Random House.

Portner, J. (1997). Zero-tolerance laws getting a second look. *Education Week on the Web*, March 26.

Prendergast, A. (1999). Doom rules. *Denver Westword*. August 5–11, 1999, pp. 1–16. URL: <westword.com>.

Saunders, C. (1997). When push comes to shove: Dealing with bullies requires adult supervision. *Our Children*, March/April.

Sebastian, S. J. (1996). Domestic violence. In A. L. Harwood-Nuss (Ed.): *Emergency medicine—A comprehensive study guide* (4th ed.). New York: McGraw Hill.

Straus, M. (1994). *Beating the devil out of them*. New York: Lexington Books.

Straus, M & Gelles, R. (1988). How violent are American families? Estimates from the national family violence resurvey and other studies. In G. Hotaling, et al. (Eds.), *Family abuse and its consequences: New directions in research.*

U. S. Department of Education, National Center for Educational Statistics, *Principal/school disciplinarian survey on school violence* (1997). (Fast Response Survey System, and FRSS 63). Washington, DC: Government Printing Office.

Weinhold, B. (1991). *Breaking free of addictive family relationships*. Walpole, NH: Stillpoint Publishing.

Weinhold, B. (Ed.) (1996*). Spreading kindness: A program guide for reducing youth violence in the schools*. Colorado Springs, CO: Kindness Campaign.

Weinhold, B. (1999a). Bullying and school violence. *Counseling Today*, 42(4), 14.

Weinhold, B. (1999b*). Raising kind kids: An activity guide for fostering kindness in families*. Colorado Springs, CO: Kindness Campaign.

Weinhold, B. (Ed.). (2000). *Kind beginnings: An activity guide for fostering kindness in pre-schools*. Colorado Springs, CO: Kindness Campaign.

Weinhold, B. & Weinhold, J. (1998). Conflict resolution: The partnership way in schools. *Counseling & Human Development,* 30 (7), 1–12.

Weinhold, B. & Weinhold, J. (2000). *Conflict resolution: The partnership way*. Denver: Love Publishing.

Teaching Children to Care Rather Than Kill

Radha J. Horton-Parker

It's a typical April morning, and school has begun like always at Columbine High School. With thoughts of graduation, summer vacation, and the vast tomorrow that seems to stretch out endlessly before them, students laugh and converse as the day proceeds. But soon carefree laughter is transformed into terror and tears as two students, armed with guns and grenades, enter the school and begin the massacre that will end the tomorrows of 15 individuals.

The recent tragedy in Littleton, Colorado, which brought immediate reactions of shock and disbelief, has begun to awaken us from the complacency that predominates in our culture. Although violence prevails in movies and video games, popular music is replete with hate-filled lyrics, guns are readily available, and bomb-making recipes abound on the Internet, we never expect our children to commit murder. Yet, when two teenagers from affluent homes with apparently caring parents went on a killing spree in a nice, suburban high school, few of us were spared the realization that major changes are needed in our society.

Although controversy abounds about what should be done, nearly everyone agrees that we must do *something*. Legislation regarding gun control, censorship in the media, greater control of the Internet, fining parents for children's misdeeds, and increased security in the schools—all have been proposed as possible solutions. On a more therapeutic note, mental health professionals have advocated diagnostic procedures to identify students who may be at risk of violent behavior, as well as counseling interventions to help alienated students fit in better with their peers.

135

Even though these ideas have merit, a more efficacious strategy might be to engage in primary prevention in early childhood rather than remediation in adolescence. One untapped resource is the potential of humanistic parenting to engender prosocial behavior in children. *Prosocial behavior,* defined as action intended to benefit others without the expectation of an external reward (Eisenberg, 1988), contrasts with aggression, defined as "behavior aimed at harming another person" (Perry, Perry, & Boldizar, 1990, p. 135). Dave Sanders, the teacher and coach who lost his life while protecting his students during the Columbine massacre, is perhaps the ultimate exemplar of prosocial behavior. In contrast, the student assassins represent extreme cases of aggression.

The key to understanding why some individuals selflessly help their fellow humans while others murder them might be found in early childhood. Much evidence suggests that parents—who serve as children's first models—can be instrumental in assisting children to develop the ability to act thoughtfully and kindly toward others (Eisenberg, 1992). Parental influence is so powerful that one longitudinal study found that 36% of the variance in adult levels of empathy could be explained by the child-rearing practices that the participants had experienced in early childhood (Koestner, Franz, & Weinberger, 1990). This is especially significant in that a meta-analysis of the research revealed that empathy and sympathy were correlated positively with prosocial behavior (Eisenberg & Miller, 1987).

Thus, a firm foundation of prosocial behavior, established when children are young, could be essential to curbing violence in the adolescent years. Perhaps, if parents acquire basic skills in humanistic parenting, today's affectionate toddlers with teddy bears will be deterred from becoming tomorrow's maleficent teens with grenades. The purpose of this chapter is to provide information that counselors can use to assist parents in developing practices that will lead to prosocial outcomes in young children that will last throughout their lives.

Our Culture of Violence

Striking insights into the psychology of extreme interpersonal violence have emerged with the advent of a new field of study: "killology." The foremost authority in this field is Lt. Col. Dave Grossman (1996), a former professor of psychology at West Point and author of the best-selling book, *On Killing.* Grossman maintains that just as AIDS breaks down the body's immune system and leaves it vulnerable to disease, so constant exposure to rampant violence in the media and video games breaks down children's natural aversion to killing, effectively "taking off the safety catch" that keeps fatal aggression psychologically in check.

To support his theories, Grossman recounts the history of the development of techniques by military psychologists to increase the kill rate of soldiers. Definitive evidence collected after the end of World War II showed that only 15% to 20% of combat infantry were willing to fire their weapons. Appalled by these findings, military psychologists began seeking and implementing new training strategies to engender a greater willingness to kill in soldiers. The needed strategies were dis-covered and successfully applied. The fire rate of infantry in Korea rose to 50%, and to more than 90% in Vietnam.

Military trainers accomplished their magic by using three tools: operant condi-tioning, classical conditioning, and social learning, focusing on the imitation of role models. Soldiers are classically conditioned by being made to view films depicting people being injured or killed in increasingly violent ways. As a result, they become able to disassociate themselves emotionally from the fear or revulsion that arises in empathy for another person being hurt or abused. Operant strategies include the use of *human-shaped* pop-up targets on firing ranges and other life-like simulated situa-tions. Soldiers trained in this way learn to target and shoot reflexively, bypassing any potential rational inhibitions, as they are reinforced by seeing their bullets make their marks.

Finally, we can credit the well known stereotype of the drill sergeant as a heroic, ultra-capable, invincible role model for the social learning component of the initia-tives we are discussing. Boot camp was redesigned to be an ever more efficient ini-tiatory rite of passage through which the neophyte soldier's previous value system is stripped away and replaced with a new ethos in which devastating physical aggres-sion and unconditional obedience become the new foundations of self-worth. These qualities are incarnate in the drill sergeant, who becomes a role model and a surro-gate father, brother, and even mother to the troops.

Grossman argues convincingly that the same conditioning techniques used suc-cessfully by the military to train soldiers to kill are present in the films, music, tele-vision programs, and video games that children regularly watch. Hyper-violent films provide an example of classical conditioning at work. The films themselves vie with each other to portray mutilation and murder in ever more graphic detail. Repeated exposure to incrementally more gruesome imagery inevitably desensitizes children and weakens their natural aversion to seeing others harmed. In a kind of *Clockwork Orange* reverse scenario, the enjoyment that derives from sitting in the comfort of a movie theater munching popcorn and enjoying the company of friends becomes paired with the aggression they are witnessing so that observing violence actually comes to evoke a pleasurable state by association.

Similarly, the principles of operant conditioning are powerfully active in chil-dren who immerse themselves in the world of violent video games. As children learn to fire weapons reflexively at pop-up villains, they receive instant reinforcement from seeing characters' heads blown off—or worse. As with films, violent video games tend to incorporate increasingly realistic weapons, wounds, and associated trauma. In some cases, the targets are not bug-eyed monsters but, instead, normal human beings, and the child plays the role of an assassin or a monster.

Through this sort of visual programming, children not only develop "auto-maticity" and learn to see the world through a gunsight, but they also can actually sharpen their shooting skills. Police officers and FBI agents both utilize the same training procedures to develop combat readiness. So effective is this training that "shoot/no shoot" programming was introduced to constrain collateral violence created by officers who receive such training. Of course, video games enjoin no such restraints.

Finally, as children watch powerful action heros successfully defeat their foes, they learn that violence is a rewarding and effective way of problem-solving. Because media characters often are shown killing others for minor slights, youth learn that murder is an acceptable response to injustice, imagined or perceived.

Grossman (1996) also offers readers a thoughtful reappraisal of the actual extent of youth violence occurring in our society. Between 1985 and 1991, the homicide rates for males 15 to 19 years of age increased 154%, with homicide the second leading cause of death for all males in this age group and the first leading cause of death in Black males. As shocking as these statistics are, things actually are significantly worse than they appear. Grossman points out that advanced medical capabilities, such as resuscitation technology, save the lives of many persons who certainly would have died in the past. Grossman cites UCLA professor James Q. Wilson's estimate that if trauma care were the same now as in 1957, the homicide rate would be close to three times what statistics reflect now.

Even though the youth violence rate is higher in the United States than in any other industrialized nation, most industrialized nations having a similar level of media violence have witnessed parallel increases in teen violent activity. The one significant exception to this rapid rise in youth aggression is Japan. Although Japanese children partake of the same violent media influences as other youth, a protective "bubble" immunizes them from acting out the aggression they observe. The key to this phenomenon is theorized to be the incredibly strong sense of interdependence between the individual and the family and social structure that is intrinsic to Japanese culture. Japanese children are taught to engage in prosocial behavior from an early age, and that lesson is reinforced at every stage of life. Perhaps by strengthening our families and helping parents learn to influence their children positively, we, too, may turn the tide of violence in our society.

Parenting Styles

Because fads in parenting come and go, parents and counselors often are left wondering what methods actually lead to the most desirable outcomes in children. The answers may lie in Diana Baumrind's ground-breaking research showing that parenting styles significantly impact children's behavior in ways that may be permanent.

In her landmark study, Baumrind (1967) observed children in a nursery school for 14 weeks. Based on their differing patterns of behavior, she categorized the youngsters into three groups: energetic-friendly children, conflicted-irritable children, and impulsive-aggressive children. Baumrind then interviewed the children's parents and observed them interacting with their children in home and laboratory settings.

On the basis of these observations, Baumrind identified three styles of parenting that appeared to be associated with the differing behavioral patterns in children. She labeled these three parenting styles as authoritarian, permissive, and authoritative. In a longitudinal study of the children from early childhood through adolescence, Baumrind (1991) found that these three parenting styles were associated with specific outcomes, which will be described in the following section.

Using Baumrind's typology of authoritarian, permissive, and authoritative parenting styles as a basis, Maccoby and Martin (1983) added a fourth category—indifferent parenting—and proposed that the four parenting styles could be distinguished by the relative balance of control/ demandingness and warmth/responsiveness present in each.

1. *Control/demandingness* refers to the extent to which parents set high standards and exert firm control to ensure that their children exhibit mature behavior. This continuum represents the extent to which parents insist that their children perform developmentally appropriate tasks that require increasing social and cognitive competence.
2. Warmth/responsiveness refers to the extent to which parents convey affection and acceptance in their communication and are responsive to their children's feelings and needs. This continuum relates to the parental warmth and responsiveness so critical to forming attachment bonds in infancy and in maintaining loving, trusting relationships with children as they mature.

The following description of the four parenting styles is based on the models of Baumrind (1967) and of Maccoby and Martin (1983). Figure 7.1 depicts these styles.

Authoritarian Parents

In the Sutter home, the parents like to think that they "run a tight ship." Frank and Miriam Sutter are strict disciplinarians and do not allow any divergence from the expected norms of behavior. When faced with any resistance from their children, the Sutters quickly exert pressure to produce the desired result. "Do it now or else" is often stated in their home, and the children intimately know that the "else" means either a spanking or a sojourn in their rooms for an extended time. When the children occasionally ask their parents why they have to do something, the inevitable reply is "because we said so," and the children then are told to "just stop complaining and do what we say."

Authoritarian parents are high in control/demandingness, but low in the humanistic qualities of warmth/responsiveness. These parents set rigid standards, demand unquestioning compliance, and allow no opportunities for their children to articulate any concerns they have about their parents' expectations. The parents show little warmth or respect in interactions with their children, and parental authority is absolute. Punishment follows quickly when their children disobey orders, and even though the children might have legitimate needs that are not being met, divergent views are not allowed expression.

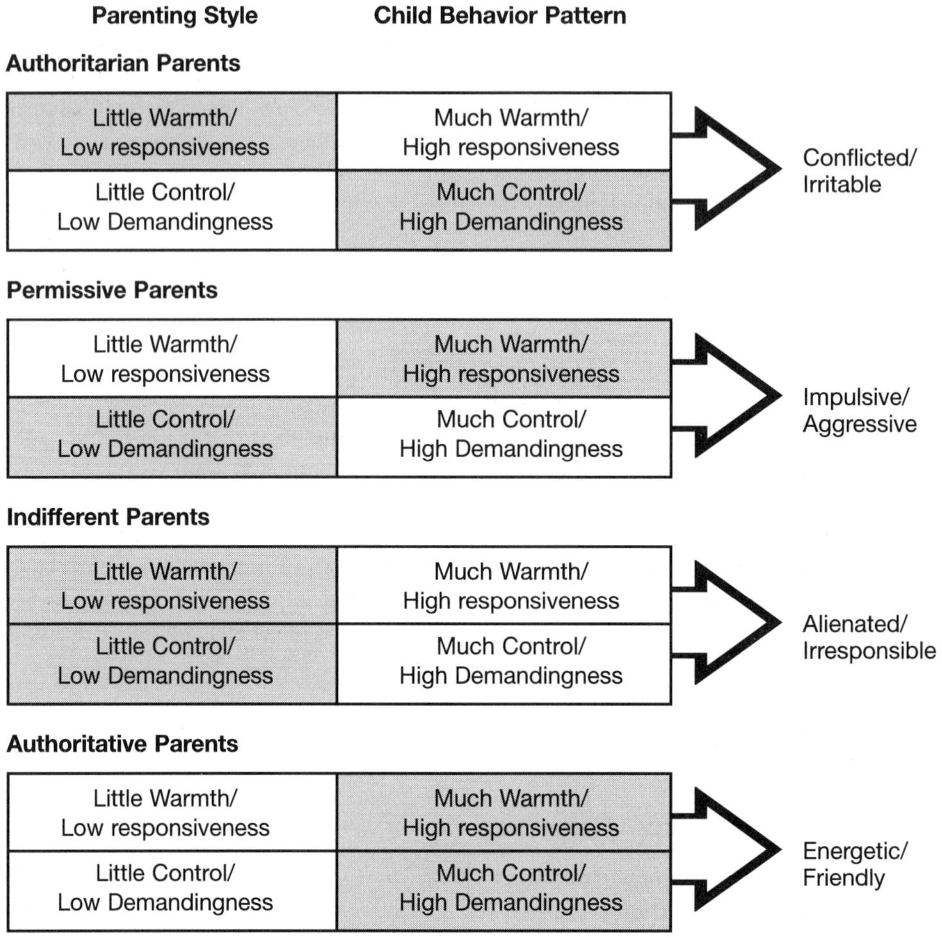

Parenting Style	Child Behavior Pattern	

Authoritarian Parents

Little Warmth/ Low responsiveness	Much Warmth/ High responsiveness	Conflicted/ Irritable
Little Control/ Low Demandingness	Much Control/ High Demandingness	

Permissive Parents

Little Warmth/ Low responsiveness	Much Warmth/ High responsiveness	Impulsive/ Aggressive
Little Control/ Low Demandingness	Much Control/ High Demandingness	

Indifferent Parents

Little Warmth/ Low responsiveness	Much Warmth/ High responsiveness	Alienated/ Irresponsible
Little Control/ Low Demandingness	Much Control/ High Demandingness	

Authoritative Parents

Little Warmth/ Low responsiveness	Much Warmth/ High responsiveness	Energetic/ Friendly
Little Control/ Low Demandingness	Much Control/ High Demandingness	

Shaded areas indicate the applicable styles.

Based on the studies of D. Baumrind, and E. E. Maccoby & J. A. Martin, and related research.

Figure 7.1

Parenting Styles Related to Child Behavior Patterns

Baumrind (1967) found the authoritarian parenting style to be correlated with the child behavioral pattern identified as *conflicted-irritable*. In nursery school, the children of authoritarian parents appeared unhappy, withdrawn, mistrustful, and socially anxious. When frustrated with their playmates, these preschoolers often responded with hostility. The negative impact of authoritarian parenting did not end when the last days of childhood had passed, but instead extended into adolescence. The effects were more pronounced for boys than girls. The adolescent sons of authoritarian parents were socially incompetent, unfriendly, and lacking in initiative and self-confidence (Baumrind, 1991).

Other studies also suggested that authoritarian parenting produced children with low self-esteem who lacked self-confidence and spontaneity (Coopersmith, 1967; Lamborn, Mounts, Steinberg, & Dornbusch, 1991; Lempers, Clark-Lempers, & Simons, 1989). Adolescents from authoritarian homes were obedient but lacking in competence (Steinberg, 1990). When corporal punishment was employed as a central component of authoritarian parenting, the results were especially detrimental. Children developed aggressive behaviors themselves when they were exposed to spanking and other harsh disciplinary practices (Dodge, Bates, & Pettit, 1990; Weiss, Dodge, Bates, & Pettit, 1992).

Permissive Parents

The Jenkins family is at the end of the continuum opposite from the Sutters. Fran and Jake Jenkins allow their children total freedom and shower them with compliments and praise. These parents rarely discipline or set limits for their children and, instead, encourage them to do whatever they wish. The children face no real consequences for failing to fulfill parental requests and often are unaware that their parents have any expectations for them other than to be themselves.

In situations in which one of the Jenkins children is asked to help with a household task, the child typically objects ("I can't. I'm busy playing this video game, and I can't stop.") When the child resists, the parents usually just do the chore themselves so their child can continue to play. Sometimes they even say, "Don't worry about it, honey. You're busy, so we'll take care of it. Go ahead and finish your game."

As this illustration shows, permissive parenting contrasts starkly with authoritarian parenting in that it is low in control/demandingness but high in warmth/responsiveness. Permissive parents offer unconditional love and acceptance but fail to provide adequate guidelines for mature, responsible behavior. Instead, they allow children to have greater freedom than is appropriate for their developmental levels and permit them to make choices that require more maturity than they possess.

Although permissive parents often believe that they are nurturing their children's growth, they could be unintentionally cultivating their children's self-indulgence and fostering a lack of social concern. By showering youngsters with unlimited material possessions and expecting nothing in return, some permissive parents think they are teaching their children to be correspondingly generous and loving. In reality, they likely are teaching their children to think only of themselves. Because this approach affords so little structure or consistency, prosocial behavior in children is not a likely outcome of permissive parenting.

Baumrind (1967) noted that the preschoolers of permissive parents exhibited the behavioral pattern categorized as *impulsive-aggressive*. These children not only had difficulty controlling their impulses but also exhibited highly immature behavior.

Lacking confidence in themselves, they were extremely demanding and dependent on adults (Baumrind, 1971). Although some of the children were creative and friendly, others were socially inept. They frequently gave up when they encountered any frustration in their nursery school tasks and became aggressive when other children's needs conflicted with their own. Later research showed that adolescents from permissive homes were likely to be self-confident but to have higher levels of substance abuse and more problems in school (Steinberg, 1990).

Authoritative Parents

Ike and Samantha Freeman clearly state what they want their children to do and how they expect them to behave. The children know that disobedience will have consequences directly related to their misbehavior. Sometimes, however, the children have valid reasons for being excused from doing expected tasks or for asking for special considerations. In these cases, the children voice their concerns, and their parents listen respectfully.

Recently one of the Freeman children asked to be allowed to stay up an hour and a half later than her customary bedtime on a school night to watch a television show about a topic she had studied in her science class. Although Ike and Samantha recognized their daughter's interest as being legitimate, they let her know that they thought it was important for her to get adequate rest. After discussing the issue, the Freemans agreed that everyone's needs would be met if the parents were to tape the show and let the daughter watch it immediately after school the next day. Although this solution meant that Ike had to make an unplanned trip to the store to purchase a blank videotape, everyone was satisfied with the outcome.

Unlike the former two parenting styles, authoritative parenting is high in both control/demandingness and warmth/responsiveness. The Freemans could have flatly denied their daughter's request and said, "You know the rules—go to bed," as the Sutters would have. Or the Freemans could have given in to whatever their daughter wished to do and said, "Sure, sweetie—we wouldn't want you to miss your show," as the Jenkinses would have. The Freemans, however, chose the authoritative approach of maintaining their parental authority while also ensuring that their daughter felt respected and that her concerns were adequately addressed. Authoritative parents set firm limits for children's behavior and also exhibit warmth and flexibility in responding to their children's needs while encouraging them to be involved in problem solving.

The children of authoritative parents exhibited the behavioral pattern that Baumrind (1967) labeled as *energetic-friendly*. Of all the children in the nursery school, this type was found to be the most well adjusted. These preschoolers showed friendliness, confidence, self-control, and high achievement. In addition, they appeared to be happy and were less likely than their peers to engage in disruptive and defiant behaviors. For these reasons, the authoritative approach is associated with the best outcomes for children. As adolescents, the children of authoritative parents continued to exhibit these positive qualities (Baumrind, 1991). Other studies have yielded similar findings, showing that children experience the most positive outcomes when parents practice child-centered patterns of discipline accompanied by clearly communicated demands, careful monitoring, and an atmosphere of acceptance (Maccoby, 1984; Maccoby & Martin, 1983).

Indifferent Parents

The Schmidts pay little attention to their children. Struggling to survive on their meager incomes, they worry more about having enough money to pay for groceries and rent than about what their children are doing. George and Bertha each work two part-time jobs with schedules that change from week to week, so their children often are left at home alone. Sometimes a teenage girl from the neighborhood watches the children, but when she is not available, the Schmidts have their own 10-year-old son attend to his four siblings.

Because their jobs are so demanding and frequently require them to work late-night shifts, George and Bertha are easily irritated when their children attempt to get their attention. The parents often respond angrily if their children make requests, as happened recently when the 5-year-old asked her mother to help her remove a splinter from her finger. Trying to get a few hours rest before going to her second job, Bertha looked at her daughter and said, "Go away. Can't you see I'm trying to sleep?" No one else was around at the time, so the daughter did go away—and began walking to her grandmother's house, 3 miles away. Concerned neighbors saw the little girl walking alone on the road and called Child Protective Services.

Indifferent parenting lies at the opposite end of the continuum from the authoritative style because it is low in both control/demandingness and warmth/responsiveness. Although Baumrind did not study this group, Maccoby and Martin (1983) described indifferent parents as being both lax in discipline and lacking in warmth. These parents show little concern for their children's welfare, are disengaged from parenting, and do not monitor their children's behavior. As a result of this parental neglect, children fail to form attachment bonds and suffer from social incompetence and low self-esteem. Indifferent parental behavior has been linked to children's non-compliance, aggression, delinquency, truancy, precocious sexuality, and alcohol problems in adolescence and adulthood (Lamborn, Mounts, Steinberg, & Dornbusch, 1991; Patterson, 1982; Pulkkinen, 1982). We therefore could describe the child behavior pattern resulting from indifferent parenting as *alienated/irresponsible*. The children of indifferent parents generally have the worst outcomes of all.

The Need for Humanistic Parenting

Because authoritative parenting has been associated with the best and most prosocial outcomes in children, counselors might help to prevent violence indirectly in the teen years by teaching parents how to interact skillfully with their children authoritatively in early childhood. Learning humanistic, authoritative parenting techniques will enable parents to respond to their children's needs respectfully while setting high behavioral standards and maintaining firm control. This balance of control and respect should provide a firm foundation for fostering positive outcomes in children and for building trusting parent-child relationships that will endure throughout the turbulence of adolescence.

Skillful parenting is not guaranteed by virtue of being able to successfully procreate. Although most parents probably have good intentions toward their children, people tend to adopt a child-rearing style similar to that of their own parents—which may or may not be conducive to helping children learn to care about others as well as themselves. More than in the past, effective parenting is critically needed.

In the remainder of this chapter, I will attempt to address the parenting-skills deficit so prevalent in our society today by presenting ideas that counselors can share with parents to promote prosocial behavior in children. The approach, which I call humanistic parenting, consists of strategies drawn from behavioral research and popular parent-training programs that adopt an authoritative child-rearing style (Horton-Parker, 1998). These humanistic parenting techniques, which can be imparted to parents via workshops, counseling sessions, and newsletters, should provide a solid basis for prosocial behavior as children mature. Because I believe that workshops can be especially beneficial for parent training, I also will include some ideas for activities that counselors can use with parents in a large-group setting.

Before introducing the techniques of humanistic parenting, I would like to point out several points. First, although I use the term "parent" throughout this chapter, it is meant to refer to any adult serving in a parental or caregiving role to a child. Because families come in many forms today, "parents" refers to any individuals serving in a parental capacity, regardless of whether they are biologically or legally related to the children they are rearing.

A second note concerns the exclusive emphasis I have placed on parenting in early childhood. Although all of the techniques contained in this chapter can be adapted with older children, my focus is on parenting the very young. Because early childhood is critical to future development, I believe that counselors can have the most impact by helping parents become more effective during children's formative years. Finding that prevention is preferable to remediation, I encourage counselors to work with the parents of preschoolers to help them develop trusting, loving parent-child relationships and exert consistent, firm control while their children are still highly receptive.

Teaching Children to Care: Humanistic Parenting

Components of humanistic parenting include respectful communication, passive listening, using I-messages, setting limits, giving choices, catching children being good, confronting misbehavior, applying logical consequences, using time-out, conducting family meetings, and conveying love.

Respectful Communication

Mental health professionals sometimes suggest that parents speak to their children as though they were their best friends. Conversely, it is interesting to consider how it might be if we spoke to our best friends as though they were our children. The following dialogue is an imaginary conversation with a couple, Mike and Judy, who have come for dinner:

> So you finally arrived! Do you have any idea what time it is? We had about given up on you two. Mike, don't you ever wear your watch? Maybe you think you can just show up any time you please. Well, think again! Now go wash your hands and we'll be ready to eat. Judy, don't drip water on the floor like you did last time. We're tired of cleaning up your mess. Mike, remember to put the toilet seat down after you use it. This isn't a bus station..
>
> Okay, dinner is served! Come to the table and have a seat. Oh, Judy, don't sit there. You and Mike can't sit next to each other tonight because you might get into another fight. We're sitting between you two so you'll stay out of trouble. You know you can't make it through a whole meal without ruining it for everyone with your bickering. Judy, wipe that nasty look off your face and do what you're told. We don't want any complaints about the seating arrangement.
>
> We're so glad you could come, since we haven't seen you for a while. Mike, how do you like your new job? Make sure that you don't oversleep too often and lose this one like you did the last one. It's about time for you to grow up and be responsible! Judy, you had said you were going on a diet. How's that going? You know, you could actually be quite pretty if you weren't so overweight!
>
> Mike, please pass the gravy. Oh, no! You spilled it again. You're such a klutz! Why do you always have to be so clumsy? Judy, what's your problem? Stop glaring at us and try to be pleasant for once in your life.
>
> Who's ready for dessert? None for you, Mike, until you finish the rest of your spinach. Judy, you may have a small piece of pie, but go easy on the ice cream, or you'll never stop looking like a big, fat pig!
>
> Well, you two certainly haven't had much to say this evening. You'd better just go home and go to bed. Come back when you can behave more like ladies and gentlemen!

This humorous example illustrates the less than respectful manner in which parents communicate with their children. While not intending to hurt their children, many parents issue directives in ways that sometimes are demeaning or insensitive to children's feelings. Disrespectful communication does not convey the warmth and responsiveness that are essential ingredients of humanistic parenting.

In contrast, when parents listen empathically and communicate respectfully, children not only feel loved and valued but also have the opportunity to observe empathy in action as their parents demonstrate. Because children imitate much of what they witness in their parents, they likely will acquire the ability to respond empathically and respectfully themselves simply by emulating that behavior. On the other hand, parental responses such as threatening, commanding, lecturing, and name-calling create roadblocks to communication and produce defensiveness in children by conveying a lack of acceptance. The following scenario exemplifies the differences in parental responding to children's expressed feelings:

When Christy Sutter came crying to her mother because her baby brother had bitten her again, Mrs. Sutter responded, "Don't be such a baby yourself. He doesn't know any better, so just ignore him and stop whining."

When a similar situation occurred in the Freeman home, however, it met with a very different response. Mrs. Freeman stopped what she was doing to listen to her daughter and replied, "That must have really hurt when he bit you, and I can tell you're frustrated because this isn't the first time he's done it. Can you tell me more about what happened?"

Passive Listening

To avoid creating roadblocks to communication, Gordon (1970) recommends that parents use passive listening (silence), verbal and nonverbal acknowledgment responses (nodding, "uh-huh"), door openers ("Could you tell me more?" "How do you feel about that?"), and active listening, which demonstrates accurate empathy by reflecting both the content and the affect of the child's message (e.g., "You're disappointed that we can't afford to buy you that game.") Empathic listening validates children's feelings and enables them to assume responsibility for their own emotions.

I-Messages

Learning to use I-messages rather than you-messages is beneficial in communicating with children. Gordon (1970) offers a simple formula for constructing effective I-messages: "When you _____, I feel _____ because _____" The first blank is to be filled in with the child's *behavior*, the second with the *emotion* the parent experiences in conjunction with the given behavior, and the third with the *reason* the parent feels that way. For example, a parent might say, "When you interrupt me while I'm talking, I feel frustrated because I don't get to finish what I'm saying." This message is likely to be far more productive than other remarks that could be said to the child, such as "Shut up when I'm talking," or "Be quiet, blabbermouth!"

Setting Limits

In addition to responding to children warmly and respectfully, authoritative parenting involves setting clear behavioral limits that provide structure and consistency.

Parents should be kind and firm in their interactions with children while clearly communicating behavioral expectations (Nelson, Lott, & Glenn, 1993). Behavioral expectations should be appropriate to children's developmental stages, and it is normal for children to test the limits as they strive for increased autonomy (Brazelton, 1992).

For example, although a 6-year-old would be expected to know that hitting another child is wrong, a 2-year-old might hit playmates as a way of getting their attention or as a means of social interaction. Although limits should be set with both children, parental reaction to the 2-year-old should take into account that the child's behavior might have been exploratory rather than hostile in nature.

When setting limits, parents should state clearly what constitutes unacceptable behavior, as well as what substitute behavior will be accepted (Ginott, 1971). For example, telling the 6-year-old, "Other children are not for hitting, but you may hit this pillow if you are angry" provides clear guidelines for what will and will not be accepted. Similarly, the 2-year-old might be instructed, "Playmates are not for hitting, but you can touch them gently like a butterfly if you want to say hi or get them to look at you."

Giving Choices

To honor and nurture children's growing sense of autonomy, parents should allow children to choose between at least two acceptable alternatives whenever possible (Ginott, 1971; Nelson et al., 1993). With very young children, the choices have to be limited—for example, "You may come and eat dinner when you are called, or you may wait until breakfast tomorrow to eat." Giving children choices enables them to assume responsibility and to learn that choices have consequences.

Catching Them Being Good

Rather than waiting for children to misbehave and reprimanding them, noticing children's appropriate behavior and praising them is more effective. When children receive positive reinforcement, such as parental approval, for appropriate behavior, they are more likely to increase the behavior and to develop high self-esteem. Parents can easily show approval for their children's behavior through words, such as "Good job!" and gestures, such as a gentle touch, loving hug, approving smile, or friendly wink.

If the given behavior is prosocial in nature, parents might articulate to the child *why* his or her actions were desirable. For example, a father might say to his son, "I really liked the way you just helped your little sister pick up her toys, because that let her know that you care about her."

Confronting Misbehavior

A common mistake that parents make is talking too much and taking too many opportunities to remind their children about what they are expected to do. As many mothers have painfully discovered, children quickly learn to ignore nagging parents as though they were noisy gnats. For this reason, it is more effective for parents to follow through on enforcing rules by taking kind, firm action than by engaging in incessant nagging or punishing (Nelson et al., 1993).

For example, if a young child refuses to stop playing outside and come inside when called, the parent could simply state, "Time to come in," and take the child by the hand into the house. If the child resists, the parent could provide a limited choice, such as, "We need to get ready to go to your grandmother's house, so would you rather get dressed first or pack your toys?"

As mentioned previously, I-messages are also helpful for parents to let children know how their behavior is affecting others (Gordon, 1970; Popkin, 1993). For example, a parent might say, "When you don't come when I call you, I feel annoyed because I have to stop what I'm doing to go and get you."

Using Logical Consequences

When children misbehave discipline is required, and parents must decide what to do. Although punishment sometimes brings an end to a given undesirable behavior, it often is accompanied by unwanted side effects. For example, when his mother yells at him for spitting on his older sibling who has called him a nasty name, a little boy might stop ejecting saliva on his big sister but might smash her porcelain horse instead. Corporal punishment, such as spanking, can be detrimental because children could learn to imitate the aggression they have experienced as they interact with others. Even subtle forms of punishment, such as ridicule and humiliation, can damage the parent/child relationship and destroy trust.

A viable method of discipline that avoids the negative effects of punishment is logical consequences. Logical consequences are actions that logically follow from the child's behavior but that are not arbitrarily punitive (Dinkmeyer & McKay, 1973; Popkin, 1993; Nelson, 1987; Nelson et al., 1993).

To be effective, logical consequences must be composed of the "three *R's*": They must be directly *related* to the child's behavior, *respectful* of the child, and *reasonable* to both child and parent (Nelson et al., 1993).

For example, if a child draws a picture on the wall with a crayon after being told that paper is for drawing, a logical consequence would be for the child to help scrub the markings off the wall. This logical consequence is related directly to the child's misbehavior and is respectful and reasonable. On the other hand, sentencing the child to a week without television for this transgression would not be related to the offense, to call the child "a moron who thinks he's Picasso" would not be respectful, and to expect the child to wash all the walls in the entire house would not be reasonable.

Logical consequences can be especially effective if parents enlist children's help in planning them before misbehavior occurs. When children are involved directly in discussing what the consequences should be for not doing what is expected, they will be much less likely to feel that they are being punished unfairly when consequences are applied. For example, a parent might ask a child, "What should be a logical consequence for splashing water on the floor as you play with your toys in the bathtub?"

Using Time-Out

When children are actively engaging in misbehavior, time-out is another disciplinary strategy that parents can employ. Time-out typically consists of removing the child from the situation in which the problematic behavior is occurring, for a short time appropriate to the child's developmental level. The child could be placed in a separate room or simply asked to sit in a chair in the same room in a designated spot away from where he or she was misbehaving.

Time-out also may consist of the parent withdrawing his or her attention from the child for a specific period. Four minutes was found to be an effective length of time for 4- to 6-year-olds, and a longer duration of up to 30 minutes could be used with older children (Howard, 1996; Roberts & Powers, 1990). Parents should explain that the purpose of time-out is to give children a chance to calm down, and that they can return when they have worked through some of their feelings and are more in control of their behavior (Nelson et al., 1993). Time-outs must be brief, and expressions of affection are important when children return. A hug and a caring message will let children know that they are loved but that they must develop the ability to behave appropriately. For example, parents might say, "I love you, but I can't let you do this. Someday you'll learn to stop yourself, and then I won't need to stop you" (Brazelton, 1992, p. 253).

Conducting Family Meetings

Weekly family meetings provide an invaluable means of addressing issues and allowing family members to brainstorm solutions to family problems. Because these meetings should be democratic in nature, leadership rotates from week to week, and all family members are allowed to raise issues. Solutions are reached by consensus rather than by majority vote, and each person in the group is allowed to give input and play an essential role in the decision-making process (Nelson, 1987; Nelson et al., 1993).

Family meetings also can be used to discuss the tasks that have to be accomplished during the week and to delegate responsibilities for attending to household chores (Eyre & Eyre, 1994). The main purpose of family meetings, however, should be to address issues that arise in the family and to resolve conflicts between family members rather than simply assigning chores (Dreikurs, 1968). For example, a family meeting might focus on a younger child's resentment that an older sibling is allowed more freedom or an older child's frustration with a younger sibling always demanding to tag along.

Conveying Love

Finally, parents must let children know that they are deeply loved and valued so they will develop high self-esteem (Brazelton, 1992). Each child should receive some special time alone with each parent every week (Nelson et al., 1993). The quality of the time spent together is more important than its quantity.

Family rituals provide an excellent means for busy parents to maximize limited time with their children and to achieve high-quality interactions with them (Parker, 1999; Parker & Horton, 1996). The rituals may be simple or elaborate, and may be short and occur daily or longer and reserved for special occasions or unique needs. Reading a bedtime story, giving a goodbye kiss, and saying "Good morning—I love you!" are all simple rituals that parents can perform daily to strengthen their bonds with their children. Other rituals, such as attending religious services or having Sunday dinner together, can be conducted at certain times during the week; and seasonal rituals, such as going trick-or-treating or exploding fireworks, might happen just once a year.

In addition to developing rituals to celebrate special events, such as birthdays and holidays, parents can create rituals to address family issues, such as dealing with grief, facing transitions, and healing from emotional wounds. For example, planting a tree to celebrate the birthday of a recently deceased loved one can help to alleviate some of the pain the family is experiencing and allow family members to express their feelings and support one another. Although family rituals might seem insignificant at the time, they often comprise some of our most lasting and important childhood memories and can be a powerful means of conveying love.

Teaching Children to Engage in Prosocial Behavior

In addition to adopting a humanistic parenting style, parents can employ specific strategies to promote prosocial behavior in children. The development of prosocial behavior can be cultivated through a variety of methods, such as modeling, induction, didactic instruction, and assigning responsibility for tasks.

Modeling

One of the best ways by which parents can help children learn to treat others with care and respect is to demonstrate these behaviors themselves. Research has shown that children exposed to models that demonstrated altruistic behavior were more likely to exhibit similar behaviors themselves, especially if the children were given an explanation for *why* the behavior was performed and that the act was done to help another person in distress (Yarrow, Scott, & Waxler, 1973). For example, the caregiver could say to the child, "He's upset because he spilled his drink and doesn't have any more, so I'm going to help him feel better by giving him some of mine."

In addition to observing models who demonstrate altruistic behaviors and giving a verbal rationale for doing them, children need to be allowed to practice these behaviors themselves. One study showed that 12-month-old infants were more likely to share things with their mothers if they had been exposed previously to models who both shared objects with them and asked them to share in return (Hay &

Murray, 1982). By asking children to share back with them, parents also teach children about the reciprocal nature of relationships.

When considering the effects of modeling on children's development, another issue that must be addressed is the influence of the media. Some television shows with altruistic models, such as Mr. Rogers, have been found to increase prosocial behavior in children (Huston et al., 1992). Unfortunately, however, children have many more opportunities to observe aggression than altruism in the media, and the influence of viewing violence begins early. Research shows that children as young as 15 months of age copy the aggressive acts of television characters (Centerwall, 1992). Young children are especially vulnerable to the effects of viewing violence because of their limited conceptual understanding of what actually is happening and the consequences of the action. For example, aggressive characters might appear to be attractive and powerful to young children who do not recognize the antisocial ramifications of their behavior. Similarly, the true impact of action figures killing others might have little meaning for preschoolers who do not understand either the finality of death or the fictional nature of the characters.

For these reasons, parents have to carefully monitor the shows children watch and the video games they play. All shows and games that consist primarily of gratuitous violence should be avoided, as they have the potential to teach children to behave aggressively and callously toward others. Even shows that are mostly acceptable sometimes contain momentary displays of aggression. Parents can counteract some of the negative influence of such media violence by watching the shows with their children and discussing with them the impact of the characters' actions on others and their own feelings.

Induction

Just as parents need to provide a verbal explanation while modeling altruistic behaviors, giving a verbal rationale is also helpful as they apply discipline for their children's antisocial actions. Induction refers to the the act of explaining the consequences of actions and suggesting solutions to interpersonal dilemmas. This promotes the development of children's inductive reasoning and expands their capacity to understand how their behavior impacts others and to empathize. For example, a mother might say to her young child, "When you hit me, it hurts and I don't like being with you when you hurt me. I'm going away from you until you can stop hitting me." The mother's explanation allows the child to understand that hitting causes pain to another person, and thus to develop empathy.

Because the ability to empathize with others is a prerequisite to altruism, induction provides a foundation for prosocial behavior. Many studies have confirmed the positive relationship between parental inductions and prosocial behavior in children (Brody & Schaffer, 1982; Dekovic & Janssens, 1992; Karylowski, 1982; Krevans & Gibbs, 1996; Moore & Eisenberg, 1984; Radke-Yarrow, Zahn-Waxler, & Chapman, 1983).

Didactic Instruction

Although lecturing children does not often bring the desired results, parents may find that providing them with moral instruction does foster prosocial behavior. One study showed that children as young as 15 to 20 months of age were more likely to show sympathy toward or attempt to help another child in distress when their mothers frequently explained to them how their behaviors affect other children (Zahn-Waxler, Radke-Yarrow, & King, 1979). Several other studies suggest that moral instruction such as, "You ought to make a get-well card to help your aunt feel better because she's very sick," can be as effective as modeling in eliciting prosocial behavior in children (Grusec, Saas-Korsaak, & Simutis, 1978; Rice & Grusec, 1975).

Didactic instruction is most effective when parents verbalize reasons for acting altruistically that evoke empathy or sympathy in children, and least effective when parents use coercive overtones or threats to pressure children. In the above example, pointing out the aunt's sickness is likely to evoke the child's sympathy and lead to prosocial behavior. In contrast, telling the child, "You'd better make a get-well card for your aunt or no television tonight," is likely to lead to resistance and to elicit little regard for the aunt's welfare.

Assigning Responsibility for Tasks

Another strategy that parents can use to nurture prosocial behavior is to make their children responsible for household tasks at a young age. Cross-cultural research in India, Kenya, Japan, Mexico, and the Philippines indicates that children from societies that make youth responsible for major domestic tasks, such as caring for younger siblings, develop more prosocial behaviors than their peers in cultures that do not promote such active involvement (Whiting & Edwards, 1988). By assisting others, children learn to think of themselves as helpful people and to develop increased prosocial behavior (Eisenberg et al., 1987).

In the process of carrying out family tasks, children discover how others feel, experience reinforcement such as parental approval, develop a sense of personal competence, and acquire a repertoire of prosocial skills they can use in the future (Eisenberg & Murphy, 1995). On the other hand, children who are given few responsibilities are more likely to have an underdeveloped ability to be helpful and to recognize the needs and rights of others.

Parents can foster children's aptitude for altruism and concern for others by establishing routines in which all family members participate in doing chores. Routines can be planned in the weekly family meeting, and visual aids, such as a pictorial chart on the refrigerator, can be used to remind each person of his or her tasks (Nelson, Lott, & Glenn, 1993). For example, the family can set up a house-cleaning routine in which each person is in charge of specific tasks, such as vacuuming, dusting, washing windows, and mopping floors.

Routines can be especially beneficial for children if the whole family performs the tasks together at a designated time during the week. Working together with parents and siblings not only helps to ensure that the tasks are accomplished but also promotes a sense of family unity and esprit de corps. Through this group effort, children can learn the tremendous value of assisting others to achieve the common good.

A common question that parents have concerns the types of tasks young children can be assigned. Children's chores must be age-appropriate, but even preschoolers can participate in family routines and be responsible for a variety of tasks (Nelson et al., 1993). For example:

- ■ 2- to 3-year-olds can do simple chores such as putting away their toys, sweeping the floor, folding socks, putting magazines in a rack, helping put groceries on lower shelves, unloading utensils from the dishwasher, clearing their own place at the table, and dressing themselves
- ■ 4-year-olds can put groceries away, dust furniture, feed pets, bring in the mail, prepare cold cereal, and help with tasks such as vacuuming, making the beds, filling the dishwasher, and yardwork
- ■ 5-year-olds can accomplish more advanced tasks, such as cleaning their rooms, scrubbing sinks and toilets, cleaning mirrors and windows, taking out garbage, making their own sandwiches, folding clean clothes and putting them away, and helping with meal planning and grocery shopping.

As children grow and mature, the variety of tasks they can be assigned expands, and they can be expected to assume more responsibility in performing family routines.

A Workshop for Parents

Although many avenues can be pursued in providing information to parents—such as written materials, family counseling sessions, and consultation—I particularly like working with parents using a workshop format. The educational nature of workshops reduces much of the stigma associated with asking for help and also provides a means for parents to see that others have similar concerns. Parenting sometimes is a lonely proposition, and parents can easily inflict guilt on themselves by assuming that everyone else knows how to do it right while they continue to struggle.

The length and format of parenting workshops should be determined by the needs of the participants, but conducting more than one session may be desirable. After attending a parenting workshop, parents can benefit from participating in support groups to reinforce each other as they practice the skills they have acquired.

In beginning the parenting workshop, I like to mention that it seems somewhat ironic that we must pass both written and performance tests to drive a car, yet no prerequisites or requirements prepare us for functioning in perhaps the most important and difficult role there is—being a parent. I emphasize that none of us are born knowing how to be perfect parents and that most of us probably are prepared inadequately for the challenges that seem to arise constantly. I then commend them for seeking help and for wanting to become better at what they do.

To introduce the topic of parenting styles, I ask parents to think about their own parents' child-rearing practices. Questions to be considered might include:

How do you feel about the way you were raised?

How strict were your parents?

What means of discipline did they use?

How did you feel about your parents when they disciplined you?

How consistently did they apply discipline?

How did each parent's method of discipline compare and contrast with each other?

What were their expectations regarding your behavior?

How responsive were they to your issues?

To what extent were you able to confide in your parents and feel understood?

Which parent were you more likely to confide in, and why?

What were some of the things you liked about the way you were parented?

If you could have changed anything about the parenting you received, what would it have been? Why would you have changed that?"

Finally, I like to ask, "How much similarity is there between how you were raised and the way that you are trying to parent your children?"

By considering questions like the above, parents begin to gain insight into the impact of parenting practices on children from a personal perspective. Sharing these perceptions with others in small groups provides a valuable means of gaining first-hand information about varying child-rearing styles and to discover that others have had quite different experiences. For partners to realize that some of their difficulties in disciplining their children stem from their own experiences in their families-of-origin can be illuminating.

In processing the information derived from this exercise, I point out that although certain forms of harsh discipline can control misbehavior effectively, these can have lasting adverse emotional consequences for children. Similarly, lack of parental control might seem desirable as a child but could have a less than positive impact on a child's overall development. Some adults who were reared by strict parents veer toward extreme permissiveness with their own children, which results in a lack of balance not unlike that of their parents.

After presenting a description of the parenting approaches and asking parents to consider which style their family-of-origin resembles and which is most like their own, I begin to explore the issue of discipline. Parents are asked to volunteer examples of misbehavior that they have found to be challenging to change in their children. In discussing these problem behaviors, I like to have them give a brief description of a specific incident in which the misbehavior occurred, what the parent did to change the behavior, and how the child responded to the disciplinary action. The behavior, the disciplinary action, and the child's response can be listed on a flipchart. After parents have volunteered a number of examples, they can be asked, "How satisfied were you with the outcome of your disciplinary action?" I then tell parents that we will return to these examples later.

As I present the techniques of humanistic parenting, I give parents opportunities to practice skills such as empathic listening, using I-messages, and giving choices in dyads or small groups. Handouts with scenarios can be provided, and the attendees can be asked to practice responding using the skills they have just learned. Brainstorming logical consequences for various problem behaviors is another excellent exercise that the workshop participants can practice with others in a small group. Their responses have to be processed so that the logical consequences adhere to the 3 Rs and are not punitive in nature.

To introduce the strategies for developing prosocial behavior, I first ask parents how they were taught to consider the needs of others and to act kindly toward them. I then ask them to volunteer any examples of altruistic behavior they have observed in their children. I also inquire if they have any ideas regarding what prompted each instance of altruism and, if so, how the parent responded. At this point, I reemphasize the importance of catching children being good and reinforcing desirable behavior, especially if it is prosocial in nature.

After concluding the discussion regarding engendering prosocial behavior, I return to the examples of misbehavior on the flipchart. Parents can be asked to use the skills they have practiced and the information they have received to brainstorm alternative ideas for dealing with each incident listed on the chart. The possible solutions and their probability for success can be processed with the whole group and fine-tuned to achieve the best possible outcome. Finally, parents can be asked to use what they have learned in the workshop to develop and commit to a simple plan to address at least one parenting issue they have encountered with their children.

Conclusion

Parents—who are children's first models—are key to instilling altruistic attitudes and prosocial behaviors in the generation of tomorrow. When parents provide a nurturing environment that abounds with both limits and love, children not only learn the art of relationship but also have opportunities to accept responsibility for their own behaviors and to develop high self-esteem.

The respectful and caring interactions that parents have with their children offer a blueprint for these youngsters to use as they develop their own modes of relating to others. By helping children understand the impact of their actions on others and develop empathy for others' distress, parents can help to prevent their children from committing travesties such as the one that occurred at Columbine High School. The isolation and alienation that fuel such desperate acts of interpersonal destruction can be displaced by the altruism and self-respect that enable us all to live up to our highest potential.

References

Baumrind, D. (1967). Child care practices anteceding three patterns of preschool behavior. *Genetic Psychology Monographs, 75,* 43–88.

Baumrind, D. (1971). Current patterns of parental authority. *Developmental Psychology Monograph, 4,* 1–103.

Baumrind, D. (1991). The influence of parenting style on adolescent competence and substance use. *Journal of Early Adolescence, 11,* 56–95.

Bombeck, E. (1974). Etiquette lesson. *The Reader's Digest.*

Brazelton, T. B. (1992). *Touchpoints: Your child's emotional and behavioral development.* New York: Addison-Wesley.

Brody, G. H., & Schaffer, D. R. (1982). Contributions of parents and peers to children's moral socialization. *Developmental Review, 2,* 31–75.

Centerwall, B. S. (1992). Children, television, and violence. In Schwartz, D. F. (Ed.), *Children and violence* (Report of the 23rd Ross Roundtable on Critical Approaches to Common Pediatrics Problems. Columbus, OH: Ross Laboratories.

Coopersmith, S. (1967). *The antecedents of self-esteem.* San Francisco: Freeman.

Dekovic, M., & Janssens, J. M. A. M. (1992). Parents' child-rearing style and child's sociometric status. *Developmental Psychology, 28,* 925–932.

Dinkmeyer, D., & McKay, G. (1973). *Raising a responsible child: Practical steps to successful family relationships.* New York: Simon & Schuster.

Dodge, K. A., Bates, J. E., & Pettit, G. D. (1990). Mechanisms in the cycle of violence. *Science, 250,* 1678–1683.

Dreikurs, R. (1968). *The new approach to discipline.* New York: Dutton.

Eisenberg, N. (1988). The development of prosocial and aggressive behavior. In M. E. Lamb & M. H. Bornstein (Eds.), *Developmental psychology: An advanced textbook* (pp. 461-495). Hillsdale, NJ: Lawrence Erlbaum Associates.

Eisenberg, N. (1992). *The caring child.* Cambridge, MA: Harvard University Press.

Eisenberg, N., & Miller, P. A. (1987). The relation of empathy to prosocial and related behavior. *Psychological Bulletin, 101,* 91–119.

Eisenberg, N., & Murphy, B. (1995). Parenting and children's moral development. In M. H. Bornstein (Ed.), *Handbook of parenting* (Vol. 4, pp. 227–257). Mahweh, NJ: Lawrence Erlbaum Associates.

Eisenberg, N., Shell, R., Pasternack, J., Lennon, R., Belber, R., & Mathy, R. M. (1987). Prosocial development in middle childhood: A longitudinal study. *Developmental Psychology, 23,* 712–718.

Eyre, L., & Eyre, R. (1994). *Teaching your children responsibility.* New York: Simon & Schuster.

Ginott, H. G. (1971). *Between parent and child: New solutions to old problems.* New York: Macmillan.

Gordon, T. (1970). *Parent effectiveness training.* New York: Wyden.

Grossman, D. G. (1996). *On killing.* Boston: Back Bay Books.

Grusec, J. E., Saas-Kortsaak, P., & Simutis, Z. M. (1978). The role of example and moral exhortation in the training of altruism. *Child Development, 49,* 920–923.

Hay, D. F. & Murray, P. (1982). Giving and requesting: Social facilitation of infants' offers to adults. *Infant Behavior and Development, 5,* 310–310.

Horton-Parker, R. (1998). Teaching children to care: Engendering prosocial behavior through humanistic parenting. *Journal of Humanistic Education and Development, 37,* 66–77.

Howard, B. (1996). The short- and long-term consequences of corporal punishment. *Pediatrics, 98,* 809–817.

Huston, A. C.. Donnerstein, E., Fairchild, H., Feshbach, N. D., Katz, P. A., Murray, J. P., Rubenstein, E. A., Wilcox, B. L., & Zuckerman, D. (1992). *Big world, small screen: The role of television in American society.* Lincoln, MN: University of Minnesota Press.

Karylowski, J. (1982). Doing good to feel good versus doing good to make others feel good: Some child-rearing antecedents. *School Psychology International, 3,* 149–156.

Koestner, R., Franz, C., & Weinberger, J. (1990). The family origins of empathic concern: A 26-year longitudinal study. *Journal of Personality & Social Psychology, 58,* 709–717.

Krevans, J. & Gibbs, J. C. (1996). Parents' use of inductive discipline: Relations to children's empathy and prosocial behavior. *Child Development, 67,* 3263–3277.

Lamborn, S. D., Mounts, N. S., Steinberg, L., & Dornbusch, S. M. (1991). Patterns of competence and adjustment among adolescents from authoritative, authoritarian, indulgent, and neglectful families. *Child Development, 62,* 1049–1065.

Lempers, J. D., Clark-Lempers, D., & Simons, R. (1989). Economic hardship, parenting, and distress in adolescence. *Child Development, 60,* 25–39.

Maccoby, E. E. (1984). Socialization and developmental change. *Child Development, 55,* 317–328.

Maccoby, E. E., & Martin, J. A. (1983). Socialization in the context of the family: Parent-child interaction. In P. H. Mussen (Series Ed.) & E. M. Hetherington (Vol. Ed.), *Handbook of child psychology: Vol. 4. Socialization, personality, and social development* (4th ed., pp. 1–101). New York: Wiley.

Moore, B., & Eisenberg, N. (1984). The development of altruism. In G. Whitehurst (Ed.), *Annals in Child Development* (Vol. 1, pp. 107–174). New York: JSI Press.

Nelson, J. (1987). *Positive discipline.* New York: Ballantine Books.

Nelson, J., Lott, L., & Glenn, H. S. (1993). *Positive discipline A ➜ Z: 1001 solutions to everyday parenting problems.* Rocklin, CA: Prima Publishing.

Parker, R. (1999). The art of blessing: Teaching parents to construct rituals. *Professional School Counseling, 2,* 218–225.

Parker, R., & Horton, H. S. (1996). A typology of ritual: Paradigms for healing and empowerment. *Counseling & Values, 40,* 82–97.

Patterson, G. R. (1982). *Corrective family process.* Eugene, OR: Castalia.

Perry, D. G., Perry, L. C., & Boldizar, J. P. (1990). Learning of aggression. In M. Lewis & S. Miller (Eds.), *Handbook of developmental psychopathology.* New York: Plenum.

Popkin, M. (1993). *Active parenting today.* Marietta, GA: Active Parenting Publishers.

Pulkkinen, L. (1982). Self-control and continuity in childhood delayed adolescence. In P. Baltes & O. Brim (Eds.), *Lifespan development and behavior* (Vol. 4, pp. 64–107). New York: Academic Press.

Radke-Yarrow, M., Zahn-Waxler, C., & Chapman, M. (1983). Prosocial dispositions and behavior. In P. H. Mussen (Series Ed.) & E. M. Hetherington (Vol. Ed.), *Handbook of child psychology: Vol. 4. Socialization, personality, and social development* (pp. 469–545). New York: Wiley.

Rice, M. E. & Grusec, J. E. (1975). Saying and doing: Effects on observer performance. *Journal of Personality and Social Psychology, 32,* 584–593.

Roberts, M. W., & Powers, S. W. (1990). Adjusting chair timeout enforcement procedures for oppositional children. *Behavior Therapy, 21,* 257–271.

Steinberg, L. D. (1990). Interdependence in the family: Autonomy, conflict, and harmony in the parent-adolescent relationship. In S. S. Feldman & G. R. Elliot (Eds.), *At the threshold: The developing adolescent* (pp. 255–276). Cambridge, MA: Harvard University Press.

Weiss, B., Dodge, K. A., Bates, J. E., & Pettit, G. S. (1992). Some consequences of early harsh discipline: Child aggression and a maladaptive social information processing style. *Child Development, 63,* 1321–1335.

Whiting, B. B., & Edwards, C. P. (1988). *Children of different worlds: The formation of social behavior.* Cambridge, MA: Harvard University Press.

Yarrow, M. R., Scott, P. M., & Waxler, C. Z. (1973). Learning concern for others. *Developmental Psychology, 8,* 240–260.

Zahn-Waxler, C., Radke-Yarrow, M., & King, R. (1979). Child rearing and children's prosocial initiations toward victims of distress. *Child Development, 50,* 319–330.

8

School-Based Violence Reduction Programs: A Selective Review of Curricula

Gerald Schamess

Several deadly and highly publicized incidents of school violence have presented educators, mental health practitioners, and policy makers with what may be an intractable dilemma: Keeping students safe within school systems that unwittingly support a culture of school violence. The incidents, both in and of themselves and as amplified by the national media, demand prompt, effective action directed toward protecting students, faculty, and other school personnel from potentially lethal violence. There is a profoundly unsettling discrepancy between the implications of the mass murders at Columbine High School and other locations around the country and the implications of statistical findings that seem to tell quite a different story. As noted by Leone, Mayer, Malmgren, and Meisel (see Chapter 4 in this volume), "Uniform Crime Reports and data from other sources indicate that schools are the safest places for children to be. Fewer homicides and violent crimes are committed against children at school than in their homes or on the streets." Depending on which behaviors are measured, current research data emphasize that school violence either leveled off or decreased between 1993 and 1999 (Leone et al., 2000). Although these data are, or at least should be, reassuring, closer examination indicates that while the direction of change is encouraging, school violence continues to be a very real and worrisome threat to children, teachers, caregivers, and parents.

According to statistics from the Centers for Disease Control and Prevention (CDC; 1999), during the 1999 academic year 14.2% of students surveyed reported having been involved in a fight on school property, 6.9% reported having carried a weapon to school at least once, and 4.9% reported having carried a gun to school on at least one occasion. Compared with data from a 1993 study, these figures reflect significant changes both in terms of direction and magnitude. They are, respectively, 12.5%, 38%, and 40% lower than the 1993 figures. Nonetheless, it is difficult to argue convincingly that American schools are "safe enough" when, in 1999, 1 in 14 American children carried a weapon of some kind to school, 1 in 20 carried a gun, and 1 in 7 was involved in a fight on school property.

Weinhold echoed this concern, describing a school- and community-wide culture of violence in which "dominator values are so tightly woven . . . they are virtually invisible" (see Weinhold, Chapter 6 in this volume). In a similar vein, in a study of child homicide in 26 industrialized nations, Bleich, Ingersoll, & Divine, (2000, cited in Twemlow, Fonagy, & Sacco, in press) found that America led the sampled nations in child homicide by a very wide margin, accounting for fully 73% of all the reports of murdered children. In the United States, adults kill children and children kill other children at rates 10 times higher than in Western Europe and Japan and 5 times higher than in Canada, New Zealand, and Australia. Clearly, being first in this regard is not the same as being best. Even the markedly improved statistics confirm that America has a long way to go before it can authentically claim that children are safe either in its schools or in society at large.

In spite of the discrepancy between intent and the prevalence of violence none of these observations are meant to challenge the nation's intermittent commitment to reducing school violence. There is nothing novel in the observation that schools are a microcosm of society and that, overall, American society is very violent (see Miller, Chapter 5 in this volume).

In addition to societal complacency with regard to violence, schools, it may be argued, create a climate that actually fosters violence. Periodically, Americans register surprise on hearing the national statistics on violence directed against children and occasionally, usually in response to a particularly deadly school "incident." As public anxiety mounts, policy makers are motivated to act (actually, to react). Consequently, federal and state money is appropriated, and government agencies actively support violence reduction initiatives. Under ordinary circumstances, however, Americans are well acclimated, not to say complacent, about this society's homegrown violence. As a nation, success and oftentimes virtue as well are measured by rank ordering one another on the basis of wealth, status, political influence, possessions ("toys"), and so forth. Thus, it is hardly surprising that schools reflexively rank order students in terms of academic achievement, popularity, winning at sports, good looks, strength, citizenship, and any number of other criteria, which, taken together, add up to an assessment of each child's overall worth. In educating to these norms, schools believe they are preparing children to function as "good citizens." Given how reflexively most Americans accept these norms, it is not surprising that so many educators are startled when reformers suggest that systematically rank ordering students perpetuates "dominator values," which encourage bullying, verbal abuse, ritualized humiliation, and other forms of emotional and physical violence.

Although most Americans seem unaware of and unconcerned about the relationship between ruthless competition ("the spirit that makes America great") and high rates of violent behavior, they also want to protect their children. Consequently, national educational policy reflects a fundamental, albeit unrecognized contradiction. From a pedagogical perspective, it is possible to teach children to work collaboratively toward achieving a common educational goal. It is also possible to teach them to be hard-nosed competitors whose primary goal is to be first and best at everything they undertake. It is not, however, possible to do both simultaneously. They are mutually exclusive goals. Given this fundamental contradiction in educational philosophy, the easy availability of guns, and the amount of violence that is casually and relentlessly displayed on television and in movies, we probably should be grateful that, so far, there have not been more instances of school violence involving multiple deaths and mass (school, community, and national) traumatization. Of course, as many students willingly tell any adult willing to listen, "minor" violence in the form of verbal abuse, humiliation, and physical bullying is endemic throughout American schools.

Despite these vexing contradictions, the available research data confirm that many school-based violence reduction programs work rather well. Although these programs do not fully neutralize America's national culture of violence or allow us to claim a more normative level of school safety in comparison with other industrialized nations, the CDC (1999) statistics suggest that the programs do play a significant role in improving school safety.

**Programs**

To advance the ongoing discussion about how to improve school safety, this chapter describes and comments on three representative school-based violence reduction programs that have been formally evaluated for efficacy. Two colleagues and I (Aronson, Schamess, & Bernard, 2001) originally reviewed these and six other programs in a white paper submitted to the Center for Mental Health Services by the American Group Psychotherapy Association. This chapter is based on program evaluations done for that review.

In addition to being well researched, the three programs discussed herein—Aggression Replacement Training (Goldstein, Glick, Irwin, Pask, & Rubama, 1989; Goldstein & Glick, 1994), Resolving Conflict Creatively (Educators for Social Responsibility, 2000), and Creating a Peaceful School Learning Environment (Twemlow, Fonagy, & Sacco, 2001; Twemlow, Fonagy, Sacco, Gies, et al., 2001)—represent major trends in contemporary school-based violence reduction programs. According to the widely utilized public health/community mental health typology, Aggression Replacement Training (ART) focuses on secondary and tertiary prevention whereas both Resolving Conflict Creatively (RCC) and Creating a Peaceful School Learning Environment (PSLE) are designed to promote primary and secondary prevention goals.

In current practice, most violence reduction programs are conceptualized as social skills, aggression management, and/or conflict resolution curricula (Aronson et al., 2001). Typically, such curricula are offered in large classroom groups to all children in a particular grade, school, or school district. For the most part these curricula attempt to modify existing cognitive schemas and teach prosocial behavioral skills. In pursuit of these goals, the programs first teach students to recognize and evaluate their typical affective and behavioral responses to stressful, frustrating, and/or interpersonally provocative situations. They then encourage students to consider alternative, more prosocial ways of managing social relationships that initially evoke angry feelings and aggressive impulses. Most school-based curricula carefully limit direct affective expression and minimize spontaneous interaction between group members, although all of the programs described herein provide students with carefully regulated modes of communication (e.g., role playing, conflict resolution rehearsals, martial arts training) that provide symbolic avenues for expressing strong feelings.

From a group dynamics perspective, all of these programs are categorized as time-limited, psychoeducational interventions. The educational orientation is both appropriate and necessary, as the interventions are designed for implementation in school settings and, accordingly, must conform to school policies that require educational relevance. Although the programs are focused and time-limited, their duration varies considerably, ranging from 10 sessions (ART) to a full school year (RCC and PSLE). Because RCC and PSLE are woven into school-as-a-whole culture, their impact is enhanced by sequential repetition as children advance to higher grades. These two programs are purposefully designed to change the fundamental culture of participating schools and thus are implemented only when school administrations express willingness to integrate them into a school's institutional system. None of the three programs utilize mental health professionals as teachers, trainers, or group facilitators even though they all make extensive use of concepts derived from different schools of psychology (cognitive theory, behaviorism, social psychology, and psychoanalysis). Teachers or other school personnel who facilitate the interventions are expected to participate in program-specific orientations (PSLE) or specialized training seminars (ART and RCC).

Aggression Replacement Training

Aggression Replacement Training (Goldstein & Glick, 1994) developed in the mid-1980s for chronically aggressive children living in detention or residential treatment centers. A later project presented the curriculum to adjudicated delinquent children living in their own or group homes in communities in which they grew up. The curriculum was subsequently expanded and refined for school-based use in small groups (six to eight members) composed of children identified as problematically aggressive or at serious risk of becoming so. ART is a multifaceted, psychoeducational approach designed to replace aggressive thinking and behavior with modified prosocial cognitive processes and social skills that are taught through a hierarchical series of structured curriculum exercises. Groups typically meet for 10 sessions, each of which addresses a particular aspect of the curriculum.

In its early years, ART focused on developing or expanding three areas of social/intellectual functioning: social skills training ("skill streaming"), anger-control training, and moral reasoning training. The original discussion topics, which are still in use, were designed to reduce aggressive behavior quickly and dramatically. More recently, Goldstein and his colleagues (Goldstein & Conoley, 1997) expanded ART and developed the Prepare Curriculum, which includes seven additional 10-session modules, each devoted to developing a particular set of social/cognitive skills. The expanded curriculum includes problem-solving training, empathy training, situational perception training, stress management training, cooperation training, recruiting supportive models, and understanding and using group processes.

Overall, ART is unique in its appreciation of the importance of social class and community factors in modifying aggressive patterns of behavior. It is one of only a very few interventions that emphasizes experiential activities specifically designed to help children function better in a range of nonschool social groups. The acquisition of collaborative/consensus building skills is viewed as essential for insulating children against peer group pressure to act out antisocially. The program is also unique in its purposeful use of the facilitator's authority. Because the program's major goal is to socialize ("train") students to conform to the psychoeducational curriculum as it is presented, facilitators model prosocial behavior and offer performance feedback that encourages compliance with the curriculum's "unchanging and unchangeable" objectives. Facilitators are selected from teachers and school personnel who work directly with children in caregiving roles. Although this is not emphasized in the program description, the caregivers are likely to be well acquainted with the group members and to have strong, positive relationships with them—qualities that are likely to increase the probability of positive outcomes.

Theoretical Framework

The theoretical framework for ART is based on the observation that middle-class children in the United States are taught to think differently and to utilize different interpersonal skills than lower-income children. According to this hypothesis, middle-class children are taught first to look inward and to consider what motivates their behavior, and then to look outward and accurately decipher the feelings of others. Having acquired these cognitive/social capacities, they are encouraged to employ restraint, affect regulation, and a growing capacity for self-control when they interact with others. In contrast, lower-class children are taught to rely heavily on external authorities for direction, to focus on how other people respond to their behavior, and to assess the consequences of their actions. Because they have been taught to rely on adults for feedback about whether a particular behavior is acceptable or unacceptable, they are less likely to develop or value controls from within. Whereas middle-class children respond well to interventions that focus on understanding motivation, discussing feelings and developing self-control, research findings (Goldstein, Glick, Irwin, Pask, & Rubama, 1989) suggest that lower-class and other similarly socialized children respond more positively to interventions that emphasize modeling, role-playing, performance feedback, and transfer training.

Program Assessment

As noted earlier, ART was initially offered in small groups to adjudicated delinquent adolescents living in detention centers. Many of the original participants were gang members with histories of physically assaulting others. Over the past decade, the curriculum has been adapted for use in schools, mostly with low-income elementary, middle, and high school students. In school programs, participants are chosen because they have been identified as physically violent or at "high risk" of becoming so. The program developers reported on three carefully constructed research studies, all of which utilized experimental and matched control groups. The first two studies involved delinquent, low-income youth incarcerated at medium-secure or maximum-secure facilities for adjudicated delinquents (Goldstein & Glick, 1987). The third study was community based and sought outcome data related to the intervention's effect on chronically aggressive youths living in their home communities with family members or in supervised group homes (Goldstein et al., 1989). The research findings documented reductions in aggressive behavior and, most significantly, a significant decrease in recidivism (measured by subsequent arrests) in comparison with the matched control groups. These findings support the view that ART is a valuable tool for decreasing violent behavior among lower-income and similarly socialized children who have physically assaulted others or are at serious risk of doing so. When used as outlined herein, ART offers effective secondary and tertiary prevention for violence-prone children (Goldstein & Conoley, 1997).

Resolving Conflict Creatively

The Resolving Conflict Creatively curriculum was developed in the mid-1980s through collaboration between Educators for Social Responsibility and the New York City Board of Education. Over the past 20 years, the curriculum has been widely disseminated across the country. Recent statistics show that it is utilized by more than 6,000 teachers and 175,000 students in 375 schools (RCCP National Center, 1997; Tugend, 2001). RCC is an important and influential model program because it is extensively utilized, committed to transforming the cultural norms of participating schools, and systematically evaluated for efficacy.

RCC utilizes curriculum material to help children develop prosocial problem-solving/conflict resolution skills. Participating schools are encouraged to integrate teaching content into their social studies curricula at every grade level. Teachers who complete a required 24-hour training program present the curriculum in regularly scheduled social studies classes, preferably in blocks of 25 or more lessons presented over the course of an academic year. Outcome studies for the program regularly show that frequency of exposure is directly related to efficacy (Roderick, 1998). Group size and gender composition vary according to class size and composition of the student body. Course content is hierarchically organized for use at different grade levels. Lessons emphasize active listening, empathy and perspective taking, negotiation (mediation), appropriate expression of feelings, and assertiveness. Teaching is done through role playing, group discussions, and brain storming. The curriculum is manualized, and teaching guides are available for grades from preschool through high school. Lessons deal with such subjects as peace and conflict, creative conflict resolution, keeping peace in the classroom, and peer mediation (Educators for Social Responsibility, 2000). A fundamental program component involves training and using student mediators to address and consensually resolve interpersonal conflicts between students.

Skill Development

Roderick (1998) noted that instruction in RCC "helps children develop skills in assertiveness so that they have other options besides passivity and aggression for dealing with conflict" (p. 4). According to Roderick, the curriculum aims to promote certain habits of thinking, including the ability to analyze a situation, avoid jumping to conclusions, listen with openness to other points of view, and see a range of options for responding" (p. 4). Desired school-as-a-whole outcomes include developing cultural norms that oppose all manifestations of violence, such as physical aggression, hurtful words, and put-downs. Other cultural norms encourage children to talk about problems as they arise, develop attitudes of mutual respect, honor diversity, and reduce or eliminate negative stereotypes. As teachers, students, and staff share power and collaborate in creating and implementing schoolwide rules, they create a democratic environment that effectively fosters the development of social and civic responsibility (Lantieri & Patti, 1996).

Over the years, program evaluators have recognized the importance of making RCC an integral part of schoolwide instructional programs. Because frequency of exposure is directly related to efficacy (Roderick, 1998), achieving integration involves recruiting teachers who are both interested in the curriculum and willing to teach it regularly in their classes. Although, typically, it is schools and/or school systems that choose to adopt the RCC curriculum, teacher use of curricula lessons is voluntary and variable. Recent RCC strategy (Roderick, 1998) has called for more fully integrating the curriculum into overall educational programming by thoroughly training five committed teachers each year in each participating school, until critical mass is achieved and curriculum integration is established at all grade levels. Orientation to the program includes formal student education in peer mediation and four 3-hour-long parent education workshops scheduled at regular intervals over the course of each academic year.

Because teacher involvement and curriculum integration depend on active administrative support, RCC representatives attempt to negotiate cooperation from superintendents, principals, and administrators before RCC is used in the school system. Thereafter, schoolwide participation is assessed and nurtured through ongoing conversations and teaching sessions between RCC representatives and key administrators. Teaching sessions assess and reconsider educational goals, program development and implementation practices.

Program Assessment

The RCC curriculum has been extensively evaluated utilizing a management information system that tracks implementation, a large-scale longitudinal process and outcome study, and teacher interviews. Matched control groups and large samples have been utilized. Measures have included pre- and post-intervention interviews that have evaluated both changes in thinking (aggressive fantasies, hostile attribution biases, etc.) and changes in behavior. Major findings have been that children exposed to 25 or more RCC curriculum lessons over the course of an academic year have shown decreases in both verbal and physical aggression when compared with peers in the control groups (Roderick, 1998; Tugend, 2001). In post-intervention interviews, teachers have reported less physical violence in the classroom. Students who were regularly exposed to the curriculum demonstrated substantial gains on academic achievement tests, while parents who regularly participated in the family workshops reported increases in communication skills. Citing a Columbia University study, Tugend (2001, p. 18) emphasized that "elementary school children naturally become more aggressive as they age." She went on to comment that exposure to the RCC curriculum did not reverse childrens' tendency to become more aggressive, but it did reduce the rate of increase. Although this may appear to be a modest effect, it is, in fact, substantial. It supports teacher reports that the RCC curriculum reduces both physical and verbal aggressiveness in the classroom. An independent evaluation of RCC over a 2-year period is currently (as of February 2002) under peer review. The research brief and executive summary of the report, both prepared by the National Center for Children in Poverty at Columbia University, are currently available from the center (www.nccp.org).

Creating a Peaceful School Learning Environment

Theoretical Framework

Creating a Peaceful School Learning Environment is a highly leveraged, cost-effective, two-pronged intervention designed to radically transform those aspects of school culture that covertly support, rationalize, or ignore violent behavior among students and/or between students and school personnel. The underlying principle asserts that patterns of bullying, whenever and wherever they occur in schools, accurately reflect the overall school culture. It further asserts that aggressive behavior can be significantly modified by interventions that systematically support anti-bullying norms and actively teach students how to disengage from and/or defend themselves against physical and verbal attacks. Schools that agree to participate in PSLE undertake three fundamental policy changes. They adopt (a) a zero-tolerance policy for bullying, bystanding and becoming a victim; (b) a disciplinary plan that emphasizes rewards and focuses on how incidents of bullying affect classroom and school-as-a-whole climate; and (c) a "gentle warrior," defensive martial arts program (Twemlow, Fonagy, & Sacco, 2001).

Twemlow (1995) postulated that the power dynamics inherent in bully-victim-bystander interactions and in "rituals of exclusion" reliably predict levels of function and dysfunction in all institutional systems. In schools, the roles of bully, victim, and bystander are dialectically structured so that individuals enact and maintain a specific role through constant interaction with individuals who enact one of the other roles. The roles (see also Slaby, Wilson-Brewer, & Dash, 1994) develop in the context of power struggles between children and adults, between individual children, and between subgroups of children. In healthy institutional systems these roles are fluid and may fluctuate from hour to hour and day to day. In dysfunctional systems, bullies and victims become locked into rigid, mutually dependent, sadomasochistic interactions that persist and perpetuate themselves over time. Persistent, unchanging interactions of this kind rarely occur unless there is covert support from bystanders, some of whom rigidly identify with the bullies and others who rigidly identify with the victims, thereby perpetuating the cycle. When bully-victim-bystander relationships become rigidly fixed and begin to cycle rapidly, tragic (sometimes lethal) consequences are likely to occur.

Operational Principles

PSLE's effectiveness depends on the program facilitators developing a psychologically informed, supportive partnership with school administrators, teachers, students, and parents. The primary goal is to modify school-as-a-whole norms to emphasize (a) learning to tolerate differences, (b) developing a habit of collaboration around issues that are not points of conflict, (c) encouraging personal relationships in which people see one another as more rather than less human, (d) modifying stereotypical racial, religious and gender perceptions, (e) developing a mutually agreed upon common language, and (f) agreeing that change occurs through collaboration rather than competition. Active endorsement by school administration and genuine, truly voluntary support from teachers/school personnel and parents are prerequisites for programmatic success.

Culture-Modifying Interventions

Twemlow et al. (2001) described the following interventions that can facilitate the necessary modifications of the school culture.

1. Establish a norm that enforces zero tolerance for bullying, bystanding, or being a victim. To help accomplish this goal, teachers and other school personnel actively reward prosocial behavior by placing posters that depict desirable behavior for "handling bullies" at strategic places around the school, by reinforcing this norm in regular classroom discussions, and third by conducting "family power struggles" workshops once each semester. A system of rewards is developed for classes that succeed in maintaining a fight-free environment.

2. Develop a disciplinary approach that encourages teachers to use rewards more frequently than consequences and that focuses on how each fighting incident affects the emotional climate of the classroom as a whole. Special reward/discipline cards are used to positively reinforce classroom discussions.

3. Encourage children to reflect on bully-victim-bystander interactions in daily classroom discussions. At the end of such discussions, classes are asked to decide whether they have earned a banner, to be displayed outside their classroom the next day, celebrating a fight-free environment.

4. Provide 12-week "gentle warrior" modules that teach *defensive* martial arts techniques. In addition to teaching specific techniques, instructors teach a martial arts philosophy that emphasizes self-respect, self-control, and respect for others.

5. Implement a program that pairs volunteer adult mentors with children. The pairs function as "surveillance teams" during recess, lunch, and the end of the school day transition. They make themselves available, as needed, to any students who wish to consult with them.

6. Initiate a peer mentorship program that utilizes students from the high school that the participating elementary school students will eventually attend. Peer mentors are supervised for an hour a week and are granted academic credit for being mentors.

7. Make experienced mental health volunteers available, as needed, to consult on school climate issues and to advise the school's existing mental health team.

Program Assessment

In its initial trial (Twemlow, Fonagy, Sacco, Gies, et al., 2001), PCLE was evaluated using a sophisticated research protocol that compared one urban, midwestern elementary school located in a violence-prone community with a second, matched school. The research protocol included three teacher-rated measures of change: behavioral scales to assess levels of disruptive classroom behavior, completion of the Child and Adolescent Adjustment Profile, and completion of a newly developed Target Behavior Scale that assesses specific behaviors such as bullying, loss of temper, distractibility, and social isolation. Data were also collected on disciplinary referrals and on academic achievement as assessed by scores on the Metropolitan Achievement Test. Student perceptions of school safety were collected using the School Atmosphere Scale.

Over a 3-year period, major findings included (a) a marked reduction in disciplinary referrals involving serious physical aggressiveness, (b) a dramatic rise in the number of in-school suspensions during the project's first year, followed by a "gradual and well-maintained reduction" during the second and third years, (c) a statistically significant improvement in academic performance for children in the experimental school, compared with no change in the control school, and (d) a statistically significant reduction in dependent behavior for children in the experimental school. One confounding finding was also reported. Despite the encouraging changes noted here, teacher ratings recorded only a "marginal reduction" in hostility among children in the experimental group.

Although the research findings reach levels of significance in only two of the four measured behaviors, the reported nonsignificant changes are also noteworthy, especially when the experimental group is compared with the control group. The positive findings support the value of replicating and evaluating the intervention through additional trials in other school systems. A follow-up evaluation of a sample of the original study participants in high school would also be instructive. Several other controlled studies are currently under way in midwestern elementary schools located in violence-prone communities.

Comments

In the initial trial, PSLE was unusually cost-effective. Because the only additional personnel required were a paid mental health professional who visited the school for a few hours a week to consult with the mental health staff and a part-time defensive martial arts teacher, costs were minimal, especially as compared with other violence reduction programs.

Creating a Peaceful School Learning Environment is designed to radically transform the emotional climate and hierarchical power relationships within participating schools. Accordingly, it requires a high level of commitment and cooperation from school administrators and teachers and is likely to evoke resistance in schools not willing to consider the possible benefits of extensive institutional change. In addition, the theoretical formulation, although well articulated and compelling, does not focus directly on learning tasks or curriculum modifications and may thus be controversial among educators. It will be instructive to review outcome findings from the ongoing research trials and to assess the degree of administrative cooperation in other participating schools.

 Program Comparison

The three programs that have been summarized constitute a representative sample of school-based violence reduction programs currently in use across the country. Of these, Aggression Replacement Training is closest to traditional group psychotherapy (see also Yaekel, & Polansky, 1967) in that it focuses on changing cognitive processes by replacing violent attitudes and impulses with prosocial thinking and behavior. Training occurs in highly structured, six to eight member, time-limited (10 session) psychoeducational groups. The training utilizes cognitive behavioral and social skills techniques. Because ART attributes antisocial levels of aggressive behavior to social class linked, internalized patterns of cognition and social interaction that determine how individuals behave, it systematically targets those patterns for change.

The second program, RCC, offers a social skills oriented curriculum that (a) emphasizes the value of peace and cooperation, (b) teaches students collaborative methods of conflict resolution, (c) facilitates increased power sharing between students and faculty members, and (d) encourages democratization of hierarchical practices and structures. Because the program is committed to framing interventions in positive terms, it tends to emphasize the value of constructive, prosocial behavior (e.g., cooperation, mutual respect, diversity, power sharing between teachers and students) without explicitly focusing on "deficits" in either students or school systems. Nonetheless, in advocating for school-as-a-whole reform, RCC seems to implicitly acknowledge previously cited observations about aspects of hierarchical and authoritarian school structures that covertly support a culture of violence. For example, the curriculum's emphasis on teaching peaceful and collaborative methods of conflict resolution strongly suggests that existing school norms are hierarchical and problematically coercive.

The third program, PSLE, identifies bullying as the prototypical expression of dysfunctional school norms. It assumes that problematic levels of aggression occur as a result of rigidified interactions in which bystanders (both students and educators) lend covert support to bullies or victims with whom they identify. Intervention focuses on generating systemwide changes in school norms and disciplinary procedures and on developing effective methods for teaching victims and bystanders how they can disengage from and/or defend themselves against bullies. One of the central underlying assumptions is that when "victims" no longer permit themselves to be bullied and when "bystanders" disengage from the frozen interactions that support bullying, problematic norms and patterns of behavior will gradually disappear. Interestingly, both RCC and PSLE (see also Corbin, Chapter 9 in this volume) seem to agree that modifying schoolwide attitudes, disciplinary procedures, and techniques for addressing interpersonal conflict is a precondition for changing the institutional norms that covertly support violence.

 **Conclusion**

Strong statistical evidence supports the view that these three programs effectively reduce the incidence of school violence. Moreover, two of the programs markedly improve both the emotional and educational environments of participating schools. ART and other similar small-group interventions show promise for reducing aggressive behavior among children identified as actually or potentially violent. Previously cited observations about "dominator values," schoolwide and nationwide cultural attitudes that covertly endorse violence, and unacknowledged contradictions in national education policy lend support to the view that school-based violence reduction protocols are more effective when they pursue primary prevention goals by modifying educational and emotional norms within school systems. Although such programs make a significant difference in participating schools, there is ample reason to think that violence reduction programs should be conceptualized and implemented as part of a larger "systems of care" (see Lightburn, Chapter 18 in this volume), public health (see Prothrow-Stith, Chapter 15 in this volume) approach that works toward creating healthier and stronger communities within schools and in the environmental surround. Ultimately, our ability to create truly safe schools will depend not only on our teaching children how to be less violent but also on our modeling nonviolent, collaborative behavior in the social structures we create and in our everday lives.

References

Aronson, S., Schamess, G., & Bernard, H. (2001). *The role of group psychotherapuetic interventions in group violence reduction and primary prevention.* New York: American Group Psychotherapy Association.

Bleich, J., Ingersoll, S., & Divine, J. (2000). *National campaign against youth violence.* (Academic Advisory Council report). Boston: Harvard University, John F. Kennedy School of Government.

Centers for Disease Control and Prevention. (1999). *Fact sheet: Youth risk behavior trends.* URL: http://www.cdc.gov/nccdphp/dash/yrbs/trend.htm

Educators for Social Responsibility. (2000). Resource catalog. (Available from Educators for Social Responsibility, 23 Garden Street, Cambridge, MA 02138)

Ganter, G., Yeakel, M., & Polansky, N. (1967). *Retrieval from limbo.* New York: Child Welfare League of America.

Goldstein, A. P. & Conoley, J. C. (1997). *School violence intervention.* New York: Guilford Press.

Goldstein, A. P. & Glick, B. (1994). Aggression replacement training. *Simulation and Gaming, 25*(1), 9–26.

Goldstein, A. P., Glick, B., Irwin, M. J., Pask, C., & Rubama, I. (1989). *Reducing delinquency: Intervention in the community.* New York: Academic Press.

Lantieri, L., & Patti, J. (1996). The road to peace in our schools. *Educational Leadership, 54*(1), 28–31.

National Center for Children in Poverty. (2002). *Executive summary.* URL: www.nccp.org

RCCP National Center. (1997). *Program report.* URL: http://www.esrnational.org

Roderick, T. (1998). Evaluating the Resolving Conflict Creatively program. *The Fourth R, 82,* 3–4, 19–21.

Slaby, R. G., Wilson-Brewer, R., & Dash, D. H. (1994). *Aggressors, victims and bystanders: Thinking and acting to prevent violence.* Newton, MA: Education Development Center.

Tugend, A. (2001, November 11). Peaceable playgrounds: Special report on education. *New York Times,* p. 18.

Twemlow, S. W. (1995). The psychoanalytic foundations of a dialectical approach to the victim/victimizer relationship. *Journal of the American Academcy of Psychoanalysis, 23,* 545–561, 563–580.

Twemlow, S. W., Fonagy, P., & Sacco, F. (2001). A social systems–power dynamic approach to preventing school violence. In M. Shafii & S. Shafii (Eds.), *School violence: Assessment, management, prevention* (pp. 273–289). Washington, DC: American Psychiatric Publishing.

Twemlow, S. W., Fonagy, P., & Sacco, F. C. (in press). Feeling safe in school. *Smith College Studies in Social Work.*

Twemlow, S. W., Fonagy, P., Sacco, F., Gies, M., Evans R., & Ewbank, R. (2001). Creating a peaceful school learning environment: A controlled study of an elementary school intervention to reduce violence. *American Journal of Psychiatry, 158,* 808–810.

9

Using a Group Psychotherapy Framework to Address School Violence

Joanne N. Corbin

The issue of school violence has been at the forefront of national attention during the past decade and on the minds of those working in schools each day. The public view of school violence focuses on the tragic events involving the loss of life within a school community. Those working in schools know that violence can be seen in non-fatal events as well, such as fighting, threats of attack, verbal assaults, and fear of unsafe conditions. As in most cases involving complex phenomena, there is no single remedy to this problem, and most schools currently have some type of formal school violence prevention or reduction program in place (National Center for Educational Statistics, 1998). This chapter looks at one school reform model, the School Development Program (SDP), through the lens of group psychotherapy and explores how this approach addresses issues of school violence.

 ## Violence Defined

Effective interventions begin with a clear definition of the problem. Violence has been defined in different ways, and thus there are multiple ways of understanding the scope of the problem and its possible solutions. Elliott, Hamburg, and Williams (1998, p. 13) defined violence as "the threat or use of physical force with the intention of causing physical injury, damage, or intimidation of another person." Their statement was meant to clarify the difference between actual violent behavior and the many other risk factors that predispose children to act violently. By this standard, verbal abuse, psychological abuse, and physical contact meant in play are not considered violent. Epp and Watkinson (1997, p. xi) defined systemic violence in schools as:

> Any institutionalized practice or procedure that adversely impacts on disadvantaged individuals or groups by burdening them psychologically, mentally, culturally, spiritually, economically, or physically. It includes practices and procedures that prevent students from learning, thus harming them. This may take the form of conventional policies and practices that foster a climate of violence, or policies and practices that appear to be neutral but result in discriminatory effects.

The literature about school violence tends to use the Elliott et al. (1998) definition as the standard for understanding, measuring, and responding to the issue of violence within schools. However, the Epp and Watkinson (1997) definition is, in many ways, preferable because it focuses on institutional and social factors that condone and support violent behavior. Reports of school violence use police or law enforcement data, meaning that violent incidents not reported to law enforcement are excluded from these reports. From an intervention point of view, exclusion of these incidents implies the underreporting of actual violent interactions within schools and does not provide a complete picture of the depth of the problem. Defining school violence within the larger social context in which it occurs as Epp and Watkinson do is necessary for the development of comprehensive interventions.

Scope of the Problem

During the 1997–1998 academic year, there were 1.2 million crimes in the United States in which students, age 12–18, were the victims of nonfatal violent acts including rape, aggravated assault, simple assault, and battery. In 1999, among students age 12–18, approximately 5% reported being bullied at school, 5% were fearful of being attacked or harmed at school, 5% avoided one or more places in school, 13% reported someone using hate-related words against them in the previous 6 months, 36% reported seeing hate-related graffiti at school, and 17% reported that street gangs were present in their schools (National Center for Education Statistics, 2000).

According to the report "Violence and Discipline Problems in U.S. Public Schools" (National Center for Education Statistics, 1998), for the 1996–1997 academic year, 57% of U.S. public schools reported at least one crime to the police. Ten percent reported that at least one serious violent crime (rape, sexual battery, suicide, physical attack, fight with a weapon, or robbery) had occurred. The number of crime incidents increased with the age of students and the size of the school. Forty-five percent of elementary schools, 74% of middle schools, and 77% of high schools reported at least one crime occurring in the school. Thirty-eight percent of small schools (300 or fewer students), 60% of medium schools (300–1,000 students), and 89% of large schools (more than 1,000 students) reported criminal incidents.

A survey of 576 school social workers (Astor, Behre, Wallace, & Fravil, 1998) found that one third of the respondents feared for their personal safety at least once a month. Of those working in inner-city schools, that figure was 71%. Thirty-five percent of the respondents reported that they had been physically assaulted or physically threatened within the past year. In these incidents, 77% of the attackers were identified as students, 49% were identified as parents, and 11% were identified as gang members. Many of the respondents reported that they consciously behaved in ways designed to increase their personal safety, for example, by leaving money at home, avoiding the school after dark, not wearing certain articles of clothing or colors, and carrying some type of deterrent. If professionally educated adults feel so unsafe working in school settings, imagine how children experience these settings.

It is hard to hear that these acts occur within public schools, places where children should feel safe enough to want to attend, feel secure enough to learn, and expect to be protected. The same can be said for adults who choose to work in schools. The issue of school violence is one that begins with an understanding of community within schools. Violent infractions against individuals within a school community occur when there is a misalignment of values and beliefs among members of that community. Any comprehensive definition of school violence must encompass the social interactions within the school community. It must encompass those interactions that damage the social climate and conditions necessary for schools to achieve their mission.

School Development Program

The School Development Program was the vision of James Comer, a child psychiatrist. It reflected his growing frustration in the 1960s and 1970s about the widening gap between minority and nonminority children, especially those with upper socioeconomic status, in terms of their relative levels of academic and social development. The sociopolitical climate in the 1960s and 1970s made him acutely aware that it was necessary to reestablish relationships between school staff, parents, and students within a context of trust and shared goals. In other words, it was necessary to rebuild the kind of community connections and social capital that were necessary to facilitate children's development. Comer (1980) shared his early experiences with the School Development Program and the responses elicited from school and neighborhood members in his book, *School Power*.

The SDP brings the necessary stakeholders together—parents, teachers, administrators—to provide leadership within schools. This process recognizes the differences in priorities, pressures, agendas, and past experiences of the various stakeholders, but it nonetheless requires individuals to come together around common goals for students within the school. The process uses data about students, staff, and parents within the school community to establish appropriate academic, social, and developmental goals (Anson et al., 1991).

Three major teams are created to facilitate this process: the School Planning and Management Team, the Student and Staff Support Team, and the Parent Team. School Planning and Management is the lead team. It is composed of representative stakeholders in the school community and makes decisions regarding school programs, policies, and practices. Although this team has representative membership, its meetings are open to anyone within the school community. Throughout this chapter, this team will be referred to as the leadership team. The Student and Staff Support Team is composed of school staff responsible for delivering educational resources in the areas of cognitive development, social-emotional development, speech and language development, and health. This team works to ensure the positive overall development of students within the school. A goal of the Parent Team is to find ways of involving all parents of students attending the school in the team's efforts, which go beyond the traditional activities of parent/teacher organizations. Because Comer realized that parents and school staff tend to be alienated from one another, the Parent Team works to create links between community and school. Parents and community members must be jointly involved in planning these efforts (Anson et al., 1991; Comer, Haynes, Joyner, & Ben-Avie, 1996).

Concepts and Team Functions

The three major functions of these teams as led by the School Planning and Management Team are to (a) develop a comprehensive plan, (b) ensure that the school's professional development program supports the plan's effective implementation, and (c) make sure the school is capable of evaluating and modifying the plan. The comprehensive plan consists of goals and objectives for the academic, social development, and public relations or community involvement aspects of the school.

The SDP operates under three guiding principles: "no fault," consensus decision making, and collaboration. These principles establish the ground rules for how teams function. "No fault" establishes a norm for not using judgmental or attacking language. When team members are attacked, they are less likely to be fully engaged as team members. Consensus decision making supports the expectation that all viewpoints will be considered and that no point of view will be ignored, as often happens when voting determines decisions. This type of decision-making process builds a sense of inclusiveness among group members. Collaboration establishes the norm that individuals and subgroups will avoid the use of power positions to muscle through decisions or stalemate the process (Comer et al., 1996).

The SDP offers a number of training opportunities that facilitate the implementation process. The foundational training consists of two 1-week sessions that prepare school staff for their roles as key change agents within a school or district. These sessions are described in more detail later in this section. The program also offers a 1-week session for principals to support and enhance their role as leaders in the implementation process. A separate week-long session geared to classroom-based teachers and support service staff is designed to integrate child development principles into their practice. Another category of training offers instruction in curriculum alignment, a literacy program (Essentials of Literacy), and an instructional dialogue program for teachers. SDP also offers specialty sessions depending on the needs of particular schools and districts.

The two week-long foundational sessions are key for building implementation capacity among groups of staff and parents from individual schools. The first session presents the basic program philosophy, team structures, and initial team activities that are specific to the SDP. This level of preparation is important because these groups will be responsible for imparting this information to the rest of their school community. The SDP prepares school staff from the very beginning to take ownership of the implementation process. A school is not helped by depending on outside "experts" to effect necessary changes. The more capacity a school has to support its own plan, the more successful the implementation process will be for the school. The second week-long session is conducted later in the year, after the school has had an opportunity to begin its work and experience some success and failure. Whereas the first session addresses the content issues of the SDP, the second session addresses both content and process. Teams learn more about issues such as child development and curriculum alignment in relationship to management and planning within schools. Teams also learn about conducting effective groups. A major part of the session is process facilitation. Participants are divided into groups of 10, including members from different school districts, and an outside observer is assigned to each group. The observer takes notes about interactions throughout the day. At the end of each training day, each group of 10 and the group's process observer have an opportunity to reflect on interactions. These conversations between group members and the process observer provide individuals with helpful and sometimes difficult feedback about interactions. It allows individuals to try different responses and interaction patterns in a safe environment. Team members come to understand the effect one person, especially someone in a leadership role, can have on group relationships and process. Participants are asked to be mindful of this process in their leadership teams after leaving the training; some teams even make a commitment to include a process observer at each team meeting.

In its current phase of systemic implementation, the SDP applies these principles to work within entire school districts and to teacher preparation programs that support school districts. This chapter describes the process at the individual school level.

One of the first interventions for SDP schools is to assess the school climate within the building. The school climate indicates the ability and potential of individuals to work collaboratively. When there are many areas of strength within a school community, the leadership and decision-making teams may begin to start work on academic and social development issues immediately. When the school climate is characterized by significant areas of weakness or disagreement, the school community may first need to find ways of increasing constructive communication and determining areas of agreement around student goals.

School climate consists of the elements within a school that affect the development and maintenance of those interpersonal relationships that are necessary to accomplish defined and agreed-upon tasks. School climate can also affect intrapersonal issues that might have an outcome on achieving these tasks. Ten elements of school climate have been identified and studied by the School Development Program. They are academic focus, achievement motivation, caring and sensitivity, order and discipline, parent involvement, sharing and fairness, the school's physical appearance and maintenance, students' relationships with teachers, students' relationships with other students, and school community relations (Haynes, Emmons, Ben-Avie, & Comer, 1996).

The school leadership is responsible for establishing the norms of behavior needed to improve school climate. This does not mean simply establishing a list of rules for students to abide by, but understanding that "in every interaction you are either building community, or breaking community" (Comer et al., 1996, p. 148). This statement puts *every* aspect of interaction within the school up for critical examination and provides a stringent standard for self-examination. The school leadership must model the desired interactions if the school community is to adopt the same norms (Comer et al., 1996). Watkinson (1997) pointed out that schools must be vigilant in examining the policies, practices, curriculum, and instructional practices that exist because these activities may fuel the culture of violence within a school.

Studies on SDP implementation have documented increases in student achievement (Cauce, Comer, & Schwartz, 1987; Cook, Hunt, & Murphy, 1999; Haynes, 1994; Haynes, Comer, & Hamilton-Lee, 1988), school climate (Cook et al., 1999; Haynes et al., 1988), and student self-concept (Haynes & Comer, 1990). In addition to these outcomes, research has found increased parental involvement, reduced discipline problems, and an increased schoolwide sense of agency to effect change (Noblit et al., 1997).

Group Psychotherapy and the SDP

Group psychotherapy is a process in which individuals come together for a common purpose or to carry out the common task of effecting interpersonal and intrapersonal change. In group psychotherapy, improvement in psychological and social functioning and symptom reduction are primary. Psychotherapy groups have leaders whose role gradually changes from being directors and initiators of process to becoming process facilitators as the group members take increasing responsibility for maintaining their norms and processes. Intrapsychic and interpersonal change tends to take place more through interaction with other group members and with the leader than through gaining insight (Klein, 1992; Yalom, 1995).

There are two major reasons for viewing the SDP process through the framework of group psychotherapy. First, the SDP facilitates change within a school community more through feedback from group members and the use of specific evaluative tools than through insight. Second, the group process in the SDP attempts to promote change at both the personal and organizational levels of interaction. Discomfort around the process immediately becomes apparent as staff members learn to share power and work collaboratively with others. SDP training prepares school leadership to give constructive feedback to others and to receive feedback. The leadership role is critical during the early stages of program implementation as individuals relearn how to work with one another.

Attention to process issues may be similar in the SDP and in group psychotherapy, but there are also important differences. In the case of a school, the principal usually does not select staff members and rarely selects students for the "group," as a group leader ordinarily would. A principal has to work with everyone who enters his or her school and must find ways of building common purpose and working relationships with all of the interacting subgroups. There are several ways to examine the various group memberships within a school. For example, one group may designate the principal as leader and enlist the other members of the leadership team as group members; another group may designate the entire leadership team as the group leader and enlist the rest of the school staff and students as group members. Finally, this larger group might even expand to include parents and other community members if the situation calls for expanded participation. A skilled principal needs to understand which group he or she is operating within at all times and understand the parallel processes that occur continuously within subgroups.

Principles of Group Psychotherapy

Although the SDP was not intended to be a form of group psychotherapy, the modalities have elements in common. Accordingly, it may be helpful to view the SDP community-building process through a group process lens to understand reasons for program implementation success and failure. Nine specific principles of group psychotherapy are explored in this section with discussion geared to their application in SDP implementation. They are primary task; open systems; maintaining, opening, and closing boundaries; authority; leadership; sociotechnical systems; social defenses; culture; and role (Klein, 1992).

Primary Task

The main purpose of an SDP group functioning within a school environment is to prepare children to become responsible citizens and productive members of society. In addition to teaching the academic content of the curriculum schools must also help students achieve age-appropriate levels of social and emotional development. When students and staff in a school come from diverse backgrounds and have diverse histories, a common platform of social and emotional development cannot be assumed. The principal must obtain agreement and support from the leadership team to accomplish this primary task. If some group members believe that academic preparation is the school's sole task, they will not recognize the need to allocate resources that enhance other aspects of school climate. Consequently, different subgroups will find themselves working toward divergent goals. The principal's ability to identify the primary task and to get the support of the school community will determine the level of success a school will experience. In schools that have experienced a breakdown of school climate, the primary task must include a social development component. Focusing solely on instructional methods ignores the fundamental premise that learning occurs in the context of relationships.

Open Systems

By their very nature, public schools are open systems that receive students from various communities. Each school responds and changes in response to the students, parents, and staff who become part of its educational community. When the educational community changes, the end result of the educational process is likely to change as well. Using the example of exposure to violence, when the number of students who have been exposed to violence at home or in the neighborhood increases and these tensions begin to infect the school climate, the school's academic focus automatically changes as staff members try to respond to the issues. This is especially true when the school does not have an effective means of mediating these tensions and continues to function as though there is no external influence. The SDP process equips the principal and leadership team to use academic and behavioral data about students to better understand strengths and weaknesses and to adjust the academic program to support students' needs.

Boundaries

The school leadership initially establishes the boundary between students, staff, and other adults who are within the school boundary and the various community members who are outside. Prosocial norms of verbal and nonverbal behavior established within a school may differ significantly from the norms that control behavior in the community outside the school. There are many stories of a student being involved in a fight with another student and being encouraged by his or her parents to retaliate. School leaders often have to convince parents that it is not acceptable for their child to defend himself or herself by hitting back and that the school will deal effectively with those who provoked the incident. Typically, the school leadership, staff, students, and others with legitimate roles within the school's boundary maintain standards for school climate and communicate those standards to parents, visitors, and community members. Some leadership teams conduct retreats in locations away from the school to create the necessary group relationships that allow the team to function as a unified group in the eyes of the larger school community. At the large-group level, schools may decide on a name that identifies their participation in the SDP, thus signaling a new boundary to the outside community.

Authority

The school principal must have both authority and credibility as the school's leader. Members of the school community must perceive and accept his or her authority. The school decision-making team is important in providing leadership for the school, but the principal is the person who represents and defends the school to the outside community, larger school district, and superintendent. In many cases, schools change principals frequently or have joint leadership shared between a principal and a CEO. In some instances, the district leadership is actively involved in the day-to-day management of the school. In such situations there may be no real authority or clear line of authority. As a result, a school may be like a ship without a captain, and usually the crew members are painfully aware of the lack of leadership. Before the reform process can effectively begin in a school, the SDP assesses the school district context to determine whether the formally designated leaders have real authority.

Leadership

The school principal and leadership team must be able to maintain staff and student focus on the task of creating a positive school climate while also mediating pressures from outside. For example, although a school district, parents, and others may demand higher test scores, the principal must protect the school community from reacting to these pressures and abandoning the work of creating the positive school climate that will ultimately facilitate improved academic work. The leadership team uses the comprehensive school plan to document school and student needs, the school's goals, and its action plan. The plan helps to keep the leadership on course.

Sociotechnical Systems

When groups attempt to carry out their work tasks, there is always the danger that they may focus solely on the technical aspects of those tasks without considering the relational aspects. In schools, the analogy might be teachers and administration focusing on a particular instructional approach to the exclusion of the sociopsychological aspects of the educational process. The teams within an SDP school must pay attention to school climate conditions that facilitate learning. Process that supports reform demands that the school leadership use information about the students when making educational decisions. Instructional practices should not drive the operation of a school. An understanding that meeting the social and emotional needs of children is intrinsic to the school's primary task should drive the process and the choice of instructional methods.

Social Defenses

In looking at the congruence between system tasks and structure, it is important to emphasize that schools can develop structures such as the three teams and still sabotage the reform process so that the school is never able to achieve its agreed-upon tasks. For example, a team may set times for team meetings but then cancel the meetings due to repeated crises, other meetings scheduled in the same time block, or requirements that staff members attend to competing tasks. The underlying unaddressed issue may be that the School Planning and Management team or the Student and Staff Support Team is either resistant to working on particular issues or reluctant to experience the pain associated with changing long-established patterns of interaction. Schools that effectively use a process facilitator or implementation coordinator will be more aware of problematic behavior patterns.

Culture

Due to the enormous pressures from external sources, school staff often behave as if they are fighting against some perceived external enemy, such as parents, community members, the superintendent, or consultants hired to institute reforms. Relationships within and without the staff may be hostile, suspicious, or impulsive. The system may lack clear goals. A major task of group work involves identifying, understanding, and changing the group culture when it impedes forward progress. It is important for the staff as a whole to understand its culture early in the process so its members can better understand interaction patterns that sustain problematic aspects of the culture. Again, the use of a process facilitator or implementation coordinator enables a school to identify problematic patterns.

Role

The leadership teams within a school implementing the SDP often use process observers or coaches (implementation support) to monitor their team process. The process observers or coaches provide feedback on the leader's effectiveness in maintaining task focus while addressing the group's interaction. Team members are assigned roles such as chairperson, recorder, reporter, and timekeeper. When these group management skills are practiced regularly, a sense of shared ownership of team process is created.

In applying these principles, it is important to remember that each step in the reform process is built on the step that precedes it. For example, the School Planning and Management Team that initiates the reform process consists of the principal as leader and the other representative stakeholders as group members. That team must first change its own interaction patterns in order to understand the nature of the reform process and to serve as a model for the larger group. The larger group, then, is composed of the leadership team, designated as group leader, with the entire school community (staff and students) enlisted as group members.

Application

Two examples of schools dealing with incidents of violence are described in this section to elucidate connections between the SDP and group psychotherapy principles. The first example involves an incident that occurred during an SDP implementation coordinator's monitoring and assessment visit to a middle school (Corbin, 1999). During the visit, the implementation coordinator observed students running down one of the main hallways, talking in loud voices. The activity was most intense at one end of the hall. A teacher arrived at the scene and directed students away from the area while attending to a male student lying on the floor. The student was in pain and holding his midsection. There had been a fight during which the student was injured. Other teachers came to help with the incident, attending to the student, getting him to the nurse's office, and clearing the area of gatherers. Less than 15 minutes after this incident the school held a Student and Staff Support Team meeting. (One of three lead teams in the school the Student and Staff Support Team was responsible for the students' overall development.) During the course of this meeting no mention of the incident in the hall was made. Some of the staff in attendance graded papers or read newspapers during the meeting. Indeed, no further mention of the incident was made by school staff during the course of the implementation coordinator's visit.

The second example concerns the Clinton Grove Elementary School Peace Program. The example demonstrates how a school community can institute practices that reduce the occurrence of violence or out-of-control behavior within a school. At the beginning of each school year, the principal discusses the Peace Program with all the students, classroom by classroom. Each class creates its own peace flag that hangs outside its classroom. The school has a peace flag that flies below the U.S. flag in the front of the school. At the end of each week, classes in which there was no occurrence of violence are given a blue ribbon to add to the class flag. At the end of each quarter the class with the most ribbons has a formal celebration, organized by the school. If there is a violent incident in the school, the offending students are photographed while they take down the school's peace flag. The principal keeps this photograph, and the students' parents are asked to come to the school to discuss the incident. In that discussion the parents are asked to make a commitment to work with their child on alternative ways of responding to difficult situations. The Peace Program was successful almost immediately. Based on that success, the school expanded the program to establish a school norm requiring the use of positive language. This initiative was viewed as a way to continue to build peace and respect for others (Savo, 1995).

The leadership team of the first school would have said they were implementing the SDP process because the team structure was in place. Their actions, however, tell another story. In this example, the nine principles of group psychotherapy were not maintained. First, there was no clear definition of the school as a community or the school team as a leadership group. In fact, there was no group. Second, the primary task of the school and the Student and Staff Support Team was not readily apparent. This raises an important point. The members of a group must behave as a definable group and also act in ways that reflect agreement about the primary task. Without a distinct group identity and an agreed-upon primary task, the other principles of group psychotherapy cannot possibly apply. School fights between students are unavoidable; however, the response to them is totally under the control of the school leadership. In this case, acknowledging within the team meeting that a fight had taken place, identifying those involved, and having the support staff resolve lingering issues between the involved students and among other students who observed or heard about the fight is the most basic intervention that a school could do. A school needs to address such issues to help ensure students' physical and emotional safety and to restore the positive school climate. Ignoring the occurrence of these events destroys a school's community.

The second example provides a different and more hopeful view of how a school can pull together as a group, separate from the larger community, for the purpose of improving students' interactions. Such a program requires the school leadership to agree to include the Peace Program as an aspect of its primary task and to support the principal in maintaining a focus on this primary task. The group realizes it will be influenced by external forces and encourages open communication with clear messages about behaviors expected within the school community. The establishment of the smaller group is possible when the principal has established his or her authority with staff, students, and parents. For this process to be effective the leadership team must be clear about its role and able to provide and receive effective feedback. The success of the Peace Program provides evidence that the sociotechnical systems of the group process are balanced. There is congruence between the group tasks and the structures needed to achieve those tasks. The culture reflects a school community that has reduced the interaction patterns that interfere with progress toward improving academic goals.

It may be unfair to draw conclusions about schools based on single incidents, but the examples cited are commonplace events in schools and provide an opportunity to reflect on all aspects of the school day. The point of the examples is to show the importance of building a school community that functions as an effective group. The philosophy and structure of the SDP allow schools to build community, recognize and use resources, and work toward preparing students to become capable, productive members of their community. School communities can accomplish these goals despite significant differences among individuals. The process allows all of the constituencies in a given school to come together around an agreed-upon task and to experience a level of change that makes it possible for each team to reach its goal.

The experiences of team members, including the students in the school community, are often markedly different inside the school, where they are members of the team, and outside the school, where they are not. The school team equips its members with new skills. For example, Comer (1980, p. 119) described an incident in which a student new to an SDP school had his foot accidentally stepped on while the students were moving around. The boy threw his hands up as if to fight, at which point another student said, "Hey, man, we don't do that at this school." The child looked around and found confirmation of this statement in the faces of the other students. In response, he gradually let his hands drop to his sides. It is the ability of the SDP to effect change within individuals as well as within the larger school community that makes the process similar to group psychotherapy.

 # Summary

The school climate and the operation of a school that is effectively implementing the SDP process are markedly different from in other schools. In SDP schools, activity in the halls and classrooms is orderly, and visitors to the school know they have stepped into a community in which expectations about normative behavior are significantly different from those in the surrounding neighborhood. Moreover, students and staff readily take responsibility for incidents and activities within the school. Principals talk of the process as saving their lives because it provides a way of working productively with other members within the school. The negative interactions within the school were extremely unproductive and diminished the effectiveness of the school program and staff. Members of leadership teams often begin to use the process with their families as a result of the school experience. These anecdotes were captured in the assessment of school climate. However, changes in individual beliefs and interpersonal functioning do not begin until the members of a school community agree on their primary task and undertake the hard, sometimes painful work of changing their interactions with others with the goal of improving conditions within the school community and the lives of children who attend the school.

School violence may be, and often is, addressed through specific "violence reduction" programs. However, it is more effective to address school violence before it has a chance to take hold. The SDP effectively addresses violence, as well as many other ills that affect schools, by building a school community that attends to the social, emotional, and academic development of students while also encouraging and facilitating supportive relationships. The school community must agree about its primary task and about the values and beliefs necessary to support that task. Moreover, the school community must agree to examine all aspects of the school day for misalignments in core values and beliefs. Building a functional SDP community begins with the leadership team and must then expand to include widening circles within the larger school community.

References

Anson, A. R., Cook, T. D., Habib, F., Grady, M. K., Haynes, N., & Comer, J. P. (1991). The Comer School Development Program: A theoretical analysis. *Urban Education, 26,* 56–82.

Astor, R. A., Behre, W. J., Wallace, J. M., & Fravil, K. A. (1998). School social workers and school violence: Personal safety, training, and violence programs. *Social Work, 43,* 223–232.

Cauce, A. M., Comer, J. P., & Schwartz, D. (1987). Long-term effects of a systems-oriented school prevention program. *American Journal of Orthopsychiatry, 57,* 127–131.

Comer, J. P. (1980). *School power: Implications of an intervention program.* New York: The Free Press.

Comer, J. P., Haynes, N. M., Joyner, E. T., & Ben-Avie, M. (1996). *Rallying the whole village: The Comer process for reforming education.* New York: Teachers College Press.

Cook, T. D., Hunt, H. D., & Murphy, R. F. (1999). *Comer's School Development Program in Chicago: A theory-based evaluation.* Evanston, IL: Northwestern University, Institute for Policy Research.

Corbin, J. N. (1999). Development: Prerequisite for learning. In J. P. Comer, M. Ben-Avie, N. M. Haynes, & E. T. Joyner (Eds.), *Child by child: The Comer process for change in education* (pp. 243–244). New York: Teachers College Press.

Elliott, D. S., Hamburg, B. A., & Williams, K. R. (1998). Violence in American schools: An overview. In D. S. Elliott, B. A. Hamburg, & K. R. Williams (Eds.), *Violence in American schools* (p. 3–28). New York: Cambridge University Press.

Epp, J. R., & Watkinson, A. M. (1997). Introduction. In J. R. Epp & A. M. Watkinson (Eds.), *Systemic violence in education: Promise broken* (pp. xi–xvii). New York: State University of New York Press.

Haynes, N. M. (1994). *School Development Program* (Research Monograph No. 1). New Haven, CT: Yale University Child Study Center School Development Program.

Haynes, N. M., & Comer, J. P. (1990). The effects of a school development program on self-concept. *Yale Journal of Biology and Medicine, 63,* 275–283.

Haynes, N. M., Comer, J. P., & Hamilton-Lee, M. (1988). The School Development Program: A model for school improvement. *Journal of Negro Education, 57,* 11–21.

Haynes, N. M., Emmons, C. L., Ben-Avie, M., & Comer, J. P. (1996). *The School Development Program: Student, staff and parent school climate surveys.* New Haven, CT: Yale Child Study Center School Development Program.

Klein, E. B. (1992). Contributions from social systems theory. In R. H. Klein, H. S. Bernard, & D. L. Singer (Eds.), *Handbook of contemporary group psychotherapy* (pp. 87–123). Madison, CT: International Universities Press.

National Center for Education Statistics. (1998). *Violence and discipline problems in U.S. public schools: 1996–97.* URL: http://nces.ed.gov/pubs98/violence/

National Center for Education Statistics. (2000). *Indicators of school crime and safety, 2000.* URL: http://nces.ed.gov/pubs2001/crime2000/

Noblit, G., Malloy, C., Malloy, W., Villenas, S., Groves, P., Jennings, M., et al. (1997). *Scaling up a supportive environment: Case studies of successful Comer schools.* Chapel Hill: University of North Carolina.

Savo, C. (1995). Let there be peace at school. *SDP Newsline, 4*(2).

Watkinson, A. M. (1997). Administrative complicity and systemic violence in education. In J. R. Epp & A. M. Watkinson (Eds.), *Systemic violence in education: Promise broken* (pp. xi–xvii). New York: State University of New York Press.

Yalom, I. D. (1995). *The theory and practice of group psychotherapy.* New York: Basic Books.

10

Escalation-De-escalation: Teacher Interventions

Marla R. Brassard and Michelle Butterfass

Aggressive behavior in schools and classrooms has been an issue of nationwide concern for many years. To identify ways to most effectively reduce this violence, it is important to understand the characteristics associated with its occurrence. These characteristics include where it occurs (ranging from certain classrooms and schools to certain locations within schools), when it occurs, who is aggressive, who is the target of the aggression, why the violence occurs, and what purpose it serves. By becoming aware of these factors and the role they play in eliciting aggressive behavior, school-based professionals will be able to use the information to develop appropriate interventions that will prevent or reduce such behavior.

This chapter describes the information social workers need to understand why, where, when, and to whom aggression occurs in their school and how to gather that information. The chapter also explains how to use this information to design simple prevention programs that can be effective and tailored to the needs of a particular setting. With several straightforward techniques, social workers can work collaboratively with teachers, administrators, and other school personnel (e.g., bus drivers, lunchroom staff) to identify the factors associated with the occurrence of aggression in their school and then use this information to find solutions that will work at their school.

The Context of Aggression

Research has shown that schools and classrooms vary dramatically in the amount of aggressive behavior exhibited. This finding was conclusively demonstrated in a very large, well-designed study by Kellam and his colleagues (Kellam & Rebok, 1992). The Baltimore public schools and some surrounding suburban districts allowed these researchers to randomly assign first-grade students and teachers to one another within a school. The researchers found that the variation in levels of aggression, as assessed by trained observers in classrooms, varied as much across first grades within a school as they did across schools within the district and the suburbs. In a follow-up study, Kellam and colleagues (Kellam, Ling, Merisca, Brown, & Ialongo, 1999) found that the earlier level of aggression was predictive of which boys would be aggressive upon entering middle school 6 years later. It was clear that having more children rated as aggressive in a classroom made some of the difference, but it was likely that teachers played a role in the level of aggression as well; however, the latter was not the focus of the study. This finding is actually very exciting because it suggests that classroom aggression might be addressed through classwide interventions, and, indeed, this is what Kellam and his colleagues did (Kellam & Rebok, 1992). They randomly assigned schools and classrooms within schools to a control condition and to three intervention conditions, one involving improving behavior (e.g., through participation in the Good Behavior Game), a second involving improving reading instruction (e.g., through use of the Distar Program), and the third involving improving both behavior and reading. The interventions focused on changing the teacher's behavior in order to change the children's behavior. By the end of the intervention, children in the good behavior program classrooms had significantly improved behavior individually and as a group. Children who had the reading instruction intervention had improved reading scores. Children who received both interventions improved on both variables. Those children in control conditions performed at lower levels for reading and higher levels for aggressive behavior.

Aggressive incidents are not only more likely to occur in some classrooms than others, but are also more likely to occur in certain locations and times on the school campus, particularly those where adults are absent. Astor, Meyer, and Behre (1999) worked with a number of high schools to develop school violence maps in order to identify which locations and times were most susceptible to aggressive behavior. Using an architectural drawing of the school campus, the researchers interviewed principals, students, teachers, janitors, school police, and others, and recorded each incident of aggressive behavior that was reported in terms of location, time of day, and who were the target and perpetrator. It became clear upon visual examination of the map that incidents clustered together both in location and in time of day and occurred primarily when adults were not present. Furthermore, the researchers found that certain groups of individuals were more likely to be victims (e.g., freshman and sophomore female students) than others (e.g., juniors and seniors). Interviews with students and staff suggested that areas where incidents of aggression clustered most were areas that they termed "unowned" by anyone. By examining the map, school personnel were able to devise effective strategies to prevent aggressive incidents by increasing ownership of these spaces and increasing the role of teachers, students, and other school personnel in reclaiming these spaces. For example, an unsupervised area behind the library began to be patrolled by teachers and aides. In addition, lights were installed in the high school parking lot, and a staff member was placed on duty there before and after school. Simple interventions like these were able to dramatically decrease the number of aggressive incidents being reported.

In addition to determining where and when aggressive incidents occur, it is important to look at the context in which aggression occurs and why it is occurring. Although the term *aggression* is often used in a pejorative sense to refer to hostile, angry, hurtful behavior, aggressive behavior is a learned behavioral pattern influenced by genetics that can be good or bad depending on the context in which it occurs. Aggressive behavior is often viewed in a positive manner when it is used in situations where one is protecting oneself or others from another's aggressive act. For example, all organisms will fight if attacked or to defend territory or loved ones that are under threat. Furthermore, a nation's success often depends on the actions of individuals in society who will engage in aggressive behavior to protect the homeland. Both nations and individuals can protect themselves from the aggression of others by making it clear that there will be unpleasant consequences if someone is aggressive toward them. However, problems arise when aggression occurs in inappropriate contexts or when alternative responses would be much better. For example, when a teacher is explaining to a student why he or she did poorly on an exam, a desirable response for the student would be to listen carefully and try to understand why he or she made errors; an inappropriate response would be to throw the paper back at the teacher and stomp out of the room.

Whether viewed as positive or negative, aggressive behavior, in classroom or school situations is influenced by a number of factors. One factor is an individual's history of reinforcement for aggressive behavior. Some students have grown up in homes where aggressively challenging a parent's demands, even for something simple, such as doing chores or completing homework, leads to the termination of the demands (Patterson, Reid, & Dishion, 1992). These children may have found that aggressively responding to parental demands or behaviors they do not like results in their parents backing off or placating them. They may then take this well-learned response to school and employ it in interactions with teachers, aides, and administrators.

Biological factors also play a role. Some children may be genetically more inclined to be irritable or impulsive or less able to effectively use language to think or communicate, making them less likely to stop and think whether there may be an appropriate, less aggressive response to use in a given situation in which they are feeling challenged or want something. Some children may have social deficits (e.g., some children with learning disabilities, children with autistic spectrum disorder) or mild thought disorders that make them vulnerable to misinterpreting social situations and responding aggressively when other responses would be far more appropriate for the situation.

Current reinforcement contingencies for behavior also play a role. Some teachers are less capable than others of maintaining order in their classrooms. Even generally well-behaved students may learn that they can take advantage of these teachers and resist their demands by behaving more aggressively. Further, although a given teacher may have good control over behavior in the school, the school as a whole may have loosely enforced rules, which can create a climate in which students think they can get away with almost anything. Knowing that aggression is mostly learned, and that its expression can be prevented through reducing opportunities and/or through providing swift consequences for misbehavior and rewards for appropriate behavior, means that prevention programs tailored to the specific needs and conditions of a classroom, school, or district can be very effective in de-escalating violence.

Methods for Gathering Information Needed to Understand Aggressive Situations in the Classroom or School

ABC Logs of Aggression in the Classroom

Many social workers are familiar with the antecedents-behavior-consequences (ABC) method of understanding problematic behaviors (e.g., marital conflicts, depressive feelings, binge eating episodes). Clinicians help clients solve problems by asking them to keep ABC logs of instances of problematic behavior. These logs can be used effectively by teachers who have an aggressive student or students in their classrooms. Once teachers are taught how to use the logs, they generally find the logs to be a very useful tool for diagnosing problematic interactions they are having with students. To use this approach, the social worker prepares an ABC chart for the teacher (see Appendix A) and has the teacher log, for several days, any psychologically or physically aggressive incidents that occur in the classroom. As can be seen from the chart, teachers are asked to first describe the incident briefly in column B, then to describe the antecedent, or what happened just before the incident, in column A. In column C, they record what happened after the incident. For example, the first incident the teacher described in the sample log in Appendix A was related to her feedback to a student on her academic performance. It seems from her description that the student involved felt put down by either the content of what the teacher said or the manner of how she said it. From examining the log, the teacher and consultant were able to generate several hypotheses about what was happening. To test some of these hypotheses, they role-played the situation that occurred and then processed how both the teacher and the student were feeling after the incident. In this situation, the teacher felt the student was not taking her class seriously, and because they did not have a particularly close relationship, her voice in giving the student feedback on her exam performance may have had a dismissive tone. The student might have interpreted this as further evidence that the teacher did not like or care about her and saw her as a stupid or lazy student who was not trying. After brainstorming and then role-playing ways that the teacher might talk to the student about her performance such that caring and concern were expressed rather than critical judgment, the teacher was able to deliver feedback more effectively to the student.

This technique can be used with teachers individually and in groups as part of professional development. We have found other teachers excellent at suggesting alternative approaches that can be used in interactions with students (see Example 2 in the Appendix A log for an alternative approach recommended by a teacher during a professional development workshop). The method is simple, is easy to grasp, provides highly relevant data for consultations, and often leads to quick, uncomplicated resolutions to common problems that can escalate into conflicts in the classroom.

Therapeutic Consultation With Teachers About Problematic Teacher-Student Relationships

Another approach for gathering information helpful for understanding aggressive situations in the classroom was developed by Pianta, a well-known theorist and researcher in the area of teacher-student relationships. The approach involves a model of teacher consultation that fits well with the clinical skills of social workers (Pianta, 1999). Drawing from systems theory, attachment theory, and developmental research, Pianta argued that children's competence is a function of the quality of their relationships with parents and teachers, who provide a context in which their behavioral competence develops. The more integrated and consistent these systems are, the more competently the child can behave in a self-regulated manner with peers, parents, and teachers. According to Pianta:

> For all school-aged children, and especially those whose caregiving relationships have not afforded them opportunities to master many of the challenges of development . . . one cannot underestimate the extent to which relationships with people and environments support or inhibit developmental progress and functioning in school. Children are only as competent as their context affords them to be. . . . Perhaps the single biggest error that educators make when working with children is to assume that competence is a property of the child and to fail to make the necessary observations of the child in context. (p. 64)

To promote better teacher-student relationships, Pianta developed the Student-Teacher Relationship Scale (STRS, Pianta, 1994), which measures the characteristics of a student-teacher relationship from the teacher's perspective and can be used in consultation with the teacher. The scale measures three factors: conflict, closeness, and dependency. Pianta reported that high conflict scores are related to behavior problems, emotionally negative interactions between a teacher and student, and ineffective behavior management in the classroom. High dependency scores have been related to the variables of children's help seeking behavior, and may be motivated by a desire for physical proximity to the teacher, as well as emotionally negative interactions and high levels of involvement by the teacher with the child. High scores on closeness are related to emotionally positive teacher-child interactions and a moderate level of involvement with the child. The STRS can be used on a schoolwide basis to identify teachers who have a disproportionate number of conflictual relationships with students, or it may be used with teachers who have a concern about a relationship with a particular child. Social workers could use this scale, along with other interview and observation measures, "to elicit teachers' perceptions of themselves in relation to a particular child" and use this information to help teachers provide a more supportive classroom context, improve problematic interactions with particular students, and prevent teacher burnout (Pianta, 1999, p. 104). Pianta's book, *Enhancing Relationships Between Children and Teachers,* provides a detailed model of his approach.

Focus Groups With Administrators, Teachers, Mediators, Parents, and Students

Focus groups have long been used in business to evaluate consumers' impressions of different products. More recently they have become popular with politicians in terms of gaining a better understanding of their image and how they might improve it, gaining a better understanding of voters and what influences them, and gathering ideas on how to market policies that may not be particularly attractive to voters. Social scientists have also become more interested in using focus groups to gain a qualitative understanding of quantitative data, such as a sudden increase in aggressive behavior at a middle school. In particular, social workers can use focus groups to identify problematic situations in the classroom, better understand their causes, and generate and evaluate possible solutions. Formal training may be useful for individuals who plan to use focus groups as a research technique. There is a large literature on running focus groups, and universities increasingly offer graduate courses in how to design and conduct these groups. Individuals with good group skills can quickly acquire the basic concepts for conducting focus groups through reading one or two of the better written guides (e.g., Basch, 1997). Social workers, with their training in group therapy, can easily acquire these skills.

Characteristics of effective focus groups include a quiet place to talk, the right group size (which varies from 5 to 12), food and beverages, and, most important, a good moderator's guide. Focus groups are most effective when the moderator carefully lays out a series of questions such as those shown in Appendix B, a moderator's guide for administrators that we designed to use with principals and vice principals in secondary schools in a district in which we were working. As you can see, the first question is designed to "break the ice" and usually elicits a laugh and a short response. The earlier questions are more general, and the later ones are more specific. This guide is designed to be used flexibly with questions and probes omitted or expanded depending on the flow of the group discussion.

We first started running focus groups when conducting research in a large school district that was experiencing multiple problems with violent behavior. In the district, 400 students had received 30-day suspensions for violent behavior, which included 120 student-teacher assaults. To get a better understanding of the problem, we conducted a series of focus groups with general and special education teachers, suspended students, parents of suspended students, and middle and high school principals and vice principals. From these groups we learned a number of interesting things.

The administrators identified three main scenarios leading to aggressive behavior that resulted in suspension: (a) behavior perceived by teachers or students as disrespectful to them (e.g., a teacher being more distant with a student, or a teacher not knowing a student's name when disciplining a student), (b) students arriving at school on edge from their home experiences so that any little thing would "set them off," and (c) teachers (often substitutes) failing to recognize that a conflict was developing between students and not taking appropriate and timely actions such as sending the students to mediation. From listening to the school administrators, we also learned that student-teacher assaults were least likely to occur when teachers and students had close relationships, such that teachers were conveying to the students that they cared about them. The administrators discussed situations in which a teacher "bawled a student out" and told the student everything he or she was doing wrong but then offered advice to the student on how to improve. According to the administrators, these teachers were perceived by the students as caring about them, and the students complied with these teachers' instructions. (Conversations with suspended students confirmed this observation.) We also learned that some of the principals felt that if they could watch each student get off the bus in the morning they would be in a position to identify those students who were going to "blow up" during the day and could make sure that a counselor or peer mediator saw them before this happened. Also, the administrators viewed peer mediators, who consisted of an informal team of students recruited by the school personnel, as very effective in dealing with students who could potentially become aggressive. Overall, the vice principals and principals had many ideas to share about how to prevent aggressive behavior and were confident that their ideas would work if they had the time to carry them out on a consistent basis.

Focus groups with two different sets of secondary school teachers also offered insight into the problems associated with the violent incidents that were occurring. We learned that the teachers in both groups recognized and were overwhelmed by the seriousness of the problems faced by their students at home related to alcoholic parents, domestic violence, abandonment by parents, and so forth. The teachers also felt that the administration in their schools showed too much tolerance for disrespectful and disruptive behavior by students, and they felt persecuted by the administration's demands that students learn, and that teachers teach, at a standard rate regardless of the ambient chaos. Two things were particularly striking about the teachers' responses. One was a failure to acknowledge that teachers' behavior might in any way contribute to the problem of school violence. The other was a failure to acknowledge that teachers' behavior might in any way ameliorate the problem of school violence. Teachers felt both blameless and powerless, and they thought that most conflicts were started by out-of-control youngsters. They thought the only solution was intensive, early intervention so that children could come to school ready to learn and behave appropriately.

Focus groups with the students who had been suspended for violent behavior identified, from their perspective, four major scenarios surrounding verbal assaults and verbal assaults that led to physical assaults: (a) being in a bad mood to start with and someone (teacher or peer) failing to leave them alone, (b) having someone (teacher or peer) behave disrespectfully toward them (e.g., "being laughed at, being ordered around in a demeaning way, being looked at as if they were nothing"), (c) having a teacher be unfair or partial in applying rules or meting out discipline, and (d) having someone (teacher or peer) trying to prove they were tough by picking on someone. What particularly stood out from these series of interviews was how upset students were when a teacher treated them with disrespect. Students were open to being disciplined by a teacher if the disciplining was done respectfully and if they knew the teacher cared about them. They reported being openly defiant to teachers who were disrespectful to them or who made it clear that they disliked them. These comments were consistent with how the administrators tended to view the cause of some student-teacher assaults. Students also conveyed a strong sense of their vulnerability to violence from others. They reported bringing weapons to school because of the dangers involved in getting to and from school. They felt forced to defend themselves and thought that it was only fair that they be allowed to arm themselves. They suggested a policy where weapons could be checked upon entry to school. No one, however, thought that weapons should be allowed in schools.

Focus groups with parents of suspended students revealed that the parents did not understand the current discipline code and suspected that it was not enforced impartially. The parents, who were all African American or Latino, implied that racial backgrounds may have contributed to this biased enforcement of rules. They were generally confused and upset about the circumstances under which their children had been suspended. They expressed their desire for a concise and clearly stated discipline code to be made available to students, parents, and teachers. From their comments, it was clear there was a cross-cultural lack of agreement about what was and was not appropriate behavior at school and in conflict situations (see also Sheets, 1996). One African American mother, who was a social worker, was very upset when her son was suspended for arguing with a teacher about his behavior. She had taught her son that he could say anything he wanted but that he could not hit someone. He had made no threatening gesture or move toward the teacher, and therefore the mother felt his suspension was completely arbitrary and unfair. Nonetheless, she instructed him that if another altercation occurred with the teacher, he was to say nothing and walk away. Unfortunately, when he tried this behavior on a subsequent occasion he was suspended for being disrespectful and insubordinate. Despite situations like these, the parents of suspended students had the same broad goals for their children as the school: successful academic achievement and good behavior.

As indicated herein, these focus groups provided a great deal of useful information for designing interventions to reduce school violence. Among the possible targets for intervention that clearly stood out were helping teachers interact in a more respectful way with students, helping teachers do a better job of identifying developing conflicts or students who are on edge and "ready to blow," working with the community to improve neighborhood safety so that students did not feel they had to arm themselves to get to school, and refining the discipline code so that it was clear and understandable to students, parents, and teachers of all ethnic backgrounds.

Review of Discipline Records to Identify Students and Teachers With High Rates of Conflict Incidents

School discipline records are another source of information about aggressive behavior that can be particularly useful in identifying both students and teachers who are typically or often involved in conflictual situations. They can also provide highly descriptive information about the conflicts that occur, which can be helpful in brainstorming appropriate and effective interventions for these particular individuals as well as for the general school population. From our review of about 300 discipline records of student-teacher assaults that occurred over the course of 2½ years in the school district described earlier, it become clear that special education classes for the emotionally and behaviorally disturbed were the most dangerous place to work in the schools studied: 40% or more of the assaults occurred in these classrooms, a higher amount than in any other location. A review of the incident reports, which were nearly all written from the perspective of the teacher, revealed that classroom rules had to be more clear, more fairly applied, and carried out in a respectful manner. The resorts also revealed that students in bad moods were more likely to respond irritably to teacher demands. In addition to student-teacher assaults, incidents included teachers getting hurt while breaking up fights among students and a teacher or paraprofessional trying to physically control a student's movements in a conflictual situation. A few incidents had clear racial overtones; however, the role of racial distrust and miscommunication may have been underreported. In this particular school district, 80% of the teaching staff were white and more than 70% of the students were nonwhite, which would suggest that more racially related incidents may have occurred. In schools with percentages such as these, it is essential that teachers, students, and administrators are aware of cultural manners, particularly in conflict situations. Furthermore, from reading these incident reports, it became clear that some teachers seemed to be provoking an aggressive response from students, perhaps to have the students removed from their classrooms. In most situations, however, the teachers were responding to situations that had already escalated out of control or were moving rapidly in that direction.

Through a reviewing of incident reports, a social worker can generate a number of hypotheses about how situations escalate and what teachers can do to de-escalate situations. Clearly, how classroom rules are administered and how students are disciplined when the rules are violated can influence the likelihood of conflict occurring. Role-playing the administration of discipline with groups of teachers may be an effective technique in helping teachers become more aware of how they are coming across to students. It can also be useful to have teachers ask themselves what students say about them. Other questions posed to teachers could be: Do you know every student's name? Do you know how to repair a botched interaction? Are you aware of the underlying message you are communicating when you give a student negative feedback or discipline a student for violating the rules? And how do students of different races perceive you? Other interventions may instruct teachers on how to break up fights among students without getting hurt or how to manage a situation in which a student is physically out of control and may be a threat to other students or to the teacher.

Discipline records can also be used to identify students with high rates of aggression in general. From reading the detailed records, a social worker can identify situations in which a particular student is aggressive and can also note situations (e.g., class periods) in which the student has no discipline referrals. From this information, hypotheses can be generated about how the environment might be modified to reduce aggression and increase appropriate behavior. The social worker might call a meeting of the student's teachers (this is much easier to do when teachers are part of a team that educates the same group of students) and ask them how the student is doing in each of their classes. Those teachers who are getting good behavior from the student might discuss what it is about the content of their courses, the other students in the courses, the relationships they have with the student, and so forth, that might contribute to good behavior in one situation as opposed to aggressive behavior in another situation.

School and Neighborhood Aggressive Incident Maps

As mentioned previously, Astor et al. (1999) developed the school violence map as a technique to identify aggressive incidents, the location, the time, and victim and perpetrator characteristics, in order to develop effective prevention approaches. His technique is fairly straightforward and is modeled after the incident maps used by law enforcement. To carry out this technique, a social worker must obtain an architectural map of the school campus. He or she would then need to obtain information about all of the aggressive incidents that occurred during a set period of time (e.g., a week). This could be done by interviewing individuals most likely to have this information, such as vice principals, or the task could be more broadly approached by announcing the study during morning announcements and asking members of the school community to report incidents that have occurred. After a week of collecting and recording this information, a social worker could share the map with representatives of the different groups involved (e.g., deans, teachers) to see if any information is missing and to interpret and make sense of the findings. This interpretation and sharing of information could be done with a fairly small but representative group of the school personnel most involved in discipline as well as a group of students who have been victimized. It also could be expanded into a much larger process in which the information is interpreted and shared with the entire school community. Reactions to the information, ideas for effective solutions to the problems, and evaluation of solutions suggested by the social worker and his or her colleagues could be made in several focus groups conducted with teachers, students, bus drivers, and others.

Observations of High-Risk Areas/Classrooms

The ABC analysis, focus groups, and school/neighborhood maps are all very useful for identifying problems and suggesting possible solutions. However, people's impressions and interpretations of what has happened recently or in the past can be fairly subjective and somewhat distorted. Direct observations can help to refine hypotheses about how an environment might be modified to reduce aggression. High-risk areas such as lunchrooms, high school parking lots, and special education classrooms for children with emotional disturbances are environments in which more detailed analyses may be required for designing the most effective interventions.

Common Areas (Cafeterias, Buses, Assemblies, and so forth)

Sprick and his colleagues (Sprick, Howard, Wise, Marcum, & Haykin, 1998) developed an extensive protocol and packet of reproducible materials for collecting information about aggressive behavior from students and staff and using the information to design interventions that improve civil behavior and reduce aggression in common areas at school. Sprick (1995) has also written an excellent monograph on lunchroom design and supervision. In it, he explained, for example, that the setup of tables in the lunchroom can result in more or less disruptive behavior. From his observations of lunchroom interactions, he noted that when tables were more spread out, children were more likely to be disruptive and it was more difficult for them to be supervised by teachers or lunchroom aides. They would engage in hit-and-run attacks on other students and easily elude pursuing adults. By pushing one end of each table against the wall so that there was only one outlet into the general cafeteria from each row of tables, misbehaving students were trapped and easily apprehended. This intervention alone dramatically reduces aggressive behavior.

Classrooms for Children With Emotional Disturbances

Observations in special education classrooms for children with emotional disturbances can be particularly helpful in providing information about the causes of aggressive behavior with this high-risk population and in generating possible solutions that can be targeted to their specific needs, which often differ from those of mainstreamed children. Our analysis of the student-teacher data for special education teachers, obtained from discipline records as described earlier, indicated that being the perfect teacher, including having close relationships with students, did not always work in terms of reducing aggression in the classroom, as it had in general education classrooms. In fact, from interviews of teachers and students involved in some of these incidents, it became clear that the students involved often had a close, long-standing relationship with their special education teacher. The teachers were, in general, very competent at managing their students' behavior and helping their students regulate their mood, impulses, and behavior. However, they did not have control of their students' lives outside of their classrooms. Students with emotional disturbances often come from very troubled families who may have exposed them to emotionally disregulating situations and aggressive behavior. These are the students most likely to come to school ready to "blow," as the vice principal described. When children with emotional disturbance come into class after having an unpleasant interaction at home, with another teacher, an administrator, or a peer, their feelings from the incident can filter into the special education teacher's classroom and can interfere with the teacher's interactions with that student. Trying to direct the behavior of a special education student who is upset is a very high-risk situation.

Colvin (cited in Walker & Walker, 1991) described this exact scenario in what he called an escalation/de-escalation sequence. This sequence typically occurs when a student who is angry, frustrated, hostile, and unresponsive to adults in general (e.g., ignoring adults' requests, commands, or demands) is upset about something outside of the classroom. This type of student wants to punish others for making any demands on him or her. Colvin described a typical chain as going like this: (a) The student is in an agitated state. (b) The teacher makes a request of the student or gives him or her a direct command (e.g., "Please take your hat off."). (c) The student asks a question designed to resist or deflect the command (e.g., "What time is it?"). (d) The teacher repeats the command. (e) The student offers an excuse, argues, whines, complains, or otherwise does not comply (e.g., "My hair looks bad."). (f) The teacher continues to pressure the student for compliance (e.g., "The rule is no hats in school. Now take your hat off."). (g) The student has a tantrum, insults the teacher, walks out of the room. By observing and analyzing this chain of events, one can assess aspects of what might have led to the disruptive behavior and make suggestions for preventing or de-escalating these events that are specifically aimed at the particular situation. The first part of this chain involves rational and appropriate behavior on the part of the teacher. Unfortunately, this behavior is addressed to a student who is in an agitated state and has a history of problematic behavior such that he or she would be placed in a special education classroom. Colvin noted that this chain starts with very trivial events early on, such as questioning and arguing, but culminates in very serious behaviors at the end of the chain, such as tantrums, verbal and physical abuse, threats, and intimidation.

Colvin argued that, after careful situation analysis and manipulation of antecedent events, the key is to anticipate and control trivial behaviors early on so that escalation does not occur. He made several suggestions for breaking this cycle or chain of events. First, he suggested that the teacher "not make demands on or initiate to students when they appear in an agitated state" (Walker & Walker, 1991, p. 22). Instead, the teacher should wait until the student's mood improves before making a direct request or demand. Otherwise, his or her command is likely to be perceived as a provocative event, particularly if it is made in the presence of other students. Second, Colvin suggested that the teacher ask what the student's problem is but not include a command until the student calms down. Third, he suggested that the teacher not get caught up in questions and answers initiated by the student. If a student asks questions or makes comments regarding the situation, the teacher should not respond. Instead, the teacher should ignore the questions and comments and simply restate what the student needs to do and say that he or she will answer the student's question after the student does as told. If the student refuses, the student should be left alone until he or she calms down. Colvin cautioned teachers to not pressure the student at this time by hovering, waiting, glaring, scolding, or making threats about future sanctions. In particular, he cautioned teachers to not touch, grab, or shake a student, noting that such behavior is highly likely to escalate a situation, something we observed in our analysis of student-teacher assault data. Fourth, if a situation calls for such action as giving a time out or a loss of privileges or points, the teacher should carry the action out in a quiet, nonprovocative way. If the situation does not call for such action, Colvin recommended that the student be left alone until he or she is ready to get back to work. In this way, the teacher retains control in the classroom, and the student has no new opportunities for noncompliance.

Fifth, if a student has persistent problems of noncompliance, Colvin recommended that the teacher discuss the situation and the patterns he or she has observed with the student when the student is calm and able to participate fully in such a discussion. The teacher can keep an ABC chart and go over it with the student, and can then work with the student to try to develop alternatives to noncompliance in these types of situations. If a student has a lot of difficulty with compliance, the teacher and student can do a daily debriefing in which they discuss what went well and what did not go well. Colvin noted that students who have difficulty with compliance often lack alternative responses to being noncompliant when they are upset. Thus, they may benefit from a family outreach or social skills training program offered by the school social worker.

Hill and Janet Walker developed a wonderful small book entitled *Coping With Noncompliance in the Classroom: A Positive Approach for Teachers* (1991). This book provides useful information for social workers who may want to consult with teachers as well as for teachers themselves, particularly teachers who work with students with emotional or behavioral disorders.

Surveys to Collect Information From Teachers and Students

Surveys can be helpful for gathering a wide range of information about students' and teachers' experiences and relationships, including aggressive behavior, which can then be used to create interventions. As part of a longitudinal study entitled "Modifiable Risk Factors for Aggression in Middle Schools," we have been administering surveys to students annually in their language arts classrooms. One of the focuses of the survey is on students' perceptions of their relationships with particular teachers and how their perception of their relationship relates to aggressive behavior in the classroom and at school, academic achievement, and discipline records. To study the relationship between a student's behavior in class and his or her relationship with a teacher without identifying teachers, we asked students to report on their experience in one of the four major subject classes that every middle school student has every semester (e.g., science). No records of the names of teachers covering these subjects were kept. Students were asked to report first on how psychologically or physically aggressive they have been to this teacher during the time they have been in his or her class (e.g., they were asked, "Have you ever talked rudely to your current math teacher?"). Students were then asked the degree to which their teacher demonstrates learner-centered practices, a factor that research has shown results in competent behavior and good academic classroom performance in students (e.g., students were given choices, such as, "My social studies teacher knows what schoolwork is hard for me"). Students were also asked how engaged they are in the class (e.g., they were given the choice, "When I am in language arts class, I usually think about other things"), how emotionally or cognitively supportive a teacher is (e.g., they were asked, "How often has your language arts teacher made you feel smart or good at something?"), and finally, their perceptions of their teachers' psychologically aggressive behavior toward them (e.g., they were asked, "How often has your science teacher yelled or sworn at you?").

This research has provided a great deal of information that is useful in generating possible solutions or interventions for aggressive interactions that occur in school. We found, for example, that most teachers were very positively perceived by students and rated as supportive, exhibiting fairly high levels of learner-centered practices and low levels of teacher psychological aggression. The survey also indicated that if a student perceived a teacher to have been psychologically aggressive to him or her, the child was more likely to report being psychologically or physically aggressive to that teacher. This was especially true of students whose teachers rated them as aggressive and who rated themselves as aggressive and delinquent. Looking at these data over time, we determined that student aggression, particularly from boys, was responsible for most of the aggressive teacher-student interactions that occurred. Students were not likely to report being aggressive to a teacher they perceived as unsupportive; rather, they reported not being very engaged in class. Students who reported having problems regulating their emotions (problems with anger, sadness, and anxiety) also reported low levels of engagement. From these data, we think a very important message for teachers is that they need to carefully monitor what they are communicating to students, especially aggressive students. Sarcasm, critical looks, calling students names, and being dismissive or in other ways disrespectful are behaviors that may have been provoked by the student and may work in obtaining compliance from aggressive students in the short term. But these behaviors also have some very real risks. Aggressive students may counterattack, and nonaggressive students may withdraw and disengage from class.

Although most teachers were rated fairly positively, some teachers were perceived by students as being less supportive, being more psychologically aggressive, and exhibiting lower levels of learner-centered characteristics. Their students reported being less engaged in class. To a surprising degree, students agreed with one another in their perceptions of these teachers. Students who had the same teacher for the same class period had the highest levels of agreement, but there was also a stable level of agreement across class periods in a day. In a few instances, a class and teacher interaction was perceived very positively by three of the teacher's classes but more negatively by two of their classes, suggesting an interaction between the teacher and a particular class.

Most social workers do not conduct research studies, but they should still obtain data from students, as students can be very accurate reporters of teacher behavior. Very brief student surveys can be gathered and analyzed, and the information can be used in consultation with teachers in helping them to improve their teaching style. These surveys may be particularly useful with new and inexperienced teachers or with teachers who report a higher than average number of aggressive incidents in their classrooms. It is important to note that confidentiality of students' responses must be kept; students should not be apprehensive about disclosing information and being fully honest in fear that their teacher will find out what they have said. Likewise, teachers must have complete confidence that the information will not be inappropriately disclosed or used against them. Ensuring that teachers' responses will remain confidential will allow for the most accurate information to be gathered.

 ## Conclusion

In analyzing aggressive behavior in classrooms and schools, social workers can use straightforward techniques to augment the interpersonal and clinical skills they already possess such as therapeutic consultation, leading groups, role play, review of records, and hypothesis development and refinement. By using these techniques to determine effective teacher and school interventions, they can de-escalate potentially violent situations and prevent unwanted aggressive incidents. The techniques do not require that social workers receive additional training or attempt to implement complicated solutions that may or may not be easily adapted to the local situation. Instead, these highly flexible techniques can be modified to gather information that is relevant to intervention in almost any classroom or school. They require only that the social worker have a good working relationship with other school personnel and a common goal of reducing aggressive and violent behavior in school.

**References**

Astor, R. A., Meyer, H. A., & Behre, W. J. (1999). Unowned places and times: Maps and interviews about violence in high schools. *American Educational Research Journal, 36,* 3–42.

Basch, C. E. (1997). Focus group interview: An underutilized research technique for improving theory and practice in health education. *Health Education Quarterly, 14,* 411–448.

Kellam, S. G., & Rebok, G. W. (1992). Building developmental and etiological theory through epidemiologically based preventative intervention trials. In J. McCord & R. E. Tremblay (Eds.), *Preventing antisocial behavior: Interventions from birth to adolescence* (pp. 162–195). New York: Guilford Press.

Kellam, S. G., Ling, X., Merisca, R., Brown, C. H., & Ialongo, N. (1999). The effect of the level of aggression in the first grade classroom on the course and malleability of aggressive behavior into middle school. *Development and Psychopathology, 10,* 165–186.

Patterson, G., Reid, J., & Dishion, T. (1992). *Antisocial boys: A social interactional approach* (vol. 4). Eugene, OR: Castalia Press.

Pianta, R. C. (1994). Patterns of relationships between children and kindergarten teachers. *Journal of School Psychology, 32,* 15–32.

Pianta, R. C. (1999). *Enhancing relationships between children and teachers.* Washington, DC: American Psychological Association.

Sheets, R. H. (1996). Urban classroom conflict: Student-teacher perceptions, ethnic integrity, solidarity, and resistance. *The Urban Review, 28,* 165–183.

Sprick, R. (1995). *Cafeteria discipline: Positive techniques for lunchroom supervision.* Eugene, OR: Teaching Strategies.

Sprick, R., Howard, L., Wise, B. J., Marcum, K., & Haykin, M. (1998). *Administrator's desk reference of behavior management: Vol. 1. Leadership guide.* Longmont, CO: Sopris West.

Walker, H. M., & Walker, J. E. (1991). *Coping with non-compliance in the classroom: A positive approach for teachers.* Austin, TX: Pro-ed.

Appendix A

Sample ABC Log

Antecedent	Behavior	Consequence
Handing back her term paper, I told Dana that her work was going to have to improve dramatically if she wanted a passing grade in my class.	Dana threw her term paper down on my desk, muttered "bitch" under her breath, glared at me, and then stomped back to her seat.	Dana refused to participate during the rest of class and made comments to other students when I wasn't looking. It was disruptive but not enough to justify giving her detention. I was angry at her and thought about getting her transferred out of my class.
I told the students they were free to work on their documentary in small groups, a project they really enjoy.	Louis, a high school student in the alternative program, grabbed the camcorder from my hand without asking.	I was annoyed but calmly said, "Let's try that again" and took the camcorder back. Confused at first, Louis then said, "May I please have the camcorder?" Mr. Jackson. With a smile I said, "Sure, Louis, thanks for asking."

Appendix B

Conducting Focus Groups: Moderator's Guide for Administrators

Purpose

We are interested in conflicts at school that lead to suspensions—conflicts that involve teachers and students, serious conflicts between students, and bringing weapons to school. The purpose of the focus group interview is to determine your ideas and opinions about these issues and what you think the district could do to help.

Guidelines

There are a few guidelines I would like to ask you to follow during the focus group interview. First, you do not need to speak in any particular order. When you have something to say, please do so. Second, you do not need to agree with what everyone and anyone in the group says. Finally, because we have limited time together, I may need to stop you and to redirect our discussion. Do you have any questions at this point?

Questions

■ How do you feel at the end of a day of school?
 — Are there some days that go better than others?
 — What are those days like?
 — Are there some days that go worse?
 — What are those days like?

■ What did you think administration would be like when you first thought about going into it?
 — Is that how it is?
 — What made you want to be an administrator?

■ Are there any negatives to being an administrator?
 — What negative things come to mind?
 — What are your greatest concerns about your job?
 — What are the causes of these problems?
 — Do you worry about conflicts with teachers, parents, students?
 — Do you worry about something you do getting into the paper? Getting hurt? Getting sued? Losing face in front of students or staff?

■ Do these concerns cause you to do anything special?
  — If so, what special things do you do?

■ How do conflicts between students get started?
  — Are there particular things people say or gestures that they make?
  — Are there particular circumstances that make conflicts more likely?

■ Why do people use critical comments, dissing, and name-calling?
  — What does it accomplish?
  — Under what conditions might it be effective?

■ How do conflicts between students and teachers get started?
  — Are there particular things people say or gestures that they make?
  — Are there particular circumstances that make conflicts more likely?

■ Are there times when you have been surprised by a student's or teacher's reaction to what you have said or done in these conflict situations?
  — Are there particular things you did or said that influenced their reaction?
  — How did you respond?

■ Are there things in the school environment that affect how you discipline or need to discipline students?
  — Student's experiences with other students?
  — How the principal/administration handles discipline, parent complaints?
  — Union, other teacher issues?
  — District discipline policy?
  — Schedule?
  — Size of school?
  — Teaching models (e.g., inclusion)?

■ Are there things that facilitate or hinder your ability to successfully resolve conflicts that arise between students? Between teachers and students?

Tell me about the most recent student-teacher assault you dealt with.
  — How did you respond?
  — Was there anything you would do different now if you could do it over again, or would you do what you did again because it worked?
  — How about student-student conflict?

■ What things could the school do to prevent fights between students?
  — What could parents do?
  — What could teachers do?
  — What could you or other students do?
  — Peer mediation?
  — Principal/counselor greet each student to assess mood?

■ Are there things the school could do to prevent conflicts between teachers and
students?
— Offer opportunity to mediate conflicts?
— Change how principal/administration handles discipline, parent complaints?
— Clarify district's discipline policy?
— Alter the schedule?
— Offer opportunities to improve teacher or student relationship skills?

Wrap-up

Unfortunately, we are close to being out of time. As I mentioned to you on the telephone, once the interview gets started it moves at a fast pace, and there is less time to express your points of view than we would like. Let me attempt to summarize the key ideas that I have heard. . . .

What would you like to add to my summary?

There were several topics that we touched upon and that we were not able to complete discussing during this focus group. Several of you . . . Another two of you . . . It is unfortunate that we were unable to spend more time discussing these topics today.

Member Check

Let me identify some key discussion points. After each point, I would like to find out how each of you feel about it by checking with each of you. At this point I am not looking for further discussion, just a general idea of how many of you feel a particular way. Again, please let me know your opinion. First, how many of you feel that . . .

(Ask each person)
Second, how many of you feel that . . .

(Ask each person)
As we come to a close, I need to remind each of you that the audiotape will be transcribed, you will be assigned false names for the purpose of the transcript and data analysis so that you will remain anonymous, and then the tape will be destroyed. We ask that you refrain from discussing the comments of group members and that you respect the right of each member to remain anonymous. Are there any questions I can answer?

Thank you for your contribution to this project. This was a very successful interview. and your honest and forthright responses will be an enormous asset to our work. Again, we very much appreciate your involvement.

11

The Use of
Debriefings in Schools

Joshua Miller

Every parent hopes and expects that schools will be sites where their children are intellectually stimulated, taught how to learn and problem solve, exposed to knowledge, socialized as citizens, and cared for. Perhaps more than anything, parents want to believe their children will be safe. But schools do not exist in isolation; they are part of communities and are subject to the same social forces that shape and influence community life. Many of these forces are positive, such as opportunity, compassion, care, and social connectedness. Nonetheless, schools also experience the destructive side of community life, including violence, disasters, and tragedies.

It is essential that schools work to prevent destructive and harmful incidents from occurring. Many if not most have excellent track records in that regard; however, schools, like all community institutions, are not immune from experiencing tragedy and disasters despite their best efforts at prevention. Accordingly, it is important that schools are prepared to respond when disaster strikes. One method of response is what is known as "debriefing."

This chapter categorizes the types of critical incidents that occur in schools. It discusses the stress, anguish, and trauma these incidents evoke and how debriefings can be helpful responses to such affective reactions. In addition to describing what a debriefing is and how it helps, the chapter gives examples of its usefulness. The chapter concludes with a discussion of special issues that must be considered when planning and conducting debriefings in school settings.

Critical Incidents and Lack of Safety in Schools

Mitchell (1983, p. 36) defined a critical incident as "any situation faced by emergency service personnel that causes them to experience unusually strong emotional reactions and has the potential to interfere with their ability to function either at the scene or later." More recently, the term has been expanded to describe "any action that causes extraordinary emotion and overwhelms an individual's normal ability to cope, either immediately following the incident or in the future" (Conroy, 1990, p. 21). Walker (1990, p. 121) defined a critical incident as a "recognized disaster, such as an airplane crash or a hotel fire; an act of nature, such as an earthquake or tornado; or any event involving death, injury, destruction and disruption." Everly (1999, p. 76) called a critical incident a "stressor event that has the potential to lead to a crisis response in many individuals." Essentially, critical incidents are traumatic; they are "powerful and overwhelming incidents that lie outside the range of usual human experience" (Bell, 1995, p. 36).

Schools can experience critical incidents as a result of natural disasters or human actions. Both types can occur either on or off campus. Natural disasters, also known as "acts of God," include floods, earthquakes, tornadoes, and hurricanes. Droughts, although less dramatic, can, over time, create a climate of despondency, especially in farming areas where the consequences affect the livelihood of many parents. Although natural disasters are not independent of human ecology (e.g., poor communities are more likely to be situated in flood plains), their cause is conceived of as beyond human control. It can be difficult, however, to make clear distinctions between natural and human-caused disasters (Lystad, 1988). A flood can become more toxic if poorly stored chemicals leach into water supplies, and the flood itself can be caused by a poorly constructed dam or by sabotage.

Schools are adversely impacted by natural disasters both outside and inside their walls. A tornado that ravages a section of a community but does not directly damage a school may still affect children who face a loss of security as a result of injury and/or damage to their homes and communities. Media-saturated events, such as a major earthquake, can affect not only children who live in the area but also children who live elsewhere whose sense of security is shaken by news reports of the disaster.

Natural disasters also occur directly in schools. An elementary school in Springfield, Massachusetts, situated in a low-lying area in a poor section of the city, was flooded by a burst water main. Fortunately, the flooding occurred on a weekend, when school was not in session, but classrooms and offices were submerged in water. Students, parents, teachers, and other staff were well aware that had this occurred when school was in session, there could have been loss of life. In addition to the trauma of the actual event and its potentially deadly consequences, students and staff experienced a secondary destabilization, as they had to be relocated until the school reopened more than a year later.

Some disasters are clearly the results of human actions. The Oklahoma City federal building bombing and the massacre at Littleton High School in Colorado are but two examples.

Whereas, many natural disasters appear inescapable, disasters caused by human actions carry the additional baggage of being avoidable. Such disasters may result from accidents, such as the Three Mile Island nuclear radiation leak, or from intentional acts, such as the 911 attack on the World Trade Center in New York City. As with natural disasters, disasters caused by human action can occur outside of a school and still have an impact on the school, as did the Oklahoma City bombing. A smaller scale but more common example is domestic violence resulting in serious injury to or the death of a parent. Such events can have a profound impact on a school attended by the deceased parent's children.

Tragedies and disasters also occur on school grounds. These range from well-publicized mass assaults and killings, such as at Littleton, to attacks or fights between individuals and small groups of students. Students also can be hurt or injured in off-campus incidents that reverberate through the school. The sudden death of a teacher is also likely to be a critical incident for students regardless of where this occurs.

Affected Groups

Typically, disasters and other critical incidents affect multiple groups of people inside and outside the school. Any of the examples that have been cited could create trauma and stress-related symptoms in students, parents, teachers, and other school personnel. The same events will have very different meanings for different individuals depending on their direct relationship to the critical incident, prior life experiences, ego strengths, personal coping strategies, and social supports. Cohorts are also likely to respond differentially to the same critical incident, particularly when there are developmental differences between the groups. Children often construe disaster and tragedy differently than adults. Professional training, culture, and values also distinguish how adults will respond; for example, teachers may find it more challenging to express their feelings to one another and their school principal than to clinical professionals such as social workers. Critical incidents that occur in schools also affect people off campus, including friends and family members, members of the community, and school personnel based at different locations.

What Is a Debriefing and How Does It Help?

A debriefing is a structured group intervention for people who have experienced primary or secondary post-traumatic stress as a result of a disaster or other crisis. Debriefings are held with groups of people and usually have the following distinct phases: (a) Participants review what occurred during the critical incident; (b) they share their cognitive, emotional, and physical reactions; (c) facilitators review typical stress responses and useful coping mechanisms; and (d) plans are made for self-care, group support, and follow-up activities. Clinical skills help in facilitating debriefings (Dyregrov, 1997; Miller, in press) but are not necessary for conducting debriefings. In practice, debriefings are often provided by community teams of volunteers (Miller, 2000).

A debriefing is not a therapy group, although it can be therapeutic in effect. The theoretical framework that informs debriefings incorporates both crisis intervention theory and trauma theory. Post-traumatic stress is viewed as a normative reaction to traumatogenic events. It is likely to occur in people who directly experience a critical incident (e.g., a child who witnesses fatal domestic violence) as well as in those who experience the incident secondarily (e.g., teachers who have the child in their classes or knew the parents). A debriefing attends to cognitive, emotional, physical, and social reactions to critical incidents in a group setting and a structured format. Debriefing facilitators lead the group through a structured series of questions that seek to elicit thoughts, feelings, and reactions. The debriefing also has a psychoeducational component in that the facilitator works with the group to describe and consider coping mechanisms. These mechanisms may include self-help, mutual support, actions, and rituals that can assist with healing. (For a detailed description of a debriefing, see Miller, 2000.)

Debriefings stress coping skills and operate from a strengths-based perspective. This is consistent with the social work profession's emphasis on client empowerment and resiliency (Miller, in press). Because debriefings are conducted with groups, they seek to stimulate affiliations and social support within the group and to connect group members with community resources and services. These goals fit well with the social work profession's tradition of group work and its emphasis on mutual aid and social support (Gitterman, 1989; Miller, in press; Schulman, 1986).

Debriefings can be offered immediately after a critical incident or weeks, even months, later. Everly and Mitchell (2000) suggested that debriefings be conducted 1 to 14 days after the critical incident; for mass disasters, they noted that debriefings can be held 3 or more weeks after the incident. Whereas debriefings held immediately after an incident have the advantage of providing a rapid response to a crisis, they have the disadvantage of asking participants to process complex emotions when they are still numb, overwhelmed, and in a state of shock. The size of the group being debriefed may vary, ranging from two or three people to large groups with scores of participants. The size of the group influences how long the debriefing takes and how actively each person is able to participate. Dyregrov (1997) argued that with fewer than 5 participants it is difficult to generate group support and resources, and with over 15 participants it may be difficult to engage people in the process. With larger groups it can be helpful to conduct a fishbowl/small-group debriefing in front of the rest of the group as a model for the process.

Warheit (1988) identified seven components found in most debriefing models:

1. Assessment of the impact of the critical incident on those directly or secondarily involved is assessed.
2. Identification of important issues resulting from the critical incident, such as safety and security, are identified.
3. Ventilation of emotions, experiences, and reactions is encouraged, and validation of participants' thoughts and feelings are validated.
4. Anticipation of future reactions and responses are anticipated and predicted.
5. Exploration of responses to the critical incident and responses to it are explored.
6. Connecting people to community resources and to bringing closure to the event.
7. Helping people to reenter their workplace or community.

Does this process really help people who have experienced post-traumatic stress in response to a disaster? There have been calls for more research, particularly randomized controlled trials, to ascertain the impact of debriefings both in the short and long term (Raphael, Meldrum, & McFarlane, 1995). There have also been questions about the negative aspects of debriefings, particularly the risk of traumatic contagion (Dyregrov, 2000). Chemtob, Tomas, Law, and Cremniter (1997) used an Impact of Event Scale, which measures psychological distress in response to trauma, to assess the effectiveness of debriefings 6 months after a Hawaiian hurricane. These authors concluded that debriefings had been effective in lowering trauma scores. Although there are potential risks in conducting debriefings and a shortage of research to help us understand their process and outcomes, they are widely used by communities, disaster relief organizations, and other organizations. The prevailing professional folklore is that they are helpful. Dyregrov (1997) suggested the following reasons for the benefits debriefings seem to provide:

- A trusting climate is created.
- Time is allowed for a common understanding to occur between group members. (In a sense, a common narrative is constructed.)
- A person can remember and reflect on what happened to him or her.
- A person can reflect on his or her emotional state, ventilate, and gain perspective.
- Processing as a group enhances group cohesion and reduces self-blame.
- Stress is normalized, and coping mechanisms are emphasized.
- The need for referrals can be identified, leading to more specialized assistance as needed.

Although further research about the benefits and risks of debriefings is called for, there is sufficient reason to believe that they are helpful for many people, particularly as part of a comprehensive disaster or crisis response system. Debriefings help people understand and process traumatic events by co-constructing a group narrative that can foster collective grieving, support, cohesion, and healing.

The Use of Debriefings in Schools

There are several important factors to consider when planning to use debriefings in schools. Perhaps the first factor to consider is who should be the target group: students, teachers, administrators, other school personnel, and/or members of the students' families? The answer depends somewhat on the nature of the critical incident and an assessment of who would most benefit. Most critical incidents, however, will have some impact on all of a school's constituent groups. A suicide by a teacher will affect students, teachers, and other school personnel particularly, but many parents may experience secondary trauma either through their children or because of their own contact with the teacher. Likewise, a student suicide, homicide, or assault will affect all members of a school community, albeit differentially. Ultimately, the unique circumstances of the critical incident, the structure, culture, and relationship of a school to its community, and the place of the school in the community will all be factors that help to determine what type of crisis response will be most helpful.

The American Red Cross (1995) applies the principle that people being debriefed should be of similar rank and status to avoid hierarchies that can lead to inhibition, deference to authority, or intimidation—perceived or real. Similarly, schools should not mix teachers and students when conducting debriefings. Whether teachers and administrators should be debriefed together depends on the size of the school and the hierarchical relationships of its personnel. For example, in a small elementary school with one principal who has close relationships with his or her teachers, it may make sense to debrief all staff together. But in a large high school with a number of administrators and perhaps more tensions between administrators and teachers, it may be advisable to offer separate debriefings to each group.

Debriefings should be adapted based on the group that is receiving the intervention. For example, teachers or guidance counselors have different needs and styles than students do. Everly and Mitchell (2000) suggested dividing children into three large, broad groups: younger than age 6, 6 to 12, and older than 12. For the first group they recommended that the debriefing be held in as natural a setting as possible. The children are usually debriefed with their teacher, so they are supported and reassured by familiar people and environments. Debriefings with this age-group should be shorter and less structured than with older children, using age-appropriate language. Because the teacher is present and likely to play an active role in the debriefing with this age-group, it is important to debrief teachers first and to prepare them for their role. A drawback to having teachers conduct debriefings with their classes is that they already know the students and are viewed as authority figures. With younger children, however, the advantage of being reassured by a known person probably outweighs this disadvantage.

For children age 6 to 12, Everly and Mitchell (2000) recommended using a scaled-down version of an adult debriefing protocol that has fewer phases (see Miller, 2000, in press, for comparative descriptions of debriefing protocols). They suggested limiting or eliminating the thought and symptoms phases, focusing more on the facts and reactions, and teaching about self-care. They also suggested shorter sessions than with adults, more directive interactions, and more active exploration of emotions. Emphasis is placed on the normalization of reactions, such as fear. Outside support from parents and caretakers is encouraged. Everly and Mitchell also suggested a follow-up debriefing after a few days to provide an opportunity to check in with the children.

For children older than 12, Everly and Mitchell (2000) encouraged full, adult-format debriefings using age-appropriate language. They did not make suggestions about the role of teachers or about how students should be grouped for these debriefings. With teenagers it might be beneficial to not have teachers present so the children are less inhibited. It might also be helpful to provide debriefings with more natural social groupings than homerooms, so participants will feel more comfortable opening up and will also be able to support one another through their natural friendship networks after the debriefing.

It is helpful to offer some form of debriefing to parents when their children are receiving debriefings at school. The debriefing can provide the parents with important information, allow them to express and ventilate their own thoughts, feelings, and reactions, and help prepare them to support their children.

Another issue for schools to consider is who should conduct the debriefings. Some organizations, such as hospitals and some school districts have in-house teams available to conduct debriefings following critical incidents (Spitzer & Burke, 1993). Other organizations including many schools use outside consultants or community teams. What will work best in any given school system will depend on the resources available, the nature of the community, and the culture of the school system. The advantages of an in-house team is that the team members' know the personnel and students and can rapidly respond. Disadvantages may include the team members' prior relationships with other staff (which may or may not be positive) and the fact that they are employees of the school system, which often raises questions about their neutrality. By virtue of being inside members of the system, they are also more likely to be affected by critical incidents that have an impact on the school and may, themselves, require outside help and support, including being debriefed. Community teams have the advantage of being able to serve a number of school systems. They often offer their services without charge, which can be advantageous to small school systems, rural communities with many school districts, and school systems on tight budgets. A disadvantage can be that they use large numbers of different volunteers, so there is less consistency. Consultants can become familiar with a school system while also having the perspective of being outsiders, but they may cost money and may not be available to cover multiple schools or regions with many different school systems, particularly in response to a large-scale disaster.

Whichever model a school system chooses, the school system should have in place, before disaster strikes, a plan for providing debriefings, other crisis interventions, and follow-ups. It is in the nature of disaster that normal coping mechanisms and responses are destabilized and disrupted, so it can be difficult to think clearly and respond rapidly. Schools should have a plan for reacting to violence, tragedies, and other disasters much in the same way that communities have civil defense and disaster relief plans. All school personnel should be familiar with the plan, and parents should be informed in advance so they are supportive of emergency responses when they are employed.

A Case Example*

In a community in the western United States, a woman was attempting to leave her husband of 20 years. She had obtained a restraining order during the day, and that night her husband broke into her parents' house where she was living and murdered her in front of her parents and four children. He then committed suicide. Two of the children were in high school and two were in a small, local elementary school. The rural community where this occurred was stunned and shocked.

The principal of the elementary school and her staff were particularly distraught. They had known both parents and were in a state of disbelief. The principal contacted a local community crisis response team and a debriefing was scheduled for the next day, 2 days after the murder/suicide.

Three volunteers, two women and one man, who had not previously worked together, were asked to conduct the debriefing. One was a social worker, another a school guidance counselor, and the third a nurse. They met in a diner near the school on the afternoon of the debriefing, with the coordinator of the crisis intervention team, for half an hour to plan the intervention. They then entered the school, met the principal, and were shown into a classroom where the debriefing would be held. They arranged the small chairs and desks in a circle and set up a flip chart to write on.

Six teachers, a librarian, and the principal, all female, attended the debriefing. Attendance was voluntary. After about 15 minutes, one teacher left saying she had a prior engagement. The debriefing followed a typical protocol: introductions, agreement on ground rules, discussion of cognitive reactions to the event, sharing of emotional reactions, consideration of self-care and mutual support strategies, and plans for follow-up. The facilitators explained during the introduction that one of them was available to meet individually if anyone found the group process too difficult to tolerate. There was much affective expression, including crying, during the debriefing. One participant found it difficult to stay in the room midway through the debriefing, because the critical incident triggered memories of another violent loss. She asked to meet with one of the coordinators in another room, and that meeting occurred while the rest of the group completed the debriefing.

During the debriefing, which lasted 2½ hours, several noteworthy themes emerged. One was that the participants doubted their ability to judge people because

---

*Details have been altered to preserve confidentiality.

they had known both parents and had not anticipated the husband's capacity to murder. Another involved the participants' feelings of a loss of security because the victim had taken all necessary steps to protect herself and yet was slain. All participants worried about how to treat the two children, particularly in a way that was sensitive and responsive without drawing undue attention to them. They also wondered how to explain the events to the other students, particularly given their own lack of confidence and security. Many participants felt guilty about not having been able to foresee or prevent the tragedy.

The principal was very upset and had asked the other staff if they would be inhibited if she participated in the debriefing. They readily assented to her involvement, and there was no noticeable inhibition. Initially the participants wanted to focus on the reactions of students, but they responded to the facilitators' suggestion that they focus on themselves. Strategies for working with the students were discussed during the last part of the debriefing as part of a consideration of future steps and activities. An internal school meeting with the school psychologist was scheduled as a follow-up to consider how to be helpful and supportive to the students. Although there was no formal follow-up by the crisis intervention team, the principal called the team coordinator a few days later to say that she and her colleagues had found the process very helpful. By collectively processing their own reactions, the staff were better able to meet the needs of students.

 Conclusion

Despite our best efforts at prevention, schools may experience violent incidents, tragedies, crises, disasters, or other traumatic and destabilizing events that occur in the community. Debriefings can be helpful to students, their families, teachers, and other school personnel, particularly as part of a comprehensive crisis response plan. One size does not fit all in this regard, and debriefings should be adapted to the group receiving the intervention, taking into account its developmental status, group culture, prior relationships, the type of critical incident, and the nature of the community. It is advisable for schools to be prepared for critical incidents before they occur and to have a crisis response plan. Further research will increase our knowledge about the effectiveness of debriefings, our understanding of how they work, and our understanding of how best to tailor and provide debriefings to meet the needs of different school systems.

 References

American Red Cross. (1995). *Disaster mental health services I.* Washington, DC: Author.

Bell, J. L. (1995). Traumatic event debriefing: Service delivery designs and the role of social work. *Social Work, 40*(1), 36–43.

Chemtob, C. M., Tomas, S., Law, W., & Cremniter, D. (1997). Postdisaster psychosocial intervention: A field study of the impact of debriefing on psychological stress. *American Journal of Psychiatry, 154*(3), 415–417.

Conroy, R. J. (1990, February). Critical incident stress debriefing. *FBI Law Enforcement Bulletin,* 20–22.

Dyregrov, A. (1997). The process in psychological debriefings. *Journal of Traumatic Stress, 10*(4), 589–605.

Dyregrov, A. (2000). Helpful and hurtful aspects of psychological debriefing groups. In G. S. Everly, Jr., & J. T. Mitchell (Eds.), *Critical incident stress management: Advanced group crisis interventions: A workbook* (pp. 47–56). Ellicott City, MD: International Critical Incident Stress Foundation.

Everly, G. S. (1999). A primer on critical incident stress management: What's really in a name. *International Journal of Emergency Mental Health, 1*(2), 76–78.

Everly, G. S., Jr., & Mitchell, J. T. (Eds.). (2000). *Critical incident stress management: Advanced group crisis interventions: A workbook.* Ellicott City, MD: International Critical Incident Stress Foundation.

Gitterman, A. (1989). Building mutual support in groups. *Social Work With Groups, 12*(2), 5–21.

Lystad, M. (1988). Perspectives on human response to mass emergencies. In M. Lystad (Ed.), *Mental health response to mass emergencies: Theory and practice* (pp. xvii–xliii). New York: Brunner/Mazel.

Miller, J. (2000). The use of debriefings in response to disasters and traumatic events. *Direct Practice: The International Journal of Continuing Social Work Education, 3*(2), 24–32.

Miller, J. (in press). Critical incident debriefings and social work: Expanding the frame. *The Journal of Social Service Research.*

Mitchell, J. T. (1983). When disaster strikes: The critical incident stress debriefing process. *Journal of Emergency Medical Services, 8*(1), 36–39.

Raphael, B., Meldrum, L., & McFarlane, A. C. (1995). Does debriefing after psychological trauma work? *British Medical Journal, 310,* 1479–1480.

Schulman, L. (1986). The dynamics of mutual aid. *Social Work With Groups, 8*(4), 51–60.

Spitzer, W. J., & Burke, L. (1993). A critical-incident stress debriefing program for hospital-based health care personnel. *Health and Social Work, 18*(2), 149–155.

Walker, G. (1990). Crisis-care in critical incident debriefing. *Death Studies, 14,* 121–133.

Warheit, C. (1988). Disasters and their mental health consequences: Issues findings and future trends in M. Lystad (Ed.) *Mental health responses to mass emergencies: Theory and practice* (pp. 3–21) New York: Brunner/Mazel.

12

The Use of Crisis Teams in Response to Violent or Critical Incidents in Schools

Verba Fanolis

Increased public awareness of violent incidents in America's schools has prompted a call for school districts to prepare themselves for such unthinkable events. School systems have developed an array of plans, including procedures to enhance the flow of communication, the installation of metal detectors or other security devices, and the formation of collaborative relationships between educational institutions and law enforcement agencies.

This chapter defines the types of violent or critical incidents that may affect schools and discusses why schools must develop plans for responding to such events. Proactive responses, including forming school crisis teams to plan interventions, developing action plans that make it possible to respond quickly and effectively to a variety of crisis situations, and establishing criteria for selecting team members, are described. The chapter then outlines the three essential components of a crisis plan and discusses the vital role social workers can play in developing and implementing such plans in school settings.

Types of Violent or Critical Incidents

Thankfully, most schools will not be confronted with massive violence of the type that has recently occurred in Arkansas, Colorado, and California. Research data published in an annual report on school safety (Office of Juvenile Justice and Delinquency Prevention, 1999) have revealed that since 1993, school crime has been declining. Moreover, the statistical findings show that violent crimes and homicides in schools are extremely rare, with the crime most frequently committed in schools being theft. Nonetheless, schools must be prepared for violence or other critical incidents that seem likely to traumatize students, families, and staff members. Critical events can include natural disasters (e.g., earthquakes, tornadoes, or hurricanes); deaths resulting from violent or natural causes that involve a student(s), parent(s), faculty, or staff member(s); and threats of in-school violence (e.g., verbal threats, bomb scares, an individual with a weapon).

It is impossible to predict the traumatic effect of any potential incident due to the number of variables that influence how students, teachers, staff, and community will respond. The most significant variables are the severity of the event, the harm inflicted, the relevant relationship of victims to the rest of the school community, and the coping skills and developmental level of the most affected children.

Preparing for Violence

If schools are to develop violence response plans, they must first recognize that violence and other traumatic events can occur within their boundaries. This fact is difficult for many people to assimilate, for it challenges the common view of the world as a safe and secure place. People tend to feel "it could never happen to us"; violence only happens to "those people." Nonetheless, violent incidents in schools have been occurring with depressing regularity over the past decade. In a survey of 1,044 students conducted by the Metropolitan Life Insurance Company (1999), 25% of the students reported that they had been victims of a violent act occurring in or around a school building. The tragedy at Columbine High School in Littleton, Colorado, rocked belief systems across the country, as people were confronted with the fact that violence can and does occur in communities of privilege. Unfortunately, violence has occurred regularly in schools in poorer communities for many years but has, far too often, been tolerated or ignored.

Preparing for violence takes several forms in schools. One perspective, typically offered by law enforcement personnel, is that preparation means installing metal detectors and instituting unannounced locker searches to keep the tools of violence out of educational institutions. Another perspective involves working with children on such issues as civility, bullying, and appropriate ways to express anger. Preparation, however, is only one component of a comprehensive plan. Ideally, such a plan would involve recruiting a crisis team; conceptualizing, agreeing upon, and implementing prevention activities; and if a violent or critical event actually occurs, implementing a mutually agreed-upon action plan designed to ameliorate the effects of the event. In a guide issued to schools by the U.S. Department of Education (1999), the attorney general and the secretary of education jointly recommended that schools create environments in which students feel connected to one another and to the faculty/administration and in which early warning signs are heeded and responded to proactively.

The Crisis Team

Responding effectively to violent incidents in schools requires the development of teams that will assess the need for intervention, develop response plans, and effectively implement agreed-upon plans. Although the composition of crisis response teams varies depending upon the particular school, all teams should include key representatives of every component of the school program. Accordingly, the response team may be composed of school administrators, teachers, paraprofessionals, nurses, office staff employees, counselors/social workers, food service personnel, custodians, and other support staff members such as speech pathologists or physical therapists. Because the team members' roles and functions within the school vary, each member contributes his or her unique perspective during the assessment and planning phases as interventions are being developed. In general, team members should be full-time staff so they can be contacted immediately in the event that the team needs to respond quickly; interested part-time personnel can be included if they are easily accessible.

Generally, because of the organizational structures of schools, it is desirable to choose as team leader a representative of the administrative staff who is committed to the team concept. A contingency plan should be developed for situations in which this administrator is unavailable. The backup person could be the principal, assistant principal, a lead teacher, or a counselor/social worker.

Team members should be evaluated carefully to ensure that they possess characteristics that will contribute to the team's effective functioning. Although willingness to participate is important, it is not the only membership criterion necessary to ensure the team's optimal development and functioning. The school social worker can play a vital role in the planning phase by helping identify appropriate staff members. Team members should possess the ability to formulate multisystemic interventions. They should also be flexible, skillful collaborators with good communication skills who are comfortable in dealing with crises and other potentially traumatic events.

Developing the Crisis Plan

After the crisis team members have been identified, the next step is to develop an intervention plan. Instead of focusing on particular types of critical incidents, the team should plan for how it will function in response to a range of emergency situations. Individual roles should be clearly delineated so that the agreed-upon intervention plan can be implemented quickly. Responsibilities that must be assigned include assembling the team; communicating with the school system's central administration; communicating with the media; providing mental health services for students, families, and/or staff members; and developing informational materials for parents.

If a critical incident occurs, the team must establish safety and security for students and faculty as quickly as possible. It is essential that this principle guide team members' thinking as they develop the crisis plan and as they intervene in the event of a crisis. The crisis plan must also consider a range of contingencies and designate backup individuals to assume responsibilities if designated team members are unable to participate. In addition, the plan should be made available to all staff in a written form that clearly describes team members' roles and responsibilities. A checklist may be helpful in guiding the assessment and planning phases of the team's response. This tool ensures that crucial aspects of the plan are not forgotten in the confusion generated by a crisis.

Communication is an essential aspect of a coordinated plan. A recognized code word should be utilized to inform all school personnel that notice of a crisis is being conveyed and that the crisis plan is being implemented. Communicating information to school personnel, parents, community members, and the media will help reestablish safety and security in the school building. Many schools use intercom systems to communicate within the building, however, a contingency plan must be developed for those times when the intercom system is disabled. This plan might, for example, involve choosing individuals to function as messengers with the task of imparting instructions and key information to school personnel. A violent act occurring in a school building will also require a response from community agencies such as the police and/or fire departments. Collaboration with these agencies in developing the crisis team and the action plan will help ensure a coordinated response and is strongly recommended.

Once a plan has been developed, all staff members in the school should attend an orientation session in which the plan's details are presented. At that time, questions can be answered and staff can become familiar with both the emergency code word and the initial steps that must be taken in the event of a critical incident, such as locking classroom doors or securing the building's outside doors while awaiting further instructions. This training should be repeated annually, and new staff should be provided with the information during their first days on the job.

Responding to a Critical Incident

When the crisis team is called upon to respond to a critical incident, the team members will move through the following three phases: assessment, planning the intervention, and carrying out the plan. A thorough assessment of the situation is necessary to determine what interventions are needed. Because each situation is different, the team must assess a variety of factors, including the severity of the incident, the number of students and/or staff affected, and the developmental level of the victims. For instance, the death of a student will have different meanings for the other students depending on their relationship with the deceased, the cause of death, and their age and culture-specific understanding of what death means.

During the assessment phase, the team must formulate its plans on a multisystemic level, taking the previously mentioned factors into account. For example, a traumatic event in the community that affects a student and his or her family may ripple throughout the entire school community. Students in the child's classroom will, perhaps, experience the most intense reaction, while staff members will have a different response, and students in other classrooms may experience the incident with less emotion. Varying reactions necessitate the development of different action plans to meet the needs of different populations.

The school social worker can play an integral role by formulating a comprehensive assessment of the situation. Social work training emphasizes collaborative skills and an ability to formulate interventions that consider how multiple systems affect individuals. These factors must be carefully considered both to reestablish a sense of safety and security within the school and to meet the needs of those people affected by the crisis.

When the assessment is complete, various interventions will be implemented. These should be targeted to specific groups, such as an individual classroom or a particular grade level. The team will need to designate individuals to facilitate the plan. Facilitators might include members of the crisis team, other school personnel, or, at times, individuals from the community. It is important that the team reconvene when the crisis is over for at least one debriefing session. During that session the interventions can be evaluated and needs assessed to determine whether further action is necessary. In addition, crisis team members should evaluate the team's functioning and process the members' feelings and reactions to the event. This is a vital but frequently overlooked team function.

Case Example: An Elementary School's Response to the Columbine High School Tragedy

In 1997, two years before the Columbine tragedy, the social worker at an elementary school in a mid-sized New England city decided it would be prudent to develop a crisis plan. The school, which served 750 students from preschool through Grade 5, operated in a large building that had some open public access because it housed a systemwide registration center for parents. The city had high rates of poverty and crime. The social worker was experienced in working with children and families affected by trauma. Consequently, she was familiar with the effects of violence and the importance of early intervention in the aftermath of a critical event. The social worker shared her concern with another school counselor, and together they approached the school principal and asked her to authorize the creation of a crisis plan. The principal agreed and strongly supported them in developing the document.

When the draft was complete, school personnel were asked to volunteer to become team members. Subsequently, other individuals were recruited to ensure that membership consisted of a representative sample of the school staff. The team reviewed the document and offered suggestions that were incorporated into the final draft. This draft was then presented to the site based management team, which approved it and forwarded it to the central office administration. The crisis plan was presented at a schoolwide staff meeting and since then has been reviewed at the beginning of each school year.

When school resumed after the spring vacation in 1999, the Columbine High School shootings had occurred. The school counselors and social workers, administrators, and a unit of social work interns convened to determine whether an intervention was necessary in the aftermath of this violent event. There was general agreement that because of the intense media coverage, most students would have heard of the incident during the vacation. The crisis team recommended a school-as-a-whole response. Counselors, social workers, and social work interns proposed to visit each classroom in teams to initiate conversations about the shootings. In support of the plan, the school administrator agreed to write a letter informing parents about the intervention. Classroom teachers were approached about their willingness to have students in their classes participate in the conversation. All agreed, and some expressed relief that the dialogue was going to occur because they had not been certain about what to say or whether it would be helpful to say anything.

The classroom conversations varied depending upon the developmental levels of the students. In the lower grade levels (kindergarten through Grade 2), students were asked what they knew about the event. Most were aware that something bad had happened at Columbine. The discussion then moved to issues of safety, and a number of children said they had not felt safe returning to school. They were assured that the adults in the building were doing everything they could to ensure a safe environment. The children were also encouraged to talk to an adult if at any time they felt unsafe or uncomfortable.

Students in Grades 3 through 5 had much more knowledge about the events at Columbine High School, and many described graphic images they had seen on television. In discussing their feelings about the events, they too expressed concerns about issues of safety. The team members outlined the procedures in place to ensure student safety. These included the security guard on full-time duty at the school, security cameras, and the policy that all visitors were required to sign in at the office. Students were encouraged to report any situations they felt might be unsafe to teachers or school administrators.

This case example illustrates that action plans must respond to events that occur outside, as well as inside, the school. Further, specific plans must be flexible enough to accommodate children's different developmental needs. And finally, it is important to note that, as in this case example, a response that addresses the entire student body may be necessary.

Conclusion

Violent and other critical incidents that affect schoolchildren are no longer impossible or even difficult to imagine. Despite one set of reassuring statistics (Office of Juvenile Justice and Delinquency Prevention, 1999), these events seem to occur with some regularity. Although a relative sense of safety is enjoyed by most schools, it is important for all schools to develop proactive plans that acknowledge the possibility that a crisis might occur. Planning should include activities directed at prevention, the development of a representative crisis team, the development of a crisis action plan, and the opening of lines of communication to community police and fire units. School staff should be oriented to the crisis plan annually, and new staff should be oriented shortly after starting work at the school, so that everyone is aware of his or her delineated responsibilities. At times of crisis, when chaos is likely, it is essential to have a clearly outlined action plan in place to ensure a prompt and effective response. A well-conceived plan guides the crisis team members as they assess the nature of the incident, conceptualize an appropriate intervention, and implement an agreed-upon intervention. The crisis plan should be flexible enough to address a wide array of crises (from natural disasters to in-house violence) and responsive enough to address the different developmental needs of children who have been affected.

References

Office of Juvenile Justice and Delinquency Prevention. (1999). *Annual report on school safety.* Washington, DC: U.S. Department of Justice.

Metropolitan Life Insurance Company. (1999). *The Metropolitan Life survey of the American teacher: Violence in America's public schools—five years later.* New York: Author.

United States Department of Education. (1999). *Early warning, timely response: A guide to safe schools.* Washington, DC: Author.

13

The Protocol Approach to School Violence

Ann Moriarty, Paul M. Kalill, and Mark Benander

Although children are generally safe at school, recent incidents of school violence focus our attention on ways to assess and intervene before violence occurs. Each time we see the horror of school violence on television we ask the same questions: How could this happen? Could it have been avoided? How can we keep our schools safe? This chapter describes the Protocol Approach to School Violence©, a model designed to recognize and respond to the early warning signs of potential violence in school settings.

Most current policies place the burden of detecting potentially violent students on teachers and school administrators, who are generally overworked, underpaid, and not trained as mental health professionals. Students are also asked to determine what is a real threat and what is not. The protocol method of evaluation and intervention is a systematic approach to school violence that allows teachers to be teachers, students to be students, and the school adjustment counselor, or the equivalent in a particular school, to be the school's mental health professional. All constituents work together to make the school safer.

Early Warning Signs

Recent investigations into the early warning signs and predictors of youth violence have identified language and behaviors that may be precursors to violent acts (Batsche & Knoff, 1994; Cornell & Loper, 1998; Dwyer et al., 1998). The challenge for schools, parents, and law enforcement officials is to determine how to recognize these signs and, subsequently, how to intervene.

Hawkins et al. (2000) identified five categories that predict violence. They include individual, family, school, peer-related, community, and neighborhood factors. Dwyer et al. (1998) identified the following early warning signs: social withdrawal, excessive isolation, excessive feelings of rejection, being a victim of violence, feeling picked on or persecuted, low school interest and poor academic performance, expression of violence in writing and drawings, uncontrolled anger, patterns of impulsive or chronic hitting, intimidating and bullying behavior, history of discipline problems, history of violent behavior, intolerance for differences and/or prejudicial attitudes, drug and/or alcohol use, affiliation with gangs, inappropriate access to, possession of, and use of firearms, and serious threats of violence.

Violence Prevention Programs

A variety of programs have been created to address the issue of school violence, ranging from educational models to crisis intervention plans. Some examples are Peace Building (Harris, 2000), Anger Coping and Management (Lochman, Dunn, & Klimes-Dougan, 1993), Violence Prevention Curriculum (Mehas, Bowling, Sobieniak, Sprague, Burke, & Hagen, 1998), and Violence Policies Implementation (Stephens, 1998). Each of these programs approaches violence from a different perspective. The programs use a variety of techniques, such as mediation, teaching antiviolence strategies as part of the school curriculum, strategies for defusing anger, and implementing standardized responses when violence occurs.

The strength of the Protocol Approach© lies in its ability to provide a structured format for the identification and prompt referral for assessment of children who present with early warning signs. Many schools have already implemented various crisis intervention models; the Protocol Approach© is not intended to replace these programs but rather to complement them by more successfully identifying students who may need additional assessment and intervention.

The Protocol Approach to School Violence©

The Protocol Approach© is a system designed (a) to identify language and behavior that may indicate significant risk of self-harm or harm to others, and (b) to implement a structured program for assessment, intervention, and follow-up. The approach consists of the following components:

- A system of five protocols that provide a standardized approach to identifying and responding to early warning signs
- Training sessions for teachers and school administrators, parents, and students

■ A training session for the protocol evaluator (the mental health professional in the school)
■ Consultation with local law enforcement agencies

The Protocols

The following five protocols are structured procedures for identifying and assessing various categories of warning signs for youth violence. For each protocol, a systematic process is provided for documenting the observed warning sign, referring the child for assessment, and initiating appropriate intervention. A sample protocol is presented in Appendix A.

Protocol 1: Verbal Threat of Harm to Self or Others

Verbal threats of harm to oneself or others may range from language that is directly threatening to language that is highly aggressive and suggestive of harm. Combined with this language is affect congruent with ideation of self-harm or harm to others. Such language can be verbal or written; played out or videotaped as part of a school assignment, letter, or school play; included on an Internet site; or presented on video or audiotape.

Protocol 2: Acts of Physical Violence With Intent to Cause Harm

An act of physical violence involves physical aggression from a student directed toward another individual, such as a student, teacher, school employee, or administrator, with the intent to cause some type of bodily harm. This is a step beyond verbalizing ideation or intent. It represents an escalation into behavior that carries with it a greater risk to everyone around the student.

Protocol 3: Bringing a Weapon to School Without Evidence of Intent to Use It

When a student brings a weapon to school, the threat of harm escalates significantly. Even if the student has no intention of using the weapon, the potential for that weapon to cause harm is a real threat. The weapon could be used unintentionally, such as when a gun is discharged by mistake, or it could fall into the hands of another student who might use it with intent to harm. Weapons in a school intensify the possibility of a violent outcome.

Protocol 4: Bringing a Weapon to School With Intent to Use It and With Evidence of Intent to Cause Harm

When a student or a group of students bring weapons to school with the intent to cause harm to others, the school must immediately initiate a crisis response mode of operation by implementing a previously determined crisis intervention plan. A crisis intervention plan is a step-by-step guide to action in the face of serious threat. All school systems should have a plan that has been developed in conjunction with local law enforcement officials. Crisis intervention plans should be reviewed periodically with faculty, administrators, students, and police and updated accordingly. It is important to inform parents through parent association meetings or correspondence about the school's plan and the steps they should follow if there is a crisis situation at the school.

Protocol 5: Aggregate Warning Signs

The presence of multiple warning signs in a particular student should inform others that the student is in need of help. Multiple warning signs are usually observed by several different people within the school system over an extended period of time. Usually, students in this category have a number of characteristics that lead school personnel to suspect an underlying problem even though the student has not triggered any of the other protocols. It is important to be clear that this protocol does not stereotype any particular group of students. Each collection of multiple warning signs may, in fact, suggest an underlying problem in a variety of different student subgroups.

A Sample Case

The following sample case demonstrates how the Protocol Approach to School Violence© would actually be implemented. This case was created to illustrate how the Protocol Approach© would be used with a particular child and was compiled from a number of actual case reports. We are presenting a sample case to protect student confidentiality.

John, an 11-year-old male, had never been in trouble at school. He was a cooperative student who did not exhibit behavioral problems in the classroom or on the school grounds. Teachers who interacted with him in various school settings reported that he was generally a good student and displayed reasonable behavior for a child of his age. They reported that, compared to his classmates, John was a cooperative student with no noticeable behavioral problems. His schoolwork was submitted on time, and no remarkable behavioral issues were noted in the first quarter of the school year.

After teacher training in the Protocol Approach©, one of John's teachers concluded that John appeared more withdrawn, with diminishing affect. Because of problems with other students, teachers and administrators did not immediately focus on John's changing behavior and demeanor. He did not say or do anything that sparked concern in any of his teachers. Not long after the Protocol Approach© training, however, a teacher noticed that a drawing John made was filled with images of death. She also recalled that John had drawn or written similar things over the previous few weeks. This teacher recognized the drawings as a possible early warning sign of violence and reported those findings to the school adjustment counselor using the standard format referral form.

After receiving the referral form, the school adjustment counselor initiated a preliminary inquiry by talking with the teacher, looking at the drawings, and calling

John into her office for a conference. Her impression was that there was enough concern to trigger Protocol 1: Verbal Threat of Harm to Self or Others, and she began an initial evaluation of the student (see sample form in Appendix A).

The school adjustment counselor used the action plan in Protocol 1 as her guide. She first conducted an evaluation using the protocol evaluation checklist.* By doing this she discovered several factors, among them John's increasing sense of depression; his being bullied by other boys at school for being "smart"; his feeling of being out of touch with his family; his inability to communicate with his family members; and, finally, his growing sense of hopelessness. John was homicidal or overtly suicidal. He had neither plan nor intent but was beginning to have thoughts about death, particularly his own.

The school adjustment counselor did an initial risk assessment based on the Protocol guidelines used. She determined the potential risks and consulted with the local crisis intervention team by telephone. After a discussion of her initial findings, the team determined that John should be seen for psychiatric evaluation at an outpatient psychiatric service as soon as possible. The school adjustment counselor determined what actions were indicated using the Protocol 1 action plan. She called John's parents at home and asked for an immediate meeting.

The family meeting was held the next day, and only one parent, John's mother, was able to attend. Using the Protocol Approach© guidelines for family meetings, the school adjustment counselor was able to obtain important information about John's behavior at home. She discovered that he was becoming more and more withdrawn and stayed in his room for longer periods. John's mother reported that John often did not want to eat dinner and talked less to family than he had before the school year began. His mother reported that the family was initially concerned but had decided that John's behavior was just part of normal adolescence and that he would get over it. When the mother was shown the drawings, she broke down and started crying, as did John. They hugged in the office and the mother reported that she had no idea things were that bad for her son.

A plan was developed in cooperation with John and his mother following the Protocol Approach© guidelines. John was referred for evaluation at the outpatient psychiatric service and was seen at the clinic later that week. Both parents came for another meeting with the school adjustment counselor the following week. The school adjustment counselor checked in with John and his teachers twice a week over the next 3 weeks and worked cooperatively with the therapist and family. John agreed that if he felt his depression getting worse and/or if he had an increase in suicidal or homicidal thinking he would immediately tell the school adjustment counselor, as well as his parents and therapist. In addition, with parental permission, the teachers were asked to monitor John's schoolwork for additional early warning signs.

---

*Requests for information on protocols and evaluation materials should be directed to: Kalill, Moriarty & Associates, 135 State Street, Springfield, MA 01103

The school adjustment counselor and the parents collaborated in identifying markers of change for John that could be monitored both at home and in school. The markers were mood, affect, and interaction with family and peers. The school adjustment counselor notified the vice principal that John was the victim of bullying by other students. She also met with John to discuss what he should do if the bullying should occur again. John was evaluated for change markers at 6 weeks and 3 months. There was clear improvement. The family continued to be involved in the process and the protocol was terminated. When the students who were bullying John were identified, protocols were also initiated with each of them.

In this case, intervention was made before violence to self occurred. The intervention was a direct result of the teacher training in early warning signs of youth violence and the systematic application of the protocol model. The school adjustment counselor had a clear action plan with guidelines provided for every step. The proper people were called because the protocol indicated who should be called, and John was able to get the help he needed before his situation progressed toward a possible suicide attempt or an attack on another student. Without the protocol model, intervention would probably not have been initiated unless John's behavior had gotten much worse or he had acted out in an overtly aggressive or self-destructive way.

Protocol Discussion

The Protocol Approach© is a tool that removes from teachers, administrators, and students the burden of assessing a student's language and behavior. It places responsibility for assessment in the hands of the protocol evaluator, who is typically the school psychologist, adjustment counselor, mental health counselor, or clinical social worker. These mental health professionals are trained to determine risk and make referrals to appropriate professionals in the fields of mental health and/or law enforcement.

The protocol model standardizes situations and conditions. Each protocol contains a checklist of actions that are triggered by certain events and followed through to an appropriate terminating point. In the protocol model for school violence, a student's language or behavior is noted by a member of the school community and brought to the attention of a designated school evaluator who implements the appropriate protocol. Each step of the protocol should be followed, with the designated individual providing relevant documentation. The documentation should occur at predetermined intervals to ensure accurate recording of events, procedures, decisions, and actions taken and to ensure appropriate follow-through.

Some school personnel may object to the Protocol Approach©, contending that the language and behaviors that trigger protocol use may not necessarily lead to violence. This is true. However, we contend that even in situations where violence might not be the final outcome, the intervention will be valuable to the student and his or her family in identifying issues important to the student's mental health.

Careful application of this approach allows the school community to avoid overreacting and guards against the unfair labeling of students. The Protocol Approach©

works to identify and assist students who may be having difficulty. For example, a protocol that is triggered by language of self-harm that the student did not mean seriously is easily terminated in the first stage with no additional intervention. Even in such instances the protocol intervention has certain intrinsic benefits. That is, the student's language evoked a response; the response showed the student that his or her well-being is of concern to adults; and the student is given an opportunity to explore issues that may be of concern.

Each protocol attempts to identify students who are in the early stages of difficulty. Accurate assessment leads to family and school intervention and to support. The early prevention mechanisms of intervention and support are clear benefits. The Protocol Approach© is designed to intervene before violent behavior actually occurs. It identifies children who may be in need of help, and its benefits are not limited to students who may be violent. Early intervention can assist a wide range of students in getting the help they need.

The Protocol Approach© also allows the school system to work collaboratively with parents, community, and law enforcement officials in creating a response program before violence occurs. It identifies roles in the evaluation and intervention process for all members of the school community, and thus helps to clarify areas of accountability. The program offers a structure for effectively handling the chain of events beginning with the triggering behavior and continuing through the process of intervention. Collaboration between outside agencies and family is supported throughout all phases of the program.

The Protocol Approach© is not a comprehensive solution to school violence; it is a tool in the fight to save children. It is a system that puts the language and behaviors of children into focus and creates a model for appropriate early intervention by properly trained professionals.

Training Component: Psychoeducational Workshops

Protocols can be most effectively triggered and implemented if all sectors of the community are willing to participate. Positive participation and collaboration involving students, teachers, school staff, parents, families, and law enforcement officials are necessary. Bringing these groups together in support of the program markedly increases the likelihood of success.

There are a number of impediments to this type of cooperation. Students are under a great deal of pressure to not report the types of language and behavior that would trigger a protocol. Even if they feel comfortable making the reports, they do not have the training to assess potential for violence. Most teachers and school administrators also are not trained to assess students' mental and emotional states or their potential for violence. In some schools, fear of retaliation may be of great concern. Further, when potentially violent behavior is reported, often little is done other than a brief punitive intervention with little long-term effect. In addition, most parents are reluctant to believe their child may have a problem or even be at risk.

Finally, law enforcement agencies are generally involved only when a situation becomes critical. Law enforcement is usually seen as a punitive step and often is not involved at the level of prevention.

The protocol model's psychoeducational workshops are designed to address the beliefs and concerns that prevent each group from participating effectively in the protocol process. They are organized around each group's level of understanding and perspective about their role in the protocol process. Each workshop addresses the specific concerns of the group and provides internal and external strategies to help the group members cope with and understand the issues in their larger context. The goal of the workshops is to stress intervention as a preventative and positive process geared toward helping students identify and deal with issues that may be present before a situation becomes dangerous. The workshops train teachers to recognize early warning signs, to implement the protocol model including the referral procedures, and to follow up with the school mental health professional. Parents are trained in the protocol system as it applies to the school, as well as in recognizing the early warning signs of youth violence in nonschool settings. The model is designed as a vehicle for parental participation. The protocol model also trains students in what they should expect from teachers, administrators, mental health professionals, and parents. Students learn about the early warning signs and are presented with a rationale for participating in early violence prevention.

In addition, the Protocol Approach© trains mental health professionals in the areas of assessment and intervention using a standard clinical interview model appropriate to the professional's scope of practice. Training includes outlines for the student interview as well as for applicable family meetings. Additional materials include referral forms for use by teachers and administrators in reporting early warning signs. Consultation is provided to the mental health professionals to help them coordinate preexisting intervention programs and referral sources.

Police As Prevention Partners

Traditionally, law enforcement becomes involved with the potential or actual commission of a crime. In the Protocol Approach©, the role of law enforcement is viewed differently. Police and court authorities can play a vital role in preventing school violence. Law enforcement can be a partner in the Protocol Approach© by becoming involved in education and community relations when appropriate. Law enforcement officials are briefed on the protocol model and the early warning signs of youth violence. They participate in the program by assisting in emergency planning as well as by helping to educate students about the consequences of violence.

Law enforcement can make an enormous impact by shifting from prosecution and punishment to intervention and support. In addition to being a deterrent, the police presence in schools should offer a support and prevention component. Law enforcement participation aids in the development of mutual respect and trust between all groups.

Documentation

An important component of the Protocol Approach© is the documentation of all steps in the process: identification, referral, assessment, and response. Such documentation provides the school with a record of all phases of the process.

Pilot Implementation at Kennedy Middle School

During the 1999–2000 school year, the Protocol Approach© was implemented at Kennedy Middle School in Springfield, Massachusetts. Training for the intervention began in October 1999, and the program was operational throughout the school year.

At the end of the school year, school suspension and Commonwealth of Massachusetts mandated reports of suspected child abuse and neglect (51-A filings) were checked to determine whether there were differences between the 1998–1999 school year, before the training and systems were in place, and the 1999–2000 school year, after training was completed and the system was in place. Any changes were considered trends as opposed to real differences due to the multiple variables that exist from year to year in any school, including different students and changes in teachers. At Kennedy, another confounding variable was the hiring of an additional adjustment counselor who was assigned to this program. Because of these variables, the results could not be wholly attributed to the psychoeducational workshops and the protocol program. Tables 13.1, 13.2, and 13.3 show the promising but preliminary nonexperimental findings.

Discussion

The discussion of results falls into two areas: the psychoeducational workshops and their implementation, and the general impact of the Protocol Approach to School Violence© program.

The Psychoeducational Workshops A range of professional literature (Kolko, Loar, & Sturnick, 1990; Stein, Cislo, & Ward, 1994; Walker, Colvin, & Ramsey, 1995) supports the effectiveness of psychoeducational workshops that follow standard practice guidelines for this type of learning. The material presented in the Protocol Approach© workshops is important, concise, and relevant to the constituencies involved. The literature also supports the educational value of identifying early warning signs of potential violence (Beaulieu, 1999).

In the Kennedy Middle School workshops, teachers and administrators learned about warning signs and about the program methodology and were thus able to implement the program. Students and parents also became invested in and supportive of the program. Because Kennedy is an inner-city school with a variety of intervention programs and a preexisting focus on violence, the educational workshops supported the view that early warning sign training is valuable. This observation bodes well for the value of this type of training in other schools, particularly those that do not have training programs in this area. The workshops facilitated

Table 13.1 SIX-MONTH COMPARISON OF SUSPENSION TRENDS
AT KENNEDY MIDDLE SCHOOL BETWEEN
SCHOOL YEAR 1998–1999 AND
SCHOOL YEAR 1999–2000

Variable	11/1/98– 04/30/99	11/1/99– 4/30/00	Percentage Change
Total Suspensions	94	67	29% decrease
Fighting	48	30	37% decrease
Bringing weapons	12	3	75% decrease
Drugs	8	3	62% decrease
Physical assaults on students	7	5	29% decrease
Disruptive behavior	7	18	157% increase*
Threats of violence	4	2	**
Hitting a teacher	2	4	**
Pushing a teacher	0	2	**
Prejudicial language	1	0	**
Suspension without data	5	0	**
30-day suspensions	17	8	53% decrease
Multiple suspensions	19	14	26% decrease

*The school is identifying and responding to these behaviors earlier. An increase in disruptive behavior with a decrease in violent behavior is an indication that early identification is occurring.

**The actual numbers of incidents were considered too small to include percentages of change; to include such percentages in these places would have been misleading.

the integration of information and helped the participants better understand the importance of early warning signs and preventive intervention.

The Intervention Program Impact The literature on school violence supports the view that early warning sign identification and response are the keys to preventing major incidents of violence from occurring on school grounds (Dwyer et al., 1998). The literature also states that the warning signs used in the Protocol Approach© program are key markers of potential violence when they appear alone or in combination (Dwyer et al., 1998).

The results of the psychoeducational workshops and the intervention program at Kennedy Middle School are very promising. In comparing the suspension data from before and after the intervention program, positive trends in violence reduction, early warning sign identification, and response were noted. There were reductions in the total number of suspensions as well as in fighting and in bringing weapons and drugs to school. There was also a substantial increase in identified disruptive behavior corresponding to an increased number of earlier interventions. We postulate that earlier intervention was responsible for the decrease in serious violent and otherwise problematic behaviors.

Table 13.2

PROTOCOL EVALUATION BREAKDOWN FOR KENNEDY MIDDLE SCHOOL, 11/1/99–04/30/00

Protocol	Number of Protocols Initiated
Protocol 1: Verbal threat of self-harm or harm to others	47
Protocol 2: Acts of physical violence	23
Protocol 3: Bringing a weapon without intent to use	4
Protocol 4: Bringing a weapon with intent to use	0
Protocol 5: Multiple warning signs	16

Table 13.3

51-A FILINGS*

School year 1998–1999	1
School year 1999–2000	1

*The increase in filings is viewed as a positive trend. Teachers and administrators are responding to these situations more frequently.

Three goals of this intervention program were (a) to train the constituencies in the early warning signs of violence, (b) to educate the constituencies concerning the Protocol Approach to School Violence©, and (c) to secure cross-disciplinary participation in the program. Our hypothesis was that the program would lead to decreased violence within the school. The literature suggests that education about and recognition of early warning signs are important aspects of violence reduction (Dwyer et al., 1998; Kolko, Loar, & Sturnick, 1990; Stein, Cislo, & Ward, 1992). The results at Kennedy Middle School tentatively support this hypothesis. The fourth goal of the program was to funnel students demonstrating early warning signs toward some type of appropriate intervention. The suspension data show a decrease in repeated suspensions indicating a positive trend in this area.

 Conclusion

The results of this project support the view that the Protocol Approach© can provide the framework for an intervention program geared toward early identification and preventive intervention. Society is searching for ways to reduce the impact of violence on children. Looking at violent acts in retrospect and asking, "What should we have done to prevent this?" is an unworkable model. Students need to be aware that adults are watching and ready to step in when language and/or behavior indicate potential violence or other mental health problems. Stopping the progression toward violence requires early intervention. Effective prevention is enhanced by educational workshops that focus on early identification and early response—that is, identification and response before violence erupts. The Protocol Approach© and its accompanying psychoeducational workshops and intervention program initially appear to meet these goals.

References

Batsche, G., & Knoff, H. (1994). Bullies and their victims: Understanding a pervasive problem in the schools. *School Psychology Review, 23*(2), 165–174.

Beaulieu, A. (1999). Atellers de prevension de la violence chez des eleves du primier cycle du primarie. *Revue Canadienne de Psycho-Education, 28*(2), 247–264.

Cornell, D., & Loper, A. (1998). Assessment of violence and other high-risk behaviors with a school survey. *School Psychology Review, 27*(2), 317–330.

Dwyer, K., Osher, D., Warner C., Bear, G., Haynes, N., Knoff, H., et al. (1998). *Early warning, timely response: A guide to safe schools.* Washington, DC: American Institute for Research.

Harris, I. (2000). Peace-building responses to school violence. *NASSP Bulletin, 84*(614), p. 5–24, March.

Hawkins, D. J., Herrenkhol, T. I., Ferrington, D. P., Brewer, D., Catalano, R. F., Harrachi, T. W., et al. (2000). *Predictors of youth violence.* Washington, DC: U.S. Department of Justice, Office of Juvenile Justice and Delinquency Prevention.

Kolko, D. J., Loar, L. L., & Sturnick, D. (1990). Inpatient social skills training groups with conduct disordered and attention deficit disordered children. *Journal of Child Psychology and Psychiatry and Allied Disciplines, 31*(5), 737–748.

Lochman, J., Dunn, S., & Klimes-Dougan, B. (1993). An intervention and consultation model from a social cognitive perspective: A description of the anger coping program. *School Psychology Review, 22*(3), 458–471.

Mehas, K., Bowling, K., Sobieniak, S., Sprague, J., Burke, M. D., & Hagan, S. (1998). Finding a safe haven in middle school. *Teaching Exceptional Children, 30*(4), 20–23.

Stein, C. H., Cislo, D. A., & Ward, M. (1994). Collaboration in the college classroom: Evaluation of a social network and social skills program for undergraduates and people with serious mental illnesses. *Psychosocial Rehabilitation Journal, 18,* 13–33.

Stephens, R. D. (1998). Ten steps for safer schools. *The American School Board Journal, 200,* 31–33.

Walker, H. M., Colvin, G., & Ramsey, E. (1995). *Antisocial behavior in school: Strategies and best practices.* Pacific Grove, CA: Brooks/Cole.

Appendix A: Sample Protocol From the Protocol Approach to School Violence©

Protocol 1: Verbal Threat of Harm to Self or Others

Date:

Student Name: ID Number:

Student Year:

1. Protocol triggered by

   ☐ The student himself or herself

   ☐ Other Student: _____

   ☐ Teacher: _____

   ☐ School psychologist or adjustment counselor: _____

   ☐ Other: _____

   ☐ Anonymous

2. Any initial corroborating information on the threat:

3. Actual language of the threat:

Protocol initiated by:

Date:

Interventions:

1. Initial evaluation by school psychologist or school adjustment counselor

    Name:

    Title:

    Date of interview:

2. Attach report of evaluation. (Use protocol evaluation checklist as guideline)

3. Initial risk assessment

    ☐ No risk determined

    ☐ Minimal risk determined

    ☐ Moderate risk determined

    ☐ Major risk determined

    ☐ Other

    Explanation of risk assessment:

4. Action or actions taken

    ☐ Parents notified of findings by mail

    ☐ Parents called and notified of findings

    ☐ Parents called and family meeting scheduled for: Date _____

    ☐ Parents called and requested to come to school immediately

    ☐ Mental health crisis team called

    ☐ Law enforcement called

    ☐ Screened out; no action taken

Protocol terminated at this time by:

Protocol continued at this time by:

5. Family meeting results

6. Plan

☐ No further action indicated

☐ No further action taken by demand of parents in opposition to school recommendation

☐ No current action taken; monitor student over next ___ weeks

☐ Student to be seen by school adjustment counselor. Appointment date:

_____

☐ Referral made to mental health professional

Name:

Appointment made by:

Date of appointment:

☐ Schedule another family meeting.

Date:

☐ Law enforcement consultation:

Name:

Date:

☐ Peer support group

☐ Family support tasks

List:

7. Identification of markers of change and progress

☐ Attitude

☐ Academic performance

☐ Interaction with support groups

☐ Appearance

☐ Mood

☐ Family interaction

☐ Others:

Specific explanation:

8. Evaluation at 6 weeks. Markers of change:

9. Evaluation at 3 months. Markers of change:

10. Protocol terminated by:

       Date of termination:

11. Protocol continued by:

12. Next evaluation date:

14

Partners for Success: A Collaborative Approach

Phebe Sessions, Verba Fanolis, Maria Corwin, and Joshua Miller

The collaborative program Partners for Success, which involves the Smith College School for Social Work faculty and some of its staff members as well as public school students and staff, was initiated in 1993 in response to the significant numbers of public school children in Springfield, Massachusetts, who were growing up in adverse environments that put them at risk for emotional and behavioral problems and for school failure. Services for these children and families were limited, and the number of barriers that interfered with their access to services had increased. In developing this program, the partners were guided by the principles and values of the systems of care model developed by the Child and Adolescent Service System Program of the National Institute of Mental Health for the delivery of mental health services to children. These principles include (a) placing services for children in natural environments such as the schools, where problems of access and stigma are reduced and opportunities for early identification and intervention are increased; (b) individualizing services for children and adapting them to meet the needs of culturally diverse children and families; and (c) offering and coordinating a continuum of services within the child's school and community setting.

Collaborating with the Springfield school system in the Partners for Success project also provided the Smith College School for Social Work (SSW) with an opportunity to develop an enriched site for preparing interns for leadership roles in school-based social work practice in urban settings. In addition, it offered opportunities to develop innovative practice methods and service delivery models that promote mental health. The evolution of this project has engaged the creative energies of numerous SSW faculty and administrators, Springfield educators and social service providers, and SSW interns. This chapter describes the development, goals, conceptual framework, operations, clinician roles, services requested, practice model employed, and program evaluation findings of the Partners for Success project, as well as some plans for future development.

Historical and Programmatic Context

Partners for Success was developed and has evolved through efforts to accommodate the service needs of Springfield children, families, and educators, as well as the training needs of the SSW and its interns. Springfield was selected as the site for this community–school–social work collaboration because it is a city with a large at-risk child and adolescent population. Many of the children being educated in the Springfield public schools are children of color from low-income families. According to the Springfield public schools, of 25,000 enrolled students, some 40% are Latino, 30% are African American, and 6% are classified as low-income because of their eligibility for free or reduced-price lunches. The communities in which these children live have high rates of substance abuse, teen pregnancy, infant mortality, HIV infection, community violence, homelessness, and out-of-home placements in foster care and kinship families (Community United Way, 1992). The public schools were selected as the project sites in recognition of the direct and profound impact that poverty, violence, and family disintegration have on increasing children's vulnerability to poor educational achievement and mental health problems. The partnership believed that early intervention could yield positive results in softening this impact. Recent studies using the Achenbach Behavioral Checklist, which measures behavioral problems, have shown that about 20% of U.S. children have symptoms that could benefit from mental health intervention. High-risk populations have significantly more exposure to community and family violence and an even greater percentage of children with symptoms of mental health problems. The need for mental health interventions in a community with as much poverty as Springfield is great, but access to such services is limited by the policies of mental health agencies that struggle to provide outreach services to impoverished families who have inadequate health insurance or none at all. In addition, stressed families have difficulty in following through on referrals to child and family mental health clinics.

The SSW was attracted to the progressive vision of the superintendent of the Springfield Public Schools. He had instituted major school reforms to make every level of management in the system more racially diverse and to improve the educational outcomes of enrolled children. Further, he was concerned that the school system had a large number of children and families who were not receiving mental health services and who could not afford to contract for or provide such services through their own resources. Children with severe behavior problems and/or other emotional disturbances were not learning in the classroom, and their troubling behaviors interfered with the learning needs of other children. In addition, a rising number of children were being referred for special education services. Many of these children required self-contained classrooms, and some required costly residential treatment settings. To address these developments, the superintendent had formed a consortium of local mental health agencies to provide on-site services in schools. Nonetheless, there were limitations on the extent of services these agencies could offer due to managed care and other billing restrictions.

The faculty of the SSW, seeking a local, urban environment where interns could train to become school-based clinical social workers, recognized the potential for synergy between the service needs of Springfield schoolchildren, the superintendent's reform efforts, and its own intern training needs. For many years, the SSW had relied on community mental health centers to help its students prepare for clinical practice with low-income children and families—that is, to learn the skills necessary to translate mental health concepts, theories, and practice models into services appropriate for underprivileged populations. With the gradual withdrawal of federal funding for community mental health centers during the 1970s and 1980s, and as the states became responsible for allocating mental health funds, outreach to impoverished urban neighborhoods and primary prevention efforts were reduced. During the 1990s, funding for mental health services overwhelmingly shifted to third-party payers, leading to greater medicalization of services and a further reduction of outreach services in community mental health centers. The restriction of community mental health services to brief, in-office, individual sessions with children resulted in sharply reduced opportunities to teach master of social work (MSW) interns about community-based practice models that emphasize access, continuity, outreach, advocacy, family and community involvement, and multisystemic interventions.

The partnership between the SSW and the Springfield schools is an example of the SSW's efforts to provide leadership toward developing social work practice models for the profession as a whole that are responsive to issues of oppression. By locating field placements within Springfield's public schools, populations in need of mental health services who otherwise would not have ready access to them could be reached, and interns could be trained in community-based, empowerment clinical practice.

In any given year, about one third of the SSW resident faculty are involved in teaching and/or administering this project. Five members of the adjunct faculty also participate actively in the interns' training program. SSW professors offer training sessions for school social workers and school adjustment counselors. These experiences create a feedback loop in which faculty members help interns integrate theoretical with practical learning experiences, and in return, interns provide faculty with input about how useful their ideas are in the real laboratory of an inner-city school. Case reports from interns have been used in several SSW classes during the school's summer academic sessions, particularly in classes on social work practice with individuals and families and classes on group therapy with children and adolescents.

Theoretical Guiding Principles

Collaboration

Partners for Success is built on the premise that the project will coevolve toward jointly defined goals. The model has evolved from a commitment to collaboration made by both institutions, which shared visions of educational reform and social service integration, toward the promotion of commonly held educational goals. Both institutions have made significant inputs into the program design. There has been shared decision making in regard to school assignment, selection of supervisors, size of intern units, components of service delivery, and, to an increasing degree, integration of program administrators into the structure of participating schools. The overall program goal is to administer the program collaboratively across the disciplines of social work and education. Shared objectives include learning from each other's perspectives and continually modifying the program based on experience and negotiation of difference.

Facilitating Environment

The project draws upon the ideas of the British pediatrician and psychoanalyst D. W. Winnicott, who wrote about the environmental experiences necessary to facilitate optimal emotional development. He richly articulated the qualities of human interaction within the social environment that enable children and adolescents to express themselves authentically and securely (Applegate & Bonovitz, 1995). To create what Winnicott called a facilitating environment, all project staff must acquire and maintain a profound respect for the subjective experiences of the people they work with, including children, parents, educational personnel, and community workers. This framework, in particular, informs the nature of the helping relationship with children who have been traumatized or challenged by multiple stressors.

Multicultural Sensitivity, Knowledge, and Skills

The administration of the Springfield public schools has established as a major goal increasing the level of multicultural sensitivity, knowledge, and skills of all professionals in the system. The SSW shares this goal and to this end promotes the values and principles of culturally competent communication and interaction.

Multisystemic and Strengths-Based Interventions

The project systematically applies the assumption that individual children, families, schools, neighborhoods, and community institutions each exert forces that continually influence one another. Interventions aimed at enhancing the capacity for change need to be made at every system level for meaningful change to occur. Many social work and educational reformers believe that the educational and psychosocial problems of inner-city children cannot be addressed by isolating one area of a child's life for change. The Partners for Success project builds networks of support for children that mobilize community resources.

The project also assumes that the most innovative approaches to working with children, families, and communities and the ones most easily integrated into a school context are based on an appreciation and understanding of the strengths and resources of the participants. Consequently, the Partners for Success program has been particularly interested in models of intervention that focus on assessing and promoting resilience. The recent development of narrative models of practice has been of great interest to the project (Durrant, 1995; Freeman, Epston, & Lobovits, 1997; Greene et al., 1998). Fundamentally, these approaches are strengths-based and problem-solving. They focus on reconstructing one's understanding of challenging life experiences in the service of developing new meaning systems that support life-enhancing choices.

Trauma and Resilience

As in other inner-city communities, many children in the Springfield schools have experienced family or community violence. Research about the effects of exposure to violence on children documents serious consequences in their ability to learn and manage aggressive behavior (Jenkins & Bell, 1997; Pynoos, Steinberg, & Goenjian, 1996). Equally important is research on resilient children who do not succumb in the face of adversity and research on those factors that promote resiliency (Garbarino, 1995). The Partners for Success project is particularly committed to both preventing and alleviating the effects of trauma on children. Key components of the project are preventive activities, such as (a) psychoeducational groups for children and parents that focus on the dynamics of family and community violence, (b) classroom teaching about mediation and anger resolution skills, and (c) consultation with teachers to help them recognize and respond to signs of trauma in children (Dore, Kauffman, & Nelson-Zupko, 1997; Eismann, 1996; Marsiglia & Johnson, 1998; Murphy, Pynoos, & James, 1997).

Project Evaluation

From its inception, Partners for Success has been committed to evaluating its service efforts to determine whether goals are being met, consumers are satisfied, and services are effective—that is, the project is committed to obtaining the information needed for program improvement. The findings from two program evaluations are presented later in this chapter.

Program Goals and Objectives

Guided by the theoretical principles just stated the following goals and objectives for the Partners for Success project have so far emerged from the collaborative efforts: (a) enhancing the capacity of at-risk children in the Springfield public schools to succeed academically and socially; (b) facilitating parental involvement in their children's education; (c) ensuring a continuum of care that is culturally responsive and appropriate to a school setting; and (d) sustaining collaborative, interdisciplinary relationships among the project partners.

Specific means for achieving these goals include the following:

1. Increasing students' abilities to participate fully in the academic and social life of the school by providing psychoeducational interventions aimed, for example, at developing social, problem-solving, and decision-making skills and by providing counseling and support services for children with emotional, behavioral, and adjustment needs.

2. Enhancing teachers' abilities to lead children toward academic success by providing teachers with consultation, support, and training to address issues that challenge class participation, including disruptive behaviors due to trauma, family crises, or difficult transitions; frequent absences; and the integration of children with special needs.

3. Stimulating or increasing parental ability to help meet children's academic, social, and emotional needs through home visits, mediation between parents and school personnel, parent education, and linkage with community services.

4. Linking students with neighborhood community agencies where they can receive support and an extension of the services provided by Partners for Success, such as tutoring, mentoring, counseling, and social skills development.

5. Heightening cultural diversity awareness of all professionals involved in the project and in the schools where the project is located so the professionals become more sensitive to the norms and values of the children, families, and communities being served.

6. Enhancing professional adaptability through interdisciplinary, collaborative program development, information sharing, and education.

7. Broadening the aspirations of children and heightening their interest in school by increasing their exposure to positive role models through joint programs with other educational and social service organizations.

8. Preventing or ameliorating social, emotional, and behavioral problems that interfere with children's development and academic performance through early intervention and crisis intervention strategies and programs.

9. Planning and implementing program goals and objectives through joint administration and program development.

Program Description: Structure and Operations

Since the formation of Partners for Success in 1993, the school sites for the internships have changed several times in response to changing needs and requests from the Springfield public schools administration. Currently the program is based in two elementary schools. Four to five Smith MSW interns are assigned to each school. The interns spend 35 hours per week on site for a period of 8 months. Two full-time on-site supervisors, one an employee of the SSW, the other an employee of Springfield public schools, administer and supervise the program. The on-site supervisors manage referrals and assignments, develop program policies, supervise interns, coordinate with the school programs, and work on school special education teams and school committees. Each social work intern also spends 5 hours per week in a community center where he or she provides mentoring and tutoring in after-school programs, individual and group counseling, consultation to paraprofessionals, and liaison services between the schools and the community centers.

Students and their families are referred to the Partners for Success program by adjustment (guidance) counselors, administrators, teachers, parents, and/or by special education planning and placement teams. The students are referred for services when they exhibit emotional or behavioral problems that interfere with their academic performance or school functioning or when their academic performance is compromised by family discord or disruption, trauma, losses, separations, or other stresses. Typical problems that lead to referral are aggression, hyperactivity, depression, anxiety, oppositional or antisocial behavior and somatic complaints.

Springfield school staff look to the Partners for Success project staff to (a) work directly with the children most in need of help; (b) establish communication with and enlist the cooperation of families; (c) advocate on behalf of children and mediate with legal, child welfare, health, and social service agencies; (d) provide crisis intervention services; and (e) provide teachers and administrators with information and insights about the needs of particular children and about managing behaviors that interfere with learning. In response to these expectations, the program offers a full range of social work services relevant to a public school setting. Among these services are individual, family, and group counseling; assessment and referral; crisis intervention (including school community crisis debriefing); consultation and collaboration with guidance counselors, administrators, and teachers; and community outreach services.

Interventions That Focus on Children and School Health Climate

Counseling with individual students is primarily supportive with an emphasis on creating a climate of safety and predictability in the counseling relationship. Students are helped to cope with stresses that leave them feeling anxious, unsafe, frustrated, angry, or quietly depressed. Through the counseling relationship, interns help students to develop a sense of mastery in some domain of their lives. This is particularly important for children whose sense of self is assaulted on a daily basis because of learning difficulties or behaviors that are maladaptive in the classroom setting. Individual counseling sessions typically occur in the project centers located in each school. However, significant interventions also occur in the classroom, lunchroom, gym, and hallways, as well as on the bus, when interns respond to crisis situations or assist children directly in managing emotional upsets or disruptive behaviors.

Students are also seen in group counseling to assist them in developing social, problem-solving, and conflict resolution skills. Peer mediation, anger management, and conflict resolution groups are offered to prevent the escalation of conflicts in the school. Groups may be developed with children who have been specifically referred because of poor social skills or with children who share common challenges, such as a death in the family, a family member with HIV/AIDS, substance abuse, learning disabilities, or foster care status.

Currently, there are a sizable number of groups in both schools because group work is the intervention the schools prefer and view as most effective. Groups are focused around two transitional periods in children's lives: entry into first grade and entry into middle school. First-grade teachers are concerned that many children have no preschool experience and are poorly socialized to adapt to a school environment. To assist students in making the transition to school, each first-grade class is divided into small groups to work on the social skills necessary to enable children to function in a classroom. These social skills groups also provide an opportunity for the Partners for Success staff to conduct mental health screening to identify vulnerable children who may need services. The transition to middle school is also a critical adjustment period, and groups are formed in the fifth grade to prepare students for this challenge.

Efforts to promote resilience in children growing up with adversity are implemented through individual and group counseling, parental involvement, and initiatives to improve the overall school health climate. (See Figure 14.1) Consultation with teachers and administrators is considered a key strategy for increasing their awareness of the impact of psychosocial stressors on children, and for helping the teachers and administrators develop the skills necessary to respond helpfully to children in distress. The goal here is to create a holding environment that allows children who are growing up in adverse environments to experience the school as a safe haven where adults are predictable, fair, and supportive and can thereby serve as buffers against adversity.

Of course, teachers and administrators vary in their receptiveness and readiness to use mental health principles in interacting with students. Many teachers are skilled in differentiating the kinds of problems interns can be helpful with and make appropriate referrals, leading to mutually beneficial collaborations. Some teachers, however, have little confidence in mental health services and are reluctant to make referrals. Other teachers have serious trouble in the classroom and want to refer

A. School Health Climate
  1. Prompt access to mental health services
  2. Interdisciplinary collaboration
  3. Teacher/intern partnerships
  4. Consultation and training on mental health issues
  5. Direct support to teachers and administrators; crisis intervention and on-the-spot behavior management
  6. Full integration into school environment
  7. Comprehensive, coordinated mental health/social services
B. Promoting Parental Involvement
  1. Mediation; facilitating communication and mutual understanding
  2. Home visits family counseling and links to resources
  3. Parent support and parenting groups
  4. Special interests groups
  5. Guidance and mediation re: special education placements
C. Promoting Individual Resiliency
  1. Competency groups; social skills, problem-solving, conflict resolution, and anger management
  2. Special needs groups; trauma, bereavement, foster care, and transition
  3. Individual counseling
  4. Mentoring, tutoring, and group work in after-school programs

Figure 14.1

Partners for Success Interventions to Promote Resilience

every difficult student. An intern entering such a classroom may hear, "You've come for Jose? Great! He's been terrible today, hasn't he, boys and girls?" Interns are encouraged to empathize with the demands of teaching and to see providing support to teachers as one of their main functions. Interns are frequently partnered with particular teachers, allowing confidential relationships to develop over time. Together, the teacher and intern brainstorm ways of reaching a child in difficulty. Interns also lend support by meeting with a child who is having a difficult day, thus allowing the teacher to regroup and attend to the learning needs of the whole classroom. In addition to providing consultation on behavior management and psychosocial stressors, Partners for Success offers in-service training for teachers in the areas of behavior management and trauma identification.

Interventions That Focus on Family and Community

In inner-city communities, many parents who visit a school about a problem fear that they will be criticized or have other negative interactions with school personnel.

Consequently, many simply stay away. Some become defensively hostile and verbally attack school personnel. In response, schools can overreact. For example, school personnel may call a parent at work and insist that his or her child be picked up even though this could disrupt the parent's work schedule and even lead to the loss of a job. Or, the school may suspend a child without first determining whether child care is available. At the beginning of the Partners for Success program, due to several assaults by parents, one school did not allow any private meetings between parents and teachers without a security guard or administrator present. The Partners for Success staff and interns helped to diminish tension and improve relationships between parents and school personnel by serving as mediators without the presence of security guards. Interns also try to promote communication between families and the school at times when there are no problems. This allows both teachers and parents to be less defensive. Interns also work with parents at community agencies, which are viewed as more neutral sites.

Family work in the schools includes counseling focusing on the difficulties of individual children, helping families understand how they can support their child's education, and helping families deal with interpersonal crises that interfere with their child's development and capacity to learn. Interns also help families navigate the often turbulent waters of special education plans, communicate more effectively with teachers, and advocate for their children with school administrators. In addition, interns assist families in accessing resources and services and in negotiating with the welfare and legal systems. Also as part of the program, families are offered resources that facilitate group cohesion and support within the school, such as parenting skills groups and a creative writing workshop (Schneider, 1991).

School social workers are drawn out into the community in part by the fact that their primary clients leave the school in mid-afternoon. After-school programs in community agencies offer both recreational and educational programming, with vital services for vulnerable children. In many neighborhoods, however, the walls of the school are very high and most of the institutional energy is directed inward. To help children experience continuity between their lives at school and their lives in the neighborhood, school social workers need to provide connecting links. SSW interns provide services directly to children in community settings through their work with individuals and groups. They may also provide consultation to paraprofessionals in community agencies on such topics as preventive work with community members affected by violence, trauma, substance abuse, HIV infection, AIDS, gangs, and other acting-out children.

Program Evaluations

The program evaluations completed thus far on Partners for Success were a consumer perspective and satisfaction evaluation and a process evaluation. The consumer satisfaction evaluation, conducted in the third year of the program, focused on the perceptions of clients (both students and families) and school personnel about the quality of the services offered. The report of that evaluation provided a description of the services delivered and statistics on the number of client contacts. The process evaluation, conducted in 2000, sought to determine the relation between the services offered and the stated program goals and objectives. It was also designed to test pilot assessment instruments that will be used in the next phase of the evaluation, during which the SSW will attempt to determine if the services offered have made a difference in each school's health climate and in the functioning of children receiving direct services.

The findings from the consumer satisfaction evaluation indicated that the Partners for Success program was delivering a wide range of services (contacts with individuals, groups, families, parents, and guardians; consultations with teachers and administrators; classroom observations; and participation in education management team meetings) and a high rate of client–school personnel contacts. Interviews with clients (children and families) and Springfield school personnel about their expectations and evaluations of the services offered resulted in overwhelmingly positive evaluations. It is significant that in this study clients and school personnel described multiple ways in which they perceived they had been helped. Their descriptions closely matched the program's stated objectives. In addition, as a result of this study, several ideas for improving the program were developed and implemented. For example, school administrators expressed concern about the interns leaving the program before the end of the school year. This concern was addressed by lengthening the internship and providing coverage for students who need to be seen until the end of the school year.

The second evaluation (the year 2000 process evaluation) focused on the outcome domains of consumers' (here Springfield teachers and administrators), perspectives and environmental contexts (Stroul et al., 1998). Separate focus groups with teachers and with administrators, and interviews with key participants in the schools and in the school project, were conducted to determine consumer experiences with the Partners for Success program, consumer perspectives on effective school-based mental health programs, the impact of the program on school health climate. Findings from this study, as with the earlier evaluation indicated an overwhelmingly positive evaluation by consumers of the types and quality of services delivered. From the consumers' perspective, stated program goals and objectives were being met.

The most significant finding in this study was the identification and description of two key components of the Partners for Success program that positively affected school health and mental health climate. They were (a) the full integration of the program staff into all aspects of the school community and (b) interdisciplinary collaboration, particularly with members of the special education team. Consumers identified the following characteristics of the program's operations as crucial elements in making the program function effectively: a commitment to teamwork, which encouraged an easy flow of information and resources across professional boundaries, and an ability to step out of traditional roles to respond quickly, flexibly, and proactively, wherever needed. Consumers valued both interventions that had an immediate impact on the daily functioning of the school and interventions that promoted the longer-term academic, social, and emotional development of children. The services identified as particularly needed and helpful were crisis intervention, outreach to families, mediation with families and community agencies, and assistance with behavior management especially in the classroom. Consumers stated that these services reduced their levels of stress and enabled them to be more effective as teachers and administrators in meeting the needs of the children in their schools. The most common recommendation for improving the program was to increase the number of interns assigned to the schools.

Whereas these evaluations describe the impact of the project on students, their families, and school personnel, future evaluations should also consider the impact of this placement on interns. Important issues to look at include how the program influences the interns' clinical capacities, professional identity, professional values, and future career trajectories.

Implications for Program Development and Practice

After 8 years of program operation, the insights gained from the program about the essential elements of a school-based mental health project include the following:

1. The time spent on cocreating project goals and objectives, and the ongoing collaborative efforts and interdisciplinary exchanges between school and project staff, have a considerable payoff in terms of consumers' continued receptiveness to and positive evaluation of the services.
2. A practice model that moves out of a traditional office-based approach and engages the child in all of his or her life space arenas, including the school, home, and community, is highly valued by consumers and appears to be effective in reducing children's symptoms of distress and dysfunction.
3. Fully integrating the program into the school environment as opposed to locating it in a satellite office—that is, establishing a special niche within the school ecology—has a positive impact on the use of services and on the overall school health climate.

Plans for Future Program Development

Three areas of identified need are being considered for expansion of existing services. The first intervention is in the area of trauma, particularly for that population of children who are in Department of Social Services custody and in foster care placement. The plan is to implement a trauma intervention program similar to the one developed by Pynoos et al. (1996), which combines individual, group, and family interventions with a mentoring program. The second area of identified need is for screening, prevention, and early intervention services in the preschool programs located at the Partners for Success school sites. A third area for expansion would involve greater coordination between the Partners for Success program and the Smith College Department of Education. Expansion of this collaborative relationship would help public school teachers gain a mental health perspective on the educational needs of children growing up in impoverished communities. It would also increase the social work interns' understanding of the complexities of educating students in inner-city schools and help them provide more sensitive consultation in working with teachers and administrators.

Conclusion

The experiences of the Partners for Success collaborative project support many of the conclusions reached by other school-based mental health programs. That is, services need to be comprehensive, preventive, child- and family-driven, integrated, flexible, responsive, and timely. In addition, program goals and services need to be codeveloped by school and mental health providers so they will be relevant and well received by their intended recipients. Finally, the implementation of a multisystemic model of practice that attempts to influence all of the psychological, family, and environmental systems that affect children's development should be a fundamental, bedrock principle of every school-based mental health program.

References

Applegate, J., & Bonovitz, J. (1995). *The facilitating partnership: A Winnicottian approach for social workers and other helping professionals.* Northvale, NJ: Jason Aronson.

Community United Way. (1992). *PACT: Planning and action for community teamwork.* Springfield, MA: Author.

Dore, M., Kauffman, E., & Nelson-Zupko, L. (1997). *Children are people too, group manual: A psychoeducational group for third and fourth graders living in homes where addiction is present.* Unpublished manuscript.

Durrant, M. (1995). *Creative strategies for school problems.* New York: Norton.

Eismann, E. (1996). *Unitas: Building healing communities for children.* Bronx, NY: Fordham University Press.

Freeman, E. (1998). Many ways of knowing: The implications for practice with youths related to substance abuse issues. *Social Work in Education, 20*(1), 3–11.

Freeman, J., Epston, D., & Lobovits, D. (1997). *Playful approaches to serious problems.* New York: Norton.

Garbarino, J. (1995). *Raising children in a socially toxic environment.* San Francisco: Jossey-Bass.

Greene, G., Jones, D., Frappier, G., Klein, M., & Culton, B. (1998). School social workers as family therapists: A dialectical-systemic-constructivist model. In E. Freeman, C. Franklin, R. Fong, G. Shaffer, & E. Timberlake (Eds.), *Multisystem skills and interventions in school social work practice* (pp. 175–190). Washington, DC: NASW Press. 175–190.

Jenkins, E., & Bell, C. (1997). Exposure and response to community violence among children and adolescents. In J. Osofsky (Ed.), *Children in a violent society.* New York: Guilford Press. 9–32.

Marsiglia, F., & Johnson, M. (1998). Social work with groups and the performing arts in the schools. In E. Freeman, C. Franklin, R. Fong, G. Shaffer, & E. Timberlake (Eds.), *Multisystem skills and interventions in school social work practice.* Washington, DC: NASW Press. 237–244.

Murphy, L., Pynoos, R., & James, C. B. (1997). The trauma/grief-focused group psychotherapy module of an elementary school-based violence prevention/intervention program. In J. Osofsky (Ed.), *Children in a violent society.* New York: Guilford Press. 223–256.

Pynoos, R., Steinberg, A., & Goenjian, A. (1996). Traumatic stress in childhood and adolescence: Recent developments and current controversies. In B. van der Kolk, A. McFarlane, & L. Weisaeth (Eds.), *Traumatic stress: The effects of overwhelming experience on mind, body, and society.* New York: Guilford Press. 331–359.

Schneider, P. (1991). *In our own voices: Writings by the women of Chicopee writing workshop.* Amherst, MA: Amherst Writers and Artists Press.

Stroul, B., Pires, S., Armstrong, M. & Meyers, J. (1998). The impact of managed care on mental health services for children and their families. *Children and Managed Health Care, 8*(2), 119–133.

PART THREE

Community Responses

15

The Importance of a Community Response to Violence

Deborah Prothrow-Stith

This chapter begins with an essay written by a young woman named Tonya Parker. I have reread this essay often since I first read it around 1990. When Tonya wrote it, she was a very young single mother and a member of a group called the Writing Crew in New York City. Terry Williams, author of *Crack House: Notes From the End of the Line* (1992) and *Cocaine Kids: The Inside Story of a Teenage Drug Ring* (1989), had organized this group of young people to teach them writing skills and to have them begin to write and publish. My coauthor and I included Tonya's essay in *Deadly Consequences* (Prothrow-Stith & Weissman, 1991). Here, then, is Tonya's essay:

> Within each and every one of us there is a fear, maybe a fear of flying, a fear of an animal, or even the fear of death. My worst fear is dying in the street. Every morning I wake up and I kiss my daughter and I thank God we have made it through the night. I live in Spanish Harlem and I'm surrounded by crack-heads and drug dealers. This is not the type of environment I want to raise my child up in, but I'm stuck here until I get to a higher level. Every night I can hear loud explosions. The children run through the streets screaming and cursing as though fighting were going on and you know a lot of time their [*sic*] just doing that for fun, because they want to be heard. They enjoy disturbing people at 4 o'clock in the morning by throwing bottles at cars just to hear the alarms go off. Sometimes I sit in the dark and I think about when

is it all going to end or is this the end. I just keep feeling pain in my heart when I look at all the children in the street suffering. It just keeps getting worst and worst. Tears run down my face when I embrace my daughter and I pray she doesn't become another victim of life. Everyone is born an innocent baby that is full of joy all they want is to be loved and comforted and they want to have play time and food. I began to wonder what goes through the minds of teenagers that still receive love and comfort and playtime from their parents. Why do they resort to violence? As a baby resorts to crying when hungry. What are they hungry for?

One thing that as a parent my children are going to figure out [is] how to get my time and my attention and my money and my resources and somehow one way or another they will get those things from me. I decide whether it will be early on in a loving and preventive way or whether it will be 4 o'clock in the morning in the middle of some crisis, but one way or the other my children get my time and my attention and my money and my resources.

It dawned on me, in thinking about Tonya's essay, that for us as adults it is true that the children around us are going to get our time, our attention, our money, and our resources, one way or another. It is through public policy that we decide whether it will be early on, in a loving and preventive way, or whether it will be at four o'clock in the morning when they are throwing bottles at cars just to hear alarms go off. So I am struck with the public policy challenge that faces us, not just as adults, but also as professionals. Tonya makes another interesting point when she asks what else children want when they already get love and playtime and food from their parents. What else are they hungry for? Teachers, social workers, outreach workers, clergy, parents, and friends have often posed this question in different ways. They say something like, "I don't know how he wound up in this kind of trouble. He's from a pretty good family." Or they say, "We don't quite know why she's in this predicament, how she got here with all the family support she has." It is an interesting question: What else do they want? Why do they resort to violence? What else are they hungry for? It is not enough to have a healthy child and a healthy family, because if the community is unhealthy, by the time that child becomes an adolescent, he or she might become involved in some bad situations. What I have learned to appreciate is that violence prevention is literally the work of building healthy communities around all children, not just the ones we know and the ones we love, but literally around all of the children.

And here is the public policy challenge. How can we, as adults and as professionals charged with serving young people, use our professional skills not only to meet the public policy challenge, but also to build healthy communities around all children? A young man was killed and a reporter was interviewing his father. The reporter said, "You did everything right and yet your son was killed. He was in the best school. He was an athlete and a scholar. He was well liked by the other kids.

You did everything right and yet he was killed." The father looked up and said, "I forgot one thing. I forgot to raise the other children."

It is almost a no-brainer to contemplate the question of why communities are important when we think about working to prevent violence and to promote peace. Why is it that we should collaborate? Why is it that we should build coalitions? Because we need each other and we need to reach all children. We also have to meet the public policy challenge. It is not enough that each agency follows the best protocol. Somehow, collectively, we must tell the story of the brilliance, the resiliency, the beauty of the children we are serving. We must tell it publicly, and we must have an impact on public policy.

I often recall a story that goes like this. Two friends ran into a bear while they were on a nature walk. They saw the bear coming at a distance and started running away as fast as they could. All of a sudden, one of them stopped, reached into his knapsack, pulled out his sneakers, and started changing shoes. The other said, "What is wrong with you? We'll never outrun the bear with you stopping." The first one said, "We don't have to outrun the bear. I just have to outrun you." I am reminded of that story because often, in our disciplines, with our professional protocols, in our individual agencies, we seek to outrun each other instead of building a community, a coalition, a group willing to have an impact on public policy. There are all sorts of turf and credit issues, but there are also substantive issues. The histories of the various professions are very different. The language is different, the values are different, and the conversations are different. It takes time and energy to become enough of a hybrid to bridge the different professional disciplines. This is particularly true with the problem of violence prevention.

Together with other public health professionals, I entered criminal justice territory and started talking about violence and violence prevention. Violence had been defined as a criminal justice problem, and the police, the police chiefs, the criminologists, and others in the law enforcement system had a way of talking about the problem, a way of describing the problem, a way of responding to the problem, that was very different, and still is, from the responses of those of us who come from the public health arena. First, we started talking about prevention. I remember being in the Boston City Hospital emergency room one night, calling the police and saying, "I'm really worried that this patient I just saw is going to hurt someone." And the response was, "We can't do anything about it until he does." Prevention simply was not a part of the criminal justice community's response system. When there was a violent event, they were going to do the best they could to respond on behalf of society. That is a very, very important job. But when people started saying, "What about prevention?" some in the criminal justice community say, "Come sit down and talk about it," while others said, "Look, get out of here. We don't know what you're taking about." But entering the criminal justice territory allowed us to understand the conflict and to realize that we were not offering a full spectrum.

In public health, there is the notion of primary, secondary, and tertiary prevention. When we offered this model, it was possible to begin a dialogue that actually became fruitful. Fundamentally, primary prevention involves changing social norms and attitudes. Do you remember when smoking was glamorous and everybody smoked? Movie stars smoked. We used to buy little candy cigarettes as children and imitate all the people smoking. I was on a trip once with my father. In the car with us, he had a friend who smoked cigars and another who smoked cigarettes. I remember having my father stop the car and saying, "Okay, now you're going to have to smoke one at time because we can't breathe in here." It is hard to imagine that happening today. Attitudes and social norms about smoking have changed over the past 30 years because of such primary prevention strategies as classroom education, public service announcements, getting information to the public, and one-on-one counseling. We have found all sorts of ways to change public attitudes and social norms about smoking.

Let us stay with the smoking example for a moment. Secondary prevention would have to do with helping people who smoke to stop, especially those who are at greater risk, in this case, for lung cancer. Secondary prevention can involve behavior modification, hypnosis, and/or group therapy. And tertiary prevention is treatment. So, for example, with lung cancer, the surgeons and oncologists respond.

When we apply the public health model to violence prevention, we start a dialogue with criminal justice that expands the thinking of many people. Public health professionals (in the very broad sense), educators, providers who embrace prevention, preventive medicine nurses, and those who work on social norms, attitudes, and education all have a major role. At the level of secondary prevention, there is shared responsibility between public health and criminal justice professionals. At the tertiary level, the criminal justice community has primary responsibility for the problem of violence.

About 10 years ago, I wrote a primary prevention curriculum for classrooms (Prothrow-Stith, 1987). The curriculum covers social norms and attitudes and redefining the hero. How do you get along? How do you give eye messages? How do you de-escalate a conflict? I was often asked, "How do you expect a gang member who has been in jail, who has killed somebody, to change just because of a classroom curriculum?" That was not the expectation. I have found the primary, secondary, tertiary prevention model very helpful, because it has allowed me to understand that when doing classroom education, we are focusing on the general population. And although the boundaries between the different levels of prevention are not rigid, the further you go in risk and involvement in the problem, the more expensive and intensive the strategies get. You begin to move into different professions, different disciplines, different sets of protocol. I think it is shameful that, as professionals, we often allow primary and secondary prevention work to fall through the cracks.

In 1987, I visited a youth detention center in West Roxbury for young men convicted of violent crimes. It was a very impressive place. Each youth had his own room, the school had a ratio of four students for each teacher, and there was a recreation area. It was actually a parenting facility where the guards were called dads. It was very intensive and very successful in cutting recidivism rates. As I toured this facility, I considered whether I had stitched up some of those young men at Boston City Hospital years before. I wondered how many of them were absent from school enough so that they had a truant officer call, how many of them were suspended regularly, how many saw the school psychologist or had the guidance counselor call. I suspect the answer was nearly a hundred percent of them. This category of secondary prevention—the actions taken before youth are placed in detention centers—requires a lot more work on our part. It is shameful that, right now, we do a little bit of bandaging here, a little bit of bandaging there, and these kids literally fall through the cracks. Then, when they commit some horrible offense, especially something involving violence, money is no limit. Then, we spend lots of money, even with the knowledge that these youth—sometimes starting from age 16—will be in jail for the rest of their lives at a cost of $35,000 a year. Have you ever heard anyone ask, "Can we really afford to send that kid to jail?"

I have found the primary, secondary, tertiary prevention model helpful also in terms of building coalitions and facilitating collaboration. Public health professionals can say: "We know something about classroom education. We know something about changing social norms." Police can say: "We know something about kids who are in trouble. We have a few first-offender programs, and we can respond." It is the dialogue at the middle level that still needs attention.

I have presented the dichotomy between public health and criminal justice practitioners, but I want to bring it closer to home. When I visit institutions serving young people, I often find the child abuse prevention program located here, the violence against women program located there, the gang violence prevention program in another building or in another institution, and so forth, even though we understand the cycle of violence. We know that witnessing violence or being a victim of violence during early childhood development is probably the most robust risk factor for involvement in violence, yet we still operate our programs in very narrow ways. The co-morbidity of child abuse and battering of the mother is in the 30% range. That means that if you are treating or helping a child who is abused, you have to ask the question: What's happening with the mother? Often, we do not think that way because we have created very narrow ways of thinking about the problem of violence.

All of this is complicated by how we deal with children who live in unhealthy families. Building healthy communities around all the children will help society, but it will not help all the children. For children in unhealthy families the intensity of risk is greater, and for those children we must move to the secondary prevention category. Probably the hardest job in any state is not in the department of public health but rather in the department of social services or the department of child welfare. It is the kind of job that has all of the challenge and all of the risk for caring for children whose families are unhealthy. Trying to serve children in that secondary category requires a great deal of work. I suggest that the solutions actually lie in community building. Boston has had a dramatic decline in its youth violence rate. U.S. Attorney General Janet Reno and President Bill Clinton visited the city at the height of the violence, when one child a month was being killed. That was in the early 1990s. We have now had 3½ years during which the number has dropped to a total of three children killed per year, representing a major change in the rate of youth violence. Victory has many handmaidens, so there are many perspectives about why that decline occurred.

I think that if thousands of people started working individually on this problem, if they literally reached out and started building coalitions and changing institutions, then things would change. For example, the violence prevention program at Boston City Hospital, which started 20 years ago, has had a significant impact on violence in the city. But there are events and situations that get in the way of building coalitions and changing institutions. For example, speaking a different language and having a different perspective are two huge issues that get in the way. Another is funding. When people talk about money, there begin to be turf divisions and issues of "my agency" versus "your agency," and we start running against one another. Another issue that gets in the way of building coalitions and changing institutions is reluctance to bring people of different perspectives together, even when we recognize that no one perspective can solve a problem.

The following anecdote illustrates this problem. I received a call one day from a friend, who said, "I want you to meet this man who has a program called Boxing Out the Violence." I said, "I really do not want to meet anybody who has a program called Boxing Out the Violence. I think boxing is part of the problem, not part of the solution." My friend said to me, "Would you just meet him? I just want you to meet him." I said, "Okay. Because you're my friend, I will meet him." I set up the meeting in a conference room and included two staff people so that I could say hello and leave. In walked this very engaging 78-year-old retired boxer who, for the next hour, explained to me what he did and how he could reach any young person in Boston. He used boxing to attract young people to his program and then, literally, did violence prevention work. One of our staff members joined his board after going to see the program and being very impressed with it.

I confess that my initial response to the program was classist. If someone had come to me and said he or she wanted to do a program with martial arts and violence prevention, I would have responded differently. As smart as I think I am about the problem of violence, and as much as I have seen by traveling around the country, my perspective alone is not enough. If you do not have room for Boxing Out the Violence, or if you do not create an environment in which someone who wants to initiate that kind of program can find support and do it, then you are not building community. So, turf issues, jargon, and professional protocol all get in the way of community building, and sometimes our individual biases get in the way as well. We start shutting out other people. I challenge especially those of you who are social work students and are moving toward a profession of serving young people to cross boundaries intentionally and to learn another's jargon. For us in violence prevention this has meant getting deeply involved with police. We have had to describe our viewpoint in ways that were helpful and that brought the police to the table. This is what literally builds community. We do not hold only lung surgeons accountable for smoking prevention. Surgery and prevention are two different skill sets. Yet we tend to hold police accountable for violence prevention. So, the police actually found some relief in the public health prevention model. To get them to hear us, we had to describe what we were doing and what we wanted in a way that brought people together. All of you will encounter and address turf issues. Everybody struggles with them. But jargon issues require that you learn another professional language in addition to your own.

But what about the issue of the personal biases we carry? We must constantly challenge ourselves to become more aware of our biases, because in the process of building healthy communities and getting everybody to the table, it is personal bias that often gets in the way of any movement. Bias keeps the coalition from gelling, keeps the full community response from gelling. Somehow, in Boston, we were able to create, for a period, a context in which, even though I thought I would never start a program called Boxing Out the Violence, a man was able to recognize his skills and bring them up without feeling judged. And in doing so, he confronted my bias. That is the kind of environment we should create when we try to build coalitions and community. There is power in numbers, and with different perspectives we get different and better solutions. Through the years, other "Boxing Out the Violence" programs have made me confront my biases. I hope I can challenge you to become more aware of your own biases and how they interfere with your ability to create an environment in which everybody can come to the table.

References

Prothrow-Stith, D. (1987). *Violence prevention curriculum for adolescents.* Newton, MA: Education Development Center.

Prothrow-Stith, D., & Weissman, M. (1991). *Deadly consequences: How violence is destroying our teenage population and a plan to begin solving the problem.* New York: HarperCollins.

Williams, T. M. (1989). *The Cocaine Kids: The inside story of a teenage drug ring.* Reading, MA: Addison-Wesley.

Williams, T. M. (1992). *Crackhouse: Notes from the end of the line.* Reading, MA: Addison-Wesley.

16

Constructing a Community Response to Violence[1]

Irene Rodriguez Martin

The massacre at Columbine High School neither announced nor confirmed the arrival of violence in schools. However, it did contribute to a confirmation of another sort. It was a dramatic and horrific testimony that violence is not relegated by income or limited to select segments of society but rather is a fact of life for today's youth and a product of our own construction in American society. No child is safe from violence, and no community is absolved of its contribution to what James Garbarino (1999) has called our "toxic environment".

After the Columbine incident, many community members across the country convened to discuss how better to understand the warning signs of youth violence, how to intervene at the right time, how to protect our children. Institutions of higher education and schools for social work must also consider their roles during such times of community crisis. This chapter presents a case study of the action taken by one school for social work toward developing a community response to violence through interdisciplinary outreach and the empowerment of local community members.

A Crisis in Community

Colorado buried its dead children and a beloved teacher in a parade of cathartic services that were as much tribute to the slain as an exorcism of inexplicable evil and a collective commitment to

carry on. But still, there were questions. Privately, residents wondered why so many warnings had been missed. By the police, by
school officials. And, most of all, by parents. Was everyone blind?

—*U.S. News & World Report,* May 10, 1999

The terror struck by the Columbine massacre was felt by communities not only
across Colorado but also across the country. One place it was felt was Springfield,
Massachusetts, the internship site of 10 Smith College School for Social Work
(SSW) students placed in two inner-city school settings. Springfield is a community
where violence is no stranger. With the support of their supervisor, the interns
quickly mobilized their best skills, organizing debriefings to reassure children who
already understood the real potential for violence in their own schools. Inwardly,
however, the interns struggled with their own anxieties as well as concerns that went
beyond their field placement. They turned to the SSW with panicked questions: Are
we prepared to read "the signs"? Could we prevent such a disaster? Would we be to
blame? What can communities do? What can social work do? What can *our* school
for social work do? Their questions, and their desire to go beyond Columbine and
their own experience in Springfield, led the SSW to mobilize its response to these
issues in its community.

The Role of Higher Education in Community: An Option or a Mandate?

In his preface to *Expanding Partnerships for Vulnerable Children, Youth and
Families* (1996), Don Beless commented that effective services for children require
cooperation and collaboration among social workers, teachers, nurses, parents, and
other stakeholders. "Although social work education serves as the cornerstone of
many collaborative efforts," he wrote, "inter-professional communication and education are critical" (p. xiii). Hooper-Briar and Lawson (1996) added colleges and
universities to this list of 8 stakeholders referring to the unique skills and resources
available in institutions of higher education. Such partnerships can promote new
synergy, as well as collaboration among faculty, students, staff, and the communities
where institutions are located (Corrigan, 1996).

In a recent study commissioned by the W. K. Kellogg Foundation (2000), institutions of higher education were challenged to take leadership in social change and
to model new leadership for their students. The report stated that effective leadership
enhances equity, social justice, and the quality of life; it expands access and opportunity; it encourages respect for differences and diversity; it strengthens democracy,
civic life, and civic responsibility; and it promotes cultural enrichment, creative
expression, intellectual honesty, the advancement of knowledge, and personal freedom coupled with social responsibility. Instead of competition, the report urged

group-centered leadership, with the group becoming an effective social change agent working toward the development of a "civil society" (Yachnin, 2000).

The question "What should social work do?" was brought to the SSW by three social work interns who had been working in the Springfield school system when the Columbine incident occurred. This crisis presented a unique leadership opportunity. Well equipped with both expertise and financial resources, the SSW had the potential to facilitate a learning opportunity for its social work students and for the larger social work community. Rather than focusing on the social work profession's contributions to violence prevention and the role of social workers in particular the interns' question back to the community was: "What can be done and how can we work collaboratively to achieve this goal?" Smith SSW offered to provide leadership in facilitating an interdisciplinary community partnership and in developing a meaningful response to community concerns around violence. Decisions about the deployment of Smith SSW resources would be directed by a community coalition—an unusual commitment. This partnership required Smith College to temporarily dismantle traditional academic hierarchies, adjusting perspectives on its professional contributions, and most important, creating a level playing field for any other discipline willing to join the endeavor.

Orchestrating a Partnership: Coming Down off the Hill

Developing a Coalition

Local residents refer to Smith College as "on the hill"—an elitist school removed from the daily struggles of its community. Developing a response directed by a community coalition meant creating an inclusive and respectful environment for dialogue.

The School for Social Work identified two cities as primary communities with which to begin this dialogue: its local community, Northampton, and the nearby major city, Springfield, both in Massachusetts. The SSW was fortunate to have developed a record of credibility and commitment through an eight-year master of social work internship program in the Springfield schools and through recent affiliations with a Northampton elementary school. In fact, at the onset of the 1999–2000 school year, violence prevention had been identified by Springfield School Superintendent Peter Negroni (Negroni, 2001) as a primary focus for the in-service training provided by the School for Social Work. The SSW set out to develop an interdisciplinary collaborative team from these two communities. As its contribution, the SSW committed funds to secure keynote speakers and agreed to provide a conference space.

In identifying the members of the collaborative team, professional leaders in each community were asked to identify representatives they felt were best able to address the needs of their disciplines within their communities. The school superintendents in both Northampton and Springfield were invited to appoint appropriate people. The Northampton School Department sent the director of pupil services, who oversaw special needs, counseling services, and bilingual education. The Springfield School Department sent the director of collaborative programs and the principal of Springfield Academy, an alternative program for violent youth. The Hampden County district attorney appointed a victim/witness advocate with expertise in working with victims of juvenile crime. Input and recommendations were also sought and received from the Hampshire/Franklin County District Attorney's Office, though individuals from this office did not participate directly on the team. The SSW appointed a social work faculty member, two social work graduate interns, and a supervisor responsible for intern learning at one of the Springfield schools. An administrator from the SSW was also appointed to facilitate the group endeavor. As conversations progressed, other professionals who became interested in the process were welcomed to join the effort; they included a Springfield school psychologist and the director of SAGE, an alternative educational program for youth. All coalition meetings were held in community settings—deliberately "off the hill."

Shared Purpose—Different Perspectives

Partnerships are sustained by pulling various entities together to define common goals, determining what each entity would do to support those goals, and designing and implementing specific interventions (Downs, 2000). Building this particular partnership with a group of professionals concerned about the occurrence of violence among and by children did not turn out to be a challenge. Each person in the group was deeply concerned and highly motivated by the opportunity to design a response. What was a challenge was the initial lack of a shared language and perspective on the issue (see Prothrow-Stith, Chapter 15 in this volume). Educators talked about the stark increase in counseling referrals for schoolchildren since the Columbine incident, the fears expressed by teachers, and the realistic limitations of teachers trained to instruct, not to assess risk or manage dangerous behaviors (see Moriarty, Kalill, & Benander, Chapter 13 in this volume). Juvenile justice representatives offered a powerful presentation about zero tolerance and their mandate to ensure safety. Social workers talked about the impact of community violence on children and the need for education and intervention with families and communities. Differences in the resources available in Springfield and Northampton were also dramatically described. As the major urban center in western Massachusetts, Springfield had access to political influence and financial resources at multiple levels. Northampton, a community of fewer than 30,000 people, struggled with very limited resources.

Although all members of the coalition shared a common purpose, their perspectives about how society had become so violent were as divergent as the route each member had taken to arrive at the meeting place: Each member highlighted distinct turns and bends, viewing influences, deterrents, and impacts through their own professional lenses. Members spoke persuasively and passionately about definitions, limitations, and appropriate interventions from their own professional perspectives, turning initial discussions into parallel conversations on a single topic. Initially, one-on-one conversations, separate from the committee process, were used to help bridge the gap between different perspectives and to refocus efforts toward a collaborative response. Professional pride and commitment fueled constructive conflict and, ultimately, achievement. The group's deep commitment to children and the professional respect members of different disciplines showed one another were most effective in keeping conversations balanced.

The Potential of an Empowered Community

These early meetings established a framework for the collaborative response that was eventually agreed upon: a day-long conference that would include (a) presentations on sociological and psychosocial perspectives about violence and the increased incidence of violence in children over recent decades; (b) a powerful appeal for interdisciplinary community coalitions and a description of their potential impact; and (c) a series of six or so workshops led by experts from different disciplines to consider violence from the perspectives of prevention, awareness/assessment, intervention, and/or response. Simple but important concerns were addressed by the planning group, including setting the date for a time not only for when the SSW was in session but also for when school personnel could take release time; developing lists of juvenile justice departments to be contacted to ensure their participation; providing continuing education credits to educators as well as social workers to make attendance a contribution to professional credentialing; and ensuring that conference fees were affordable for all.

James Garbarino (2001) and Deborah Prothrow-Stith (2001) were quickly identified and secured as ideal keynote speakers to present a psychosocial understanding of violent behavior and the importance of community collaboration, respectively. At this point in time, however, the tenor of the planning group again grew complicated as it considered limiting the number of workshops to only a half dozen. The list of important, even essential, questions to be addressed through the workshops seemed endless: How do we foster resiliency? How does one intervene around the development of gangs? What is the role of spirituality in responding to violence? What about bullying? Is zero tolerance the best choice for schools? What about the needs of a system after it has experienced violence? The list was overwhelming. Thus far, the conference had been organized with the premise that resources provided by Smith SSW would fund major speakers and the meeting space and that workshop speaker stipends would be covered by modest conference fees. Responding with workshops on each of the many concerns would certainly outstrip the committee's means if it was to maintain its goal of making the conference financially accessible to all professionals from every area of the community.

As the group struggled with a brainstormed list that kept getting longer, members also spoke about the need for networking and sharing resources across disciplines and between communities. A conscious decision was made to have workshops presented only by area practitioners in order to encourage networking, emphasize local expertise, and foster a sense of potential for those struggling with limited resources. The group was impressed by the list derived from this new focus. Dozens of local projects and/or experts whose individual endeavors were addressing some aspect of violence in their communities were identified from a wide range of backgrounds. Committee members used their personal relationships to solicit the participation of these experts; professional after professional offered to share his or her expertise—pro bono. In all, committee members scheduled more than 40 workshops to be presented at no cost by local practitioners committed to the notion of building a coalition against violence.

A Conference, a Network of Experts, and an Ongoing Learning Opportunity

On June 9, 2000, nearly 700 social workers, social work students, teachers, principals, juvenile justice workers, community police, child welfare workers, and community leaders attended an all-day conference entitled "Safe Schools: Building Fortresses or Opening the Doors to Community?" The conference featured two internationally known keynote speakers and 42 workshops (quite an increase from the 6 workshops that were originally planned) presenting expertise and models that addressed the issue of violence in local communities. At information tables, reference materials and business cards were offered to facilitate the sharing of knowledge and future collaborative work.

Although the total attendance nearly doubled the original projections, over 200 professionals were turned away due to space limitations. In response to the information needs of those unable to attend, and to further extend the resources made available that day, the SSW agreed to publish the conference papers in the March 2001 issue of *Smith Studies in Social Work*. In addition, all lectures and workshops were taped and made available throughout the summer of 2000 to SSW faculty wanting to incorporate themes of trauma, resilience, or violence into their teaching.

Smith SSW College students were especially affected by the day's event because of their role in spearheading the conference and planning the day. The W. K. Kellogg report (Astin & Astin, 2000) on colleges dedicated to leading social change noted that when students exercise leadership, they become more deeply involved in and committed to shaping the educational experience—for themselves and for others. Plus, they are more likely to exercise leadership in their lives beyond college. In addition to their contributions to organizing the conference, many SSW students presented workshops at the conference based on their research and clinical experience (e.g., "Bully-Proofing Your School," by Karen Brazda and Sarah Toig; "Youth Empowerment as Prevention," by Bill Macomber and Shalini Sharma). The students also organized a White Ribbon–of–Hope campaign, which involved pinning white ribbons on conference participants as a reminder to bring the experience of the day's meetings back to their workplaces and to their communities. The students urged participants to sign a 30-foot-long, 5-inch-wide ribbon with personal messages of hope. This ribbon was eventually sent to Washington with a letter urging President Clinton to provide leadership on the critical issue of children and violence. The ribbon was circulated on the Smith College campus and at various community events before it was sent to the White House. In this way, students were instrumental in transforming the conference from a day of learning into a program of community action.

The event inspired hope and potential for change on an issue that normally evokes despair and immobilization. Garbarino spoke for many of us when he commented before making his presentation, "It's a great pleasure to [participate in this event]. At a time when people around the country are mindlessly talking about zero tolerance, video cameras, and cracking down, it is refreshing to come to Smith College to speak at a conference titled "Safe Schools: Building Fortresses or Opening the Doors to Community?" It gives us reason to hope."

Conclusion

Institutions of higher education have unique resources and opportunities to contribute to social change in their communities. In times of community crisis, schools of social work offer particular expertise because of their ability to build coalitions and coordinate multidisciplinary partnerships to address community needs. Achieving a true community response, however, involves aggressive outreach on the part of institutions of higher education, a temporary dismantling of traditional academic hierarchies, and an expanded perspective on multidisciplinary cooperation.

Several factors are key in developing and sustaining a partnership to guide such a community response. First, it is essential to acknowledge community leadership and to solicit participation from community leaders and other community stakeholders at multiple levels. Once a group is convened, it needs to be empowered to define and to take leadership in shaping the community response. In identifying stakeholders it is important to consider not only different disciplines represented in the community but also the diversity of the community. The goal is to ensure that all voices are represented.

A second key factor is access. Institutions of higher education are often insular. Access to institutions of higher education can sometimes begin with a strategy as simple as having members of the institution join planning sessions in the community rather than having community members come to campus. Promoting access also involves careful consideration of issues that can either restrict or support the participation of various sectors of community: Are planning meetings closed? Is the defined response focused on community needs and concerns from the perspective of multiple disciplines? Is the planned response financially accessible to all community members? And finally, facilitating the development of a community response requires a generous commitment from the institution of higher education. It must invest time and resources in the community and develop long-term respectful relationships with a wide range of community professionals and paraprofessionals. The end result of such endeavors is their positive effect on communities, on the institution's perception and place in community, and on the development of community leadership skills among the institution's students.

References

Astin, A., & Astin, H. (Eds.). (2000). *Leadership reconsidered: Engaging higher education in social change.* Battle Creek, MI: W. K. Kellogg Foundation.

Beless, D. (1996). Preface. In K. Hooper-Briar & H. Lawson (Eds.), *Expanding partnerships for vulnerable children, youth and families* (p. xii–xiii). Alexandria, VA: Council on Social Work Education.

Corrigan, D. (1996). An educator's view of expanding partnerships. In K. Hooper & H. Lawson (Eds.), *Expanding partnerships for vulnerable children, youth and families* (p. 113–120). Alexandria, VA: Council on Social Work Education.

Downs, M. (2000, August 18). Researchers reach out to "stakeholders" in studies. *Chronicle of Higher Education.*

Garbarino, J. (1999). *Raising children in a socially toxic environment.* San Francisco: Jossey-Bass.

Garbarino, J. (2001). Lost boys: Why our sons turn violent and how we can save them. *Smith Studies in Social Work 71*(2), 169–182..

Hooper-Briar, K., & Lawson, L. (Eds.). (1996). *Expanding partnerships for vulnerable children, youth and families.* VA: Council on Social Work Education.

Moriarty, A., Kalill, P., & Benander, M. (2000). The protocol approach to school violence. *Smith Studies in Social Work 71*(2).

Negroni, P. J. (2001). Preface. *Smith Studies in Social Work 71*(2).

Prothrow- Stith, D. (2001). The importance of a community response to violence. *Smith Studies in Social Work 71*(2).

Streisand, B., & Cannon, C. (1999, May 10). Exorcising the pain: Littleton buries its dead and tries to understand. *U.S. News & World Report.*

Yachnin, J. (2000, Oct. 26). Report encourages colleges to assume a role in promoting leadership. *Chronicle of Higher Education.*

Notes

[1] Appreciation is extended to the following individuals for their contributions described in this article: Devonna Amis, Isabelina Rodriguez Babcock, William Cosgriff, April Ely, Verba Fanolis, Alex Gillat, Irenne Magoulas, Joshua Miller, Sheila McCarthy, Jennifer Seydel, Shalini Sharma, Sarah Toig, and Dennis Vogel.

17

Reflections on Family Traditions

Monica Herrera Perez

These reflections are rooted in life experience and 15 years of work in the justice system. While I was in law school, I worked as a parole officer and was assigned to the Hampden County Jail and House of Correction in Springfield, MA. It was there that I first met, up close and personal, those individuals called gangsters who were feared by all. It was there that I first met the families who loved them, supported them, and committed crimes for and with them. They educated me about the lifestyle, but none of those experiences prepared me for what I would see when I moved on to work in the juvenile justice system.

It is in this youth serving system that I have come to know the children and victims of my former clients. There are legions of children whose lives are lost as a result of their believing in the myth of a better life that is offered by gang membership. I have learned that there are many ways to die, including losing your family, losing your identity, losing your freedom, and losing your own life whether it is a physical death or being sent to prison for life without the possibility of parole. I have learned that the grief of families who lose children to gangs is no less intense than that of families who mourn a death.

Over the course of time, I have become increasingly impressed with the ways in which gang culture negatively mirrors the institutions and values of the dominant culture. It is no accident that gangs are so effective at promoting antisocial beliefs and behaviors. They purposefully incorporate norms, mores, rituals, "business practices," and patterned relationships that have proven successful in acculturating people from time immemorial. Their tactics are well designed to attract and acculturate young people who are alienated from their families, especially when they live in communities that are forgotten or exploited by the larger society.

Living and working in our midst are countless numbers of people who prefer to believe that bad things happen only to bad people living in lousy neighborhoods. I have met people like this during the 15 years I have worked in the criminal justice system. I meet them when I conduct workshops designed to enhance awareness of gang-related activity. I am constantly amazed at how people from all walks of life can stubbornly refuse to acknowledge that the foundation that supports our society is slowly crumbling. Gangs are in the vanguard of the assault that undermines social values and institutions. In this chapter I discuss the parallel universe gangs have created for themselves and compare it with the dominant prosocial values of our society. The discussion aims to advance understanding of gang practices and gang members while also challenging the commonly held belief that gangs are inherently "other," that they are fundamentally different from the organizations we uphold and belong to as law abiding citizens and fundamentally different from who we are and how we conduct our lives.

How Gangs Represent Family

Families are the most significant component of the foundation that supports our society. The birth of children into most families is a long awaited and joyous event. Ideally, the child is welcomed into a family that is committed to providing, among other things, unconditional love. Almost immediately, the traditions and rituals of life begin. Spirituality and religious education begin with a ceremonial initiation into a faith and often result in lifelong participation in a formal, organized religion.

Sadly, children are "born" into gang cultures every day, having been conceived in families and communities driven by endless cycles of abuse, neglect, rejection, isolation, lack of privilege, poverty, and lack of opportunity. Their birth into gang membership is defined by the pain of the ritual beating endured during the "jumping in" initiation ceremonies of traditional street gangs. In gang culture, it is said that the beating ritual represents the pain of the mother while giving birth. In recent years we have seen how, even in more affluent communities, personal experiences of neglect, rejection, and isolation can manifest themselves in waves of retribution involving unexpected violent outbursts.

"Healthy" families promote spiritual growth and development by teaching their children socially acceptable philosophies and values; they actively participate in organized religion, take their children to religious services, and enroll them in religious study. Rituals are practiced, prayers are learned, and religious milestones are celebrated.

Similarly, in their own way, gangs provide many opportunities for spiritual enrichment. Outlaw motorcycle gangs have "church services" almost every Sunday. While members have a business meeting at these services, their significant others prepare a meal for all to share afterward. It is during this time of fellowship that achievements are acknowledged, celebrations are held, losses are mourned, and new members are welcomed. Other gangs, such as the Latin Kings, have prayers that must be said each night before bedtime or prior to engaging in a battle. Gaining membership into the Kings while incarcerated can be achieved as simply as by saying the prayers for a certain number of days in a row while witnessed by a full member.

At the appropriate time, we introduce our children to learning. Healthy families send them to school as required, but watch them and their school systems carefully. If facilities and resources are inadequate, most of us demand better. If our children are being mistreated, most of us notice and demand change. If children have special needs, we insist that programs be developed to help them learn in the same classrooms as the other children.

Consider now that in many schools children are faced with facilities that lack the basic amenities. Utility rooms double as classrooms. There are not enough supplies to go around. The school is neither user friendly nor parent friendly. Teachers are spread so thin that they cannot give adequate attention to their students overall, never mind the ones who need extra help.

Meanwhile, the Latin Kings conduct mandatory classes for prospective members. During their probationary period, prospective members learn about the philosophies of the Nation as embodied in the King's Charter. They must rate the instructor after each class and write a short essay about what they learned. This sounds amazing considering that most of the recruits are youngsters who have dropped out of school. Many of them are significantly delayed academically, yet they are required to learn complex rules similar to those written in the Constitution of the United States. Such academic deficiencies present no problem for the Latin Kings. They provide tutors—free of charge. Therefore, for children who have no support, gangs provide protection, acceptance, and what is perceived to be respect, despite the "antisocial" behavior in which members engage.

While many children are enjoying the playground and learning the alphabet, there are growing numbers of children who are learning gang signals and how to identify the police in order to warn their older counterparts. While many children are learning advanced math, there are growing numbers who are learning how to move vast quantities of illegal drugs and goods undetected, and to mentally calculate the street value of their product. While many children are taking comprehensive assessment tests to determine if they will be honored with a high school diploma, gangs are conducting their own final exams. Gangs require an act of brazen violence performed with distinction to determine if a prospective member will be welcomed into the fold. The reward is a permanent marking that identifies you as a member of the gang *por vida* (for life).

Advanced education and a career are the goals most families have for their children. They are the dream of many and a reality for those who persevere. Parents plan ahead for a child's advanced education and encourage his or her personal growth and development. Children often follow in their parents' footsteps both in college and careers. Witnessing academic and career success is a great source of pride for all family members.

It is no different in a gang. Continuing education is encouraged. Crimes of increasing difficulty are taught to different age-groups. Upward mobility is encouraged and supported. Support shifts daily to whoever has the most power (brute strength, numbers of followers, years of survival, or skill at "strategic planning"). Achievements are celebrated. Failure is unacceptable and may be life threatening. If you fail often enough or appear weak, you die. In the gang world, it is survival of the fittest. The criminal behavior that is required results in an adolescence of delinquency. Members graduate the day they go to prison.

Prison opens up an entire new realm of opportunity for gang members. It is there that power and authority are tested. Success is measured not only by survival "inside" but also by the ability to control matters on the street despite being incarcerated. For every prison "bid" (sentence) completed, a "badge" is earned. It may be represented by a tattoo or by increased power within the gang. It is the equivalent of a bachelor's or postgraduate degree.

Exporting the Lifestyle

How does any of this apply to people who live outside of economically distressed, dangerous, drug-infested neighborhoods? Simply stated, the world has gotten a lot smaller. Those bad people from lousy neighborhoods are remarkably mobile. They go on vacation. They go to the mall. They go to theme parks and the arcade. They go to the movies. It is in these places that they interact with people, usually unsupervised children, who are utterly impressed by them.

In addition to mobility, there is another vehicle for the "export" of this negative and violent lifestyle to suburbia and rural America. It is the media. There are countless movies that glorify the gangster lifestyle. Many of these movies portray gangsters as oppressed people who finally stand up against the establishment and win. The perception is that they have tired of being excluded, isolated, and disenfranchised and, therefore, launch a war on the oppressors.

Each week, another gangster rap CD makes it to the top of the charts because middle-class and upper-middle-class white kids are buying the music on the black market faster than it can be produced. This musical advertisement for violence against such institutions as law enforcement and against others, specifically women, cannot be heard on regular radio stations, but it can be purchased easily and virtually anywhere by kids who have a great deal of disposable income. And the evening news caps it all. In any metropolitan area, on any given night, there are precious informational minutes dedicated to honoring the dark work of gangs by publicizing the latest results of violence in living color.

Is it any wonder, then, that individuals in "good" communities who are experiencing the same feelings of exclusion, isolation, oppression, and disenfranchisement look to such widely advertised behavior as a solution? Manifestations of this trend are evident in such places as Littleton, Colorado; Springfield, Oregon; Paducah, Kentucky; Los Angeles, California; Houston, Texas; Detroit, Michigan; and Boston, Massachusetts. These are all places where very bad things have "happened" in the past months—things that are virtually inexplicable in the context of such communities as we ordinarily think of them. Bad things are happening to "good" people in places where we least expect it.

In Littleton, Colorado, two youths who seemed totally disenfranchised from their community developed new identities for themselves. They became "scary," and they also became active in creating weapons. For some reason, adults thought this would be a phase they would grow out of. They did not grow out of it, and at least 16 other youngsters will not grow up at all. In Springfield, Oregon, a young man killed his parents. This event occurred without warning or any prior signs of trouble. In Paducah, Kentucky, a youth went to school and shot classmates who were gathered for morning prayer. The incident may have had something to do with a girl, but no one knows for certain. In Detroit, Michigan, a first-grader brought a gun to school and shot a classmate dead because they had engaged in a disagreement. This child had been left by his mother to live with his drug-dealing uncle. The father was unavailable because he was in prison. In Houston, Texas, and Los Angeles, California, traditional street gangs run rampant in certain sections of each city striking fear in the hearts of citizens. In Boston, Massachusetts, not nearly long enough ago, an Assistant U.S. Attorney was shot dead while waiting for a train; gang members he was prosecuting murdered him. Bad things, good people, just another day.

In nearby suburban communities, we see young people in so much pain that they begin using drugs and quickly develop a dependency. They engage in frighteningly risky behaviors to feed their drug habits. These behaviors include prostitution, drug dealing, theft and armed robbery. In this increasingly mobile and busy society, we leave young children and teenagers alone for extended periods of time at theme parks, arcades, concerts, and shopping malls. They meet people none of us know, and we are later shocked to find out their new friends are gang members. They trade phone numbers with complete strangers who they later invite to parties at their suburban homes while their parents are away. Gang members never travel alone. For a variety of reasons, these suburban teens crave attention. Alcohol is consumed. Sexual assaults occur. Burglaries occur. Dreams and expectations are shattered. The gangsters say to suburbia, "Welcome to our world."

 **Turning the Tide**

Traditions are born within cultures when people create rituals to celebrate events. The rituals are repeated consistently over time and are taught by older generations to the younger ones. Traditions identify who we are and how we move through the life we are given. It takes time to teach prosocial traditions to our children, and time is one thing nobody can buy. Time and tradition create lasting ties that bind our children to their families. The greatest return on that investment is the fact that nobody else will identify who they are. That is a family tradition.

18

Systems of Care: Expanding the Response to School Violence

Anita Lightburn

Clinical practitioners are opening new doors to community collaboration through their work in school-based mental health settings. Effective community-based clinical practice depends on the development of prevention and intervention programs beginning with early childhood programs through high school that are anchored in larger systems of care. A vision of "what can be" is derived from successes in the systems of care movement, which is at the frontier of 21st century mental health services for children and adolescents. The gap between what we now know service should be and current programs can be narrowed if this vision is realized. The systems of care concept and philosophy are explored in this chapter as a response to the challenge of preventing violence in schools. Systems of care are the best positioned policy and practice approach to meet the complex mental health needs of those children, youth, and families at risk because of violence.

In a dramatically changing mental health service delivery environment it is vital that community-based clinical social workers take leadership in collaborations that build systems of care (Stroul, 1996). The philosophy of this relatively new mental health paradigm emphasizes effective collaboration between mental health providers, schools, child welfare agencies, and the juvenile justice system. The result has been more responsive, timely services. In the systems of care model, practitioners provide vital clinical services. For most clinicians who have not been part of community-based practice programs, this involves translating traditional clinical practice into more flexible, responsive forms that fit with the systems of care concept and philosophy. Change is called for to move past resistance anchored in traditional practice

279

approaches and to advance collaborative innovations that make it possible to respond more effectively to the crisis of care for children and adolescents. It will be possible to make schools safe when the mental well-being of all children is addressed. The potential of community-based practice and the paradigm shifts involved in practicing within the model are illustrated in this chapter with case examples.

Unsafe Schools: A National Mental Health Concern

Senseless acts of tragic violence in schools in Arkansas, Colorado, and Kentucky, where many young people and teachers died or were injured, loomed large in our collective consciousness in the spring of 1999. In the high state of anxiety about safety that followed these tragic and deadly events, explanations and answers were sought by all school personnel as well as by many educators preparing mental health professionals for practice in this environment. Attention was focused on the unmet mental health needs of children and youth. Conversations began in earnest about how schools could be made safe from such senseless acts. A White House Conference on School Violence was called in 1999, and a National Summit on Children Exposed to Violence was cosponsored by the U.S. Department of Justice, the Department of Health and Human Services, and the Federal Communications Commission. At the summit, Eric Holder, deputy attorney general, called for participation in "a national action plan that would address the needs of children at each stage of their lives so that they don't start off as victims and end up as suspects and arrestees" (Beaucar, 1999b, p. 15). Millicent Williams, the National Association of Social Workers (NASW) senior staff associate for child welfare policy, commented that "the most resounding message gleaned from the White House conference was that adults need to start listening to children and make more of a concerted effort to work in interdisciplinary teams" (Beaucar, 1999a, p. 15).

Dealing with the problem of violence requires the development of conceptual tools. As James Garbarino emphasized in Chapter 1 of this volume, thinking more deeply means grappling with the realities of risk and resilience and with the legacies of racism, sexism, and classism. The multiple influences on child development, the absence of opportunities, and the psychological cancer of rejection all need to be considered within an ecosystemic perspective. Aspects of popular culture that champion aggressiveness and aspects of peer culture that view gun violence as a symbol of masculinity affect all children and young people in both middle-class and inner-city neighborhoods. The mental well-being of our children and youth depends on attention to violence prevention and on effective advocacy for policies, programs, and practice methods that respond to what we are learning. In addition, practitioners need to acknowledge and integrate an understanding of the healing power of spirituality. With good theory and research to draw from, community-based clinical practitioners are changing the norms of traditional practice by daring to "go up the road, in the dark places"[1] and to work with those most at risk. These practitioners need the support of reliable collaborators to ensure that financial and service resources are available to support the necessary continuum of care in communities.

Seriously disturbed children and youth need more than what schools or any single mental health provider can offer. In communities where violence is rife on the streets and in homes, where schools become bunkers for children at risk, a community response that goes from the schools to the community and back to the schools is required (Hernandez & Goldman, 1996; Richters & Martinez, 1993). It is abundantly clear that many environments place children and adolescents at risk of becoming violent because of such factors as poverty, exposure to violence in the community and family, fractured families, lack of nurturing adults, and an absence of opportunities that counterbalance risk (Beaucar, 1999a; Beaucar, 1999b; Dryfoos, 1994; Garbarino, 2001; Garbarino & Kostelny, 1994; Glodich & Allen, 1998; Marans, Berkman, & Cohen, 1996; Richters & Martinez, 1993; and Schechter & Edleson, 2000). Youth who live in "war zones" and/or with deprivation, racism, and sexism struggle with emotional and behavioral problems that can easily overwhelm educational and mental health systems (Knitzer, 1996a). With an estimated 14% to 20% of all children (Stroul, 1996) requiring mental health care, the challenge is to reach beyond traditional intervention procedures. This involves collaborating across disciplines to create integrated systems of care (Knitzer, 1996a; Knitzer, Steinberg, & Fleisch, 1990; Stroul & Friedman, 1996; Weist, 1997).

The System of Care Paradigm as an Answer to the Mental Health Needs of Children and Adolescents

There is growing evidence that the system of care paradigm, a dynamic concept and philosophy, merits serious attention. As a major shift in thinking about the provision of mental health services, it has continued to develop over the past 15 years as a progressive response to the limitations in traditional, categorical mental health services (Epstein, Kutash, and Duchnowski, 1998; Friedman, 1996; Macro International Inc. Staff, 1998; Stroul, 1996). Systems of care are organized to provide a broad continuum of coordinated community-based programs involving flexible clinical and wraparound services that include family support. The systems of care concept was developed in response to the critical needs of emotionally disturbed children and adolescents. Jane Knitzer, director of the Center for Children and Poverty, emphasized that "system of care reform appears to be a vehicle for underscoring the need for, and developing strategies for, substantive school based change"(Knitzer, 1996b, pp. 205–206). Knitzer has long advocated for the integration of mental health services in schools. A system of care model would make this possible and, at the same time, would provide in-house mental health support for efforts directed toward school reform.

Guiding Philosophical Principles

Because it brings together professionals from many disciplines, community members, and parents, the systems of care model has the potential to restructure and integrate community services in ways that better protect children and families. The model offers a clearly conceptualized philosophical framework for establishing programmatic directions and goals. Rooted in strategic principles, the model facilitates accountability and communication while providing a well-coordinated, comprehensive spectrum of mental health and other necessary services that are well designed to meet the multiple and changing needs of children and adolescents (Stroul & Friedman, 1996). Over time, the systems of care paradigm has been impressive in transforming the way care is given. The "centering" power of collaboration shapes policy, planning, financing, training, and service provision. The core values of the model emphasize that services should be (a) child centered and family focused, with the needs of the child and family dictating the types and mix of services provided; and (b) community based, with the locus of services as well as management and decision-making responsibility resting at the community level. Systems of care must also be culturally competent—that is, they must be responsive to the cultural, racial, and ethnic differences of the clients who utilize the services (Stroul, 1996). Of community and based within community, systems of care constitute extended holding environments. They are purposefully and collaboratively constructed in a process that pools commitments, goals, and resources from a variety of service providers.

Federal and state governments have, through legislation and policy direction, been instrumental in stimulating the development of new systems of care. Of special note are programs in California, Pennsylvania, Virginia, Kentucky, Texas, Oregon, and the District of Columbia. In all of these localities, legislation has played a central role in supporting the ongoing development of unique systems rooted in a creative response to particular needs, a vision of what is possible, and a realistic evaluation of how best to utilize available financial resources. At the state and local levels, localities have supported needed and innovative community services within parameters designed to ensure cost effectiveness.

An Example in Which a System of Care Program Led to Legislative Change

In Ventura County, California, a community mental health center took the lead in developing a well-documented system of care that has been recognized as an influential example for other counties in California and elsewhere. The system of care developed in Ventura County made a significant difference in the quality of service provided, and by redeploying the resources available, it was also cost-effective. Both in concept and in philosophy, the Ventura Planning Model provided a framework that guided system development. It supported "a new way of doing business for public mental health agencies, other child-serving public agencies, and communities interested in helping their highest risk and most vulnerable children" (Hernandez & Goldman, 1996, p. 177). The model was developed in three phases, focused first on reducing the country's population of children in the state hospital. The second phase was a human service delivery demonstration project and the development of an outcome based plan. The final stage included legislation and replication of the planning approach (*ibid,* 178). The planning model incorporated five essential characteristics: identifiable target populations; measurable goals; coalitions or interagency partnerships; an array of services tailored to the needs of the target populations; and evaluation and continuous monitoring of client outcomes. Specific goals included reductions in out-of-home placements, juvenile justice recidivism, psychiatric hospitalization, out-of-county non-public-school placements, and school failure. An array of services, part of a service continuum of alternatives to restrictive, intrusive, and costly care, "filled the wide gap between once-a-week therapy and hospital admission" (*ibid,* 185). A balance was worked out to meet the needs of individual children and their families through intensive in-home services, family support, enhanced special day classes in schools, school-based day treatment, respite care, and emergency in-patient services. Individual psychotherapy, group therapy, and family therapy were provided in concert with case management and crisis response. Key to the program's success was the method of service integration made possible by careful collaboration in how each major agency processed and made decisions about a child's life over time (Hernandez & Goldman, 1996).

Because of its cost effectiveness and its success in exceeding all client outcome goals, the Ventura County system of care was replicated in three other California counties. The new systems of care had comparable rates of successful outcomes. In 1992, this impressive record led to important new legislation. As described by Hernandez and Goldman (1996),

> the Children's Mental Health Services: County Contract (AB 3015) was passed and signed by the governor in order to add more definition and clarity to the requirements for a system of care model. It also expressed the governor's commitment of the model's statewide expansion. The bill states that "an interagency system of care for children with serious emotional and behavioral disturbances provides comprehensive and coordinated care based on the Ventura Planning Model." . . . Furthermore, the bill directs that "the State Department of Mental Health adopt as part of its overall mission the development of community based, comprehensive, interagency systems of care." (p. 181)

Thus, a "vision generated as a reaction to the philosophical and service limits that marked the traditional children's mental health paradigm" has resulted in local mental health reform. In California, and for a wide range of other systems of care reported in states throughout the country, these new networks all include preventive approaches (Knitzer, 1996a, pp. 209–211; Macbeth, 1996; Stroul, 1996).

Limitations of Traditional Mental Health Approaches

According to Knitzer (1996a, p. 210), government records estimate that only "one third of children and youth with emotional and behavioral problems receive services, and even for those, services were inappropriate." There is ample evidence that traditional mental health service systems have failed those most in need. Limitations in traditional services have been attributed to their narrow focus and isolation in relationship to systems in which children and families grow and learn; inaccessibility because of location, expense, and waiting lists; unresponsiveness to cultural differences; and reactivity. Furthermore, there has been and continues to be lack of available care for the most seriously disturbed children and youth, and in the case of the services that are provided, fragmentation and lack of coordination are persistent problems. Not only do these problems exist, but there has been a failure to address them. For poor children who live in impoverished environments, all of these problems are exacerbated (Catron, Harris, & Weiss, 1998; Friedman, 1994; King & Meyers, 1996; Knitzer, 1996a; Sessions, 1998; Stagner & Duran, 1997; Stroul, 1996).

The mental health service terrain changes continually. Services are restructured through legislation and collaboration in the midst of the disintegration and collapse of service agencies that have lost ground in the fiscal struggle for survival. Buyouts and reconfigurations wrought by managed care have, for the most part, limited services instead of expanding the service continuum. Adding to the problem, fewer and fewer services have been available to the children and youth most at risk. Further, there has been a shift from inpatient care to outpatient services. Yet, current practices that finance mental health services through private insurers who control service provision have resulted in fatal fractures for many outpatient mental health programs and increasingly limited service options for seriously disturbed youth (see, for example, discussions by Edelstein, Braverman, and Sessions in Schamess and Lightburn, 1998).

Support for Developing Systems of Care

As traditional outpatient agencies that serve children have been fractured, creative co-location of services has increased access to mental health services supported by managed care organizations for at least some low-income children and adolescents (Armbruster, Andrews, Couenhover, & Blau, 1999; Armbruster & Lichtman, 1999). Unfortunately, colocation and expansion of services for those most in need have been limited. For example, essential preventive services have been sorely neglected (Knitzer, 1996a; Weist, 1999). It is significant, therefore, that new community-based, integrated programs are beginning to have long enough histories to establish a track record. Because community-based systems are capable of transforming traditional services, they hold exceptional promise for the future. Beginning in 1984, some of the major systems of care initiatives were supported by federal and state legislation. Critical to the success of these initiatives was leadership from the National Institute of Mental Health (NIMH), which established the Child and Adolescent Service System Program (CASSP). NIMH not only supported program development but also provided essential training resources for new community-based mental health work. Major support from the Robert Wood Johnson and the Annie B. Casey foundations significantly influenced the development and evaluation of these new systems of care. These far-reaching collaborative efforts provided indispensable support for the hard work of revolutionizing the focus, priorities, and process of delivering integrated services. New, more effective approaches evolved to support the emotional well-being of vulnerable children and youth (Cole, 1996; King & Meyers, 1996; Lourie, Katz-Leavy, DeCarolis, & Quinlan, 1996; Pires & Ignelzi, 1996).

Major Challenges for Systems of Care

It is heartening to review the range of approaches being crafted in these evolving partnerships. The strength of purpose demonstrated by the many states enacting legislation to develop or expand systems of care indicates extraordinary progress and commitment toward meeting the mental health needs of children in more realistic and effective ways. At the same time, system change of this magnitude brings major challenges. In looking to the future, Stroul and her colleagues (1996) cited the most pressing issues as deficiencies in infrastructure and resource capacity, with many systems of care experiencing both problems. Resource constraints include a lack of "quality" community support services as well as a lack of community-based clinicians who are trained in comprehensive care models and who are capable of using creative means for overcoming resistance to treatment (Henggeler, et al., 1997). It is not surprising that Friedman (1993) observed that the system of care movement is relatively new and requires a paradigm for practice that is dissonant with many professionals' training and experience. Reformation in mental health service delivery systems will depend on the openness of professionals to expanding their conceptualization of practice and to fostering new attitudes with multidisciplinary colleagues.

Managed Care and Funding Systems of Care

Experience over the past 15 years provides strong models for funding systems of care (Armbruster et al., 1999; Behar, 1996; Friedman, 1994). Informed advocacy can fortify a team's approach to successfully developing funding. Without the development of such funding, financial constraints can become a barrier to change. Financing for systems of care has been described as a "patchwork enterprise" that requires creative approaches. While commonly shared values and principles underpin a team's efforts toward developing resources that can be pooled by restructuring financing mechanisms; collaborative advocacy in pursuit of funding from state, federal, and private sources, such as managed care, is also essential (Behar, 1996; Dupper & Evans, 1996; Freeman, 1996; Weist, 1997). Funding often goes unused because it is not applied for. According to the Connecticut Commission on Children, only 20 of 167 eligible school districts applied for available aid from Medicaid, leaving unspent 3.3 million dollars in special education funding (Children and Youth Funding Report, 2000, p. 12). Support for systems of care depends on successful financing strategies (Freeman, 1996).

Managed care funding for school-based mental health services should be negotiated with the appropriate state and local managed care provider. There is evidence that funding of school-based health and mental health services can expand through children's managed cared health plans (Armbruster et al., 1999). However, as the Connecticut experience demonstrates, careful attention should be given to funding complexities that can jeopardize programmatic goals, especially those intended to support preventive services (Armbruster et al., 1999; Prothrow-Stith, Chapter 15 in this volume; Weist, 1999/2000).

Community-Based Clinical Practice and Systems of Care

Clinical social workers involved in community-based clinical practice must work with systems flexibly and collaboratively. A range of examples drawn from community settings provides an overview of how systems of care are evolving. In school settings, the possibilities currently include (a) colocation of mental health clinics in schools as an integrated component in a collaborative school–community agency program that provides a range of school linked services, (b) full service schools, where the school is the community "hub" for a wide range of services; and (c) university-based programs, which emphasize collaborative interdisciplinary practice (Armbruster & Lichtman, 1999; Bosch, 1998; Bronstein & Kelly, 1998; Dryfoos, 1994; Sessions, Fanolis, Corwin, & Miller, Chapter 14 in this volume; Tourse & Mooney, 1999; Weist, 1997). There are also a growing number of examples in early intervention programs, including family support programs in community centers, day care, and Head Start programs (Lightburn & Kemp, 1994a, 1994b) as well as programs that operate in homes and neighborhoods (Eismann, 1996, Chapter 19 in this volume; Lindblad-Goldberg, Dore, & Stern, 1998). Family support can also be implemented through partnerships between mental health and community policing programs (Marans et al., 1996).

These examples of community-based practice illustrate and define principles of practice that are similar to and compatible with the systems of care philosophy. Each example represents a segment of a continuum of services that depends on coordination and multidisciplinary work. The programs are not, however, a formal part of a larger system of care as described in the Ventura case example.

Another instructive example is the family home-based service developed in response to the serious mental health needs of children and adolescents in

Pennsylvania. This innovative program is situated within the larger context of federal and state mental health reform. Creating competence out of chaos is the description Lindblad-Goldberg and colleagues (1998) gave to their program, which emphasizes the practice goal of working collaboratively with parents to build skills and promote competence. Practice and program principles drawn from this and other programmatic examples, as well as formal research on systems of care, are summarized in Table 18.1. The table broadly characterizes the pertinent differences between traditional mental health services and community-based multidisciplinary services.

The continued creative work of community-based clinicians will also depend on clearly conceptualized, described, and evaluated practice interventions. Accountability and the establishment of a track record are fundamental to program viability. For example, testimony based on the success of the California programs was presented to Congress in support of requests for additional funding (Hernandez & Goldman, 1996). The testimony of practitioners was especially important because the practitioners had actively participated in developing outcome measures and in collecting data. And in Pennsylvania, when resources were needed to continue the innovative home-based services, advocacy with the state legislature was successful because program evaluation supported the efficacy of the approach (Lindblad-Goldberg et al., 1998).

Paradigm Shifts From Traditional to Community-Based Clinical Work

Working productively in a system of care program requires a paradigm shift for those whose only experience is in traditional practice models. Useful information can by gleaned by reviewing the characteristics of traditional programs and contrasting them with more successful community-based innovations (see Table 18.1). The characteristics described in Table 18.1 can be used to assess current practice with children and families and to envision what is possible (Armbruster & Lichtman, 1999; Corwin, 2000; Eismann, 1996; Epstein et al., 1998; Henggeler et al., 1997; Kagan & Pritchard, 1996; Knitzer et al., 1990, 1994, 1996a, 1996b; Lightburn & Kemp, 1994a; Lindblad-Goldberg et al., 1998; Sessions et al., Chapter 14 in this volume; Stroul, 1996; Weist, 1997; Zigler, Finn-Stevenson, & Stern, 1997).

In the remainder of this section, two examples drawn from elsewhere in this volume are discussed to illustrate some of the characteristics of innovative, community-based programs and the paradigm shift they represent. For a more substantive description of these complex innovations readers should refer to the authors' descriptions (see Eismann, Chapter 19, and Sessions et al., Chapter 14). In particular, notions about capacity building, normative provision of services, systemic interventions, and the development of community support are described.

Table 18.1

CHARACTERISTICS OF TRADITIONAL AND
INNOVATIVE MENTAL HEALTH SERVICES
FOR CHILDREN, YOUTH, AND FAMILIES

Characteristics of Traditional Services and Practice	Characteristics of Community-Based Innovation and Reform for Mental Health Services
Reactive when client at crisis point; targets mental illness; provider driven	Focus is the promotion and protection of emotional well-being and behavioral health of children and their families with a continuum of services; involves consumers in the service design
Insufficient attention to prevention and early intervention	Broad perspective of prevention, with early intervention a priority; prevention is not targeted to a specific narrowly defined group (e.g., emotionally disturbed)
Fragmented and overlapping services; uncoordinated and unintegrated	Coordinated, networked systems; interagency collaboration and alliances for practice
Unresponsive to multiple and interrelated problems experienced by disadvantaged children and youth	Systems of care concept and philosophy set as priority support and resource to respond to the multiple problems of disadvantaged children and youth
Institutional, office-bound, unfamiliar environments that are artificial; inpatient, outpatient, and residential treatment; inflexible services	Colocated, community-based services in schools and community centers; use of care coordinators and case managers; in-home and community crisis intervention; home-based services; wraparound services
Culturally insensitive and linguistically incompetent programs and practice without accountability	Cultural competence developed and promoted with culturally sensitive programs and services involving accountability
Relatively indifferent to the family and neighborhood; rhetoric without action; maltreatment, disenfranchisement, blaming of families, or distancing from families, who are seen at infrequent intervals	Families are partners and collaborators; capacity building with families and community; supports families; family-centered philosophy
Single-system solutions	Multisystemic and multisystem solutions through linkages in the system of care
Lack of consistent use of developmentally appropriate services and practice	Founded on developmental principles and with consonant programs and practice

Table 18.1   *(continued)*

Characteristics of Traditional Services and Practice	Characteristics of Community-Based Innovation and Reform for Mental Health Services
Limited training and professional development	Interdisciplinary and cross-professional inquiry into practice and program solutions, with continued professional development and training
Stigmatizing, labeling, blaming practice and programs	Normative provision of services emphasizing strengths, opportunity, and humanizing descriptions of emotional and behavioral struggles
Isolating practice, commitments, and management	Develops community, support, mutuality, responsibility to and for others, and collaborative alliances for achieving system of care goals
Toxicity of environment not a major priority or focus of service or practice	Ensures safe place, havens, refuge, and retreats as a major priority
Inflexible financing: limited to allocated traditional services; vulnerable financing due to changes in state and federal allocations as well as managed care policies	Restructuring of financial practice and policies with necessary flexibility to ensure pool or resources for service in neighborhood; a patchwork of resources developed for stable support for flexible programs
Therapist autonomy in practice and philosophy of participation in services and programs	Professionals and staff oriented to systems of care philosophy; committed to the mission and goals of the system of care
Disregard for communities as social structures	Focus on communities and neighborhood as resources to develop and utilize in service provision
Top-down organization management	Blending of top-down with bottom-up management
Limited policy support	State and federal legislative and policy support
Limited research and evaluation	Evaluation and research built in from the beginning so that outcomes are readily known

Source: Armbruster and Lichtman, 1999; Corwin, 2000; Eisman, 1996; Epstein et al., 1998; Friedman, 1994; Henggeler et al., 1997; Kagan & Pritchard, 1996; Knitzer et al. 1990, 1996a, 1996b; Lightburn & Kemp, 1994a; 1994b; Lindblad-Goldberg, et .al. 1998; Marans et al, 1996; Sessions, Fanolis, Corwin, & Miller, Chapter 14 in this volume; Stroul & Friedman, 1996; Tourse & Mooney, 1999; Weist, 1997; Zigler, Finn-Stevenson, & Stern, 1997.

Unitas

As Eismann demonstrated in developing Unitas[2], a program for street kids in the South Bronx, it is critical to engage distressed young people where they are most comfortable, on the street. The unmet mental health needs of street kids made it necessary for Eismann to abandon the comfortable and contained interview room. The success of Eismann's program was based on his ability to enter the children's culture and space. He had to learn how to build a symbolic family system that could nurture and hold needy young people in a circle on the street where they hang out. His translation of traditional clinical theory involved extending the use of relationship. He built capacity in a community of street kids by encouraging them to nurture others as they, themselves, were being nurtured by him. He expanded his relationship to the children by creating a community group that tapped their strengths, hopes, and capacity to grow by offering "corrective emotional experiences" in repeated encounters on the street. His flexibility and responsiveness to the themes of street life brought repeated dramas of conflict and aggression into focus. In effect, the crisis of the moment became the way to connect. Unmet needs required active outreach. It was the only way to engage and re-engage these young people who needed to have adults interested in their own struggles and/or in protecting themselves. Basic to the Unitas's success was enlarging the network of relationships so children, themselves, could create a holding environment that would "live on for generations" outside the home. Older children would continue to nurture the unnurtured for their own as well as for the younger children's emotional well being.

Partners for Success

Partners for Success (see Sessions et al., Chapter 14 in this volume) is a school-based program designed to meet the mental health needs of children and families. In addition, it fosters collaboration between social work supervisors, interns, the school community, parents, and the broader community. It was initiated by the Smith College School for Social Work with the aim of developing partnerships with community agencies to provide inner-city children and families with a multisystemic, nontraditional approach to prevention and practice. Priorities include capacity building in systems that are important to children and schools. Work that is flexible and responsive to the needs of schools, families, and communities occurs in classrooms, hallways, cafeterias, offices, and homes. As described in Chapter 14 of this volume, the program has made notable progress toward developing responsive interventions with children, teachers, administrators, parents and the community centers that are afterschool havens for children and parents (see also Corwin, 2000).

Within the school, children receive help, as needed, through individual and group sessions. Family work, consultation, and advocacy with teachers and administration are augmented by work with other community service providers. Similar to Unitas (Eismann, 1996), Partners for Success emphasizes the importance of working interactively with clients and caregivers in their own social environments.[3] This work may, for example, take the form of interns consulting with teachers and/or school administrators about a student's difficult behavior that is "triggered" by something that evokes previous traumatic experiences. Through such collaboration, social workers begin to understand the complex dimensions of the teacher's work as well as the relationship between a child's experience with others in the class and his or her experiences with parents and community. Consultation between teachers and social workers also initiates a feedback loop that builds capacity for both the teachers and the social workers, strengthening both in understanding and mastery. Again, the approach is similar to Eismann's in focusing on expanding the network of relationships and increasing the network's capacity to respond to children's emotional distress and unmet needs.

Collaborative work extends to community center paraprofessionals, who also become involved with school social workers. The focus of these supportive and enabling relationships is to help community center staff develop knowledge and competencies in preventive work with members of the community who are affected by violence, substance abuse, HIV/AIDS, and gangs. Similarly, the recursive process that develops between the collaborating program staff deepens understanding for both school social workers and paraprofessionals, as both become better able to respond to whatever stresses the community experiences.

In this model, prevention and intervention are intertwined, as strengths and competence within the system are enhanced. Once a systems of care environment has been established it is possible to respond to the developmental needs of both normal children and those with serious emotional and behavioral problems. It has been deeply gratifying to review the progress Partners for Success has made. The student interns and social work supervisors are valued within their schools. In addition, both the schools and community have increased their capacity to meet the needs of very troubled children.

Effecting Paradigm Shifts and Changing Systemic Norms

The two examples presented illustrate paradigm shifts in theories for practice. These shifts evolved through collaboration and a willingness to take risks in extending the traditional boundaries of practice. Building on these programmatic examples cited previously, a larger frame of community-based clinical practice founded on new principles can be identified. This new frame of practice fits well within the systems of care philosophy. Mental health service reform prepares the ground for change. Describing, conceptualizing, and evaluating practice initiates a recursive process that advances the development of responsive community-based models of clinical practice.

Working With Dissonance

Practitioners often experience paradigm shifts as being dissonant with cherished beliefs and ways of knowing and working. A recent regional report on systems of care development identified an urgent need for training programs in mental health. As stated in Knitzer (1996a),

> human resource development issues related to the new children's mental health paradigms are of equal or greater concern than funding issues to state officials, parents, advocates and providers. . . . The *bottom line is that there must be mental health professionals excited about working in new ways and invested in continuing to move the field forward* [italics added]. (p. 223)

It is telling when state officials, parents, advocates, and providers all agree that providers need to learn to work in new ways. Single-system solutions, isolation from community life, indifference to families and culture, and inflexible, office-bound methods of providing service are too familiar problems in practice settings that serve children and adolescents (see Table 18.1). The forces that circumscribe practice are many, including ideology; finances; programmatic priorities; agency traditions and structures; lack of training and skill; productivity overload; shrinking opportunities for supervision, consultation, and reflection; lack of information and outcome evaluation; and "politics." Strong resistance also stems from territorial imperatives even when ideology is agreed upon. Bowman (1994) discussed this phenomenon in examining the tensions that typically arise between home and school even when both fully agree about the importance of education. In contrast, Delgado's (1998) exploratory research with Latino parents illuminated the parents' desire to be involved in school programs both as a way of relating to their children's education and as a way of satisfying some of their own service needs through linked services.

Understanding resistance, assessing the nature and reason for the "frozen state of practice," is a step toward progress and prepares the ground for risk taking. Reflection is indispensable, and reflecting in dialogue with others is enabling. As William Torbert (1976, p. xiv) wrote: "We need to create a world wide community of inquiry, concluding that transforming ourselves is a place to begin." Reflection, dialogue, and a willingness to challenge assumptions are indispensable to the spirit of inquiry. They enable us to deal with dissonance. As Garbarino so dynamically demonstrates in Chapter 1 of this volume, perspective is possible only when you aggressively inquire into the complexity of the problem.

Summary

Leadership in clinical social work requires a loosening and redefinition of the boundaries of traditional practice. Promoting and developing systems of care requires us to challenge and change norms. It also means changing systems and practice paradigms. Vision, conceptual clarity, and a philosophy that can be clearly articulated are all essential. Along with these qualities, social work must strengthen its commitment to evaluation as well as its willingness and capacity to continually translate theory into practice and practice into theory. The potential already demonstrated by systems of care can be further realized by developing funding resources that include managed care organizations and community-based service providers. Progress requires advocates who are not discouraged because the task is difficult and who are heartened by the synergy of collaboration intrinsic to building systems of care. It also requires social workers who believe in community. It requires champions.

References

Armbruster, P., Andrews, E., Couenhoven, J., & Blau, G. (1999). Collision or collaboration? School-based mental health services meet managed care. *Clinical Psychology Review*, *19*(2), 221–237.

Armbruster, P., & Lichtman, J. (1999). Are school-based mental health services effective? Evidence from 36 inner city schools. *Community Mental Health Journal, 35*(6), 493–504.

Beaucar, K. O. (1999b, November). Action plan on youth violence urged. *NASW News*, p. 15.

Beaucar, K. O. (1999a, November). Research links crime to child abuse history. *NASW News*, p. 15.

Behar, L. B. (1996). Financing systems of care. In B. Stroul (Ed.), *Children's mental health: Creating systems of care in a changing society.* Baltimore: Paul H. Brookes. 299–312.

Bosch, L. (1998). Early intervention in the new millenium: The critical role of school social workers. *Social Work in Education, 20*(2), 139–143.

Bowman, B. (1994). Home and school. In S. Kagan & B. Weissbourd (Eds.), *Putting families first.* San Francisco: Jossey-Bass. 51–72.

Braverman, A. (1998). Losing innocents. In G. Schamess & A. Lightburn (Eds.), *Humane managed care?* Washington, DC: NASW Press. 240–246.

Bronstein, L. R., & Kelly, T. (1998). A multidimensional approach to evaluating school-linked services: A school of social work and county public school partnership. *Social Work in Education, 20*(3), 152–164.

Catron, T., Harris, V., & Weiss, B. (1998). Post-treatment results after two years of services in the Vanderbilt school-based counseling project. In M. H. Epstein, K. Kutash, & A. Duchnowski (Eds.), *Outcomes for children and youth with emotional and behavioral disorders and their families.* Austin, TX: Pro-Ed. 633–656.

Children and Youth Funding Report. (2000). *State and local news.* Silver Spring, MD: CD Publications.

Cole, R. F. (1996). The Robert Wood Johnson Foundation's mental health services program for youth. In B. Stroul (Ed.), *Children's mental health: Creating systems of care in a changing society.* Baltimore: Paul H. Brookes. 235–248.

Corwin, M. (2000). *Evaluation of Partners for Success: Collaboration between Smith College School for Social Work and the Springfield public schools.* Unpublished manuscript.

Delgado, M. (1998). Linking schools, human service, and community: A Puerto Rican perspective. *Social Work in Education, 20*(2), 121–130.

Dryfoos, J. G. (1994). *Full service schools.* San Francisco: Jossey-Bass.

Dupper, D. R., & Evans, S. (1996). From Band-Aids and putting out fires to prevention: School social work practice approaches for the new century. *Social Work in Education, 18*(3), 186–192.

Edelstein, C. (1998). Notes from a sinking ship. In G. Schamess & A. Lightburn (Eds.), *Humane managed care?* Washington, DC: NASW Press. 247–254.

Eismann, E. (1996). *Unitas.* New York: Fordham University Press.

Epstein, M. H., Kutash, K., & Duchnowski, A. (Eds.). (1998). *Outcomes for children and youth with emotional and behavioral disorders and their families* Austin, TX: Pro-Ed.

Freeman, E. M. (1996). The art of forecasting: Shaping the future of school social work. *Social Work in Education, 18*(3), 131–134.

Friedman, R. (1994). Restructuring of systems to emphasize prevention and family support. *Journal of Clinical Child Psychology, 23,* 40–47.

Friedman, R. M. (1993). Preparation of students to work with children and families: Is it meeting the need? *Administration and Policy in Mental Health, 20,* 297–310.

Friedman, R. M. (1996). Child mental health policy. In B. L. Levin and J. Petrila (Eds.), *Mental health services: Public health perspective* (pp. 234–248). NY: Oxford University Press.

Garbarino, J., & Kostelny, K. (1994). Family support and community development. In S. Kagan & B. Weissbourd (Eds.), *Putting families first.* San Francisco: Jossey-Bass. 297–320.

Garbarino, J. (1996). Lost boys: Why our sons turn violent and what we can do to save them. *Smith College Studies in Social Work, 71*(2), 169–181.

Glodich, A., & Allen, J. G. (1998). Adolescents exposed to violence and abuse: A review of the group therapy literature with an emphasis on preventing trauma reenactment. *Journal of Child and Adolescent Group Therapy, 8*(3), 135–154.

Henggeler, S. W., Cowland, M. D., Pickrel, S. G., Miller, S. L., Cunningham, P. B., Santos, A. B., et al. (1997). Investigating family-based alternatives to institution-based mental health services for youth: Lessons learned from the pilot study of a randomized trial. *Journal of Clinical Psychology, 26*(3), 226–233.

Hernandez, M., & Goldman, S. (1996). A local approach to system development: Ventura County, California. In B. Stroul (Ed.), *Children's mental health: Creating systems of care in a changing society.* Baltimore: Paul H. Brookes. 177–196.

Kagan, S. L., & Pritchard, E. (1996). Linking services for children and families: Past legacy, future possibilities. In E. F. Zigler, S. L. Kagan, & N. Hall (Eds.), *Children, families, and government: Preparing for the twenty-first century.* New York: Cambridge University Press. 378–393.

King, B., & Meyers, J. (1996). The Annie E. Casey Foundation's mental health initiative for urban children. In B. Stroul (Ed.), *Children's mental health: Creating systems of care in a changing society.* Baltimore: Paul H. Brookes. 249–264.

Knitzer, J., Steinberg, Z., & Fleisch, B. (1990). *At the schoolhouse door.* New York: Bank Street College of Education.

Knitzer, J. (1994). Empowering families and changing systems: Toward a new ecology. *Empowering families.* Riverdale, IL: National Association for Family-Based Services. 117–126.

Knitzer, J. (1996b). The role of education in systems of care. In B. Stroul (Ed.), *Children's mental health: Creating systems of care in a changing society.* Baltimore: Paul H. Brookes. 197–214.

Knitzer, J. (1996a). Children's mental health: Changing paradigms and policies. In E. F. Zigler, S. L. Kagan, & N. Hall (Eds.), *Children, families, and government: Preparing for the twenty-first century.* New York: Cambridge University Press. 207–232.

Lightburn, A., & Kemp, S. (1994a). Family support: Opportunities for community-based practice. *Families and Society, 75*(1), 16–26.

Lightburn, A., & Kemp, S. (1994b). Urban family support: Empowering high-risk minority families. In R. Fong, P. Sandau-Beckler, & D. Haapala (Eds.), *Empowering families.* Riverdale, IL: National Association for Family-Based Services. 77–86.

Lindblad-Goldberg, M., Dore, M. M., & Stern, L. (1998). *Creating competence out of chaos.* New York: Norton.

Lourie, I. S., Katz-Leavy, J., DeCarolis, C., & Quinlan, W. (1996). The role of the federal government. In B. Stroul (Ed.), *Children's mental health: Creating systems of care in a changing society.* Baltimore: Paul H. Brookes. 99–114.

Macbeth, G. (1996). Profiles of local systems of care. In B. Stroul (Ed.), *Children's mental health: Creating systems of care in a changing society.* Baltimore: Paul H. Brookes. 131–148.

Macro International Inc. (1998). *Annual report to Congress on the evaluation of the Comprehensive Community Mental Health Services for Children and Their Families Program, executive summary.* Atlanta, GA: Author.

Marans, S., Berkman, M., & Cohen, D. (1996). Child development and adaptation to catastrophic circumstances. In R. Apfel, & B. Simons (Eds.), *Minefields in their hearts: The mental health of children in war and communal violence.* New Haven, CT: Yale University Press. 104–127.

Pires, S. A., & Ignelzi, S. (1996). The role of the state in system development. In B. Stroul (Ed.), *Children's mental health: Creating systems of care in a changing society.* Baltimore: Paul H. Brookes. 115–130.

Richters, J. E., & Martinez, P. (1993). The NIMH community violence project: I. Children as victims of and witness to violence. *Psychiatry, 56,* 7–21.

Schamess, G., & Lightburn, A. (Eds.). (1998). *Humane managed care?* Washington, DC: NASW Press.

Schechter, S., & Edleson, J. L. (2000). *Domestic violence and children: Creating a public response.* New York: Center on Crime, Communities and Culture for the Open Society.

Sessions, P. (1998). Managed care and the oppression of psychiatrically disturbed adolescents. In G. Schamess & A. Lightburn (Eds.), *Humane managed care?* Washington, DC: NASW Press. 171–179.

Stagner, M., & Duran, A. (1997). Comprehensive community initiatives: Principles, practice and lessons learned. *Children and Poverty, 7*(2), 132–140.

Stroul, B. (Ed.). (1996). *Children's mental health: Creating systems of care in a changing society.* Baltimore: Paul H. Brookes.

Stroul, B. A., & Friedman, R. M. (1996). The system of care concept and philosophy. In B. Stroul (Ed.), *Children's mental health: Creating systems of care in a changing society.* Baltimore: Paul H. Brookes. 3–22.

Stroul, B., Friedman, R. M., Hernandez, M., Roebuck, L., Lourie, I. S., & Koyanagi, C. (1996). Systems of care in the future. In B. Stroul (Ed.), *Children's mental health: Creating systems of care in a changing society.* Baltimore: Paul H. Brookes. 591–612.

Torbert, W. (1976). *Creating a community of inquiry: Conflict, collaboration, transformation.* New York: Wiley.

Tourse, R. W. C., & Mooney, J. F. (Eds.). (1999). *Collaborative practice.* Westport, CT: Praeger.

Wadock, S. (1999). Socioeconomic forces and educational reform. In R. W. C. Tourse & J. F. Mooney (Eds.), *Collaborative practice.* Westport, CT: Praeger. 33–55.

Weist, M. D. (1997). Expanded school mental health services: A national movement in progress. *Advances in Clinical Child Psychology, 19,* 319–352.

Weist, M. (1999/2000). Focusing on strengths within and around youth. *On the Move With School-Based Mental Health,* 1.

Zigler, E. F., Finn-Stevenson, M., & Stern, B. (1997). Supporting children and families in the schools: The school of the 21st century. *American Journal of Orthopsychiatry, 67*(3), 396–407.

**Notes**

---

[1] This phrase is drawn from Garbarino's parable of the lamppost (see Chapter 1 in this volume), which illustrates the need to go beyond the place where the light is shining and, in this application, where services are funded, to find answers to dealing with violence. In Garbarino's words, this can mean going down the road into violent areas where funding may not exist. Drawing from another metaphor, it means going into the heart of darkness.

---

[2] Unitas is introduced briefly in this volume and fully described in Eismann (1996).

---

[3] This notion is drawn from Winnicott's concept of the facilitating environment, that is essential in nurturing development.

19

Unitas: The Street as Therapeutic Community

Edward P. Eismann

It is 1:30 on a hot, summer afternoon as I pull into Fox Street in the South Bronx. Gutted buildings and trash-strewn streets announce its stature as the worst of New York City's slums. I am surrounded by kids chattering in English and Spanish, all wanting something from the beat-up van that serves as the play closet of my "traveling clinic": bats, balls, paper, crafts, ropes, games. Gently, but firmly, I pull their attention aside, directing it instead to the teenagers lounging against the chain fence enclosing the street's vacant lot. This is Unitas, a community mental health approach to hard-to-reach youth who would rather die than come to a traditional mental health center for therapy. Unitas aims to teach its youth how to find supportive resources and how to master the tasks of daily living, not through formal mental health interventions or from me personally, but through mutual influence and, in this street system, through learning from the teenage role models who live with them right there—the caretakers I have found, conveniently, right in their own backyard. To put this story into context, I need to back up a bit, however.

 ## Theoretical Framework

Unitas owes much in concept to the ideology of the community mental health movement, with its emphasis on primary and secondary prevention. Community mental health practice stresses that the resources people need can be found in the interpersonal networks all around them and in relationships that need only be recognized so they can be cultivated and reinforced for helping or healing purposes. Community mental health theory stresses the impact of social, group, and environmental forces on peoples' mental health and aims to alter those systemic influences that are unhealthy. Relevant literature from the early years of the community mental health movement, as reviewed by Langston (1970), identifies five categories of need that are essential to the concept of community mental health. They are as follows:

1. A need to focus on all members of a designated community, functional as well as dysfunctional.
2. A need to address primary prevention through interventions aimed at identifying and responding to potential disturbance in people who are normally well.
3. A need to establish social treatment goals aimed at promoting social adjustment in ordinary life rather than at reconstructing personality organization.
4. A need to provide continuity of care by ensuring that clients are integrated in a comprehensive network of care.
5. A need to work collaboratively with other community caretakers in order to extend one's effectiveness. Change is facilitated by working through and with other people.

No description of historical timeliness and ideology could be more in sync with these principles than the arrival and development of Unitas. It was conceived and implemented in the early years of the community mental health movement as a preventive and alternative system of mental health care and has been sustained without interruption over three decades and into a new century. In keeping with this ideology, Unitas focuses on a designated community of functional and dysfunctional youth. The program initially worked through and with its own community caretakers and developed a social support structure aimed at promoting social adjustment in one small influential system of children's lives—namely, the open system of the street. It eventually moved into schools and settlement houses as well.

But why the street? The street is simply the second home for most alienated and hard-to-reach youth. For many, it is the first place, the closest place to home they know. All the power and influence these youth have is located there, and they live substantially on the street. And so, in this setting, using the banquet of play as a golden apple, Unitas seeks to create a therapeutic structure in the form of a symbolic family. This symbolic family is composed of neighborhood youth of all ages. It serves the majority of local youth as well as drifters from surrounding streets, most of whom are at risk in some way because of the emotional and physical poverty of ghetto life.

# Developing Relationships

Armed with notions about community mental health practice that emphasize systemic interventions and community caretaking, I decided to get as close as possible to the lives of my ghetto children and their potential caretakers by enmeshing myself in their street culture (Eismann, 1996). The decision to enmesh myself, first as a participant observer and then as an active practitioner, was not just the result of my theoretical persuasion, however. It was born of the terrible frustration I felt as an office-based clinician at the local Lincoln Hospital Community Mental Health Center—a center whose services few youth were using. The absence of troubled youngsters from the Mental Health Center caseload made it obvious that children were not responding to the services offered by the formal system. Driven by frustration as well as intense curiosity regarding this clinical conundrum, I walked the center's catchment area for months, sitting in school yards, on tenement stoops, on curbs and car fenders, and "hanging out" in alleyways, bodegas, and social clubs. I made connections and "friendships" as did the friendly visitor of bygone settlement house days. People wanted to know who I was. I explained that I was Dr. E. from Lincoln Health Center and that my job (self-defined) was to hang out and talk to youngsters who had problems or worries.

The floodgates opened. Children poured out their hearts about family, bullies, violence, and drugs; teens accepted my mediation in street conflicts. I still talked the language of therapy, but I did so in their systems and in the midst of their networks. There was no dearth of customers; in fact, it was difficult to hold back the tide. This experience taught me not only that the youngsters were not resistant to mental health interventions but that they sought me out with undaunted motivation as long as two elements were present: my immersion in their social setting and in the company of their social network. Those elements made the difference.

So I began to dream about developing a model of intervention that would provide an alternative form of mental health care. The influence of the naturally existing network in the children's social setting would be recognized, organized, and then cultivated for healing purposes. I noticed that in this street system, children often hung around groups of teenagers who were their natural role models. I slowly engaged these streetwise teenagers as my "consultees" in the networking venture. Recognizing the emphasis on family relationships prevalent among the heavily Hispanic and African American population and, over time, placing myself in the symbolic role of grandpa, the court of last appeal, I enlisted the neighborhood young men and women to serve as caretakers—co-padres, co-parents, symbolic "mothers and fathers" to the children who lived on their own streets. I began meeting with these teens to provide them with structure and training in their child-caring work, while also giving them direct help with their own concerns. I arranged for these young caretakers to meet with children in schools, libraries, recreation centers, and church settings. This brought me into contact with the larger network of agencies that serve youth and permitted me to open doors for the children and teen caretakers with minimal bureaucratic constraints. And everywhere I went I was met with openness and support. But all of this is another story. For a fuller description of the steps in this initial journey, I refer readers to other sources (Eismann, 1996; Farber & Rogler, 1981; Procidano & Glenwick, 1985).

Large-Group Processes

My digression finished, let me return to Fox Street. As I prepare for the afternoon it becomes clearer to me that the street scene is to be taken as seriously as the rituals I need to enact there in the form of interventions that inculcate structure and love. These two items—structure and love—are the most lacking among wayward, emotionally starved youngsters. At 1:45 two teenage caretakers, Eric, 17, and Cheo, 16, emerge from the church where Unitas stores its larger props. They are carrying a carpentry table and tools, which they set on the curb under a spindly tree. Paper and fabric scraps make their way to a worn stoop for the art groups, headed this afternoon by 16-year-old James. Hulking and brown skinned, Ian, 17, dumps tumbling mats on the sidewalk's shady side while three other teenage caretakers, Ada, Angel, and Maria, anchor the volleyball net to parked cars. Then, in twos and threes, led by 18-year-old Papo, who is as cool and taciturn as any Puerto Rican John Wayne, and 16-year-old Elena, children from 5 to 15 years of age emerge with push brooms and trash cans. While I watch approvingly, Hector, Jesus, Chico, Juan, and Alex, along with Magdelena, Ernesto, Bobby, Renee, Raoul, and the rest of their street compatriots, whisk the street clean of broken glass, paper cartons, and orange peels, the ubiquitous garbage of the slum, polishing it better than many a living room. That is exactly what I have in mind. If they can work out these details of living together then they can probably get their heads straight in other ways too. Begin where the client is.

It is now 2:30 in the afternoon. Continuing a daily ritual, I take my place sitting cross-legged on the asphalt, in the gutter, the first point of a circle that falls into place without any further announcement. We are ready to begin the "Family Circle," the therapeutic community session that kicks off each day. Within a few minutes, 75 to 100 children and teenagers have followed suit, arranging themselves in their own little family groupings in the circle with me. The circle radiates to 30 feet in diameter. The youngsters know the rules: We begin when all are quiet. And so around the group can be heard "sh-sh-sh" as the children shush each other, anxious to get on with the meeting and the play to come. In this stillness, Hector and Jesus, two 14-year-olds, both of whom are chronic truants and troublemakers in school, seem to ignore the group. They persist with a ball game, hanging back, hanging tough. I say to the group with a smile, "They are enjoying their game so much. I wish they were here." It is a signal to the caretakers that it is not up to me, but to them, to take care of their neighbors. Seven, eight voices call out to the two while Papo, quietly authoritative, leaves for a word with the outsiders. Slowly, smirking and gesturing but drawing near, they come to listen, leaning on a parked car not quite in the circle, but close. This has been a victory of sorts. For days the two have refused to join at all.

And so I begin: "Hello, my friends. As you know, this is Unitas, and Unitas is a wonderful community of boys and girls, young men and young women, and some older men and women, that meets like this each day to play together and talk together about better ways of getting along and settling problems peacefully. If you have anything you would like to say today, just raise your hand as I come around so I can see how many have something to bring to the family today." I make eye contact, at least momentarily, with each child as I go around the circle. Several look away; for them the exercise is unbearable. Most are silent. Then, 8-year-old Chico waves his hand. "Alex," he wails, "took my quarter." His gang vigorously nods agreement. Chico explains that he gave Alex, a 9-year-old newcomer, a quarter that morning to bring him a snack. But no quarter and no snack ever arrived, even though Alex, a tough acting but withdrawn child, has been skulking around ever since. Chico, plagued by his own hostile nature, is furious. "Alex spent my quarter. That is why he is not here," he announces with total conviction. "He's afraid to come to the circle. But I'll get him."

That, too, is a matter for the community. I send another child to find Alex, an easy task because the boy is moping alone in the Unitas sandbox in the back of the street's vacant lot. As Alex, head down, reaches the circle, caretaker Ada, heretofore listening intently to the furor, speaks up first. "Do you have Chico's quarter?" she asks simply. Shuffling, the child nods yes. "Then give it back to him," she commands, "and come sit next to me here because you are part of this family." While Chico stares, stunned at getting his quarter back, Alex joins Ada's family—a true son and brother. "What has Ada done?" I ask. "Found the quarter," chirp the children happily. "Solved a problem," I reinterpret, "and reconciled Alex and Chico. That is why we meet like this, to help each other the way Ada did."

There is still tension. There was some conflict this morning on the way to the city pool between two factions that have developed among the group. One faction sided with Eric, the acknowledged leader of the caretakers, the other with Angel, a competitive youth who would like the glory attributed to Eric. A disruption took place along the way with the group split in two and each leader facing each other from different street corners. Whose fault was it that the group was not together? Finally, Elena, a clear-eyed, gifted youngster and one of the youngest caretakers, breaks the ice. "We broke into two groups this morning," she announces, opening the wound to air. "I don't think that was safe or right."

Angel, seething, bursts forth with his version of the power struggle. "Eric was late," he charges. "We'd all crossed the street when he comes along behind because he wasn't keeping up. Then he wanted us to come back to his side of the street. That was stupid and I didn't because I was right."

Eric, brooding, is equally angry. "I lagged behind," he admits, "because I was trying to get Juan (a 7-year-old impulsive, hyperactive child and one of Eric's "sons") to keep together with us. He kept running the other way, and no one even noticed. But no one should cross the street until the whole group gets there including me. I'm in charge." Angel blows his top, "If we stop on every corner and take attendance we'll never get anywhere. It's Eric's responsibility to keep up. Besides, does one person have the power here or does the group?" "Ideally the group has the power," I say, attempting both to acknowledge and quell Angel's rage, "and it is the group that helps, but anger is getting in the way here of listening and helping."

Deflecting the tense energy away from the protagonists, I continue: "But I want to know what the rest of you think." Magdelena, age 10, raises her hand and declares, "We should all stay together on a trip." Next, caretaker Maria notes that both parties were wrong. "Eric should have told us through someone else that he was having a problem. Angel shouldn't have gone ahead without checking what the problem was." The group nods in agreement with Maria as their spokesperson. I say, "So you, as group members, were neglectful. You didn't communicate to Eric and Angel that anything was wrong. Instead, you left them all alone to decide what to do. And, in their own ways, each of them did what he thought best." With this reinterpretation of the problem in which I emphasize that the entire group shared responsibility, Eric and Angel exchange smiles. They have been affirmed and neither has lost face. The problem was aired, the struggle is over, and less than a half hour later the two youths, having become friends again, are working smoothly together at a favorite sport, flipping giggling children through the air to tumble on the sidewalk mats.

The Use of Psychodrama

From the corner of my eye I detect another conflict emerging in the circle among caretaker Felix and two of his oppositional "sons," Antonio and Adam. Felix has been trying to control their disruptive behavior in the group, and they in turn have been increasingly defying his power over them. Taking authority into his own hands he starts to remove them physically from the group. The situation threatens to develop into a real fracas. I quickly intervene: "What is happening over there?" "These stupids are not listening to me," Felix responds, "so I'm kicking them out." Felix has overstepped a community rule: Whenever caretakers have problems they cannot handle alone they are to ask the community for help. I say: "You need some help; thank you for making that known." I rise from my community space and enter the special space in the circle reserved for psychodrama. I say to Antonio and Adam: "I don't want you to leave. Would the two of you be willing to come to the middle of the circle and tell us what went on that you were asked to leave so you have a chance to speak your heart? And you, Felix, would you come over here to speak your heart to your sons so they know clearly what it is that you expect of them as their caretaker? Have a seat here, and you over there. Is there anyone else who has some thoughts on this matter?" Caylene raises her hand and is invited to join the inner circle of protagonists and antagonists. I turn around and say: "Listen up, all of you, there was this problem between Antonio and Adam and their caretaker, Felix. Also, Caylene who is a caretaker in a nearby family has something to say, too. Felix was telling these two brothers to be quiet but they were not listening to him. That was the problem. So, let's find out more about this. Felix, what happened? What did you actually say to them?" Felix recounts his words: "I said, 'Please shut your mouth,' but they did not listen, so I said it again, 'Shut your mouth.' They still paid me no mind, so I finally shouted, 'Shut up!' to them." I said, "You finally became forceful after nothing else seemed to work. Then, when I questioned what was happening, you asked for help by stating the problem. That is where the rest of us come in. Is that it?" Felix says, "Yeah, that's it." I say, "Thank you."

Turning to Adam, I invite him to tell us what happened from his point of view. Adam says he remembers being yelled at to "shut up . . . shut up." I comment that he seems to say this with a lot of anger; what actually was he feeling at the time? He shrugs. "Who thinks they know how Adam might have felt?" I ask the group. A child raises his hand and is invited to join the psychodramatic enactment. "Sit next to Adam," I tell him, "and make out you are Adam himself. I will call you Adam II." Adam II comments strongly that he would have felt very mad to be talked to that way. Adam agrees with bobbing head. "Antonio, how about you? Why didn't you quiet down when asked? What is your story?" Antonio states that it is the same and that he didn't think it was right to be cursed at that way. I summarize: "Do you all see now what went on? The caretaker of the family was doing his job, responsibly so, in making sure his sons were paying attention in the circle. He exercised his rightful authority in his own way of speaking. The sons here are saying they heard him but didn't like being told to shut up or 'shut your mouth.' How many of you here like it when people say 'shut up' to you?" The group is awake. The question has landed on empathic ground. "So you know how the brothers felt."

I have neglected Caylene. She has been bursting at the seams as I have tediously labored to bring focus to this confrontation in the middle of the street. Containing herself no longer, she says with passion: "It is not just how *they* felt; they were talking constantly. I saw them and even motioned to them to quiet down, but they sneered at me." Looking directly at them, she added, "I don't like that kind of disrespect." I comment, "So this was your observation from sitting nearby. You were feeling as frustrated and annoyed as Felix; you know through your own anger how the caretaker might also have felt." In defending Felix, Caylene has loyally implemented another community rule, namely that caretakers should support and back each other up as members of an "executive system." I turn to the community and say, "This is getting more and more interesting; there seem to be two sides to this story, as in all stories. Let's see how the story will unfold." I look firmly but in an engaging manner at Antonio and Adam and say, "You have heard what Felix said. He was backed up by Caylene. I am going to push you a little bit to continue this wonderful cooperation you are showing by asking if you could talk to Felix respectfully, but in such a way as to win his attention. Tell him you don't mind being told what to do but the words he uses make a big difference. Talk to him now about this."

Both boys respond to my direction, and Adam, taking the lead, says squarely to Felix, "We don't like it when you curse at us to make us do something. That's not right." I say, "Good words, nice way of directly talking to someone you have a gripe with . . . very manly." Felix says back, "You don't want me to say 'shut up,' right? Well, then, when I tell you to be quiet I expect you to do that . . . okay? I don't want to keep telling you to always do that. Be quiet when I tell you. I did ask you nice, but then you gave me no choice." I comment, "You want them to respect you as much as they want you to respect them with the words you use." Caylene, undaunted in her support of Felix, adds: "You know he's right and so do I, so remember what he is saying to you." Adam and Antonio each say, "Sorry for talking." "Thanks for apologizing," Felix says, and he adds, "Next time I won't curse at you, but you have to listen to me the first time." I look with admiration at Felix and say, "Listen, these brothers had a lot of courage to get up here and voice their problem. And Felix, you had courage too, together with Caylene's backing. Great . . . wonderful work, all of you." As all return to their places in the outer circle a round of applause gives recognition to their courage. "Thanks to all of you," I say. "This is not easy; it is our work together."

It is almost time to close the meeting, so I conclude: "Listen up, all of you, especially you caretakers. Next time, take care of things the way we did here, speak up sooner and respectfully to each other whether on a trip or right here in this circle. I want you to remember that problems are opportunities to learn from, not excuses to slug things out. If you don't act on this thinking, how will your children ever learn to get along with others?" Having rationalized my advice, which was given as a psychoeducational intervention, I conclude the session: "As we finish up, what do you think of the courage shown here today by Ada and Chico and then Elena and Maria, a while back, and then Felix, Caylene, Adam, and Antonio? They were the ones here who had the courage to speak up and help this group." A chorus of yays and a hearty round of applause reverberate around the circle, clear as the grin on my face. The heroes and heroines in today's mini-drama of life, enacted in this therapeutic theater, also beam and bask in their deserved recognition.

Anger and Managing It

The problem of anger, even rage and its violent expressions, is ubiquitous among street youth. Equally so are its counterparts, sullenness and withdrawal. One is outward, the others inward—same DNA, just juxtaposed. The courage to communicate is key to balance. When the children learn to communicate within a safe support network where no one loses face, and where empathy for their plight is reflected, they are in recovery. I never have to go far to find intense anger or opportunities for intervention in its social context occurring interpersonally right in front of me.

At 2:45 the Family Circle breaks up. Ernesto, another of Eric's sons and, at 10, still famous for his tantrums and oppositional behavior, takes his station at the carpentry table. While several children wait, fidgeting, Ernesto monopolizes the group's one vise, sawing slowly away on a tennis racket. Finally Cheo, the carpentry caretaker for the afternoon, loses patience. "Here," he says, gently pulling Ernesto aside, "I'll finish it for you." While Ernesto stands by, barely quelling his fury, Cheo, unseeing, saws rapidly through the work. As he nears the end, a chip falls out, only slightly marring the racket's shape. But that is all Ernesto needs. "You goddamn motherfucker, " he screams, arms flailing at Cheo. "You'll pay for this. I hate you." Cheo tries to hold Ernesto to embrace him and calm him as a mother would calm a distraught infant. But Ernesto is too wild, and, picking up a stray piece of wood, he swings it, hitting Cheo in the face. That is too much for the older boy. He smacks

Ernesto hard. Stunned but still furious, Ernesto charges back for a full-fledged fist-fight. With this, however, all the support mechanisms and ties I have carefully cultivated among the caretakers make themselves felt. Papo suddenly materializes from the volleyball games he has been supervising and grabs Cheo. "Hey, cool it, man," he says, quietly leading his friend off with an arm around his shoulder.

Just as quickly, I seize Ernesto, managing to hold him firmly in a gesture aimed at physically imparting structure and restraints. In response to Ernesto's feelings, I say, "You have a right to be angry at Cheo; we'll take care of him later." At the same time I scratch the boy's head and shoulders until he stops shaking and screaming. "Why don't you tell Eric what happened and see what he thinks about this?" Within minutes, Ernesto remembers that Eric is in the sandbox and dashes off to spend the next half hour tunneling happily in the sand near his best friend and only ally. Later, Cheo and Ernesto make up over ice cream and talk about what happened, but as designed, it was the wider resources of Unitas as a whole that restored both teenager and child. I do not discount firm physical restraint or hugging in this population of chaotic street children, but there must be a balance between the two. As I watch Eric leading Ernesto and carrying tiny Juan lightly on his shoulders through the vacant lot, there appears to be no question that Eric's influence lies in his relationship with his "sons," so physical restraint becomes less necessary.

A little later in the afternoon I hold court behind the trunk of my van, taking special requests from a line of young petitioners. Renee, the first, a sturdy, well-balanced 12-year-old, classified normal as are some 40% of Unitas's children, is making a clear case for more material for the art group where, with paper crowns and scissored capes, a dozen children are turning themselves into the kings and queens of Fox Street. Then Bobby, hyperactive, constantly demanding attention, breaks into the line. "I want a ball," he insists over and over. Instead of imposing my authority, something Bobby is patterned to resist, I turn to Renee and ask, "Will you tell Bobby what he's doing wrong?" Renee responds quickly. "You know, Bobby," she says, "you have to wait your turn. This is like going to lunch in school. You'll get your lunch, but you have to wait your turn." Without a word, Bobby takes his place and waits.

Unitas as a Therapeutic Community

The therapeutic community dimension of Unitas works in simple moment-to-moment interactions. It understands that human behavior is determined to a significant degree by the influence of the active social network one is embedded in. And so, Unitas enlists the influence of everyone in the already existing network and uses each to bring about behavioral change in the lives of the others. Because the power came from a peer, Bobby took it, and because Renee is a normal child with no defensive axes to grind, she knew just what to say in a child's idiom. All I have to do is be a sensitive navigator. The troops do the work as long as I believe in them.

This theme of the troops doing the work is the core idea in the support community. I carry it into every area of Unitas, relying mainly on the teenage caretakers as the community's healthy, giving components. It is the teenagers who, with my guidance, deal almost solely with even the most disturbed of the Unitas children, taking them for extra one-on-one sessions during the day, talking with their parents, even bottle-feeding them at times to give the angriest youngsters an opportunity to recapture some of the early nurturing they have missed. This was just the strategy used with Ernesto and eight other oppositionally defiant children whose presence daily reminded me of war on a battlefield, with each child strategically planning what was necessary in the service of survival and always questioning on which side the victory would eventually fall. It was the ancient story: good guys versus bad guys. Of course, I was the good guy.

The battlefield being a given, the strategy I proposed was determinedly psychodynamic and aimed at repairing early deprivation by providing "symbolic realization" (Secheheye, 1951) and a "corrective emotional experience" (Alexander, 1948; Bowlby, 1966). My theoretical arrogance knew no bounds. And so, armed with these theories and with metaphorical imagery, I linked the most deprived youngsters with selected caretakers who would feed them milk in the quietness of the fire escape behind the church lot, caringly cradling them in a one-to-one relationship. Each day at a prescribed time in the afternoon, consistent with regularity and predictability to inculcate security and expectation at an infantile level of experience, there they were, children and caretakers, equipped with cartons of milk saved from the city lunch program, in a feeding scene equal to Bruno Bettelheim's (1950, 1955, 1974) accounts of his regressive therapy at the Orthogenic School[1].

One day, in the midst of this radical drama, I was confronted by Jason, a chunky, pint-sized Sherlock Holmes and a "non milk" recipient, who had discovered the nursery. "How come those kids are getting milk and not the rest of us?" he cried. And with the pause that precedes all deliveries of clinical wisdom, I looked him seriously in the eye, eyeball to eyeball, and said: "You know, Jason, you are right. You ask a wonderful question, and it would be nice for everyone to have milk, but let me tell you why those boys are getting milk and not you. You know how badly behaved those boys always are, always fighting, always stealing, always cursing, always bullying?" His curiosity engaged through my use of his own question and his deep attention attracted, he responded with a hypnotic "yes." I continued, "That is because when they were younger, even babies, they did not get enough milk. When you don't have enough milk as a baby, this kind of behavior happens later on. In order to help them change their behavior, I am providing the milk they didn't have. You will see how their behavior improves from this. You don't need the milk because you did receive enough. That is why you are well behaved and a joy to have around. That's the reason they're getting milk and you are not." And as we stand for a moment in time suspended, still eyeball to eyeball, Jason, stunned and speechless at this brilliant explanation and true to an insight that has met its mark, comments, "Oh!" Then, spotting a friend, he shifts out of his elevated state of awareness and says, "I gotta go." And with hurt pride I say to myself, "That's all he has to say? At least he could have said 'huh!'" As I look up at the fire escape, the feeding time is over. And you know, those boys do seem better.

A Dynamic Perspective on Community

As I emerge from the lot, walk away from the fire escape, and make my way to the noise and activity of the street, I scan all the caretakers with their symbolic sons and daughters. I think, "Who are the feeders and the feedees here, anyway, and why is absenteeism so rare among these caretakers, these symbolic 'mothers and fathers,' and their symbolic children?" I conclude that for the caretakers particularly, it must be a hunger that the sense of community, *communitas* gives them in terms of inclusion, belonging, nourishment, and affirmation as well as a thirst for connection with a nurturing, symbolic parent of their own, expressed in their relationship with me. Through transferential dynamics, these relationships with me and each other provide them with a corrective experience that begins to heal the abuse and neglect so many of them had suffered in their lives. And while this reflection applies to all, children and caretakers alike, it seems that the caretaking teens are among the biggest gainers in this picture.

For Papo, who by his own admission "made a habit of not talking" (an elective mutism) until 3 years earlier, when he became part of Unitas, the desire to be a symbolic father was the wedge to opening communication with the world. For Wilfredo, a teen lost in the middle of a large multi-problem family, it was the personal attention that alleviated his loneliness and that engaged his constant presence. As he said, "It was the way I was treated here that made me want to treat someone like that too. I experienced a lot here, and to one who never got that, you are a brother to him" (Eismann, 1996). For Eric, who came to Unitas as a shy child of 12, only to grow into the open, outgoing leader he has now become, "Unitas is kind of a perfect place." He adds, "I was the quietest one when I first came. I didn't want to do anything, just sit and watch TV. But now," grins the lanky teenager, rakish with an orange comb stuck into his short Afro, "I'm the busiest, noisiest one of the lot."

Pascual, an overanxious and overachieving caretaker, speaking of James who had been his symbolic father, says, "If it weren't for James in my life . . . I was full of anger and wanted to hurt people because I was hurting and it did not feel right for anyone else to be happy. I hated everyone, and James took that hate away from me" (Shapiro, 1988). And James, who had been sullen and uncommunicative, and who eventually grew into the role of model caretaker, touching the lives of innumerable youth, reminisces:

> I was also bitter and angry and did not have a father in my life. And then this man, well not only this man, but this white man came along and was selling black and Hispanic people something I had not ever heard before. He said, as he pointed to all of us, "You have the power to have an effect on other peoples' lives, and I want you to be as mothers and fathers to the neighborhood

children." In my youth and in my anger and frustration, I said, "How do you expect me to be like a mother or father to some little brat when I never had that in my own life?" Yes, I was challenging him because I was angry. And he said something to me that I hope I will always be able to do. He said, "James, what is it you want from your father . . . wanted from your father? When you can think of those things you would have liked, then you will know what to do with someone else." I will never forget the experience of not having a father. I would never want anyone else to have that experience. It is like my quest in life is to be available to anyone who missed a mother or father in their life. I was lucky though because I had a special experience with Doc, Papo, and the other brothers who nurtured each other, and that is what made me strong and able to go on. (Shapiro, 1988)

I could continue describing the narratives of a legion of caretakers over 30 years, the influence Unitas has had on their lives, and how they have influenced one another, but I need to stop somewhere. What I have not indicated are the failures. That, too, is another story with a hypothesis.

 **Conclusion**

As I reflect on my decades of listening to the needs, hopes, and dreams of thousands of youth in schools, churches, settlement houses, and street settings, the message is the same. They cry out for inclusion, for personal empathic attention, and for a relationship with an accepting father[2] who provides reason and constancy in their chaotic lives. When offered these three experiences, not so far removed from the essential taste of treatment itself, they seem to internalize what they receive in the service of their own maturation. Doing so enables them to provide the same experience, in turn, to their own symbolic children, who again, in turn, become caretakers to the next generation of symbolic children. The call to youth in 1968, to serve as community caretakers remains unbroken into a new millenium. What also remains unbroken is the realization of one of the community mental health movement's most cherished dreams, namely that primary, secondary, and perhaps even tertiary prevention can be actualized when mental health professionals who believe in this vision use themselves to organize any given social setting to enlist, support, and develop the positive potential influence of whatever social network already exists in order both to bring about changes among its members and to modify the environment itself.

In the midst of the street was the tree of life . . .
And the leaves of the tree were for the healing of the nations.

—Apocalypse 22:2

References

Alexander, F. (1948). *Fundamentals of psychoanalysis.* New York: Norton.

Bettelheim, B. (1950). *Love is not enough.* New York: Free Press.

Bettelheim, B. (1955). *Truants from life.* Glencoe, IL: Free Press.

Bettelheim, B. (1974). *A home for the heart.* New York: Knopf.

Bowlby, J. (1966). *Maternal deprivation and the growth of love.* Baltimore: Penguin.

Eismann, E. (1996). *Unitas: Building healing communities for children.* Bronx, NY: Fordham University Press.

Farber, A., & Rogler, L. (1981). *Unitas: Hispanic and black children in a healing community.* Bronx, NY: Fordham University, Hispanic Research Center.

Kaufman, I., & Reiner, B. S. (1959). *Character disorders in parents of delinquents.* New York: Family Service Association of America.

Langston, R. (1970, October). Community mental health centers and community mental health ideology. *Community Mental Health Journal, 6,* 387–392.

Procidano, M., & Glenwick, D. (1985). *Unitas: Evaluating a preventive program for Hispanic and black youth.* Bronx, NY: Fordham University, Hispanic Research Center.

Secheheye, M. (1951). *Symbolic realization.* New York: International Universities Press.

Shapiro, S. (1988). *Unitas: Ties that bind* (video documentary). Bronx, NY: Channel L Working Group and Unitas Therapeutic Community.

Notes

[1] The concepts referred to in this section, "symbolic realization," "corrective emotional experience," and "regressive therapy," are highly interrelated, and so I will comment on them collectively, to demonstrate, at least, the significance they hold historically in psychodynamic thought, even if the concepts are controversial. Bowlby (1966), reviewing international evidence of the effects of maternal deprivation in early life, commented that although many experts were pessimistic about the rehabilitation of people who as infants had suffered rejection or had never had a libidinal tie, "others are more hopeful and believe that if the child is permitted to regress to completely infantile modes of behavior, there is a chance of his developing afresh along better lines" (p. 50). Such regressive experiments were seen in the Children's Village at Ska near Stockholm and at Bettelheim's Orthogenic School in Chicago, where children were encouraged to become highly dependent on their caretakers and permitted to regress to such infantile behavior as taking food from a baby's feeding bottle in the context of a nurturing relationship in order literally to gratify an unresolved psychosexual need of an oral instinctual nature. This approach of oral restitution, drive theory in perspective, was also demonstrated in Secheheye's (1951) highly successful treatment of Rene, an adolescent schizophrenic girl. By providing her with an experience of symbolic breast feeding (which Secheheye called "symbolic realization")—feeding her green apples together with the warmth of motherly care while reclining the girl against her breast—Secheheye's treatment goal was to undo the effects of infantile trauma, which the girl compensated for through psychotic symptoms. The emotional aspect of this experience appears in part to be what Alexander (1948) subsequently spoke of as the "corrective emotional experience," in which the therapist provides an empathic reparative relationship as an antidote to the assumed rejecting or ambivalent relationship with the mother.

Although the "nursery children" at Unitas would not be classified as psychotic (nor were many of Bettelheim's, either), they did appear to fall into a character disorder category described by Kaufman & Reiner (1959), in which the individual's emotional growth was interrupted and distorted by early trauma or an unfavorable milieu. For these children, Kaufman claimed that "treatment that does not operate within the clients' developmental structure and the defenses associated with it may actually be reinforcing the pathology" (p. 67).

With this foregoing rationale, I instituted the "nursery of the street" and attempted to provide a treatment intervention aimed at repairing developmental arrest by a "relationship through feeding" experience that was dyadic, instinctively pleasurable, relational, kinesthetic, and predictable in the interest of behavioral change. With the expansion and modification of classical theory since that time, derived from object relations, self psychology, and social systems theories, emphasis has been placed on the primacy of significant others in affectional bondedness and continuity of relationship and a de-emphasis has been placed on others considered primarily as sources for instinctual satisfaction. That is how I explain things now. This expansion of psychodynamic theory and the integration of social systems thinking appear to explain in a richer way why these boys seem better than would be understood by limiting such an explanation to some version of the classical theory of that time. It must be remembered, however, that the relational aspect of healing has major significance in classical as well as post-classical theory.

---

[2] I specify father rather than parent in general because of a repetitious theme in the verbal dialogues of both boys and girls that related to the longing for and anger at the absent father. Being male, I am more directly the object of positive or negative transference.

Acknowledgment of the author is extended to Barbara Davidson, freelance journalist, for many descriptive observations contained in this chapter that were taken verbatim from her writing.

NAME INDEX

SUBJECT INDEX

315